SCHOLAR EXTRAORDINARY
The Life of Professor The Rt. Hon.
FREIDRICH MAX MÜLLER, P.C.

Max Müller, an oil painting by Sir Hubert von Herkomer

SCHOLAR
EXTRAORDINARY

The Life of Professor the Rt. Hon.

FRIEDRICH
MAX MÜLLER, P.C.

By

NIRAD C. CHAUDHURI

New York
Oxford University Press
1974

Printed in Great Britain

ACKNOWLEDGEMENTS

LADY BLENNERHASSET, a well-known literary and social figure of the last quarter of the nineteenth century, wrote to Mrs Max Müller after the death of her husband: 'My admiration for your husband makes me envy the task of him or her, who will be his biographer. There are few lives so rich, so attractive, so truly interesting, from the intellectual and purely human point of view.'

During the four years which I took to write this biography I have felt that she was right in saying so. It has been a memorable experience for me, and not merely a task. The introduction which follows will explain why I undertook to write Max Müller's life anew after the first and last biography so far written was published in 1902. Here I shall only set down my obligations.

First and foremost, my thanks are due to my friend, Laurens van der Post, for having suggested the project to me. After him I am indebted to the two grandsons of Max Müller, Mr Charles and Mr J. H. Max-Muller, *(anglicé)* for the interest they have taken in the work, and especially to Mr J. H. Max-Muller for the readiness with which he has helped me with documents and books. A very large volume of Max Müller's papers have been deposited by Mr J. H. Max-Muller in the Bodleian for the use of those who might be interested in his work and life. He has also given me access to papers which are still with the family. Without this help this book could not have been written.

Dr Hunt, Keeper of the Western MSS in the Bodleian, and the staff of Duke Humphrey's Library—Mr Vaisey, Mr Porter, Mr Harris and their assistants—have been very helpful and courteous, so making the consultation of the papers in the Library not only research but an agreeable spending of time. I am indebted to Mr Alexander of the Library for helping with passages in Greek and Latin, not all quoted in the book.

In India I would record my obligation to Margaret Chatterji and Parimal Goswami for supplying me with certain information I wanted, and also to my dead friend Gopal Bhattacharya for the same kind of help.

I must next thank the helper without whom this book would not have been published. As written by me, it became too long to be a commercial proposition, and since I did not have the time to carry out the editing it was undertaken by Ingaret Giffard. As the author of the book I would say that the omissions have been made and the editing done with extraordinary skill. There is nothing more delicate and difficult than to deal with another man's writing. Ingaret Giffard's handling of this tricky task was such that when I read the results of her editing in the proofs—not

ACKNOWLEDGEMENTS

having looked into the edited typescript, I could not be sure where the cuts had been made, and I discovered them by an effort of the memory. I think no author could say more about the editing of his work.

But skilled as the editing has been, it has also to be pointed out that it was bound to have another aspect. Max Müller's life was so many-sided and information about it is so voluminous that even in the original version I could not include many things which I should have liked to have dealt with. If all the details could have been retained, the book would have been more colourful, but, on the other hand, the streamlining will make for a coherent and clean-cut impression. And I would stress that only illustrative details have been cut, no basic feature of the book has been interfered with, and its spirit has been wholly preserved.

My publishers have been very generous and forbearing with me during the long gestation of the book, and without prodding me have taken keen personal interest in its progress.

I want to acknowledge the authority that has been given me to use manuscript material: the telegrams from Queen Victoria and Albert Edward (Prince of Wales) on the illness and death of Max Müller have been reproduced by the gracious permission of Her Majesty Queen Elizabeth II; and the letters from Lord Salisbury and Lord Curzon by the courtesy respectively of the Marquess of Salisbury and the Viscount Scarsdale.

Last of all, I must set down my gratitude to Oxford, where I wrote the book. Of course, since the papers were in the Bodleian, I had to be here. But I did not work at Oxford only as a research student. I had to imbibe the spirit of the place where Max Müller spent his life, and the book would never have been what it is if only its materials were gathered at Oxford.

Oxford   NIRAD C. CHAUDHURI

IMPORTANT NOTE

The fact that Max Müller was German by birth and spent his early life in Germany, has quite unnecessarily fixed the idea that he was a German scholar writing in German. Actually, he was naturalized in England and *always* wrote in English with complete mastery of the language, except when he employed German for a special purpose in a book, article, or his correspondence. The lists given in the two appendices specify which books or documents are in German. All others are in his *own* English.

CONTENTS

ILLUSTRATIONS

PLATES

TEXT FIGURE

INTRODUCTION

THIS book is a biography, that is to say, an account of the life of a man who was a scholar and a thinker; it is not except incidentally a discussion or evaluation of his work in the fields of knowledge with which his scholarship was concerned. But a biography should not be inflicted on a reading public without proper justification, I do not think that a man is entitled to such treatment only on the strength of his position and fame in his own age, unless in addition he played so important and significant a role in history that he remains an element to be reckoned with in understanding the continuing evolution of a particular people or humanity in general; nor unless his personality and activities belong to a type whose presence and functioning is continuous and universal, so that no outstanding individual of the type ever loses his relevance to all ages.

Whether Max Müller deserves a new biography in the light of such a criterion cannot be discussed without taking note of two indisputable facts about him: the first, that he is almost completely forgotten today; and the second, that when he died in 1900 and for thirty years before that he was a world figure. Both of these have to be considered, more especially his great contemporaneous reputation.

In Britain, which was his adopted country and where he spent all his working life of over fifty years, his name means nothing outside the circle of professional Indologists, linguists and mythologists, and even within it the recollection is dim. It is the same in Germany where he was born and brought up, though above all it was he who was responsible for building up the reputation and prestige of the Germans as the most admiring, sympathetic, and profound interpreters of Hindu civilization and spirituality. Even in India, where he was a legend and an institution combined, he is now only vaguely remembered as a German intermediary between India and Europe, and Indians hardly remember that if Max Müller was a German, he was equally an Englishman. It is only very recently that the cultural projection of western Germany of today has revived his name by calling its centres in the big cities of India Max Mueller Bhavans or Houses. Through this the Germans have put the memory and prestige of Max Müller behind their cultural propaganda though he was interested only in presenting the rediscovered ancient India, and not Germany, to modern Indians.

His contemporary position has now to be set against the current eclipse. His prestige was as impressive in its geographical range, extending from the United States to Japan, as it was by its recognition by all social classes from royalty to common people. Witness the reaction to the news of his death. He died at half-past eleven in the morning of Sunday, October 28, 1900. Immediately, messages of condolence began to pour in to his home at Oxford from all over the world, sent by emperors and kings as well as persons of less exalted worldly status. One of the first to come was that from Queen Victoria, herself to die in less than three months. She wrote to Mrs Max Müller: 'It is with the truest concern that I learn that your dear and excellent husband passed away today.' There were also telegrams from her son, the future Edward VII; her daughters, the Empress Frederick and Princess Christian; her grandson, Kaiser William II; and many more royal personages. The most touching and intimate among these came from the Queen of Rumania, a German princess by birth and better known under her pen name of Carmen Sylva. She wrote:

Last night the King woke me in the first sleep with the sad, sad news. Of course, I did not sleep again, thinking of you, and watching with you through this long night, and its loneliness! Oh, how I wish I could fly to you, and look once more into that most beautiful face, in which harmony of thought, and love, and noble refinement met, in every curve of the lip, in every line, that had been marked by the intensity of thought and feeling.

From an Indian social reformer, Malabari, came the message, 'All India mourns with you', and that embodied the feeling of all educated Indians.

The funeral took place on November 1. Early in the morning of that day the coffin was moved from his home to St Mary's (the University church), and placed in Adam de Brome's chapel, where the mourners assembled. Though no invitations had been sent out the large church was entirely filled by people from all walks of life, including representatives of the Queen and the German Emperor. The Crown Prince of Siam was also among the mourners. The congregation followed the coffin on foot to the Holywell cemetery, where the body of the scholar, who had come to Oxford as an unknown and poor youth fifty-two years before, was laid to rest. A friend who was attending the service noticed that a little bird sitting on a branch nearby went on singing all through the service, un-scared by the crowd and the noise. Remembering that Max Müller was a philologist, one could say that it was like the grammarian's funeral in the epoch of the Revival of Learning described by Browning:

> Hail to your purlieus,
> All ye highfliers of the feathered race,
> Swallows and curlews!
> Here's the top-peak; the multitude below
> Live, for they can, there;
> This man decided not to Live but to Know—
> Bury this man there?
> No! yonder sparkle is the citadel's
> Circling its summit.
> Thither our path lies; wind we up the heights . . .

For in that bygone age even the grammatical knowledge of a dead language was the key to a new life. Max Müller's speciality was knowledge of Sanskrit which, though a pioneering study when he was young, had hardened into a narrow academic discipline when he died. Yet his funeral was a throw back to an older tradition.

On the following Sunday memorial services were held in many churches in England, including Westminster Abbey, and the whole world press published editorials and obituary notices. These were not just matter-of-fact accounts of his scholarly work, but tributes giving expression to a feeling that an epoch was closing. *Le Temps* of Paris summed up his special contribution to knowledge with the observation: 'It is a figure from the heroic age of Oriental and linguistic studies which disappears', and the *Journal des Débats* recalled his work in its widest scope and wrote: 'The death of Max Müller not only creates a sadly felt gap in historical and philological studies, but also extinguishes the beacon of light to which over the whole world thinking men turned their eyes.' In India distinguished scholars like R. G. Bhandarkar and R. C. Dutt paid tributes to him.

Similar interest mixed with concern was also shown during his serious illness the previous year. Examining a volume of his papers in the Bodleian I found at its beginning a whole sheaf of pink tele-gram forms. The very first telegram was: 'Sept. 23: '99—To Mrs

Max Müller. I heard with great regret of the serious illness of your husband and am anxious to hear how he is and hoping he is better. V.R.I. [Victoria, Regina Imperatrix], Balmoral.' The next telegram was also from her, and the third ran: 'Much grieved to hear how seriously ill your husband is. Trust you are able to give me better accounts. Albert Edward [Prince of Wales and the future Edward VII].' There were many more from royal and other personages.

But I consider a letter about this illness from an ordinary middle-class Hindu in Madras to be the most significant. He wrote:

> Madras, December 13, 1899.
> Most respected Sir, Sunday was the mail day, on which English mail letters are delivered at Madras. That morning, while I was eagerly expecting the postman, he gave me a card received from you, in which the following lines were written: 'Professor Max Müller is seriously ill and not able to attend to any letters.' When I saw these lines tears trickled down my cheeks unconsciously. When I showed the card to my friends who spend the last days of their life like mine in reading the Bhagavatgitha and some such religious books, they were also very much overpowered with grief.
>
> Last night when we were going to Sri Parthasarathy Swami temple as usual for devotions, one thing suggested to me, and that was that I should have some special service performed to God (Sri Parthasarathy Swami, the presiding deity in the temple here) by the temple priest in your name for your complete recovery. When I expressed my suggestion to my friends that followed me to the temple they were unanimous in their opinion that it was the best that can be done for a gentleman like you who has sacrificed his health and wealth to the good of India and the Hindus in particular. The temple priest was immediately sent for and we disclosed to him our object. He raised many objections to have our object accomplished, and the chief one of his objections was that he can't offer prayers and enchant *mantrams* to God in the name of one who is not a Hindu by birth, and if he does so in the name of a Christian he will not only be dismissed from the service of the temple, but will also be excommunicated from his caste . . . But, when one of our friends promised to him to pay ample renumeration for the purpose, he acceded to the request. Then the next day each of us subscribed our mite and paid to the priest some rupees.

The rest of the letter (which is given by Mrs Max Müller in her biography in a paraphrased and corrected form) described how they went to the temple the next day with the usual offerings of coconut, flowers, and sacred leaves and had the rite for recovery performed.

Max Müller's relations with India and Indians were a major element in his life and an essential part of his vocation. So they will have to be described and considered as fully as possible in this book. Here I shall quote some general statements. One comes from an American writer, Moncure D. Conway, who had known him for thirty years and contributed the obituary article in the *North American Review*. In it he wrote: 'Wherever I went I usually met the students and the pundits, and a number of the titled men, and all of these, of whatever caste or sect, regarded Max Müller as the greatest of mankind, and I was charged with messages entreating him to visit India. This enthusiasm of the cultured influenced even the illiterate.'

To this I would add the tribute of one of the greatest of modern Indians, Swami Vivekananda, the preacher of neo-Hinduism. 'There are a number of great souls in the West,' he wrote in Bengali —and I am giving a translation—'who undoubtedly are well-wishers of India, but I am not aware of one in Europe who is a greater well-wisher. He is not only a well-wisher, but also a deep believer in Indian philosophy and religion . . . Though all through life he has lived with and steeped himself in ancient Sanskrit literature the India of the Professor's imagination is not simply that which resounded with the chanting of the Vedas and from which sacrificial smoke rose to the sky . . . he also is ever alert to whatever in the way of new developments is happening in every corner of India and keeps himself well-posted about them.'

I could illustrate the nature of Max Müller's influence on India even better by giving a humbler example; for instance, how as a child I came to know about him. My father was not a highly educated man in the formal sense, for he had received only a school education and that too in the backwaters of East Bengal and not in Calcutta, the centre of modern Bengali culture. None the less, it was he who explained to me how Max Müller had established that our languages and the European languages belonged to the same family; that our words, *pita, mata, duhita*, etc., were the same as the English words, 'father', 'mother', 'daughter', etc.; that Sanskrit *Dyaus Pitr* and the Greek *Zeus Pater* were identical; and that we Hindus and the Europeans were both peoples descended from the same original stock.

This leads me to Max Müller's position and influence in the West. It could be expected that he would impinge on the learned world, be in personal communication with front-rank scholars in many lines, and also that he would receive attention from men and women interested in things of the mind. But his influence overflowed into very much wider areas, and indeed they ramified beyond the field of scholarship into the sphere of public affairs, and beyond that even, as in India, into the interests of common people. Among his friends, acquaintances, or correspondents in England alone were literary figures like Macaulay, Tennyson, Thackeray, Ruskin, Browning, Matthew Arnold, and political figures like Gladstone, the Duke of Argyll, Lord Northbrooke, Lord Granville, Lord Stratford de Radcliffe, the Marquis of Salisbury, Lord Curzon, and among ecclesiastical personalities there was, to mention only one name, Archbishop Tait. This list wholly ignores the wide circles of his friends and acquaintances in Europe and America.

No contrast could be more striking than that between the contemporary fame of Max Müller and its posthumous decline, and this by itself might inspire a moralizing biography to demonstrate the vanity of fame. I would not admit that this would be more shallow than airing intellectual conceit towards men of the past out of uncritical satisfaction with the present. But historically neither would carry us very far. The reputation of Max Müller and its eclipse have to be correlated with his intellectual function so as to bring out the real significance of his life. But scholars, scientists and historians belong to the times in which they worked, and if any new biographies are to be written of them these must either show what historical role they played in the development of the subjects they dealt with; or illustrate the particular incidence of a general human phenomenon.

A life of Max Müller can be written from both points of view. Of course, the illustrations I have given of the kind of fame he had and its range do not by themselves prove the value of his researches and ideas. To be admired in this way may be regarded as being nothing better than a popular fetish. Some of his rivals in scholarship did at times rate him as nothing more important, and made the kind of reputation he enjoyed the ground for denying his scholarship. But his popular fame, so far as it could be related with his specialized scholarship, was only the penumbra of a hard core.

One of the ironies provided by specialized learning is that though only a specialist can pronounce a competent judgement on a fellow-worker, it is rare to get a fair judgement from him. It is always possible to find minor mistakes in the works of the greatest scholars, and a rival scholar can always dismiss him as worthless on the strength of these mistakes. But Max Müller's position and reputation were not that of a specialized scholar; he was an intellectual playing a part in the mental history of his times by making people aware of new ideas and extending their view to new horizons. His fame spread out from the scholarly field to the lay world like that of Darwin or Einstein, but with a stronger and wider impingement which bore practical results in some countries.

This standing becomes still more remarkable when one considers Max Müller's own outlook on life. Generally such fame as he had, comes only to men of action, religious, moral, or political preachers, i.e., those men of ideas who provide driving power for action. But Müller disavowed both roles. His view of his own life was set down by him in very clear language at the very end of his autobiography.

> I have never been a doer [he wrote in it]. Many people would call me an idle, useless, and indolent man, and though I have not wasted many hours of my life, I cannot deny the charge that I have neither fought battles, nor helped to conquer new countries, nor joined in any syndicate to roll up a fortune. I have been a scholar, a *Stubengelehrter*, and *voilà tout* . . . Much as I admired Ruskin when I saw him with his spade and wheelbarrow, encouraging and helping his undergraduate friends to make a new road from one village to another, I never myself took to digging, and shovelling, and carting. Nor could I agree with him, happy as I felt in listening to him, when he said: 'What we think, or what we know, or what we believe, is in the end of little consequence. The only thing of consequence, to my mind, is what we do.' My view of life has always been the very opposite. What we do, or what we build up, has always seemed to me of little consequence. Even Nineveh is now a mere desert of sand, and Ruskin's new road also has long since been worn away. The only thing of consequence, to my mind, is what we think, what we know, what we believe.

In theory, he equally rejected the role of a man of ideas as the priest behind the warrior.

> I cannot claim [he further observed], to have been a man of action in the sense in which Carlyle was one in England, or Emerson in America. They were men who in their books were constantly teaching and preaching. 'Do this!' they said, 'Do not do that!' The Jewish prophets

did much the same, and they are not considered to have been useless men, though they did not make bricks, or fight battles like Jehu. But the poor *Stubengelehrter* has not even that comfort . . . I felt satisfied when my work led me to a new discovery, whether it was the discovery of a new continent of thought, or of the smallest desert island in the vast ocean of truth.'

Nothing could be more free from ambiguity. None the less Max Müller did intervene in practical affairs, both political and social. But as a definition of his major intellectual vocation his words were true, and his wide fame was based mainly, not on his involvement in practical questions, but on his work in the scholarly field. Therefore his life has a bearing on a very large and important question: Can a man who has deliberately chosen to devote himself to the pursuit of knowledge *qua* knowledge, and to ideas *qua* ideas, ever hope to make an impact on the minds of men in general? Max Müller's life would show that ideas do travel from the scholar's study over the wide world of the mind. For this demonstration alone his life would be revealing.

A life of Max Müller is also justified if it can show what the scholarly life and the scholar's personality really are. Those who are not familiar with either tend to take too simple a view of both. They assume that life runs a straight and a tranquil course whereas even when there is a strong sense of direction in it, it can be as winding as a river running to the sea. Writing this life at Oxford I cannot forget that in order to go to London by train I have to cross the Thames six times. The life of an Oxford don might not be less winding.

As to the scholar's personality, it is neither less complex nor less varied than that of poets. I would even say that scholars are more varied in type than are poets. The Renaissance humanists were not less colourful than the courtesans of their times. The fact is that scholarship is a matter of temperament. As I have written in my autobiography: 'The greater part of the scholar's *métier* is the capacity for experiencing the emotion of scholarship. Without this there is no genuine scholarship but only a juggling with books for the sake of making money in a small way, or a career of sorts.' It is impossible to understand Max Müller's adherence to the scholarly life without assuming a temperamental compulsion behind it. Indeed Max Müller, who was often regarded as a very Germanic pedant by those who did not know him, was looked upon even by the very temperamental Oxford dons of his times as a very temperamental person. In any case he, with all his individuality, is an example of a certain type of scholar-thinker, and this type recurs. Therefore it never loses interest or the challenge to understanding.

Last of all, the life of Max Müller as lived by him faces us with an absolutely fundamental question, to which I shall certainly try to give an answer. It is this: Is the life of a scholar-thinker worth living? It is no use dismissing this question by taking for granted the scholar's role in a civilized society. Most of our incomprehension of life comes from not facing up to this sort of question; for disregarding Plato's profound maxim that the unexamined life—*anexatastos bios*—is not worth living.

Just to accept the incidence of the scholarly life as a necessary part of civilization is hardly better than accepting motor-cars as a phenomenon which must be accepted. Perhaps, in our age scholarly activities in the universities all over the world have assumed a character which makes scholars provide grist to a colossal mill turning out information as consumer goods, and these multiply themselves in obedience to their own Parkinson's Law. But that does not make an understanding, evaluation, or validation of the scholarly life less needed than the administrator's life in the modern bureaucracy.

So I have always put to myself the question of the basic significance of all lives. I have seen, come in contact with, or read about many of the highest of my countrymen—Tagore, Gandhi or Nehru. At the death of each of these men I have been terrified by the sudden onset of a conviction that their lives ended as ghastly tragedies and were not very far from that when they were living. Again, at the death of many of my contemporaries who in their careers achieved a worldly success which has never come my way nor will, I have asked—What did they gain which I should have liked to have had and have lost? In each case I had to justify their life by faith, and hardly ever by reasoning. But for me it was impossible to avoid the question.

I have considered it in connexion with the life of European scholar-thinkers, and above all Karl Marx. Did his ideas contribute anything to the understanding of human life or to enhancing its value? Or was he only the priest and propagator of a cult more bloody than that of our Kali or of the Aztec war god Huitzilopochtli, to be himself dragged to the altar of his own cult as a sacrificial beast fattened in the British Museum?

Max Müller put forward his ideas as explanations of some of the deepest facts of life:—religion, mythology, language. Neither he nor anybody else has been able to say the final word on any of these. But at all events, his theories, provisional as they were bound to be, touched on universal and timeless interests. The question is whether these have that amount of relative or absolute value which makes any life-long pursuit of them worthwhile.

I am bound in this book to attempt an answer to this question. But it has to come out of the book as a whole, and even then only by implication. To close this introduction I shall set down what my feeling about his life has been while I have been writing this biography. I have felt that it was as tragic in one way as it was successful in another. This biography should bring out the *grandeur et misère de la vie savante* as Alfred de Vigny's stories brought out the *grandeur et servitude de la vie militaire.*

I would, of course, say that of any scholar or man of action who has played a part in history. At many moments a man who feels deeply about life is seized with a conviction, terrifying though it is, that the significance of life and its vanity are almost equally matched. But perhaps we should expect nothing else. Significance of life must be found in grains after sifting the immense amount of chaff of insignificance which covers it. The really unintelligent reaction is to be clever and blasé, and not to be excited by the grain and saddened by the chaff.

PART ONE

INCIPIT VITA NOVA

BEGINNINGS IN RURITANIA

FRIEDRICH Max Müller was born on December 6, 1823, in the town of Dessau, now in eastern Germany, but then the capital of a sovereign State, though a very small one. Indeed, Anhalt-Dessau was so small that when in the revolutionary days of mid-nineteenth-century Germany, a troublesome political agitator was expelled from the principality he threatened to break the windows of the ruler's palace by throwing stones from across the border. That would have been, not petty mischief-making, but a very appropriate symbolic gesture, for the Schloss or the ducal palace was the focal point of the life of the whole population of the State, irrespective of class and station. The building itself was both old and imposing, with a large quadrangle in front, from which staircases supported by turrets led up to the reception rooms. The impression it made on Müller as a boy, he put in the mouth of the young hero of the only story he ever wrote:

> Not far from our house, and opposite the old church with its golden cross, stood a large building, larger even than the church, and with many towers. They, too, looked very grey and old; but there was no golden cross, only stone eagles were placed on the pinnacles, and a great white and blue flag waved from the highest tower, just over the lofty entrance where the steps went up on each side, and where two mounted soldiers kept guard. The house had many windows, and through the windows could be seen red silk curtains with golden tassels; and all round the court stood old lime trees, which in summer overshadowed the grey stone walls with their green foliage, and strewed the grass with their fragrant white blossoms. I had often looked up there; and at evening, when the limes smelt sweetly and the windows were lighted up, I saw many forms floating here and there like shadows, and music echoed from the palace above; and carriages drove in, from which men and women stepped out and hastened up the steps. And they all looked so kind and beautiful; and the men had stars on their breasts, and the women had fresh flowers in their hair; and then I often thought, 'Why do you not go there also?'

Though Müller did not accept any identification of the Schloss

of his story with the ducal palace at Dessau, there can be no doubt
that the real castle inspired the description. But in offering it he was
not whipping into it any worked-up romantic feeling. The account
was truthful and natural from one who as a child saw the castle as
the material embodiment of a historical identity—that of the little
principality in which he was born and brought up.

This principality was the Duchy of Anhalt-Dessau. In Max
Müller's time it was ruled by Duke Leopold Friedrich, who succeeded to his inheritance in 1817 and did not die till 1871. Its identity, like that of many such States in Germany, was the product of
a long and characteristic political evolution which at the beginning
of the nineteenth century left the country with nearly three hundred
and fifty petty States in addition to the big ones like Prussia,
Saxony or Bavaria. Britain and France had, of course, become
unitary and centralized politically. These principalities were looked
upon as a drag on the process of making Germany a national
State, and with the exception of some twenty they were all swept
away by the upheavals of the Napoleonic Wars and the reorganiza-
tion carried out by the Congress of Vienna. That brought down
the number of States in the amorphous pan-German political
structure from the three hundred and sixty of the Holy Roman
Empire abolished in 1806, to the thirty-nine in the Germanic Confederation created in 1815.

The Duchy of Anhalt-Dessau was among the few that survived
the process and were recognized as constituent sovereign States of
the Confederation. But even these were considered too many and
denounced by the champions of German unity, and more especially
by those historians and publicists who wanted the unity to be
brought about by Prussia. But Max Müller did not share this attitude. Though he too was an ardent believer in German unity and
in some sense a supporter of the Prussian cause, he did not think
that the small German States wholly deserved the contempt and
ridicule with which they were treated. He admitted that the etiquette kept up by some of the courts and their sense of self-
importance were at times very ludicrous, but he also asserted quite
deliberately that without the small principalities 'German history
would often be quite unintelligible, and Germany would never
have had so intense a vitality, and would never have become what it
is now'.

This was putting it strongly, but not uncritically. The piety that he felt for his native State, and gave expression to in his reminiscences, did not make him blind. A great majority of these States had indeed become completely obsolete, but those that were left intact by the Vienna settlement—which with the exception of the four Free Cities, were all monarchical—had still left in them some of that vitality which had kept them alive down to the nineteenth century in a line of organic succession from the earliest political organization of the German people. The Prussianizers called these princely States feudalistic, and in our time the world of these little kingdoms has been romanticized in fiction under the name of Ruritania. None of these labels were inappropriate. But the reality was quite solid, and, though composite, it had been fused into an organic whole.

As seen in the early nineteenth century, this princely order was showing the latest form of the German tribal organization. In these courts and kingdoms the power, prestige and influence of the princes did not depend on extent of territory or military strength, but on certain qualities of personality and life. The whole community from the prince to the peasant was animated by a coherent *Volksgeist* (spirit of the people) which made it favourable ground for that kind of cultural creation in which the individual personality mattered.

The Duchy of Anhalt-Dessau was a typical principality of this species. To begin with, it had a very old dynasty whose princes held a distinguished record in the whole course of German history. The line was very old—in fact, older than the Habsburgs and the Hohenzollerns, and it could trace an unbroken descent from Albrecht the Bear who became Margrave of Brandenburg in A.D. 1134. The dynasty was called the Ascanian, which prompted some fanciful genealogists to claim its origin from Ascanius, the son of Aeneas. But even without any eponymous ancestor, many of these dynasties had lasted long enough to have become rooted in the hearts of their people without any reference to their personal merits.

The princes of Anhalt were, at all events, able and good men. They never acquired large territories. At their most extensive, their land embraced only the whole of Anhalt, but even this was split up from time to time owing to a curious law of succession which did not recognize primogeniture, but required that at the death of a father each of his sons would get an equal share by means of partition. Thus, at the time of Müller's birth, there were three duchies of Anhalt—Anhalt-Dessau, Anhalt-Cöthen and Anhalt-Bernburg.

In actual fact, the importance of the principality as well as of the dynasty was due, not to territory, but to the personality of the princes and their achievements. In the Middle Ages the Ascanians took an active part in the conflict between the Teuton and the Slav in eastern Germany. At the time of the Reformation the princes of Anhalt were prominent champions of the Protestant cause, and both Luther and Melancthon paid tributes to their zeal, ability and piety. During the Thirty Years' War again they commanded the Protestant armies. In the eighteenth century Leopold of Anhalt, famous under the name of the *Alte Dessauer* (Old Dessauer), was one of the leading generals of Prussia, and fought at Höchstadt, Blenheim and Malplaquet. He also organized the armies of Frederick the Great's father, and afterwards commanded part of Frederick's forces in the War of Austrian Succession.

The personal role of the Dukes of Anhalt continued in the second half of the eighteenth century, when Duke Franz of Anhalt-Dessau became one of the most outstanding representatives of the Age of Enlightenment. He had travelled widely in Italy, Holland and England, and though he had avoided France as a country dangerous to young German princes, he was liberal enough to erect a monument to Rousseau in his park at Wörlitz. He loved England, and used to say that 'in England one becomes a man'. There he studied agriculture, architecture, gardening and even manufacture, so that he might be able to introduce improvements in the manner of living of his people.

He spent his time and efforts not only in trying to improve the conditions of living of his subjects, for which he was loved by his people and called Father Franz; he also tried to inspire them with high ideals and to raise their mental level. After seeing the English parks he laid out many in and around Dessau, and some of them were as fine as any in England. In Italy he studied both ancient and modern art with the pioneer art critic Winckelmann, and collected works of art. These he arranged in his museums and palaces which were open to the people. Like Weimar, Dessau also attracted great literary figures of the age—Goethe, Wieland, Lavater, Matthieson and many more, who came to the Duke's palace as guests. He patronized the educational reformer, von Basedow, who was the precursor of Pestalozzi and Froebel, and gave him a home in Dessau when he had to leave Hamburg after a riotous mob had burnt down his house. Even Treitschke, the champion of Prussia, who had no sympathy to waste on the small principalities, called Duke Franz, 'the honourable doyen of the house of Anhalt and a prince of imperishable memory'. Not the least of the attraction of these princes was that they were all tall and handsome. Winckelmann spoke of the visit of young Duke Franz to him as the visit of a young Greek god. His successor, Leopold, too, was very tall and handsome.

Towards the end of Duke Franz's rule Napoleon appeared at Dessau after crushing Prussia at Jena. Max Müller's mother, as a child of six, saw her venerable and beautiful prince standing at the foot of the stairs bareheaded to receive the pale and small Corsican. Even then he was wearing the Prussian Order of the Black Eagle on his breast. Napoleon inquired if he had sent a contingent to the Prussian army, and when he said that he had not, asked him why. 'Because I was not asked,' replied the Duke. 'But if you had been?' 'Then I should have sent my soldiers,' said the Duke, and then he added, 'Your Majesty knows the right of the stronger.' Napoleon was rather pleased, and said that he would respect the neutrality of Dessau, provided the Duke repaired, at his expense, the bridges destroyed by the Prussians. He even inquired further if he could do anything for the Duke. 'For myself,' the Duke replied, 'I want nothing. I only ask for mercy for my people, for they are all like my children to me.'

Duke Leopold Friedrich, who succeeded in 1817, continued the traditions of Duke Franz. In Anhalt-Dessau there was neither restoration nor reaction. It was as if the twenty-five years of upheaval, from 1789 to 1814, which created modern Germany, formed no part of the history of the principality. It remained untouched by the currents of change which were powerful in Prussia in one way, and in the southern German States like Bavaria in another. The first was reconstructing its political and economic organization under the shock of defeat, the southerners were doing so from their association with Revolutionary and Napoleonic France. The rest of Germany was more or less stagnant. But Dessau was not stagnant, it remained traditional but healthy in its unchanged state. It had both stability and tranquillity. Though the old order remained intact in it there was no conscious theory either of restoration or reaction. It carried on the pre-Revolution existence of the principality with its benevolent despotism and spirit of Enlightenment. Duke Leopold was able to rule his Duchy in this manner till 1848.

Max Müller, who was born and brought up in this Dessau,

described the Duke as the most independent sovereign in Europe. He was not accountable to anybody in the exercise of his power, a constitution did not exist, nor was it allowed to be mentioned. All appointments were made by him, all salaries were paid from the ducal chest, and whatever existed in the Duchy belonged or seemed to belong to the Duke. There was no appeal from him. He imposed the taxes, and if money was wanted introduced a new tax. But the taxation was low, and, what was more remarkable, if there were wars or distress the taxes were actually remitted. The only outside opinion that counted was that of the civil service of the Duchy, which was the custodian of the established traditions of government and in such a strong position that its advice, though not binding, could not be disregarded by the Dukes.

The Dukes were rich. Not only did the Duchy belong to them virtually as private property, they also had properties elsewhere. They used this wealth as much for their people as for themselves. All the public buildings, theatres, libraries, schools, and barracks were erected by them, and in addition they also provided residences for their high officials. Though formally the land belonged to them, most of those who had houses of their own enjoyed their property in freehold.

Personally, Duke Leopold was a splendid example of the best type of paternal ruler, just and fair, very hardworking, and accessible. Besides, he was very cultivated, and his Duchess, a Prussian princess—a niece of Frederick William III—was equally well educated and cultivated. Both were popular with their subjects, and to the common people and to the young they were little short of a god and a goddess. The peasants as they caught sight of the Duke's carriage shouted '*Hä Kimmet*', and the whole village gathered round him.

The Duke was completely feudal in his love of hunting. The beautiful oak forests of the Duchy were stocked both with deer and boars, and he would not allow anybody else to hunt them. When he did, that was considered a great favour. The deer came to recognize and dread his approach so much that even when they heard his carriage coming they scampered away, though they did not budge in their grazing when other carriages passed. The boars destroyed the crops of the peasants, who ran after his carriage asking for compensation, and he made up the losses. When these amounts became too much the officials demurred. But the Duke still compensated them from his private funds, and asked them not to tell his ministers.

Max Müller's relationship with the ducal family was closer than that of others. For one thing, his father was the Duke's librarian, and was held in great esteem and affection by him. Secondly, his grandfather on his mother's side was the Duke's chief minister, or President of the Duchy. He was the son of von Basedow the educationist, and after him his son also became the chief minister of Dessau. Even after Müller's father had died, leaving his wife and two very young children unprovided for and in genuine poverty, the Duke continued to take an interest in the boy and helped the family. As Müller became a very competent musician even as a boy, the Duchess would ask him to come to the Schloss and play duets with her on the piano. When the Duke sent for him he would look up at him with fear and trembling, though nothing could be kinder than the reception of the boy by the tall and handsome old man, with his deep voice, slowly uttered words, and very quiet manner.

The landscape of the Duchy was beautiful. The Elbe was not far away, and its tributary, the Mulde, ran by the town. All around were magnificent forests of oak, as well as of firs, which stood in rows like so many grenadiers. But the town, except for the ducal Schloss and the other palaces, had no architectural pretensions. It was also very small, with no more than ten to twelve thousand inhabitants in Müller's childhood. It was still walled in, and at night the gates were shut. The oil lamps swung across the streets, and the night watchmen walked along them.

It was a curious town with one long main street running through it, called Cavalierstrasse. This street was very long, and had pavements on both sides. But so little traffic passed over it that it had to be weeded from time to time to get rid of the grass which came up through the chinks of the stones. The houses generally had only one storey, and some of them were mere cottages. Almost every house had a mirror fastened outside the main window, like the driving mirrors of today, so that the inmates could get notice of an approaching visitor. It was the fashion to paint the walls white, green, pink, or blue, and above there were waterspouts like real gargoyles which not only frowned on those who passed below, but during rainstorms poured water by the bucketful on their red and green umbrellas.

The population of the town was divided into two classes according to Müller—the educated and the uneducated. The first, without reckoning the princely families, consisted of the officials, the clergy, the school teachers, doctors, artists and the military officers; and the other class, of tradesmen, mechanics and labourers. Trade was almost wholly a Jewish monopoly, and Dessau had its ghetto, for a former Duke who had granted them leave to settle in Dessau without any fear of persecution also insisted that they should live only in certain streets. But the Jewish quarters in Dessau did not show the squalor which the ghettoes in other German towns did. There was no particular prejudice against Jews. None the less even as a boy Müller felt that they were only a tolerated community.

Max Müller's classification of the population of Dessau by education was significant, because in the world in which he lived mental status was more valued than wealth. In any case, nobody outside the ducal circle had much money. None the less, the community of the educated in Dessau lived happily enough. One thing which helped the peace of the town was the absence of newspapers. In his young days at Dessau Müller knew only one, which gave nothing but reports of actual events on one, or half, or even quarter of a sheet.

The horizon of this world was narrow, but for that reason it was also stable. Everybody performed his work honestly and conscientiously, and everybody was the keeper of his brother's conscience. As Max Müller says in his autobiography, 'everybody knew everybody else, and every thing about everybody. Everybody knew that he was watched, and gossip, in the best sense of the word, ruled supreme in the little town. Gossip was, in fact, public opinion with all its good and all its bad features.' The result was that no one could afford to lose caste, and everybody behaved as well as he could. The society being on the whole blameless, it was all the more merciless towards sinners, whether the sin was small or great.

But even this small world did not impose its limitations on mental growth. For so small a town, the education provided was as good as any to be had in a large German city. At the beginning of the century the eyes of the whole of Germany, and even of Europe, were turned on the educational experiments carried out by von Basedow in the Philanthropium which he had established in Dessau. The Dukes took great interest in education, and everything possible was done to keep the different schools—elementary, middle and high—on the highest level of efficiency. Besides, in the small élite of the town, the cultural level was very high, and there was music of a type which could be heard only in the great cities. There was a first-rate theatre, both for plays and opera, and also a small but real intellectual circle.

The society of the educated at Dessau exhibited a mixture of simplicity in living with the highest kind of mental enjoyment. At the evening parties in the house of Müller's maternal grandfather there would be playing or singing of extracts from *Don Giovanni* or *Fidelio* and readings from the latest works of Goethe or Jean Paul along with drinking of wine and tea. In the house of his parents a more learned company would enjoy their Shakespeare, Dante and Calderón in the original languages with his mother as well as his father.

The Müller family were old residents of Dessau. Max Müller's grandfather was only a tradesman, but he was very much respected as such, and he was also the founder of the first lending library in the town. Müller never saw him, nor his grandmother on the father's side. The old lady whom he knew as granny was his father's stepmother, who was a rich widow before her second marriage. Müller was told that his grandfather married her for her money, so that he might be able to give his son a liberal education.

She grew to be very old, and when Müller and his sister, who was two years older, were sent to visit their grandmother they were terrified by her thin, white face, her piercing eyes, and her dishevelled clothes—all of which made them think of her as the old witch of German fairy-tales. This notion she strengthened by telling them stories of ogres, ghosts and witches, which kept them awake at night from fear and, on Müller himself, left a very deep impression. She did not know her stepson at all well, and for preference she would talk of her own young days and of her first husband, but in such language that if the children repeated it at home they were severely scolded.

Max Müller's father, Wilhelm Müller (1794–1827), did get his liberal education, and under F. A. Wolf acquired enough classical scholarship to be able to write a book on Homer, *Homerische Vorschule*. Besides being the Duke's librarian, he was also a teacher in the Gymnasium of Dessau. But he became more widely known, and even famous, as a poet. Müller never claimed that his father was one of the great poets of Germany, and he was not. But he was very popular as a writer of lyrics and songs. Among his best-known song cycles are the still well-known and sung *Schöne Müllerin* and the *Winterreise*, set to music by Schubert. He also wrote poems inspired by the nationalism of the age in its most fiery form. These were contained in a collection called *Griechenlieder*, and in them his love for ancient Greece mingled with his enthusiasm about the Greek war of independence and admiration for the heroes of this war. These songs were at one remove an expression of his ardent German nationalism. Under the Metternich System it could no longer be directly voiced in Germany, so it broke out in phil-Hellenism. The Greeks did not forget him. When a monument was erected to him at Dessau in 1891 the Greek government of the day sent Pentelic marble for it.

On his mother's side Max Müller was connected with the highest in Dessau's public service. As has been already mentioned, his grandfather and uncle were successive presidents or chief ministers of the principality. Another uncle was the commander-in-chief of the army; he had fought with the Prussians at Jena, and marched into Paris twice. The Basedows were a handsome, high-tempered and imperious tribe, and when Müller was told that he took after his mother's people, he was ready enough to admit it as regards looks, but he hoped he was not a Basedow in temper.

His mother, Adelheide von Basedow, was very beautiful, very small and very passionate. She was very highly cultivated, and knew English, French and Italian perfectly. She was not the Pedagogue Basedow's granddaughter for nothing. Goethe and old Basedow were friends, and the poet mentioned and praised the educationist in his poems. But he also complained bitterly of Basedow's never being without a pipe in his mouth, and of lighting it with the most offensive tinder, *Stinkschwamm*, as Goethe called it. Müller's mother knew that, of course, and when she and her husband went to see Goethe, and the latter asked what her maiden name was, she replied laughing: 'Your Excellency ought to scent it, I am the granddaughter of Basedow.' This was a very great liberty, but as she was young and very beautiful Goethe characteristically did not mind.

It was Wilhelm Müller's personal qualities and his standing with the Duke which made his marriage into the Basedow family possible. But he and his wife were most devoted to each other, and even on their very small income they lived pleasantly in a house provided for the ducal librarian, with a pretty garden behind it. This home was the rallying point of all the cultivated, scientific and artistic society of Dessau. Wilhelm was also a most devoted father, and would play for hours with the children as though he were a child himself. These games, together with a vague picture of his father making him and his sister sit on his knees and telling them stories, were the only recollections Müller had of his father. He was four years old when his father died at the age of only thirty-three, on October 1, 1827.

This was a sudden and terrible calamity for the family. One day Wilhelm Müller had gone to Oranienbaum, a park near Dessau, to see the Duke, and returned late in high spirits. In the night his wife woke up to find him dead by her side. The death was due to paralysis of the heart. Adelheide Müller was twenty-eight, and unprovided for. But more than that she felt the loss of a beloved husband. She remained inconsolable, and though she lived for fifty-six years as a widow, she never married again. She would take her children with her when she went to her husband's grave in the cemetery at Dessau, which was called *Göttesacker* or God's Acre, and was planted with acacia trees. She stood there for hours, sobbing and crying, and saying that she wished to die in order to be with her husband. Her children, when they heard that, only hoped that she would not leave them behind but take them with her. This restful place planted a life-long love in Max Müller for acacias. But at that time the inscription over the gateway of the place puzzled him very much. It ran. '*Tod ist nicht Tod, ist nur Veredlung Menschlicher Natur*'—'Death is not death, 'tis the ennobling of man's nature.'

Although Max Müller from his early childhood grew up in the shadow of death, he came on both sides from a stock which possessed great vitality and as a small boy he was full of fun and mischief. His mother's old servant, Hanna, who called him *Dieser infame Junge*, this terrible boy, and who lived to a great age, never tired of asking for news of her early tormentor.

After the death of her husband Frau Müller lived for some years with her father, and then settled herself with her children in a very small house, consisting of a ground floor, a storey above, and a loft under a high-pitched roof. With that there began a life of great hardship for the whole family. The widow had been granted a pension by the Duke, who had himself written to her expressing his sympathy, and informing her of the grant. But it was only 150 thalers (£15) a year, and from the life insurance which was compulsory for a civil servant there was a little more. All of it was quite inadequate for any kind of comfort. If it had not been for the extreme cheapness of living at Dessau Frau Müller would not have been able to feed her children. As for clothing, it was always thin and extremely well-cared for. In winter there was positive suffering. Müller often woke up to find his breath frozen on the bedsheet into a thin layer of ice, and he had to wash after breaking the ice in the ewer, which left only a few drops for use. The snow-covered windows did not admit light. For breakfast there was only coffee and a roll. This hard life made Müller a sufferer from acute headaches throughout his early life, and from their recurrence even later. It remained a riddle to Max Müller that his mother was able to bring up her children at all.

Naturally, religion was an important element in his early life. Of a winter's evening his mother would sit by the warm stove, and in candle light would read out from a book in her hand, while the servant woman went on turning the humming spinning-wheel:

> *O Haupt voll Blut und Wunden,*
> *Voll Schmerz unde voller Hohn . . .*

As he listened, the boy Müller saw the bleeding head before his eyes, and cried until his mother comforted him by saying that the sufferer was now in heaven, and it was only a song to be sung in church. Another experience, too, left an indelible impression on him. The house in which Müller lived looked into the churchyard of the Johannis Kirche, which in itself was not beautiful. But on one Easter Day, it was transfigured for him—the sun had risen in full radiance and the old church, with its grey slate roof, the high windows and the tower with a golden cross, shone with marvellous brightness, and suddenly music began to come out of it. When he asked his mother what it was, she said that it was an Easter hymn which they were singing in the church.

But willingly as he listened to religious readings at home, and full as his heart was with love towards Christ, he suffered intensely when taken to attend the church service. Though he liked the singing, the sermon was a real torture, and the large church was so cold that he felt as if he was in an ice-cellar, and would have allowed his teeth to chatter if he had not been told that it was wrong to make any kind of noise in a church.

Music was the greatest enjoyment of his life at that age. Dessau at the time was steeped in music. The Duke kept a first-rate orchestra, and his *Capellmeister* was a composer of the old school, Friedrich Schneider, who was also the head of the conservatorium or the music school. He scolded Paganini, Spohr, Sonntag and Mendelssohn. Apart from the general musical atmosphere, his mother and her sisters sang well. His mother had a perfect contralto voice, and was often invited to sing solos at musical festivals. At home she and Müller played *à quatre*, and soon he began to accompany her when she sang. Hearing his mother and aunts, he could sing all that they sang, and was once put on the table to sing a great aria of Handel. His parents were friends of the Webers, and also of Mendelssohn who once took the boy Müller on his knees as he was playing the organ in the *Grosse Kirche* and made him play the choral, while he himself played the pedal.

Müller's formal musical education began very early, but it began secretly. He was five years old, and his mother was staying with her father. The neighbour on the right-hand side of the house took lodgers, and one of his lodgers was an ex-theology student, now studying music and taking lessons from Schneider. He often talked to Müller across the hedge. He had noted the child's love of music, and one day, lifting him over the hedge, he took him to his room and asked him if he would like to play the piano. When Müller agreed with eagerness, he said that he would teach him for half an hour every day, provided he told nobody, not even his mother. So Müller had his lessons for about six months, keeping it quite secret. He at last sat down to the piano in his grandfather's salon, and to the amazement of everybody played some easy pieces from Mozart and Diabelli. The young man, whose name was Kahle, was at once formally engaged to be Max's music teacher, and he charged sixpence for a lesson. Müller made very quick progress.

Young Max was, of course, sent to school, first to the elementary school and after that to the higher one. His school work, which at the higher level included elements of Latin and Greek, was not heavy. The teachers were very conscientious, and though they taught well they did not make the life of their pupils a burden. Müller's record was good at school, but in no way very outstanding. His musical interest and his constant headaches interfered with his work in school.

At this stage it was a young teacher who first told Max Müller that he ought to be worthy of his father—an idea which had never before entered his mind, for he was not old enough when his father died to have any correct idea of his literary eminence. This teacher, a Dr Hönicke, had an attractive appearance, though there was a very sad air about him, due to the fact that he knew he was dying of consumption. Besides, he was a liberal and was politically persecuted. He died soon after Müller had left Dessau, but Hönicke's suggestion that he should remember what he owed to his father, and the feeling of piety that went with it became strong influences on the boy's life.

Max Müller's headaches often made him lose two or three days a week in his lessons, for he felt as if the skin of his forehead was peeling off and he had to lie down and try to sleep. Yet he had to do his work, even though he did it carelessly, and in consequence was scolded and punished. Finally, when all remedies had failed, he was sent to the famous founder of homoeopathy, Hahnemann, who had taken refuge in the Duchy of Anhalt-Cöthen, and from there visited Dessau as a consulting physician. Hahnemann was a very imposing personality, a powerful man with a gigantic head and strong eyes, and a most persuasive voice. He made the boy Müller swallow a good many of his globules, but did not succeed in curing him, and it was not till 1860 that he was finally cured of his migraine at Oxford.

Max Müller visited his grandfather Basedow's house as a matter of course. But the old president did not have much time to attend to the children in the family, and in any case he made no secret of his preference for his son's son. So when his cousin was taken out by his grandfather to shoot with him, and came back with a hare, Müller felt somewhat jealous. But he was soon cured of that jealousy, for one day he was also taken out to shoot, and his grandfather, who could not see very well, shot a doe with two young fawns. The death cries of the mother, and the whimperings of distress of the young ones, which kept trying to suckle their dead mother, horrified Müller, and he made a vow never again to go out shooting or to kill an animal. This vow he kept, though he was laughed at for it.

Once, when he was twelve, Müller's mother went with some friends for a holiday to Heligoland, leaving her son with her mother, the Frau President. The reports of the old lady to her daughter of her grandson's doings showed that he did have his due share of being spoilt by grandparents, at all events by his grandmother.

We shall miss him very much [wrote the old lady] when he leaves us. He has become quite one of us. You would be amused to see him smoking a pipe with his grandfather, he can also take a pinch of snuff, and he does not refuse a taste of liqueur. The father has a very quiet horse on which he can ride alone, so you will find him quite a grown-up man in all the fine arts. His trousers indeed have a very variegated appearance from cherries, bilberries, and ink, but a young man does not think much of that.

Soon after his grandfather, President Basedow, died. Müller was twelve, and his mother thought that it would be better for him to be with other boys and under the supervision of a man. He had been spoilt by her love, and also by her severity in punishing him. So, after having risen from form to form in the school at Dessau, he was sent to the famous Nicolai School at Leipzig. That was at Easter 1836.

For the next eight years Max Müller lived at Leipzig, taking five years to finish his school education, two and a half to obtain his doctorate from the University of Leipzig, and spending about six months in literary work and exploring openings for a career. During the last three of these his mother and sister came over from Dessau, and they lived together in order to economize and also to enable Müller to live in greater freedom and comfort. But during the school years he was separated from his mother, and much as both wished to meet each other he could not always afford to go home as frequently as he wanted. The distance was only thirty-five miles and the journey by coach cost only one thaler (approximately three shillings). To save even that Müller at times walked home all the way, and in the last lap felt so tired and cramped and stiff in the legs that he sat by the roadside and rested before he actually entered the town. So, the agonizing separation between a fatherless only son and a widowed mother, both of whom passionately loved each other, began for Müller at the age of twelve, and lasted for forty-seven years. During the whole of this period he wrote regularly to his mother, and every letter was preserved by her. Bound in five volumes they are now in the Bodleian.

The extraordinary thing was that even as a boy he unconsciously assumed a role of guardianship over his mother, and as he grew older it became quite conscious, of course. The following letter was written when Müller was just short of thirteen:

My dear good mother—Today for the first time, I have to be far away from you on your birthday, and you can fancy how sorry I am. I think it grieves you too, little mother, for I know your love for me. Oh, how I long to be with you, only for a moment, only to press you in my arms, only to tell you how I love you: but it cannot be. Your birthday is always doubly dear to me, first because it is your birthday, and then because it was the first day that you roused yourself again from your sorrow, to which just in these weeks of the year you gave way more than usually. [Wilhelm Müller died on October 1, and her birthday was October 12.] You were right to grieve, and it would not have been proper to try to console and amuse you. You must have sorrowed this year more than usual, as the birthday of our good grandfather was this week. [The first birthday after his death in 1835.] But I will not write more about this; it will but renew your sorrow. I will only say that God has replaced something of what you have lost, in giving you two beings who love you as no others do. You best know whom I mean. Your Max.

When at school in Leipzig Müller lived with a friend of the family, Professor Carus, whose son, Victor, was the same age as he was. The Professor would not accept any money, nor could Müller's mother offer any. He was treated as a son of the family, and the two boys slept in the same room, worked together and had everything in common. They remained friends all their life. Frau Carus, who took care of him like a mother, was called *Tante* (Aunt) by Müller. The house had a large garden, and it was also an orthopaedic institution for girls. About thirty of them were either boarders or attended daily. Their joyful company made the place pleasant.

The Nicolai School, into which Müller had secured admission, was one of two famous schools in Leipzig, and when the boys of the schools met, their rivalry often showed itself in blows. These German public schools were not residential; the boys lived at home and spent about six hours at school. Therefore the influence of the teachers on the boys was less continuous than in English schools. Also, they were mixed in their social affiliations. The son of a minister and the son of a well-to-do butcher or blacksmith had to sit together, and the more delicate boys were exposed to bullying by their rough and muscular school-fellows. Max Müller however, was well able to hold his own both at Dessau and at Leipzig, and many of his masters, who knew his father, took a personal interest in him.

The emphasis in teaching was almost overwhelmingly on the

classics, and the grounding given in both Greek and Latin was very thorough. In the higher forms the boys were expected to speak Latin fluently, and Müller when he left school did so easily. Modern languages, mathematics and science were looked upon as poor relations, and the boys, who were aware of the relative prestige of the subjects, often absented themselves from the science classes.

Therefore, as was only to be expected, the headmaster was a well-known classical scholar, Dr Nobbe, whose edition of Cicero was used even in England. Another teacher was a specialist in ancient geography, one an annotator of Demosthenes, and yet another a Greek lexicographer. Max Müller became very proficient in Greek as well as Latin. But being the son of a German poet and a reader of contemporary German literature, and too young to appreciate the kind of greatness the classics had as literature, he could not help feeling that, compared with the great German writers of the day, the Greek and Latin poets were somewhat overpraised.

He did well at school and often carried off prizes, to which at times a warning was attached that he ought not to become conceited on account of them. At that stage he wrote poems, and some of them were read on important occasions. In 1839 three hundred years had passed since Luther had preached in the church of St Nicolai at Leipzig, and for the tercentenary celebrations in the city a poem of Müller's was selected for him to recite before a large audience. He was only sixteen, and went through it with fear and trembling.

But good as he was at bookwork, his most active interest at Leipzig was music. By that time he could hum all the arias and symphonies of Beethoven. He was asked at times to play at the houses of friends. But his most memorable experiences were of listening to the most famous musicians and composers of the day. From 1835 to 1843, during the whole period of Müller's stay in Leipzig, Mendelssohn was conductor and director of the *Gewandhaus* concerts in the city. Though only twenty-six at the time of his appointment, he was already famous, and he made Leipzig the musical capital of the country. So Max Müller was able to hear the most distinguished artists and composers of his time. Moreover, on account of his intimacy with Mendelssohn, he was actually invited to many performances, sometimes to listen, and at other times to take part in them.

Professor Carus was himself very musical, and his wife sang

beautifully. His son, Victor, played the violin, and Max the piano and also sang. Many celebrities of the musical world came to his house. One evening Müller got the autographs of five of them on a slip of paper which he kept till the end of his life. They were Mendelssohn, Liszt, Kalliwoda (violinist, composer, conductor), David (violist), Hiller (conductor and composer).

Soon after his arrival in Leipzig as a boy of thirteen, he was invited to the house of Mendelssohn, and there he found not only his host, but his host's sister, Fanny, and her husband the painter Hensel, besides David and the pianist Dreyschock. He walked in bravely, and was received with the utmost kindness.

Young Müller sent a report of the evening's experience to his mother, and showed remarkable maturity in his appreciation of the performance, Dreyschock's playing on the piano.

Mendelssohn [he wrote] stood close to the piano, and I sat where I could watch Dreyschock with great comfort. He is still the first of the pianists, and quite a young man. He played here last winter, and was taken for Thalberg. He played marvellously, so that Mendelssohn wondered at his skill, though he [Mendelssohn] immediately afterwards played an imitation of Dreyschock's composition. I must say, I much prefer Mendelssohn, even if the other has more skill, particularly in octave playing, in which he is decidedly the first of artists.

Later, Müller also heard Thalberg, and wrote to his mother: 'Now I have heard Thalberg . . . It is indescribable. I am still enchanted by it: there can be nothing else like it. He is quite young, handsome, and very distinguished looking, beautiful hands and such skill, execution, and power.'

Max Müller also saw the first entry of Liszt into Germany after his triumphal tours in France and elsewhere. In March 1840 this blazing meteor struck Leipzig, and both dazzled and repelled the musical Leipzigers. He was only twenty-eight, very theatrical and immensely attractive to women. His style of playing was quite new then, and many lovers of music who heard him for the first time were repelled by the flamboyance both of his playing and of his appearance and manners. At one concert he came in Magyar costume, and the ladies offered him a golden chaplet of laurel and a sword. Max Müller went to three of his concerts, one of them public for which he bought a ticket, and the other two at Mendelssohn's invitation.

The public concert was advertised long before Liszt's coming, but when he heard that tickets had been sold at one thaler (three shillings) he was very annoyed and decided that he would play only part of the programme. The house was crowded, but when he appeared there was a terrible hissing, and Liszt glared like a demon at the audience. However, when he began to play there was thunderous applause. There was more hissing later at his manager, who was really responsible for the arrangements. The next day it was advertised that the full original programme would be played, but as it was higher priced only fifty tickets were sold, and Liszt showed his displeasure by pretending to be ill and not going at all. Though many of those who heard him were dazzled by his playing, Leipzig as a whole was not pleased with the new musical genius. Even young Max felt that his technique was a little mechanical, though of the highest perfection.

Mendelssohn, however, was delighted with Liszt, and with his usual generosity arranged two concerts for him—one a musical soirée and the other a musical matinée. At the soirée, to which four hundred people came, Müller was invited because he was one of the tenors in the chorus which was to sing an oratorio.

At the matinée, at which many famous musicians of the day were present, Liszt appeared in Hungarian costume, wild and magnificent, and told Mendelssohn that he was going to play something specially written for him. Then, sitting down and swaying right and left on the music stool, he played first a Hungarian melody and then three or four variations, each to Müller, more incredible than the last.

Those who heard were amazed, and all paid compliments to the hero of the day. Mendelssohn's friends gathered round him and said: 'Ah, Felix, now we can pack up—*(jetzt konnen wir einpacken)*. No one else could do that, it's all over with us!' Liszt then came up and asked Mendelssohn to play something, and the latter laughed and said that he hardly played any more. Liszt, however, would not take a refusal, and so at last Mendelssohn said playfully: 'Well, I'll play, but you must promise not to be angry.' Then he sat down and played the whole of Liszt's Hungarian melody, and after that all the variations. He even imitated Liszt's movements and raptures, and the audience was a little afraid that the guest might take offence. But when it was over Liszt laughed, applauded and observed that no one, not even he, could execute such a bravura.

2*

At Leipzig Müller also saw another musical genius, soon to be recognized as great. He was Robert Schumann, then poor and striving for recognition, and engaged in an almost public struggle with the father of Clara Wieck, whom he loved and wanted to marry. Max Müller did not see much of Schumann in later life, and he recollected him only as a young man generally sitting in a corner of the orchestra listening to one of his works being performed under Mendelssohn's direction. He remembered his very large head and his drooping eyes, and that he smiled but rarely.

Max Müller completed his school education early in 1841, but for his final or *abiturienten* examination he had to go to Zerbst in Anhalt, so that if he passed he might qualify for a scholarship from Dessau, without which he could hardly go to university. He passed and got his scholarship; it was only £6, but it was an important help to him. Before the examination his headmaster, Dr Nobbe, wrote to his mother: 'I rejoice that I can see him leave this school with testimonials of moral excellence not often found in one of his years, *possessed of knowledge first rate in more than one subject, and with intellectual capacities excellent throughout.* May this young mind develop more and more, and may the fruits of his labours be hereafter a comfort to his mother for the sorrows and cares of the past.'

After Müller's death in 1900, at a gathering held in the memory of the old boys of the Nicolai School, the Director ended his reference to him with the words: 'He was without any doubt, next to Leibnitz, one of the greatest of our pupils.'

Before he left the house of Professor Carus, Müller recalled the letter to his mother in which he had sent her birthday greetings, and looked forward to the next stage of his life. He wrote:

When I remember the time when I first sent you my birthday greetings from Leipzig, and now see that this period of life is nearly over, I must gratefully acknowledge how good God has been to us in various ways, and has given us many compensations. But above all, how grateful we should be that God has preserved you, our dear mother, to us, to sweeten for us all that is bitter, to reward all effort. How I rejoice over next year, in which a new existence opens for me, a higher aim in life floats before me, and I shall have you both [his mother and sister] with me. I cannot tell you how I rejoice at the thought of this time, when I must take another step forwards, and shall again, at all events for a time, be with my own people.

He was then just over seventeen.

Max Müller joined Leipzig University in the summer term of 1841, and left with a doctorate in September 1843, that is to say, after spending less than eighteen months there, and before he had completed his twentieth year. That was, by our standards, a very short period for going through university disciplines, but perhaps the length of the process did not, in his case, matter so much as its intensity. The University of Leipzig for long had a very high reputation in Europe, and was looked upon, if not as the first, certainly among the best. Other universities had come up in the early part of the nineteenth century, but even so the standing of Leipzig was very high.

The German universities were quite different from English universities in their teaching methods, and in them professors had a status and prestige which they never acquired at Oxford or Cambridge. It was they who imparted university education, and not the tutors, and they expounded the subjects without supervising the work of the students. Personal attention was given only to those students who became members of seminars or societies, to which admission was obtained by submitting essays. As to lectures, the young men were left to choose whatever they liked, and the variety as well as interest of the subjects was so great that the students had great difficulty in choosing what lectures they would attend, and on what subjects they should concentrate. Thus what a student might get out of his university depended more on himself than on his teachers. Max Müller exercised the freedom to widen his reading, but he also knew how to concentrate, and since he was a member of two societies concerned with Greek and Latin he received some personal guidance and advice. In addition, he sampled an enormous number of subjects of which he had known nothing at school, and as a result during his stay at the university his mind passed from one stage of formation to another, which in a very German fashion I might describe as passing from a state of *being* to one of *becoming*.

The growth of his mind till it was ripe enough to realize its potential, and of his character till it had acquired its individuality, will be traced in a later chapter. Here only the external events and the incidental activities of his life in Leipzig University have to be set down and these latter were not at all like the so-called extra-curricular activities of modern universities. At Leipzig the university authorities did not have anything to do with them, neither organizing nor supervising in any way; they were in fact part of the private life of each student, and the most noticeable feature was their freedom. In regard to student discipline, the German universities of those days differed radically from the German schools of the same period. They gave as much freedom as the schools imposed discipline and supervised conduct. So young German university students, when they moved from the strict control by the schools to the unrestricted freedom of the universities, fully exercised and thoroughly enjoyed their freedom. They gave immediate expression to it in their pranks which as Max Müller said later, would have brought them into conflict with the university authorities if indulged in at Oxford or Cambridge.

Then there were duels, which though illegal, were connived at by the university, unless they resulted in serious wounds or death; and they were universal. The university itself had a fencing school, the *Fechtboden*, to which Müller went. During his university days he fought three duels, wounds from two of which left him with permanent scars. One was fought to defend the scholarly standing of Professor Hermann who taught the classics. Müller was listening to one of his lectures, when a student sitting at the table made some disrespectful remark about the Professor. He asked the youth to be quiet, and when he went on with his foolish remarks Müller stopped him by calling him out. It was obligatory on any German university student to cease from any further provocation when once challenged.

In the duels the accepted etiquette with seconds was strictly observed. The most usual weapon was the sword, but theological students preferred pistols because they could not easily get a living if their faces were scarred. However, the last thing a German student desired was to kill his adversary, and though in Max Müller's time there were four hundred duels in one year, only two fatal accidents happened, and, as he observed in his autobiography, that could happen even at football. A beautiful wood near the city was the usual rendezvous of the duellers, and there was a small river close by to enable the duellers to escape if the police arrived after hearing any report. Formally, duels were forbidden and punished; but unless something serious happened the punishment for mere duelling never went beyond loss of the club uniform and flag, of the arms, and of the barrels of beer.

When Müller went to the duelling ground to defend the reputation of his Professor of Greek, there were thirty or forty other couples ready to fight their duels, and there was a throng of spectators—of course, students—gaily attired in their club uniforms, with beer barrels pushed up on one side; and the surgeon with his instruments, waiting. Many of the combatants came on horseback or even in their carriages.

In spite of all his effort to remain calm and unconcerned, Müller could not help being nervous before his first duel, and he saw himself being carried severely wounded or even killed to a house where his mother and sister would be waiting for him. But everything went off well, and after the duel he and his friends enjoyed a good breakfast.

Though in his autobiography, written almost at the end of his life, Max Müller said that duels could never be defended, it was remarkable that even at that age, he should justify them, at least for German students. In the German universities, he said, the society of students was very mixed and perfect equality reigned among them —all of them addressed one another with the 'Thou' (Du). So a gentleman's son required some kind of protection against the son of a butcher or of a day-labourer. Crude fighting with hands was entirely forbidden among German students, so that there remained nothing to a student who wanted to escape from being insulted by a young ruffian but to call him out. Müller deliberately set down the view: 'Of course, duels can never be defended, but for keeping up good manners, also for bringing out a man's character, these academic duels seem useful. However small the danger is, it frightens the coward and restrains the poltroon.' Still, he hoped for a time when it would be possible for men to defend their honour without recourse to sword or pistol.

Of social life in the ordinary sense of the word Müller had very little during his university days. He would not even have an evening suit made. But he joined a student club which formed part of the famous German *Burschenschaft* or Students' Association which played such an important part in the war of liberation against Napoleon, but which on account of its political associations had to go under the name of *Gemeinschaft* under the Metternich System. To his club he went to smoke and drink beer, and there he acquired a number of friends. Some of his acquaintances resented the loss of political freedom, and were ready for any wild scheme in order to have Germany united and respected abroad and to establish constitutional government at home. Being very young Müller generally kept aloof while his older friends talked of their plans *pour culbuter toute l'Europe*, and he followed the rodomontades with the shrewd bright face of a squirrel.

But that did not prevent his being locked up in prison for two days by the police for wearing the ribbon of a club which lay under their suspicion. His friends were however allowed to visit him and to smoke and drink beer with him. What he really dreaded as a consequence of this escapade was the loss of his stipend without which he could not continue his studies at Leipzig, and scholarships were forfeit for political offences. So after his release he saw the Rector of the university and explained the circumstances of his imprisonment—how he had been arrested simply because he was a member of a club which was suspect to the police. He assured the Rector that he was not involved in any political agitation or propaganda. The old gentleman relieved Müller by saying: 'I have heard nothing about this; and if I do, how am I to know that it refers to you, for there are many Müllers in the university?'

If Max Müller's principal recreation in his school days was music, at the university it became literature, and more especially poetry. From time to time he fancied he would become a poet, which was not unnatural in the son of a poet. He became an active member of a literary society formed by like-minded fellow-students. It was called 'The Elegant World', or 'The Elegant' for short. Two of its members became literary figures in later life—Wolfssohn as a poet and Theodor Fontane as a very popular and widely read novelist and a minor poet. But none of these aspirants could at the time imagine themselves to be destined for real greatness.

Max Müller appeared for his doctorate earlier than he had intended, in September 1843, and as he was not sure of success he did not inform his mother for fear of disappointing her. But he passed with ease, received his doctorate in a borrowed dress-suit, and got his cards printed with 'Dr Max Müller'—and placed them himself on his mother's lap. During the years she lived with him she never interfered with his full freedom, and yet she loved him passionately as he also loved her. After her death her feeling for the relationship was found set down on a scrap of paper in words which she had copied from some English book: 'The tie of mother and son, of widowed mother and only son, the tie unlike all others in the world, not only in its blessedness, but in its divine compensation.' None the less, she had realized what few mothers or wives do, that

love which at its best and strongest obliterates the separateness
of selves, cannot also exist without respecting the freedom of each
self.

The last months of Max Müller's stay at Leipzig were devoted to
two literary projects, the publication of a new edition of his father's
Griechenlieder, and of his own translation of the Sanskrit *Hitopadesa*,
a collection of moral fables. To Leipzig society he remained, as he
informed his friend, Fontane, incognito because he had paid all his
farewell visits and felt no inclination for society. To the new edition
of his father's lyrics of ancient and modern Greece, he added a few
new poems and the hymn to Raphael Riego, the Spanish revolutionary. He also wrote a preface to the new edition, showing the
poems in relation to the reaction against all liberal movements which
had followed. In writing this, his object was to excite a feeling of
contempt for those who had betrayed the struggle for liberty of a
whole people. But in the political conditions of the times—five
years were still to go before the suppressed revolutionary feeling
was to burst out in 1848—it could not be printed. Max Müller told
his friend Fontane that he was very annoyed, but he also observed
philosophically: 'You see there is nothing left but to avoid all living
subjective topics, and take refuge in the objective past.' So he added:
'I have picked out a work from hoary antiquity and my first *opus*
will soon appear, a German translation of the oldest Indian collection of fables. You will find many acquaintances of childhood's
days, from Gellert, La Fontaine, etc., and the interesting thing is
that one can follow the wanderings of these fables, through twenty
different languages, from the oldest to most recent times.' This
book Müller dedicated to his Professor of Sanskrit, Brockhaus.

Chapter 2

WANDERINGS OF YOUNG MAX MÜLLER

EVERYTHING in Max Müller's social antecedents, taken with his education which was typical for a young German of his birth and times, destined him for the career of an official or teacher. But he exercised his own choice and launched himself into a vocation which, despite the feeling of uncertainty and groping he felt for many years, inevitably made him the Erasmus of the nineteenth century. Nevertheless the very first plan for settling him in the world envisaged an official's life for him. He was offered a position in the Austrian diplomatic service.

The source of the offer was romantic. His mother had a cousin with whom the brother of the reigning Duke of Anhalt-Dessau, Prince Wilhelm, fell in love. There was naturally a great outcry in the Ruritanian circle, but the Prince would not give up his love, and finally he was allowed to marry her morganatically. However, she was raised from the position of a commoner by being made Baroness Stolzenberg, though to Müller she always remained Cousin Emilie. This lady had as her childhood's companion a mysterious individual who became known as Baron Hagedorn. Nobody knew who his parents were. His mother had given birth to him in a forester's cottage near Dessau, and disappeared for ever. He was brought to the house of Müller's mother's aunt, Frau Klausnitzer, and lived in her family as a schoolboy. Thus he and Emilie became play-fellows. Hagedorn never did anything, but was never in want of money. Large sums were paid annually for his maintenance by a Frankfurt banker.

So his main activity was to wander about Europe, and stay in the great capitals where he had comfortable apartments. He had a large country house near Munich, and a prettily furnished flat in Rue Royale, opposite La Madeleine, though *au cinquième*. Once he took Max Müller on a tour of Germany.

Müller had not as yet taken his doctorate when Cousin Emilie and Hagedorn devised their joint plan for him. He was to join the Oriental Academy in Vienna, in order to qualify for the Austrian diplomatic service by learning some Oriental languages. As Cousin

Emilie and her husband the Prince were childless, they wanted to adopt him and give him a new name and also a title. Furthermore, they offered to find a wife for him. Max Müller shook his head, and without hesitation declined all the honours; he wanted to remain independent and true to his first love, Sanskrit. All the decisive turns in his life were unexpected, almost accidental, but there did appear to be an inevitability in all that happened to him.

To begin with, Max Müller himself decided to go to Berlin and join the university there. His object was partly to hear Franz Bopp, author of *Comparative Grammar* and the most eminent philologist of his age, and partly to study philosophy under Schelling. He also wanted to examine the Sanskrit manuscripts which the King of Prussia had just bought from the executors of Robert Chambers, an English Orientalist. Müller's sister had been married in February 1844 to Dr Krug, a physician and son of the well-known philosopher, and they proposed to live at Chemnitz. His own financial position was not such that he could take his mother with him to Berlin, and so it was decided that she should go and live with her daughter and son-in-law.

But even for himself Max Müller's finances were not adequate. The scholarship of forty thalers (= £6) which he held was to last only one more year, and at his majority in 1844 his mother's pension was going to be reduced from £15 a year to half that amount. Therefore on his way to Berlin he stopped at Dessau in order to find out if he could obtain a grant from the Stipendium founded by Duke Leopold for poor scholars. But no one gave him any hope. The Duke and Duchess expressed a desire to see him, and he explained his position, but there was no practical result. He then went to the family friend, Advocate Richter. From him, too, he could get no hope. At last he resolved to help himself, drew fifty thalers (= £7.50) from his savings bank, and started for Berlin.

He arrived there at the beginning of April, and at first stayed in the house of relatives, his uncle and Aunt Hake, who said that he could stay with them as long as he liked. He gratefully accepted the offer, but began to look for lodgings at once. He wanted a really nice room, and informed his mother that in two days he had seen forty, and was dead tired. He explained that he could not pay any visits until he was settled, but added in despair: 'But when will that be?' However, in two days he found a room very near the Unter den Linden, becoming the lodger of a cobbler. He paid 18 shillings a

month for the room, service and cleaning of boots, and found the
people of the house to be clean and respectable.

But the cobbler's workshop was next to his room, and the beating
of leather went on all day long and tried his patience very much.
However, the room was on the third floor and commanded a wonderful view. To look at it was a solace to him, and he held out against
the noise.

In Berlin he had access to influential persons. Though the
Duchess could not help him about money, she had given him an
introduction to Alexander von Humboldt. More significantly, she
asked him to see Rückert, the famous poet and Orientalist. Max
Müller's father and he were friends, and Müller himself was very
fond of Rückert's poetry, which he had read since boyhood. But he
had a fair warning that the man might be different from the poet.
Before he left Dessau the Duchess told him: 'When you go to Berlin
you must see Rückert, but don't be frightened.'

Max Müller found Rückert to be the broad-shouldered giant
described to him, and, besides when he went to see the poet, he was
in his dressing-gown, with his hair parted in the middle and hanging
wildly about his temples. The opening of the acquaintance did not
promise well. When Max Müller requested the professor to enrol
him for the lectures on the Persian poet Saadi and his *Gulistan*, he
was asked: 'Why do you want to learn Persian?' He humbly explained his reason, but Rückert observed: 'It is no use your learning
Persian unless you know Arabic.' Müller said that he had studied
Arabic for a year under Professor Fleischer at Leipzig. But the
real reason for Rückert's unwillingness was that he was anxious to
get away from Berlin to his country place, Neusses, near Coburg,
if only he could find a good excuse for not lecturing to give to the
Minister of Education, who grumbled at his absences. So he said
to Müller: 'You know *tres faciunt collegium*' (without three there
cannot be a class), and he added, 'I cannot lecture for one.' Müller
went away to find two more listeners, and came back with them,
making up the required three. All of them said to the professor
that they were most anxious to learn Persian. One of them really
wanted to learn the language, and indeed subsequently became a
great scholar; the other was only a makeweight. Seeing no way out,
Rückert agreed to remain in Berlin and give his lectures.

Nevertheless, when lecturing he told them that he had forgotten his Persian, and confessed: 'I cannot teach you Persian.

I can only show you how to learn it. I learned everything by myself, and so can you. We will work together, but that is all I can do.'

Müller found that Rückert's informal teaching was more useful than that of many learned professors who year after year read the same lectures to admiring audiences. Rückert was extremely adventurous in his linguistic excursions. Nobody in Germany in those days thought of learning Tamil, but he showed Müller a large treatise on Tamil which he had himself copied and amended. He also studied Chinese, and was fairly advanced in Sanskrit and Zend. According to Max Müller, the secret of success of the German professors was that they took their pupils into the worshops and did not keep them standing and gaping at the show window. Something like the tutorial teaching at Oxford and Cambridge was given by the German professors in the seminars and societies, where the students were shown how to work rather than simply crammed for examinations. Afterwards Rückert learned that Max was the son of his friend Wilhelm Müller, and he became very friendly to him. Treated with cordiality and admitted to intimacy, Max Müller felt that it was a privilege to know him.

Max Müller's acquaintance with Bopp was not so fruitful. He received Müller most kindly, but was very infirm though only fifty-three years old. In his lectures he simply read his *Comparative Grammar* with a magnifying glass, and added very little that was new. He lent some Latin manuscripts to Müller, but could not help him with the really difficult passages. This at first surprised Müller, for he had assumed that every professor was omniscient. Then he realized that even at fifty-three a scholar might forget many things he had known.

He paid more attention to Schelling, and attended his course of lectures more diligently. He saw the philosopher as soon as he could after his arrival in Berlin, and sent an account of the first meeting to his mother. Müller was an obscure student not yet twenty-one, and the other was a famous philosopher of sixty-nine. He had heard that Schelling also could be abrupt with his visitors. But he was received kindly, and when after the preliminary talk about his lectures and Müller's own interests the subject of Indian philosophy came up, the eminent elder allowed the younger man to tell him a good deal. Müller dwelt especially on the likeness between the Samkhya system of Hindu philosophy and Schelling's own system, and remarked how an inclination to Vedanta also showed itself.

Schelling asked him more about this. He was specially interested in knowing what the Vedanta said about the existence of God, how it proved His existence, whether it said that God had created the world, and also whether it said that the world had any reality. He was at that time very much occupied with the essays of the English Orientalist Colebrooke, and wanted to learn more, even asking Müller if he could explain a text. At last he inquired where Müller lived, told him that he had known his father as a poet who had written on Greece and worked on Homer, and dismissed him with a cordial 'Come again soon'. Müller attended Schelling's lectures, and even translated a portion of one of the *Upanishads* for him.

The first few months of Müller's stay in Berlin were very pleasant socially. His connexions, the Hakes and the Krügers, regularly asked him to meals, and as his friend he had Fontane, once a fellow-student at Leipzig. He met his teachers from time to time, and even visited Bettina von Arnim, one of the Egerias of the Romantics. But his closest friends were the Hensels, particularly the artist's wife, Fanny, who was the favourite sister of Mendelssohn. They always sent him invitations, and he went to them more often than he could really spare the time. He described one of his early visits in a letter to his mother:

> I went at twelve, for a large musical matinée; they sang the choruses of *Antigone*. Then I stayed in the garden with the tutor, and we played with Hensel a sort of ninepins; then came dinner, and they asked me to return in the evening, as Oehlenschläger, the German poet, was coming to them, so I spent nearly the whole day there. I have not played there yet, as she has not asked me to do so, but when I told her I wanted to hire a piano, cheap but not bad, she offered to lend me an English one, on which she used to play. He, too, is most friendly.

As to his studies, they were more desultory than concentrated. He attended lectures on many languages and subjects, and even matriculated in theology. His mother felt glad that he was not working too hard, but he wrote in his diary: 'Worked early, but could not concentrate. Dreaming, and a little poetry, and very little work. I must work more in future.' Even in respect of Sanskrit, on which he wanted to specialize, he could not get permission to read the manuscripts at home until many months later von Humboldt intervened for him. But he made translations from Sanskrit, read Pali and Hindustani, and learned the elements of Bengali by himself.

What distracted him was anxiety about money combined with total uncertainty about the future. His scholarship was small enough, but even that was going to be stopped at the end of a year. At first, to economize, when not asked out he dined at a restaurant which supplied a dinner, considered good by him, for only sixpence. Later he lived on only bread and butter at home, and coffee without milk or sugar. In the diary which he kept then such entries as 'no dinner' or 'dinner of scrambled eggs' (prepared by himself) occur frequently. Despite all this, he wrote to his mother that he was doing well and nothing was wanting to him except his dear little mother. He even admonished her: 'Don't say again you do not like Chemnitz—a contented spirit is happy anywhere.'

He could struggle with poverty but he saw no end to it, and was troubled by doubts whether the vocation he had chosen of scholar was likely to lead anywhere. On June 26, less than three months after his arrival in Berlin, he wrote to his mother:

> Where I am to go next Easter is not at all certain. I hesitate between Paris, Vienna, and Bonn. I am attracted to Vienna by the thought of studying Persian and Turkish, for which there are better means there than in Paris, and they are certainly necessary should I ever have the chance of employment in the East. You can fancy that these plans often disturb me, as for the nearest future I have no certain prospect; and the university course is so expensive and wearisome, that I cannot reckon on it, as generally for the first three years, that is six years after leaving school, one is not admitted to anything. Well, one must console oneself with the lilies of the field!

Two days later he set down in his diary: 'I *cannot* give up Sanskrit, though it holds out no prospect for me.' Two months later he reached even a deeper level of dejection and wrote to his mother:

> I am longing to be away from Berlin, to get a thorough change of thought, as I really think I have every chance here of becoming a confirmed hypochondriac. This is no mere transitory feeling, but it is founded on my circumstances, which have cost me many sad thoughts latterly. I acknowledge that the plan of life I had formed is not to be realized; that it is difficult for me to part with all these favourite ideas you can well imagine. And yet it would be folly in my circumstances to attempt a university career.

His mother had assured him that he still had 800 thalers ($= £120$), the money left by his father to start him in life. But Müller told her that it would last only until he had settled where to live, and thus he would continue to study and starve, in order not to relinquish an idea which he had taken up for his own pleasure and for which he had sacrificed much money and time. He added, with injustice to himself, that if he had more courage and a firmer point to cling to, he could perhaps still try his luck, but as things were nothing remained for him but to become a sensible schoolmaster, and this at least would give him bread and butter. 'You will find,' he commented, 'that a certain amount of resignation is needed for such a decision.'

For the moment he was cheered by the prospect of seeing his mother and sister, for he was going home for his vacation and for a respite from all his anxieties. Early in October he returned to Berlin, and was relieved to get the news that the Duke had extended his mother's full pension for five years, writing to her: 'I hope that your promising son may continue to give you as much cause for joy as hitherto.' But his depression returned, and he wrote to his mother:

I hope you make yourself as happy in the backstream of life as I do. As I sit here in my garret and for days together see no one I know, I fancy myself as a bird alone in its nest on a tall tree, and Leipzig, Chemnitz, and Dessau appear perfect Eldorados. But I am quite happy and amuse myself, by myself, as far as possible . . . Well, I have enough for the present, and I think of the birds in the sky. They have no fire, yet they don't freeze, but I do freeze.

Relief came to Max Müller within a month or so in the shape of his capricious friend, Baron Hagedorn. He suddenly appeared in Berlin, and invited Max to stay with him in Paris and carry on his Sanskrit studies. Max immediately fell in with the proposal, and on his twenty-first birthday, December 6, 1844, wrote to his mother:

My dearly loved Mother, As I am sitting here quite alone on my birthday I must give myself at least the delight of writing to those who love me so, and whom I dearly love. And first of all comes my darling little mother. My best thanks for your love and goodness, which in many things are far too great . . . I wish I could see you, darling mother, and talk over all the unexpected and undeserved kindness that has been shown me. I went Thursday early to Hagedorn, and we talked over everything; and the result is he has asked me to go to Paris with him, to live with him there and work. So in about four weeks from today I shall be in Paris. Hagedorn will tell you all this himself more fully.

As it happened, at that time another choice was open to him. Baron J. von Bunsen, then Prussian Minister in London, had heard about Müller from Humboldt as well as from Baroness Stolzenberg, and he at once wrote to his English friend, Archdeacon Hare, asking whether he could think of any openings for a young German who was at twenty-one already a distinguished scholar and wanted to live for some years in England. As a result, there came an offer to go to London as tutor in an English family. Müller was in great indecision for some time, but finally decided in favour of Paris and pleasant independence.

But Hagedorn disappeared, and Max Müller had to go in pursuit to Dessau, where he was dawdling. At last he settled everything, and on February 26 set out with Hagedorn for Paris. At Cöthen the train was stopped by snow and they had to return to Dessau, where Hagedorn found business letters awaiting him which kept him there. So Max Müller set out alone, and after a number of halts arrived in Paris at three o'clock on March 10, 1845.

The arrival was an unsolicited adventure. Hagedorn's address was given to him as 25 Rue Royale St Honoré, but he had forgotten the word *Royale*, and had himself driven in a fiacre to 25 Rue St Honoré. The concierge stared at him, told him that no Baron Hagedorn lived there, and suggested he try 25 Faubourg St Honoré, where the same scene was repeated. It was a rainy afternoon, and Müller was both tired and hungry. He was being taken along the Boulevard des Italiens, when looking out of the window of the carriage he saw a familiar figure on the pavement, an old acquaintance from Dessau, a half-French half-German hunchback named Gathy who was a student of music under his own teacher and had become a musical writer in Paris. 'Gathy, Gathy!' Müller cried out, rescued from his despair, and jumping down told his story. Of course Gathy knew both Hagedorn and his apartments, and guided Müller to the proper place. The concierge was prepared for him, and took him to the *cinquième*. He lay down exhausted on a sofa and cried out in what French he could command: *'Donnez-moi quelque chose à manger et à boire.'* That took some time, but food was brought, and restoring himself Müller discussed the most necessary matters with Gathy.

The immediate problem was money. Depending on Hagedorn, Max Müller had brought very little with him, and there was no Hagedorn. But Müller remembered the name of a friend of the Baron's who was with Rothschilds, and went over to the bank. This man too was away, but another bank official told him that he could have as much money as he wanted until the Baron himself or his friend returned. Then came the larger question of financing his whole stay in Paris. Müller was to have stayed with Hagedorn, but throughout his sojourn in Paris his friend never came there. So, apart from rent, he had to bear all his own living expenses. The free lodging was an immense advantage, but still he needed 100 francs a month for food and service, without taking into account lighting, heating, laundry or clothes. His situation in Paris was worse than in Berlin.

He had breakfast of bread and butter without coffee, and dined at the Palais Royal for two francs. This he found too expensive, and discovered that beyond the barrier, where there was no octroi, he could eat much more cheaply. Yet the problem remained of providing his daily bread while eking out what money he had for the longest possible stay in Paris. 'I am spending a lot of money,' he wrote within days of his arrival; and less than a month later in a letter to his mother he reverted to the theme: 'How gladly I would have put something in the letter for Auguste's [his sister's] birthday from the Paris shops, for the sight of the splendid and tastefully arranged windows is most tempting. But, alas! my purse suffers from chronic consumption; you know this family complaint, which has followed me to Paris.' Within another month he again wrote: 'One's money runs away here, one does not know how, and though of course it costs one more in the beginning, the daily wants do not lessen. That I am saving as much as I can you may be sure, for it is my greatest wish to stay here as long as possible, where I have found so much necessary to my studies.'

He got offers of help from friends, but refused them. He had at times to borrow money to tide over a temporary difficulty, but he never did so unless he knew that some money due to him would soon arrive. He could also give private lessons, but he had a strong dislike of that kind of drudgery. In fact, once he got a very handsome offer to go with Baron von Cetts, the Bavarian Minister to

London, as tutor of his children, all expenses paid and 3,000 francs a year. But the Minister required a promise that Müller would never leave his children even for an hour, and such a condition appeared so degrading and foolish to him that he declined. He wrote to his mother:

> It was a substantial position, which would free me from many disagreeable things, and in which, instead of taking money from you, my dearest mother, I could have given you some little pleasure. But it was impossible, unless I sacrificed my whole future, and wasted the little I have already done; and I hope that as I feel I have little to reproach myself with, I shall not be blamed by others.

What he would do to earn money was to copy Sanskrit manuscripts for the Orientalists who wanted copies. Even this meant very hard work, and his plan was to sit up the whole of one night, take three hours' rest the next night without however undressing, and then take a full night's rest, and repeat the sequence. This was not good for his health. He suffered both in body and in mind, and at times felt very lonely and homesick, all the more so because of his strong attachment to his mother. He often wrote about it; for example, on April 10: 'You can fancy that in this utterly strange land I sometimes feel lonely and forsaken, and would gladly find myself for a few hours in Chemnitz with you.' But he also knew that the poverty as well as the separation was of his own choice. At the end of his life he wrote in his autobiography: 'It was, indeed, a hard struggle, far harder than those who have known me in later life would believe. It was a hard fight, and cannot have been good for me physically, but I do not regret it now.' He told himself that he had mapped out his course of life and, as he added: 'It was in my own hands whether I should swim or sink.'

He kept his resolution and swam, but it was at first like the swimming of a shipwrecked sailor who clings to a plank without seeing anybody near him, and then suddenly catches sight of a rescuing boat. All the early openings in his career came unexpectedly, and were almost like windfalls. While waiting for them he sought relief from his anxieties in work, and for his sorrow at separation from his family in religion and philosophy. As he wrote to his mother:

> Separation loses its bitterness when we have faith in each other and in God. Faith in each other keeps us close together in life, and faith in

God keeps us together in eternity. But I see I am talking Sanskrit philosophy instead of simply telling you not to be unhappy, not to make yourself and others uneasy, but try to enjoy life in this lovely spring weather, whether in Chemnitz or Dresden . . . [Or again]: But enough of these lamentations, which are of no use, least of all in Paris. Melancholy and frivolity are the two scales in which men here go up and down; happy he who sits in the middle quiet and observant as an Indian Muni [Sage].

Max Müller was only twenty-two when he wrote that, and was amazed to find that he was so old.

There was however something deeper in his moods of dejection than could be accounted for by their apparent and tangible causes, such as lack of money, separation from family and friends, struggle to make a career and great uncertainty over it. Even when he was happily settled and prosperous at Oxford, sudden fits of depression and restlessness would come over him. But such swings are habitual to those who begin life and spend their first years in an environment which is socially and culturally stable, and then take the road to other worlds in which they can never again take root.

But it is wrong to say that they become mentally, socially, or culturally *déraciné*. On the other hand, they can develop a very high capacity to assimilate themselves into any environment and move naturally in it. This is true cosmopolitanism, which in spite of its diverse elements is a stable, though compound, product. The unity of such lives is that of harmonic and contrapuntal music. The basic strand in it is always the deep bass of the early environment, punctuating the other melodic lines and sometimes surging above them. Then comes the middle register of work and workaday life, and, above all, there is the treble line of creative moods and moments of revelation, all accompanied by the trills and other decorative figures of sense experience. Such a life is no more ill-organized than a symphony. But it is not easily put together.

However, the initial homesickness is made more painful if a man has migrated from a small town or village. It is these men who feel most cruelly the truth of the saying that a great city is a great desert. Müller had come from Dessau, and even at Leipzig his life was not different in kind. But when he went to Berlin, Paris and London, he saw an agglomeration of people and not a community. He suffered cruelly at this contrast.

But of course the other parts of his mind remained active, and he could amuse himself with what he saw. As he wrote to his mother: 'For interesting observation there is no place like this.' Only he wished his mother there too. At first he took to that absorbing occupation of a visitor, *Flaner à Paris*, lounging about in the city and taking in its outward beauty, and also taking delight in the rush and bustle of the streets. The contrast of such scenes with the quiet of Dessau and Leipzig made him laugh out loud. Soon after his arrival he found that the days which, in the serious world, were called Holy Thursday and Good Friday, were known as *Longchamps* in Paris, and he saw magnificent equipages, ladies in splendid dresses and well-groomed gentlemen, driving out through the Champs Elysées to the races.

Müller had come to Paris in the last days of the Orleanist Monarchy, when the middle-class regime created by the July Revolution fifteen years before had become stagnant but had not yet provoked another revolution. In the Place du Carrousel at only twenty paces from himself he saw the bourgeois King Louis-Philippe as he was riding with his whole suite to watch the craze of the day, the midget General Tom Thumb, who held receptions in Rue Richelieu and drove out in his carriage the size of a child's go-cart.

Life in Paris did not then have the garishness it acquired under the Second Empire. But it had its lurid lights. Müller saw some of these. When dining *hors de la barrière* he once noticed a strange lady sitting not very far from him, and learned that she was the well-known Louve of Eugene Sue's *Mystères de Paris*, or, in other words, she belonged to the Orleanist prototype of the world of Toulouse-Lautrec. At the end of his stay he went to a masked ball at the Opera, which he described as odious, full of vulgar people, wretched dresses, noise, tumult and at the end drunken stupor for all. But the music, he added, was excellent.

He also saw the flaming comet of the day, the actress Rachel in Racine's *Phèdre*. He described what he saw to his mother: 'From the beginning to the end Rachel was nothing but a pale shadow whose only life is passion and despair, but passion which fails in all tragic effect because it has no influence on one's feelings. It is a crude and painful passion with which she is possessed, and in which there is nothing to awake our sympathy.'

But the most exceptional experience Müller had in Paris was his acquaintance with a wealthy Bengali from Calcutta, who was creating as great a sensation in the French capital as Dumas's *Count*

of Monte Cristo. He was Dwarkanath Tagore, father of Debendranath Tagore, the religious reformer, and grandfather of the
great Indian poet, Rabindranath Tagore, the only Indian to have
received the Nobel Prize for Literature. He had taken the best
suite in one of the best hotels of Paris, and was spending lavishly.
Not only did King Louis-Philippe receive him, he even came with
his court to a grand party given by Tagore, who had the room hung
with real Cashmere shawls, then the ambition of every fashionable
woman, and as she left placed a shawl on the shoulders of every lady.

Tagore had been told that Müller had already copied and collated
the MSS of the *Veda* in Paris, and so showed lively interest in the
young German, inviting him to his hotel. Müller went there often,
and spent the mornings discussing India and Indian customs, and
also practising English and Bengali. He discovered that Tagore was
very fond of music, was in fact an accomplished musician himself,
and had acquired a taste for Italian music.

One day Müller asked him to sing something Indian, and Tagore
at first sang a Persian song. Max Müller did not want to hear that,
but genuine Indian or Hindu music. Tagore smiled and turned
away, saying: 'You would not appreciate it.' But as Müller went on
pressing, he sat down at the piano and accompanying himself began
to sing. Müller could discern neither melody, nor rhythm, nor
harmony in what he sang. When told this, Tagore shook his head
and said: 'You are all alike. If anything seems strange to you and
does not please you at once, you turn away. When I first heard
Italian music, it was no music to me at all; but I went on and on,
till I began to like it, or, what you call, understand it.'

Then he began a general homily.

It is the same with everything else, [he went on]. You say our religion
is no religion, our poetry no poetry, our philosophy no philosophy.
We try to understand and appreciate whatever Europe has produced,
but do not imagine that we despise what India has produced. If you
studied our music as we do yours, you would find that there is melody,
rhythm, and harmony in it, quite as much as in yours. And if you would
study our poetry, our religion, and our philosophy, you would find
that we are not what you call heathens or miscreants, but know as
much of the Unknowable as you do, and have seen perhaps deeper into
it than you have!

He became very eloquent, and so excited that Max Müller pacified him by saying that he was quite aware that India possessed a science of music founded on mathematics.

This speech of Tagore's has a profoundly significant historical importance as one of the earliest utterances of the polemical position of modern Indians against their British rulers and detractors. These Hindus were accepting the West and rediscovering their ancient civilization at the same time, and creating a liberal nationalism based on a cultural synthesis to which the British never had an effective answer. Max Müller was to remain in touch with this nationalism all his life.

He also found another expression of both liberalism and nationalism in Dwarkanath Tagore and that was in his cynicism towards the Brahmins and also towards what he called the 'black-coated Brahmins', the Anglican clergy.

The dislike which Dwarkanath and all Hindu nationalists felt for English clergymen, in spite of their sincere admiration for so many other things English and also their gratitude for what the missionaries were doing for India in the way of education, was due to the fact that these men aired, in the most arrogant and frigid form, the moral superiority which the British in India felt towards the natives. Thus Dwarkanath, who read many English newspapers, copied out in a sort of black book he kept all the reports which did not redound to the credit of any bishop, dean, or priest, and he took great delight in bringing out this collection of every kind of ecclesiastical scandal whenever the talk turned on the respective merits of the Hindu and the Christian religions. Max Müller could only reply that no religion, whether in Italy, England, or India, should be judged by its priests.

Müller had opportunities to meet the foremost literary and intellectual figures of France of that epoch through Baron d'Eckstein, who gave him plenty of work in the way of copying Sanskrit manuscripts and paid him liberally, thus helping him to keep financially afloat in Paris. Eckstein was a notability in Paris, and had acquired his position as a propagator of Hindu wisdom and as an intermediary between Hindu thought and spirituality and the greatest writers of the day. He offered to introduce Müller to George Sand, Lamennais, Daniel Stern (Comtesse d'Agoult), Lamartine, Victor Hugo and others. But Müller had neither the time nor the money to take part in social life, nor did he have the inclination to make formal calls on celebrities. But he regretted it afterwards, and said that one result of his seeing so little of French life was that his spoken French remained imperfect.

But in connexion with his own interests he was bound to meet French Orientalists, both old and young, and he moved in their set. His first desire was to meet Burnouf, whose works he had read and for whom he had acquired a very great respect. But he did not know his address, and had to wait until Gathy discovered it for him. He then summoned up his courage and called on him. When he walked in he found a dear old gentleman in his dressing-gown, surrounded by his books and his four little daughters who were helping him to collect and arrange alphabetically a number of slips on which he had jotted down whatever had struck him as important in his reading during the day. Müller saw that the scholar was small, with a face that was decidedly German but became distinctively French when lighted up by a sparkle. Burnouf could hardly understand Müller because his French was very poor. But he showed him a civility such as he had not met with before. He inquired warmly after his German teachers, Brockhaus, Bopp and Lassen, and even mentioned a small book which Müller had written. He told him that he might attend his lectures in the Collège de France, and added that he would be most happy to give him any advice or help he wanted. Müller at once felt perfect trust in him, and was *aux cieux*, as he put it, to have found such an adviser.

Müller attended the lectures which Burnouf gave on the first book of the *Rig-Veda* as published by Rosen, and discovered Burnouf was a different type of lecturer. He had a small and select audience of young scholars like Roth and Goldstücker who were to become great specialists in Sanskrit, and also older men like Barthélemy St Hilaire, once a Minister of Foreign Affairs in France, and the Abbé Bardelli. He would explain his method, give his students all the new information he had collected and make them his fellow-workers. All this Müller found to be very inspiring, more especially because Burnouf was very generous in his approval and if his pupils found out anything new he was delighted to give them full credit for it. They all worked as a team, exploring, mapping out and prospecting a new and unknown country—which indeed the world of Oriental scholarship then was.

It was in Paris and at the express direction of Burnouf that Max Müller finally canalized his Sanskritic studies into the highly specialized research project which was to gain recognition for him in the world of scholarship: that of editing and publishing the *Rig-Veda*, the oldest scripture of the Hindus.

While working on the manuscripts of the *Rig-Veda* in Paris he often felt the want of some essential manuscripts which he knew were in the library of the East India Company in London, and therefore he wished to go over to consult them. But he did not have the money even to make the journey, far less for a stay. At last, in June 1846, when he was six months short of being twenty-three, he scraped together enough for a flying trip. Though Müller could not afford to cultivate the celebrities of Paris, he had made many personal friends, among whom were not only fellow-workers in the Oriental field but also a Duchess and a Countess, both of whom were musical and made much of him. These and others, including Burnouf, gave him farewell parties, and many of them came to the post-house to see him off. He left Paris at 5 p.m. on June 9, and arrived at Boulogne by the diligence at 11 a.m. the next day. He had never seen the sea before, and the sight of the wide, dancing expanse excited him so much that he hardly had the patience to go into the hotel, but set off at once for a long walk along the shore, and wandered about for five hours until forced to return by sheer hunger.

At ten o'clock that night he went on board the ship which was to take him direct to London. It was almost full moon, and he remained on deck taking in the beauty of the scene. But soon a rough passage brought on an onset of seasickness, and turned his delight into misery. A young Englishman, who was a fellow-passenger, found him holding on to the stays, trying to resist the attacks, and watched him with interest. This was William Howard Russell, who was to become the most famous war correspondent of his time, and was then working for *The Times* as well as studying law.

In the morning, once the ship had entered the Thames, Müller recovered. Russell saw a young man with regular features, fine intelligent eyes, most engaging expression, thick, dark hair but no trace of whiskers, beard or moustache, neatly dressed in a suit which showed his erect, slight, but well-built figure to advantage. The melancholy expression of the previous night had vanished from his face, and he was standing with an alert air and penetrating gaze. When a question from him to another passenger produced a misleading answer, Russell stepped up and gave the true explanation. Then they became acquainted. Müller said that he was going to

London to pursue his studies in Oriental literature, and Russell
said that he was a law student in the Middle Temple.

At the Customs House above Blackwall Müller found that his
portmanteau with all his worldly goods, and particularly his papers
and letters, had not arrived. He was in a panic and told Russell that
if it was lost that would be ruinous to him. The luggage of all the
passengers was gone over again, but there was not a trace of the
missing trunk. Seeing Müller's distress Russell offered to take him
to his chambers, give him a shakedown for the night, and come back
the next day to look for the box. Very much moved, Müller accepted
the offer, was driven to the Temple, and after dining at Andertons
in Fleet Street, went to sleep on a comfortable couch and in a sleeping suit provided by the laundress. The next day Russell and
Müller went back to the Customs House and found the trunk, and
Russell secured a decent bedroom for him at 10s. a week at the
house of a tailor in near-by Essex Street. Max Müller settled himself in, and in two days had seen Hyde Park, St James's Palace,
Westminster, St Paul's and the Tower, besides calling on Professor
Wilson to obtain permission to examine manuscripts in the library
of the East India Company.

During the first months of his stay in London Müller and
Russell met almost every day. In those days students could take
friends to their rooms after dining in hall at the Temple. Müller was
always a welcome guest at Russell's, and he provided novel and
exhilarating entertainment by singing, *Edite, bibite, conviviales,
Cramambuli* and other *studentenlieder*. Those who had rooms at the
Temple were eager to secure a special right to one performance,
which was always applauded and encored. That was *O Tannenbaum, O Tannenbaum!*, an imitation of the whole orchestra, trum-
pets, drums, bassoons and what not, delivered with the greatest
perfection.

Russell as a newspaper reporter got free tickets to concerts and
theatres, and the two went night after night to Drury Lane, the
Haymarket, the Adelphi, Her Majesty's, Covent Garden and others.
Müller's enjoyment of the opera was intense, and after seeing the
Italian opera he wrote to his mother:

A friend took me to the Italian Opera, which I had not yet seen either
here or in Paris. It was wonderful. A larger house than I have ever
seen, and every one in full dress. The boxes filled with the nobility,

and I saw Queen Victoria and Prince Albert, the Duke of Cambridge, etc. The music absolutely perfect; *Anna Bolena*, sung by Grisi, Mario and Lablache; all the highest artistic perfection. And then a ballet to which there can be nothing equal, and *Jugement de Paris* with Taglioni, Grahn, and Cerito as the three goddesses. The decorations were beautiful.

Müller's work in London offered no difficulty. Wilson at once gave him permission not only to examine the manuscripts, but even to take them home. On the very first day he invited him to dinner. Müller also paid visits to the British Museum, and made pleasant acquaintances there.

His first great difficulty was with English, which he could not speak well enough to make himself easily understood. He wrote to his mother that he hoped to improve, and his struggles with the language began soon enough. The morning after he had moved into his room in Essex Street, his landlady came in to inquire how he had slept, and then put another question: 'But, sir, don't you want another "pillar"?' Müller's bed was an immense four-poster, and as he had never seen such a structure before he had been in constant fear the previous night that the top would fall upon him and smother him. Bewildered by his landlady's pronunciation, he looked at the posts of the bed and asked in his turn: 'Why, what shall I do with another pillar, and where will you put it?' She then touched the pillows on the bed and said: 'Well, sir, you shall have another "pillar" tomorrow.' Müller said to himself: 'How shall I ever learn English if a "pillar" means a soft pillow?'

But his greatest problem was still money. He found that his German money did not go far in London, and he thought of supplementing it by giving private lessons. At the same time he economized as much as he could. He was paying 1s. 6d. for his dinners, but moved to new lodgings where he could eat with a German fellow-lodger for 1s. He walked with armfuls of books and papers from the library in Leadenhall Street to wherever his rooms were. Sometimes he was even roughly treated. He had taken his broken spectacles to be repaired at a shop in the Strand, and when he went to fetch them he laid down a sovereign. The salesman gave him change for only half a sovereign, and when Max Müller pointed out the mistake he became abusive to the foreigner in a well-worn coat. Sadly he left the shop, aware that the ten shillings represented several dinners, and actually some days passed dinnerless. One evening, however, as Müller was passing the shop the man rushed out, saying: 'Oh, sir, I have watched for you several days. You were right; I found that I had ten shillings too much when I counted up my money that evening, and I have longed to get it back to you,' and then he added, 'for you look as if you wanted it.'

His long-term worries were more harrowing. He found that there was so much material in London and so much work needing to be done on it, that unless he was to lose the benefit of all that he had already done he must stay there for years. As he wrote to Burnouf:

> The MSS are splendid, but in such masses that to copy all that concerns the *Veda* and my work would take at least two or three years of merely mechanical labour. So I must stay in England ... I shall do this if I can possibly, by private lessons and copying MSS, make enough to face the great expense of life here ... I do not deny that it is perhaps foolish to make such a sacrifice, and lead this anxious life for another five years without doing anything that can secure a settled post; but as I have once begun the work it must be finished, and I see no other way of doing it.

Burnouf replied to say that his plans were excellent, and hoped that Wilson would do something. 'Mr Wilson,' he wrote, 'will indirectly render a great service to Indian letters if, with the benevolent liberality with which he meets all those who ask his support, he makes it possible for you to stay in London as long as the task of publishing your *Rig-Veda* with its commentaries and indispensable indices may require.' To his mother Müller gave an estimate of five years, and said that his work was full of interest, and kept him straight, but he also added: 'Yet sometimes one longs for more in life than this everlasting struggle.'

Wilson was always sympathetic and willing to help, but for the present he could not help practically. That help came from another source, Baron C. K. J. von Bunsen, Prussian Minister in London. He was one of the most remarkable men of his age, a scholar who thought of himself as a student, a seeker of the origins of religion and spirituality, a man of bold and original ideas which were considered unorthodox; and possessing a warmth of heart not usual in the intellectual type. Yet he was a diplomat and a man of the world, with such social talents that the whole élite of London cultivated him.

He had formed the idea of writing a history of spirituality when he was only twenty-five, and had actually planned to go to India to find the *Veda* which was believed to embody the earliest spiritual expression of man. But while waiting in Rome on his way to the East, he became a friend of the Prussian Crown Prince, the future King Frederick William IV, and eventually joined the diplomatic service of his country. But though he gave up the idea of studying the *Veda*, he never lost his scholarly and philosophical interests. He worked hard at his books, and published the first of his many large works on religion and philosophy, *Christianity and Mankind*, in 1854.

On the strength of recommendations from Humboldt and Baroness Stolzenberg he had in 1844 secured for Max Müller the offer of a tutorship, which Müller had rejected. But the two had never met. Now they did, about three weeks after Müller's arrival in London, when he called on Bunsen at 4 Carlton Terrace. At that time, Bunsen was fifty-five and Müller still not twenty-three. Müller was astonished by the warmth of his reception. This meeting was a turning-point in his career, and to the end of his life Müller felt that he could never adequately express what he owed to Bunsen.

Bunsen told him how glad he was to see the son of his old friend, and advised him to continue his researches without giving thought to anything else. When Müller told him about his work and his financial difficulties, Bunsen at once assured him that he had found a friend (meaning himself) who would care for him as a father for a son. And he kept his word. He asked Müller to trust him absolutely, for he was going to take all responsibility on himself. For nearly a year Müller was supported by his patron, and without that help he would have had to abandon his researches and go back to Germany.

What attracted Bunsen to Müller was in the first instance the *Veda*, whose quest he had to renounce. Thus whenever he was shown some portion of Müller's work, he said: 'I am glad to have lived to see the *Veda*. Whatever you want, let me know. I look upon you as myself grown young again.'

But if Bunsen himself was attracted by what he knew of Müller's mind, the ladies of the family felt the attraction of his presence. Mme Bunsen cherished the remembrance of his first appearance at her house for, as she wrote, he astonished the family by his youthful looks and cheerfulness.

Though Müller did not live in Carlton Terrace, he made it his real home in London, and came and went whenever he pleased. Often, even during receptions, Bunsen would sit with him in the library discussing all sorts of subjects with him. They did not always agree. During his stay in Rome Bunsen had become acquainted with Champollion, the decipherer of hieroglyphics, and had shifted his interest to Egyptology. As a result, he inclined to give primacy to Egypt and not to India in respect of the first emergence of thought and civilization. Max Müller did not deny that Egypt had older historical records, but he said that his interest lay in thought. Bunsen at times got very excited, for in argument he could be very violent, but that never made any difference to his affection for Müller, who was invited to all parties and special occasions besides being taken to Bunsen's country-house at Totteridge.

Everybody who was anybody in London came to Bunsen's house, and there Max Müller saw such personalities as the Archbishop of Canterbury, the Duke of Wellington, Sir Robert Peel, also divines, intellectuals and scholars in many fields of knowledge: Connop Thirwal, F. D. Maurice, Rawlinson, Layard, Hodgson and Birch. The discussions mostly took place at breakfast parties, which were in fashion then in London as they remained for many more decades at Oxford. They were quite new to Müller and he enjoyed them very much, though he thought that they broke too much into the day. Some of Bunsen's parties were very grand affairs, and some idea of them can be formed from a description that Müller gave to his mother three years later:

They had asked 750 people—the whole Corps Diplomatique and the élite of English society. The whole house was like a garden, the balconies covered with awnings from which one had a splendid view over London, the garden of the house illuminated, beautiful music, German songs with a full chorus, from the German opera now in London. I cannot describe the diamonds and dresses, but I have never seen such a crowd of beautiful women and girls together. Guizot was there, and Palmerston; in fact, all the lions and lionesses of the season.

The normal parties were, however, much more intimate, and Müller liked the whole family. Besides having Müller in his own house, Bunsen also took him to his friends, both in the country and in London. One day he took him to the house of his friend, Archdeacon Hare at Hurstmonceaux. Another time he was taken to Lord Ellesmere's house, famous for its priceless collections of books and pictures. He wrote to his mother: 'Only think of looking round in the middle of a conversation and seeing on all sides Raphaels, Titians, Murillos, Carlo Dolcis—all originals!' He added a comment which makes me feel that things have changed since his days: 'This sort of thing only exists in England.'

At first this kind of life was a great trial for Müller, for he committed any number of gaucheries from his ignorance. He did not know, as he wrote in his autobiography, that potatoes could not be eaten with a fork, nor fish touched with the table-knife (for fish-knives did not exist then), and he could not understand why it was worse manners to divide crisp pastry with a knife than with a fork scattering it over the table-cloth. He also had difficulties in addressing and writing to people. Once, having been told to address a person exactly as he was addressed by him, he wrote a letter to the Bishop of Oxford, Bishop Wilberforce, with the superscription, 'My dear Sir,' because the Bishop had written to him in that way. Bunsen remonstrated with him for not returning calls nor leaving cards after dining with people. Yet Bunsen took delight in inviting Müller whenever he had a prince or some such grandee to lunch or dinner.

These were kindnesses meant to lick the German bear cub into shape, and Bunsen showed no less kindness when he found that Müller could not go to see his mother in Germany when she was seriously ill. He at once sent him to Berlin with despatches, and this also gave him an opportunity to meet his German friends and patrons. After he returned from Berlin, Bunsen helped Müller in another way which relieved him of all anxiety and dependence in regard to money, and put his plan to publish the Rig-Veda on a sound financial basis.

Max Müller had begun to copy and collate the MSS of the *Rig-Veda* with a view to printing it eventually, but he worked in complete uncertainty, because he did not know who might be willing to publish it. He sounded out the Prussian government for financial support, but without success. In Paris, too, he had no luck. An offer came from the Academy of St Petersburg, but on such conditions that he could not accept it. At last a German publisher of Königsberg came forward, but he would undertake the actual work only if a sufficient number of copies were subscribed for beforehand. By way of publicity Müller had a prospectus printed in a number of languages. The Prussian and the French governments agreed to take a large number of sets, but the subscription was still short, and the East India Company was approached with a request to take one hundred sets. At the suggestion of both Bunsen and Wilson, Müller called on the Directors, but they were unwilling to give financial support to a work carried out in a foreign country. Then Bunsen, who had influence with the Directors, stepped in energetically. It was no easy task to persuade the Board of Directors, all practical businessmen, to authorize considerable expenditure on an old book which none of them could read and many had not even heard of. But Bunsen saw the Chairman as well as the Directors, and represented to them what a disgrace it would be if some other country than England published this sacred book of the Hindus. Professor Wilson too threw in his weight. At their insistence, the Directors agreed to the project in principle.

But the working out and consideration of the details took time, for the commitment was not only to be large but also uncertain. During this period Müller was very restless and uncomfortable, and thought that the uncertainty was making him unfit to do any work. As he wrote to his mother: 'The whole month has gone in hopes, expectations, disappointments, and rejoicings, and though it is possible that I might hear today that all is settled, it may dawdle on to next year, and even fail entirely.' But he had confidence in Bunsen. It did dawdle on, to the April of 1847, but on April 15 he informed his mother joyfully that the matter was decided. He could hardly believe that the struggle was ending and the independence he had hoped for had at last come. He was to get £4 for every sheet printed, which, according to the programme of editing and printing Müller had worked out would give him £200 a year, which would enable him to live at ease, and the income was guaranteed for the duration of the whole work, which might be many years.

As it happened, there came to him at the same time an offer of a post as assistant librarian in the British Museum at £150 a year. But on Bunsen's advice he declined it, preferring his freedom and trusting to time to bring him some means of livelihood which would be permanent. Among all his feelings the gratitude he felt towards Bunsen was the strongest. He wrote to his mother:

I knew that none of my relations and friends agreed with me; on the contrary, that they all thought my plans foolish and exaggerated, and I had no one from whom I could expect support—I mean, who would have lent me a small sum for a few years. In fact, all my time, money, and work, indeed my whole life perhaps would have been sacrificed and lost, had not Bunsen, who had once been in the same position, without my saying anything to him, stood by me, and in this way made it possible for me to struggle on with joyful confidence and firm faith towards the goal I had set before me. I do not know whether I should thank God more that I have at last attained my long-desired and long-sought object or that I have gained the friendship of so noble and distinguished a man as Bunsen.

The work of printing began at once at Oxford, though he sent the text and corrected the proofs from London. But in February 1847, before the question of printing had been decided, Max Müller had to come to Oxford to consult a manuscript in the Bodleian, and that was his first visit to the place where the following year he was to settle and spend the rest of his life. He was enchanted by what he saw, and informed his mother: 'I have seen the most interesting and beautiful city in Europe. The whole town is of the Middle Ages, and consists almost entirely of churches, monasteries (now colleges), castles, and towers, all in old English or Gothic, and the whole life is of the Middle Ages.' What struck him no less strongly was the contrast presented by the students and teachers going about in their black gowns, to what he had seen in German university towns like Leipzig or Jena where the students walked about in the streets in pink cotton trousers and dressing-gowns.

He came to Oxford four months later to pay a more formal visit, to read a paper before the seventeenth meeting of the British Association for the Advancement of Science held in 1847. One day, when he had gone to see Bunsen with some of his work, Bunsen said: 'You must come with me to Oxford to the meeting of the British Association.' Müller asked him what this was, and Bunsen replied that he would explain it later, but Müller was to sit down at once and write a paper. He himself was going to read a paper on the 'Results of the recent Egyptian Researches in reference to Asiatic and African Ethnology and Classification of Languages', and he wanted Dr Karl Meyer to support him with one on Celtic philology, and Müller with another on the relationship between the Aryan and aboriginal languages of India. Müller was thoroughly frightened, but Bunsen would not take a refusal, and said: 'We must show them what we have done in Germany for the history and philosophy of language, and I reckon on your help.' But also he was anxious to advance Müller's career, and wanted to introduce him not only to the world of learning, but to all important people who might be able to help him.

Müller prepared the paper, but remained nervous, for he knew that, generally speaking, English scholars were hostile to German scholarship. More especially, he was afraid of some not very friendly ethnologists like Dr Latham and Mr Crawford, the latter well known in British learned circles as the Objector General. As he expected, he was criticized when in his paper he tried to prove the Indo-European and Sanskritic affiliations of the Bengali language, which were being denied by a school of English philologists. But the opposition was not so much against him or his views, as against what a group of English scholars called the 'German clique' headed by Prince Albert and Bunsen; and the Prince too was present at the congress. However, Dr Pritchard, the pioneer British anthropologist, defended him very generously. Later, there was even objection to including Müller's paper in the proceedings, but Bunsen declared that he would not allow his own paper to be printed unless Müller's was also, so it was. Max Müller never reprinted the paper because he thought it was very immature. But I found it extremely interesting as the first formulation of his linguistic ideas. I have also been surprised by the knowledge he showed of the Bengali language, which he had learned in Berlin and then practised with Dwarkanath Tagore in Paris.

Though this was his first participation in a learned conference, Max Müller was not very much impressed by the discussions, the wranglings of scholars as he called them, but he found the social occasions connected with the conference very interesting. Being with Bunsen, he was invited to all the official dinners, at which the grave Vice-Chancellor, Dr Frederick Plumptree, presided. At one of these Prince Lucien Bonaparte delivered a eulogy of British freedom. 'In France', he declared, 'with all the declamations about *Liberté*, *Egalité*, *Fraternité*, there is very little freedom, but you in England; you have your old tree of liberty, which is always flowering and showering *peas* on the whole world.' A titter went round the table, stopping only at the Vice-Chancellor.

Max Müller went back to London to resume his work on the *Rig-Veda*. But in order to establish a text he had to go to Paris early next year. He also wanted to consult a particular manuscript in the Bibliothèque Nationale, and to see Hagedorn. But he was caught in the February Revolution. From the windows of Hagedorn's apartment he saw the fighting and the tumult, and gave an account of his experience to his mother:

I am still so excited that I can hardly describe all that I have seen and done. Since Tuesday last [Feb. 24] I have had sleepless nights from fighting, the roar of cannon, burning of houses, fall of buildings, etc., men murdered by hundreds or simply shot down in the streets. No one's life was safe, for there was neither Government, police, nor soldiers. The man in the blouse was lord of all, and blood ran in the streets, which were filled with barricades. Women on horseback, ruffians on the finest officers' chargers paraded the streets, carrying Louis-Philippe's throne in triumph . . . One could see all that went on from Hagedorn's windows; the bullets whistled on every side, and yet ladies went out on foot *pour voir la Revolution*. We did the same, and were more than once pursued by the cavalry. I saw barricades built up of omnibuses, tables and pianos, attacked and taken, and again built up, till at last the soldiers fraternized with the people, gave up their weapons, and finally withdrew. There was nothing grand in it.

When too many bullets began to come through his windows, Max Müller thought it prudent to leave Paris. But the problem was to take back his trunk full of precious manuscripts, all belonging to the East India Company, for though the railway line to Le Havre was open, the station had been burnt down, and in order to get to the trains he would have to climb over three barricades. He offered his concierge five francs to carry the box, but the consierge's wife would not hear of it. He raised it to ten francs, with the same result. But when he held up a *louis d'or* she said to her husband: '*Allez, mon ami, allez toujours.*'

As soon as he arrived in London he went to see Bunsen, and Bunsen took him at once to Palmerston, to whom Müller gave the first news of the deposition of Louis-Philippe, and he also showed him a bullet which he had picked up in his own room. After that he went on with his work, but found that the work of reading the proofs from London was slow as well as tiring. So he decided to migrate to Oxford. Another reason which inclined him to do so was that he thought he was getting too gay in London. In addition to Bunsen's parties he had his own social engagements. For instance, he went regularly to the suppers given by his friend Vaux of the British Museum, whose invitation cards were adorned with pictures of Assyrian bulls and hawk-headed Egyptian gods, and he also went to balls at the houses of his English friends, and danced away in his old coat, finding the English girls to be very beautiful and pleasant. He wrote to his mother that 'one hardly sees a single ugly face in a

3*

ballroom—which one cannot say in either France or Germany'. Then he had his German circle, consisting of German Sanskrit scholars as well as the German merchants at Denmark Hill. All this came in the way of his work. So in May 1848, he went to Oxford, and took rooms in Walton Street. As it happened, this turned out to be the beginning of a lifelong stay.

But even at Oxford Max Müller was not to live the life of a recluse. His paper had been printed along with Bunsen's by that time, and in academic circles he found it to be 'a good visiting card', as he told his mother. His handsome looks, extremely youthful appearance, the unfamiliar subject with which he was occupied and the kind words spoken about him by Bunsen and Dr Pritchard were remembered, and he was received very kindly by the heads of colleges, the younger teachers and the undergraduates. But on account of his age, and in spite of his scholarship, he moved most naturally and happily among the younger fellows and undergraduates. A majority of them were Balliol men, which meant the most brilliant young men at Oxford in those days. Morier, Grant, Sellar, Palgrave, Spottiswoode, Walrond, Earle, Church, Butler, Thomson, Story-Maskelyne, all to rise to one kind of distinction or another, were among his intimates. He also knew Matthew Arnold, Clough, Jowett, Stanley, Froude, Coxe, Johnson, Acland, Donkin and many others. They were a happy company, and recalling them Max Müller wrote at the very end of his life: 'Those early Oxford days were bright for me, and now, when those young and old faces, whether undergraduates or archbishops, rise up again before me, I being almost the only one left of that happy company, I ask again, 'Did they also belong to a mere dreamland, they who gave life to my life, and made England my real home?'

He was noticed by the town, as well as the gown, as a rare and exotic bird in the streets. As he passed among them he observed people staring at him and whispering to one another. A vague notion had got about that the handsome young German had discovered a strange religion older than the Jewish or Christian, which also contained the key to many religious mysteries. That should speak to us in favour of the 'man in the street' of those days.

His settling at Oxford is the point at which it is necessary to take an observation, to use a nautical expression, in order to determine Max Miller's position in his voyage through life. He was under twenty-five, yet he had completed the transition from the Ruritanian principality ruled by Duke Leopold to England under the young Queen Victoria, to the Oxford of Jowett and Mark Pattison soon to be remodelled by Gladstone. It was a remarkable feat for a man so young, so poor and so obscure, and the passage was no less long in terms of cultural distances than it was in space. In Anhalt-Dessau he was in the Age of Enlightenment and Benevolent Despotism, in England people were exulting over the march of industry, science and democracy. He had also reached the place where he was to spend the rest of his life, and had at last ensured a means of living which would free him from literally praying for his daily bread.

But still he had not arrived at certainty or security. He did not know how long he would remain at Oxford or in England, and he was not settled in a career which he could look upon as permanent. The last billet was yet to be found. Whatever he had obtained was promise, not fulfilment. But that was the most significant feature of his early life and choices—his regular preference for freedom to pursue what he felt as his vocation, at the expense of security and ease. He never played for safety, and paid no heed to the dictum that a bird in hand is worth two in the bush. This sort of behaviour which worldly wisdom regards as perversity is not found in anybody who does not possess or, to be more correct, is not possessed by a very strong sense of vocation. But this sense is not a rational driving force, it is always a supra-rational motive power, almost as compulsive as submitting to love for a woman without knowing why.

But the strength with which such a sense of vocation can take hold of a man is wholly determined by his character and temperament, which make him attack the eternal problems set by life in his particular way. Nothing is more profoundly true than the saying that it avails nothing if you gain the world and lose your soul. But it is also terrifyingly true that the first problem for a man is to remain alive in the world before he can even dream of conquering it. So livelihood and vocation are always at loggerheads. In this situation most men concentrate on livelihood, raising it if they can to security and comfort, or finally to affluence and luxury. A minority, however, stick to vocation. The former make their work conform to their means of livelihood, the latter contrive to gain livelihood out of their vocation. Certainly, it is the most difficult thing in life to make vocation and profession merge. Max Müller had arrived at the starting-point of that process without achieving finality.

It must however be pointed out that even this beginning would not have been possible solely through his own determination and effort, unless there was something in the spirit of the age that could help him. At extremely critical points of his life he had received help which came to him as if by complete chance, and he had also received general aid and encouragement which he could not have reckoned on. One has to admit that a young man in Müller's position would never have got all this in our age. Quite apart from ministers, politicians, eminent divines and men of letters, would a university don of today receive a penniless beggar such as Müller appeared in the eyes of the world? Would any head of a college at Oxford invite to his house a young and unknown foreign scholar working in the Bodleian? The truth of the matter is that in our age, in spite of all its talk about equality of opportunity and the iniquity of class distinctions, successful and established men are infinitely more exclusive, set-conscious, stand-offish and snobbish than men in their position were in any aristocratic age. Our age has erected such psychological barriers between men of different positions that the outcome has been the creation of a rancorous hatred by the have-nots for what they call the 'Establishment', which is mistakenly taken for a revolutionary movement. Our times have recovered the primitive's hostility for the 'unlike'. Today an exceptional man is swamped by sheer numbers. The aristocratic age recognized classes, but never made them over-rigid. Its élite needed new blood continuously, and so just as it maintained its economic prosperity by marrying into wealthy bourgeois families, it welcomed talent to maintain its mental level.

There is always something mysterious about the rise of a man to fame and spectacular worldly success. It presents such a complex interaction of circumstances and genius that it cannot be fully explained. At the beginning nothing is seen nor even suspected. The ladder is hidden, but suddenly the heights reached are perceived, and then the whole process appears to be the result of something like determinism. When one considers how and where Max Müller began and where he finally arrived, his success and fame too would seem to have been due to predestination. After he became famous, young and struggling men wrote wanting to know how he had managed to keep his head above water and yet rise in life without sacrificing his independence or his vocation. He gave a modest answer to this question in his autobiography, in which he said:

'Everything in my career came about most naturally, not by my own effort, but owing to those circumstances or to that environment of which we have heard so much of late.' That appears to be the theory of natural selection applied to personal success.

Max Müller had a clear idea of how this principle worked in England, and he could see the illustration of the process in the lives of many of his friends and acquaintances who rose to eminence in different lines. More especially, he gave his explanation in regard to the fame and standing of Charles Kingsley, about whom he said that whenever a social or a religious or a great political question stirred the people, they thought of Kingsley. Nothing in Kingsley's worldly position could have given him this influence, but only the view generally held of the quality of his mind and character.

Now, Max Müller attributed the creation of such a view to a 'very minute organization of public feeling in England', of which, he added, people abroad had no idea. Then he described the basis of this organization:

> This close intellectual organization is favoured in England by many circumstances. The number of public schools is limited. Of the universities there are, or there were till lately, two only. Most men of note are acquainted with each other from school or from university, and whoever has gained the trust and love of his friends at Eton or Oxford, retains it mostly through life . . . Add to this the innumerable societies, clubs, charitable institutions, political associations, and last, not least, the central hearth in London, Parliament, where everybody appears from time to time, if only to have a warm shaking of hands with old friends and acquaintances, and you will understand that England hangs more closely together and knows itself better than any other country in Europe. As a natural result of all this there is a very sharp control. A man who has once attracted public attention is not easily lost sight of.

This is a very perceptive account of the social and psychological process in nineteenth-century England which promoted men of talent from private to public status and function, and it certainly leads to the conclusion that a social and intellectual élite can do much more to utilize the available talent among a people than an egalitarian community.

Anyway, through his life at Oxford Max Müller had come into close contact with many Englishmen who belonged to this élite working as a clearing house of ability. Besides, he had also secured the good opinion of men in his line who counted, in Berlin, Paris and London. In his personal affiliations he was well placed, and it now depended only on him as to how high he would rise.

Chapter 3

FORMATION OF MIND AND CHARACTER

WHEN Max Müller ended his *wanderjahre* by taking up residence at Oxford, he was six months short of being twenty-five, and his personality, in its dual aspect of mind and character, was already formed in its structure and functioning. After that, so far as his own development was concerned, he was to go on adding to the content of his mind. But henceforth he was also to give his mind a new role —that of impinging on other minds as teacher and writer. The publication of the first volume of his edition of the *Rig-Veda* in 1849 was symbolic of his transition from purely internal growth to external projection, which gained strength from year to year until in the last quarter of the nineteenth century he came to be accepted as one of the outstanding figures in the world of European thought.

At this point of transition it is necessary to take stock of his mind and character as these were then, and also to consider the influences which shaped them. Perhaps the scope of this chapter will be more correctly stated if I say that in it I shall analyse young Müller's personality as the product of a historical process. What was distinctively personal in his qualities and activities will come out of the whole account of his life. What it is necessary to examine here is the relationship between his personality and the particular environment, both social and psychological, in which he grew up. This alone can place his individuality in its rightful historical setting.

The particularity of individual human-beings is generally very much exaggerated, and in regarding every person as unique, as he in one sense certainly is, it is invariably forgotten that his particularity is only the psychological counterpart of what is known as continuous somatic variation in zoology, which makes every cat or dog equally particular. It is only in the case of very exceptional persons that it is safe to attribute true individuality, and even then it cannot be assumed absolutely, for such men would also be found to be the products of a particular historical process. Real originality is the surplus value which enables the exceptional man to give an added momentum to the process of which he is the product.

The foundations of Max Müller's mental life were laid in

Anhalt-Dessau, and under the control of the social and geographical environment which that principality constituted. He made a symbolic confession about this himself. He wrote in his autobiography, published after his death, that the Dessau dialect remained with him for life, and his friends told him that though he had spoken English and French for years they could always detect from his German accent that he came from Dessau or Leipzig. One might add that there remained a dialectal or local accent in his thinking and feeling.

The first evidence of this is to be found in his religious beliefs. All of pre-Reformation Christianity in the Protestant parts of Germany was remoulded by Lutheranism, which I might describe as the transforming of the deep, dark, warm and mysterious forest of German medieval Christianity into the good arable land of Protestantism. Those who adopted this form of Christianity also thought that it was the most basic, simple and therefore indestructible form of the religion. Luther himself was thought of by these Protestants as a saint. His hymns were sung in churches, and seemed to singers and listeners alike to be little different from the psalms of David. This musical expression of Lutheranism reached its fullness in Bach. Sharing the worship of Luther at Dessau, Müller was shocked when after coming to Oxford he found him spoken of as just another mortal, or even as a heretic, and a most dangerous one at that.

Max Müller came into his Protestant religious inheritance at Dessau through his mother, to whom he owed all the practical side of his religion. He came to hold the view very strongly that any true religious feeling can only be planted deeply at home, and by a mother even more than a father. Max Müller also believed that the sense of a divine presence everywhere, once implanted in the heart of a child, remains for life.

So it was with him. His simple faith remained unshaken through all storms. As he himself put it: 'In its extreme simplicity and childishness it answered all the purposes for which religion is meant.' It seemed to satisfy all his religious needs. So what he read later in Strauss or Ewald, Renan or Colenso, never disturbed his faith or his life with and in God. Nor was he interested in the question of the improbability of the Christian miracles, which for many of his contemporaries had a crucial bearing on faith. He wrote:

Suppose it was proved to me that, on geological evidence, the earth or the world could not have been created in six days, what was that to me? Suppose it was proved to me that Christ could never have given leave to the unclean spirits to enter into the swine [on the assumption that He could not be so unjust and unkind to innocent animals] what was that to me? Let Colenso and Bishop Wilberforce, let Huxley and Gladstone fight about such matters; their turbulent waves could never disturb me, could never even reach me in my safe harbour.

So he remained outside the religious controversies of Oxford; and the crises of faith which formed an essential part of Oxford's religious life never touched him. He could never share the doubts and agonies of his friends at Oxford—Froude, Liddon, Clough, Arnold or Kingsley—and he even tried to show them how self-made their difficulties were. His own faith had little burden to carry, and no impedimenta bore it down.

This kind of faith made him take the duty of church attendance more or less lightly, and this attitude, he said, was typically German. 'The religious and devotional element,' he wrote, 'is very strong in Germany, but the churches are mostly empty. A German keeps his religion for weekdays rather than for Sunday.'

At a higher level his simple faith made him suspicious both of the Church and of theology. This was stated by him most emphatically, not in any formal pronouncement on religion, but in his novel *Deutsche Liebe (German Love)*. Its hero, who certainly represented Müller's own feelings, says:

The cause of many heated and violent conflicts lies in this,—that the doctrine of Christ, instead of winning our hearts gradually and irresistibly as it won the hearts of the Apostles and early Christians, meets us from our earliest childhood as the incontrovertible law of a mighty Church, and claims from us an unqualified submission, which we call faith. Doubt will arise sooner or later in the breast of every one who has the power of reflection and veneration for truth, and then whilst we are just in the right way to gain our faith, the spectres of doubt and unbelief rise before us, and hinder the quiet growth of the new life.

He always made a distinction between the Christ of faith and the Christ of the Church and formal theology. He set forth the distinction in a letter he wrote to his wife after she and his second daughter, Mary, had seen the Passion Play at Oberammergau in 1880. He wrote: 'It must have been very powerful—and I feel sure just now nothing is more wanted than to be powerfully impressed with the truly human character of Christ. It has almost vanished under the extravagant phraseology of hymns and creeds—and yet how much greater is the simple story of his unselfish life than all the super-latives of later theology.'

The same opinion he repeated to Renan in another letter: 'My wife and daughter are still away; they were quite overpowered by the Passion Play at Oberammergau. We have lost far too much of the reality of Christ, and I have always thought that your work has done most good by restoring that reality, so far as it can be, in dia-metrical opposition to Strauss.'

This feeling had begun to grow on him very early in life, and he put it quite explicitly in the novel. 'It is only a wonder,' to quote its hero again, 'that theologians have not yet deprived us of all religion; and they will do so if the believers do not determinately oppose them, and say to them, "Thus far, but no further."' Though he knew that each church must have its ministers, he had also learned from history that 'there has as yet been no religion in the world which the priests—the Brahmans, the Shamans, the Bonzes, the Lamas, the Pharisees and Scribes—have not corrupted and de-stroyed. They quarrel and argue in a language which is incompre-hensible to nine-tenths of their community.'

He quoted with approval the saying of an English writer that 'truth makes revelation and not revelation truth', and so if certain writings were required to be accepted by believers as the inspired truth and as the basis of the *only saving* religion, the question arose as to how anybody was to be sure that they were inspired without imputing to himself an equal degree of inspiration? They could avoid doing this only by admitting inspiration in the Apostles and early Fathers. But that, too, was bound to raise the question of how was one to know which early bishops were inspired and which were not. In the end, the last desperate step was unavoidable; to accept apostolic succession by the laying on of hands as the channel of inspiration, making all inward conviction, all self-surrender, all faithful introspection superfluous.

His Lutheranism made Müller unsympathetic even to medieval German mysticism which gave expression to one of the most beauti-ful aspects of Christianity in Germany. He could not share the current admiration for the *Theologia Germanica*, whose authorship was unknown. So, in his novel, he made the hero say that according to his feeling it was wanting in the sense of the human and the real.

'The whole mysticism of the fourteenth century,' he said, 'seems to me useful as a preparation; but it first attained its solution in that manly and courageous return to actual life which we find in Luther.'

Müller would have none of the ecstasy in annihilation which is the essence of Christian mysticism. He accepted it as the first step. 'Man must, once in his life,' he said, 'perceive nothingness; he must feel that of himself he is nothing; that his being, his beginning, his eternal life, are rooted and hid in something supra-terrestrial and incomprehensible.' But that negative return to God could never lead to the goal, though it could create a divine longing after a true home. The truth was that man could not abolish the act of creation, as the mystics desired. Though formed from nothing, that is to say, by and of God alone, he could not through his own power return to nothing; and the self-annihilation of which the mystics spoke was hardly better than the Buddhistic Nirvana:

> But this annihilation of the creature was not the will of the Creator, for He had created it. 'God makes Himself into man,' says St Augustine, 'not man into God.' Mysticism should only be, as the ordeal by fire, to steel the human soul, not to dissolve it away into vapour like boiling water in a cauldron. He who had perceived the nothingness of Self should also recognize this Self as a reflex of the truly divine Self.

But the invalid princess to whom the hero of *Deutsche Liebe* says all this, replies: 'Health and strength are required for your faith, but there are also life-weary souls who long for rest and sleep, who feel themselves so lonely, that when they fall asleep in God they will miss the world as little as the world will miss them.'

That was the crux of the matter: Max Müller's faith belonged to a robust and active world in a particular age. There was, however, in him a very strong mystical element or predisposition, but his religious conviction did not want to admit it. So it passed over to his mode of thinking. All his speculation, even though it concerned language, had a supra-rational streak in it, and he might be said to have been a mystic in philosophy, or for that matter in linguistics.

But this line of thinking and feeling about Christianity did not make Müller reject the historical approach to the religion. In fact, there was no question of his rejecting that approach during the course of his education at school and university. At school his religious teaching was chiefly historical and moral. So from his earliest youth he was taught to look upon Christianity as an historical fact; on Christ and his disciples as historical characters; on the Old and New Testament as real historical books.

At the university stage the historical study of Christianity became as familiar as the study of Roman history. The professors he looked up to as great authorities, such as Lotze and Weisse at Leipzig and Schelling and Michelet in Berlin, left him with a firm conviction that the Old and New Testaments were historical books which should be treated in accordance with the same critical principles as any other ancient books, including the sacred texts of the East. He was taught to see that they contained only what, under the conditions in which they were written, they could contain, namely, a number of traditions of great antiquity collected by men who gathered together all that they thought would be useful for the education of the people. As a result of this teaching, Müller left behind him the idea that the Christian scriptures contained revelation in the sense that they were verbally communicated by the Deity. What occupied his mind at that stage were questions as to the date and authorship of these books and the historical sequence of the doctrines embodied in them.

This shows that Müller was coming into the great movement of thought regarding Christianity which had been started at the end of the eighteenth century by Reimarus with his tentative attempt to distinguish between the historical Jesus and the theological Christ. In this antithesis Max Müller did not go over to the historical school entirely. In fact, after leaving university, he became somewhat suspicious of it. During his stay in Paris he frequently discussed the historical aspect of Christianity with Renan, who was already adumbrating his idyllic view of Christ and his imaginative reconstruction of Judaism and Christianity. By that time Müller had moved to the philosophical stage of his mental growth. Under the influence of Kant, he was thinking more about the limits of knowledge, even in respect of the early history of Christianity, than of the specific problem of the date of, for instance, the fourth gospel. Renan and Müller agreed that the evidence on the life of Jesus and on what he actually taught was very slender. But while Renan still directed his attention to the historic aspect, Müller wanted to find out how the religious truths proclaimed by Christ could spring up in His mind at that time. He doubted very much whether any scholar would be justified in giving his interpretation of the life and teaching of Christ from the historical fragments at his disposal. He objected to Renan's idyllic leanings, and when his *Vie de Jésus* was published in 1863, he called the image presented in that book, 'Renan's ghost, or rather his corpse of Christ', which was very severe. In the end Müller came to believe that each man had the right to believe in his own Christ, and to this view, he remained true, all through his life.

It was also from his Dessau upbringing that Max Müller derived the ethical counterpart of his religious principles—a simple and solid moral consciousness which developed robust convictions. All through life nothing repelled him more than untruthfulness and deception, cowardice, idleness and self-indulgence. His sense of moral responsibility was very individualistic, due in part to the spirit of the age, but also to the fact that he grew up in a very small community. In his autobiography Max Müller wrote that it was dangerous to go through life with so imperfect a knowledge of the world, and with so small a viaticum of wisdom. None the less, all this stood him in better stead than a more sophisticated and complex view of life could have. His early struggles were stark and bare, and they needed stark and bare qualities to be mastered. Certainly, he could never have gone through what he had to endure and fight against without the aid of these elemental or even elementary prescriptions for tackling life. As we have now seen, for practical purposes the only alternative to these moral precepts are sleeping tablets.

But even as a schoolboy Max Müller had begun to realize that however useful the moral rigidity of Dessau might be in practice, it could not be maintained in the sphere of moral concepts, for which a tenable view of moral evil was essential. Curiously enough, this kind of introspection was set going within him by reading Goethe's *Wilhelm Meister* in the last years of his school life. He knew that his mother would not like his reading the book, and so he wrote:

> I had already said to myself that you would not be pleased that I had read *Wilhelm Meister*, and in some respects you are quite right; not that it can exactly hurt me, but that it might occupy my thoughts too much. On the evil influence of reading or other temptations, I could not point out any better passage than the Latin verse in *Faust* which Mephistopheles repeats to the student, that God is holy and good just because He knows what evil is. This is very true if only further explained; i.e. because He knows evil, He never commits it. If we could

imagine that God did not know what sin and temptation are, we could not call Him God, for we should have an imperfect God.

So he assured his mother that the more dangerous things he read, the stronger he became to wage war against them. He was, however, quite ready to admit his mother's argument that it was foolhardy to throw oneself into temptations without thoroughly knowing oneself and ascertaining how far one could stand firm. This was a remarkable letter from a boy of some sixteen years.

Nevertheless, the moral rigidity of Dessau adhered to him in his dealings with other men, and it developed in him certain incapacities for living in the wider world into which he moved later. He had to acquire the capacity to do so from painful experience. At Dessau he saw those whom he liked, and those whom he did not, and there was no compulsion on him or anybody to cultivate unpleasant fellow townsmen. Therefore he did not become aware until very much later that in any community there might be a large intermediate group of people whom it was neither necessary to admire nor to despise, and with whom one could be civil without caring whether one met them again or not.

So, there grew up in his mind in his early years the image of a community divided into two classes; one quite perfect, pure as angels, and the other consisting of black sheep. There were no intermediate links, no shading of light and dark. As a result, he became used to approaching people with complete trust, and it took him many years before he learned to make allowance for human weakness. He lost, as he admitted, many a charming friend because he weighed them in his rough Dessau balance. At the end of his life he grew more tolerant, without losing his moral strictness. He came to see that even disloyalty or untruth in certain circumstances might not be a deadly sin. He realized that a man known to be guilty of falsehood to himself might yet be looked upon as perfectly honest and trustworthy by others. He suspected also that moral severity could often be sharpened by self-interest. But this tolerance did not come to him easily. Nor did he have it when he came to Oxford at the age of twenty-five and most needed the capacity for making allowances.

On the other hand, the smallness of the human community in Dessau developed in him a very strong awareness of personal responsibility for social welfare. To help others was a duty, and he considered that a tenth of his income should be the least that he gave away in charity. In his days of prosperity he far exceeded this sum. To his mother and sister he was most generous, and though he preferred the best cigars he gave up smoking altogether in order that his 'charity purse', as he called it, might not suffer.

There was another attitude which influenced his social and political outlook, perhaps due also to his growing up in the small principality of Dessau and having associations with the ducal family. It was what might be called his special brand of royalism. Max Müller came to know a large number of monarchs, from emperors to princes, and generally regarded them with respect and appreciation. He also enjoyed his acquaintance with them, and when he wrote or spoke about them, he did so not only with a certain amount of admiration, but also with deference. He was often criticized for this, and described as too courtly or even sycophantic.

But Max Müller's attitude to princes had no touch of obsequiousness in it. Nothing reveals his own attitude so clearly as a passage in a private book of thoughts which he maintained over years after the death of his eldest daughter. In this book, written in his own hand, I read under the date May 2, 1881, the following observations in regard to Disraeli's relations with Queen Victoria: 'Nothing is so dangerous in England than a Minister who bids for Court favours—nothing easier—nothing therefore more contemptible. The true friend of royalty would speak out at Court more even than in Parliament, and nothing keeps up my faith in Gladstone so much as his unpopularity at Court. It is due to such men as Gladstone that monarchy in England has a future.'

There was no consciousness of inferiority in Max Müller's attitude to royalty, far less any readiness to be a flatterer. His royalism, if it can be described as such, was a projection of his own notion of and belief in aristocracy:

> It has been my good fortune to see a good deal of royalty during the whole of my life [he wrote]. I say good fortune on purpose, for, with all the drawbacks inherent in court life, royal persons enjoy some great advantages. Their position is assured and well defined. It requires no kind of self-assertion, and wherever they appear, they have socially no equals, no rivals, and hardly any enviers. They seldom have any inducement to try to appear different from what they are, or to disguise what they think and feel. A king or a prince does not generally want to become anything else, and as they want nothing from anybody, they are not likely to scheme, to flatter, or to deceive.

Of course, he was aware that there were differences among the royalty as among the commonalty. But he said that many bishops displayed their mitres and crosiers before other people's faces much more than kings waved their crowns or sceptres. Many people who become something, he added, forget that they were already something, and seem to assume that they were created afresh when they were made peers, temporal or spiritual. The princes, on the other hand, were to their business born; they did not become royal, but were born royal.

Müller's mental growth had begun when he moved to Leipzig and to a larger world in which he met many musical celebrities. A new stage in his intellectual development was marked by his joining the University of Leipzig in 1841. Though he had done very well at school he also became aware when he went to the university that his school education was entirely passive. He was now to pass from intellectual tutelage to freedom in educating himself.

He was not eighteen when he joined the university, but at school he had received a thorough formal grounding in classical philology. He could understand both Greek and Latin with ease; he could also speak Latin easily, and follow the lectures of his professors when they delivered them in Latin. But he could not resist the lure of unknown subjects, and spread himself over many of them even at the risk of attempting too much.

German students were required to keep what was called a *Collegienbuch*, in which the professors attested what lectures the student attended. Müller preserved his book to the end of his life. It contains an impressive list of subjects: German literature, aesthetics, anthropology, harmonic composition, Hebrew grammar, psychology, German grammar, medieval German literature, Hegel, modern history, Sanskrit grammar Sanskrit literature, Arabic grammar, the history of Oriental literature. In his second year the emphasis transferred to philosophy, and philosophy and Sanskrit were combined with history, both ancient and modern. In his last term he began the study of both Persian and the *Veda*.

Finally, however, he had to decide what he would concentrate on. He found little to rouse his enthusiasm for Greek and Latin. Everything seemed to him to have been done, there was no virgin soil left to plough, and as he significantly added, 'no ruins on which to try one's own spade', which showed that his mind was feeling the attraction of what might be described as the archaeology of ideas.

His work in Greek and Latin had been on established scholarly lines. He respected his teachers in classical scholarship. He saw that they taught the principles of criticism, both external and internal, very thoroughly, and made the student realize what accuracy meant. But he regretted that he had failed to acquire a larger knowledge of Greek and Latin literature, and of the character and spirit of each author. He wanted to break out of this closed world into the open air of a wider mental world. So he betook himself to philosophy.

This was perfectly intelligible, for his natural interest was in ideas, and in language as the vehicle of ideas. At that time, although Hegel had been dead for more than ten years, Hegelian fever still ran high. To be a Hegelian was considered a *sine qua non* not only among philosophers, but also among theologians, men of science, lawyers, artists and everybody else who pretended to have any kind of mental life. If Christianity in its Protestant form was the State religion of Prussia, Hegelianism was its State philosophy. To be a Hegelian was supposed to be a help to advancement in life. All the young spirits at Leipzig had heard of Hegel's Idea, and looked to the dialectic process as the solution of all difficulties.

There followed a strong reaction, and even in Berlin Hegel's standing suddenly collapsed. After that no truly scientific man liked to be called a Hegelian.

Max Müller made a sincere and determined attempt to understand Hegel's philosophy, especially the concept of the Idea and the dialectic method, and he had a very sound teacher, Professor Weisse, a Hegelian, but a sober one and as much a critic as he was an admirer. Weisse was convinced of the truth of the dialectic method, but differed from Hegel in its application. From his study of history and philology Max Müller felt, like Weisse, that there was a contradiction between the theories of Hegel and facts. He was confirmed in this opinion by the teaching of a young professor at Leipzig, Lotze, whose *Metaphysics* he later got published by the Clarendon Press at Oxford.

The teaching of another professor, Drobisch, also served Müller as an antidote to Hegel. Drobisch taught Herbart's philosophy, whose chief object was to analyse and clear up concepts. As Müller was occupied with the problem of language he was stimulated by the philosophy of Herbart to seek accurate definition of words. But the kind of thinking which finally turned Müller away from Hegel was historical. In developing a historical attitude to the growth of human thought, Max Müller was influenced and guided by another professor, Dr Niedner, whose manual for the history of philosophy he found useful all through life. In contrast with Weisse and Drobisch, the teaching of Niedner was wholly historical. This appealed to Müller, and as he said, his own philosophical interest became strong and healthy only after he had heard the lectures of Niedner.

Meanwhile, his special philological interest had also taken a turn which was to lead him to a study of the early history of languages and of thought. The immediate impulse came from his desire to take up some language which others did not know, and he tried three Oriental languages. Finally he chose Sanskrit as his own special field, prompted by an inner urge which came from an early experience, combined with a very important aspect of the spirit of the age: the rising interest in India.

When he was a small boy at Dessau, one of his copybooks had a large picture of Benares on the outside. It was a very rough picture, but he could still see the figures of men, women and children as they stepped down the ghats to bathe in the waters of the Ganges. As everyone who has seen that view knows, it is one of the most moving and impressive to be seen in all India. The picture caught Müller's fancy. He had already heard about India, but knew nothing more than that the people were black, that they burnt their widows, and that to go to heaven they had first to be mangled under the wheels of the car of Juggernaut. At Leipzig University a remembered vision of childhood was reawakened when he heard that a chair had recently been established for Sanskrit. Afterwards he also saw lectures advertised by Professor Brockhaus.

He had heard also about Hindu philosophy, though very vaguely. Afterwards he had read Schlegel's *Über die Sprache und Weisheit der Indier* published in 1808, and Windischmann's *Die Philosophie in Fortgange der Weltgeschichte* (1827–34), both pioneering books which had ushered in new ideas, and left on many minds, as they did on Müller's, a feeling that new fields were waiting to be prospected which would yield gold if only there were the people to dig. This general inclination took a practical form when Müller heard of the professorship in Sanskrit.

Professor Brockhaus held the professorship from 1841. It had not been easy to institute it, for at that time there was a good deal of prejudice in scholarly circles against Sanskrit, especially among the classical scholars. The number of men who stood up for it were still very small, though they were all eminent, e.g., Wilhelm von Humboldt, and the two Schlegels.

But Brockhaus was established at Leipzig, and Müller called on him, and got himself enrolled. There were only two other students to attend the lectures, both very much his senior. One was Spiegel who became a Professor of Sanskrit as well as Zend, and Klengel, a scholar, philosopher and musician, who gave up Sanskrit after a term or two. He encouraged Müller, however, and told him that something might be made of Sanskrit by a philologist and a philosopher. So, under Brockhaus, he began with simple grammar and went as far as the *Rig-Veda*.

With the choice of Sanskrit as his main scholarly pursuit, Müller's vocation, and with it his profession, became, so to speak, predetermined. But even in Sanskrit his interest was not to be purely linguistic. In the university, it has been seen, his dislike for formal classical philology was strengthened. On the other hand, his inclination for philosophy grew, and for a time he thought of becoming a philosopher. Thus, dreaming of a chair of philosophy in a German university, he began to feel that he must know something which other philosophers did not know, and having heard of Oriental philosophy he was led to learn Oriental languages, and finally settled down to Sanskrit.

This wider background to his philological studies must never be overlooked, and from the very first he thought of his knowledge of Sanskrit as a key to another mental world. By the time he came to Oxford to deliver his address before the British Association, this view of philology was fully developed in his mind. Technically, his paper was on the linguistic affiliation of Bengali, whether it belonged to the Indo-European family or not. But while trying to establish that it did, he was fully aware of the immensely wider background of the question. So he said:

What does it matter whether Bengali belongs, by its grammatical structure, to the Indo-Germanic or the Turkish family of languages, provided that a man knows enough of it to express what he wishes? My answer is this: from comparing languages, from finding out analogies between them, from tracing the origin of forms in modern languages down to the living roots of more ancient languages, and from going back, as far as it is allowed to us, to see the first manifestation of the human mind by human speech, we derive, I think, a threefold advantage—an historical, practical, and philosophical.

According to him the historical gain was this:

> When poetical tradition is silent, when historical records are lost, when physiological researches fail, language will speak and decide whether there has been a community and connection in the intellectual development of different people.

The philosophical vista opened out was even vaster:

> Language stands in the system of the intellectual world as light stands in the system of the physical world, comprising all, penetrating all, and revealing all. There is more indeed to be read in human language itself than in anything that has been written in it.

Thus he thought that a scientific study of language would help to reveal the prehistory of the human mind, and disclose the mental affinities of different human groups. Actually, in this paper written before Müller was twenty-four, the whole sweep of his scholarly career is already foreshadowed.

By that time he had not only arrived at a definite idea of his scholarly interest, but also of the kind of life he wanted to live. It could only be a life devoted to thought and contemplation. Even at school his ideal was that of a monk, undisturbed in his monastery, surrounded by his books and a few friends. But as there were no Protestant monks among whom he could become a Protestant Benedictine, he thought he would become an assistant in a large library. From a very early period of his life he became conscious of the narrow horizon of human life on earth, and the purely phenomenal character of the world in which he assumed he was to move, live and have his being for only a few years.

Such a view of life neither did nor could exclude music, not only as an accepted element but also as a theoretically justified element, for Müller came in the end to hold a supra-rational view of music.

It remained an enjoyment to him, and more than that, a spiritual experience. He grew into the belief that music was, of all the arts, the least worldly, that it was not of this earth at all. He saw that music was not an art of imitation and that it did not reproduce, improve or sublimize (as he put it) anything that we could hear with our ears in the external world, not even the song of a lark. So he declared that neither history nor evolution could help anybody to account for Schubert's *Tröckne Blumen*, and he added that Schubert's melodies were picked up, not in the Prater, but in another world. In simple words, Müller thought that music was an absolute art, even in its vocal form.

He began with Haydn, Mozart and Beethoven, lived on Mendelssohn, rose to Schumann, and reached even Brahms. But he never learned to enjoy Wagner, except, as he qualified his statement, in his lucid moments. He confessed his failure with Wagner in these words: 'I have tried in vain to find out what prominent music connoisseurs admire in Wagner. I have shunned neither time nor trouble, but without results; the swamp in which we find a few lilies is too deep for me.'

At all events, he admitted that enjoyment of music was very much a matter of habit. He himself was most happy in the early morning of romantic music in Beethoven and Schubert. In his enjoyment of execution too Max Müller remained attached to the early nineteenth century. He shied at the virtuosity which was ushered in by Liszt, and sighed for an *allegro* or *andante* by Haydn or Mozart played as they were in his young days with simplicity on very imperfect instruments. As he grew older and had to hear more and more technically faultless playing he thought that these performers thought more of themselves than of the musician-poets whom they were rendering. He recalled that with all their technical skill even Mendelssohn and Clara Wieck (Schumann) acted only as faithful interpreters. Therefore even when he listened to the exquisite performances of these latterday virtuosi, he himself thought more of *what* they were playing than of *how* they were playing.

When Max Müller settled at Oxford at the age of twenty-four, music was still an active pursuit for him, but in the next five years he found that he had to be economical of his time and he gave up many things which were a pleasure to him. So in November 1854 he wrote to his mother about his musical interest:

One's delight in music always lasts, and I owe the old instrument so much—not only the enjoyment one has had, and the use my music has been as an introduction in a foreign place, but also the happy frame of mind which music unconsciously produces in one, and it smooths many little roughnesses which one often sees in those who have no taste for music. People who cannot sing are almost as badly off as people who cannot cry, but one does not always want to cry, nor always to sing; if we know we can, it is enough.

So far the mental development of Max Müller has been traced as it proceeded from his own internal impulses, but these very impulses were also the products of the spirit of the age, and in their expression were wholly controlled by the same spirit. Therefore it is now necessary to examine the movement of the human mind, the European mind, in the age in which Müller grew up. The most important movement was the Romantic Movement, and it may be stated as a brief enunciation of the formation of Max Müller's mind that he was a child of that movement.

I do not think there is, even now, a full realization of the sweep, depth and significance of the Romantic Movement, and of its revolutionary impact on the European mind. Actually, it was a new force in the evolution of European civilization. I regard it as the last Renaissance of Europe, as the final phase of the development of the European mind in the long historical process that began with the fall of the Roman Empire. It was certainly not less important than the Renaissance, and its impact on the human spirit rather than on human activity, was more creative than that of the French Revolution.

It stimulated every aspect and kind of mental activity, passional, ratiocinative, scholarly, imaginative and artistic, and gave to each a special motivation, method and expression. Under its influence people loved and worshipped differently, studied and taught differently, wrote books and composed music differently, and all these departures from the established pattern were made possible because, in the first instance, it created a different type of European mind which would not stay within the limits set by the eighteenth century. To the Romantics the eighteenth-century attitude, the classical attitude, the rational attitude, the whole extrovert thinking, feeling and moralizing of the *Aufklärung* seemed to make a man an object with surface and no depth. So the Romantics deprecated rationalism and extolled intuition, thought little of sense but much of sensibility. And in their groping and unsystematic way, they even dived down into the subconscious long before Freud.

Any sudden or fresh intensification of feeling and thinking within an individual makes him first of all aware of himself as the most vivid reality and, realizing the truth of the philosophical dictum *cogito, ergo sum* in his throbbing being, he also becomes egoistical, and at times even goes over to an egregious puppyism. The Romantic Movement glorified the self above everything else, and naturally it arrived at the conviction of the autonomy and irrepeatability of the individual. From this it was only one step to the feeling that the most valuable thing for an individual was experience in itself, rather than the fruit of experience. A book like Senancourt's *Oberman* would not have been possible without a new attitude towards introspective brooding, even to the point of enjoying nothingness, *vide et néant*.

The trend continued in Amiel, whose *Journal* Müller enjoyed very much when it was sent to him by a friend, to whom he wrote in reply: 'A delightful book—how little we know of the untold wealth of the world! In the eyes of the world, who is Amiel? and is he not ten times richer than Lord Overstone?'

I am inclined to think of Walter Pater as fighting the battle of Romanticism belatedly at Oxford, and I am surprised neither by his quoting Novalis when the latter says, '*Philosophiren, ist dephlegmatisiren, vivificiren*' (To philosophize is to dephlegmatize and vivify), nor at his being accused of Cyrenaicism or an unmanly hedonism by the Oxford of his times. It is the Romantic credo that we read in the beautiful conclusion to his *Studies in the History of the Renaissance*:

> To burn always with this hard gem-like flame, to maintain this ecstasy, is success in life. Failure is to form habits; for habit is relative to a stereotyped world; meantime it is only the roughness of the eye that makes any two persons, things, situations, seem alike . . . With this sense of the splendour of our experience and of its awful brevity, gathering all we are into one desperate effort to see and touch, we shall hardly have time to make theories about the things we see and touch.

If the Romantic Movement enlarged the mind internally by diving or dredging deeper within it, externally the widening was brought about by sending it wandering into space and time. The Romantics broke out of the mental baroque palaces and formal gardens of the eighteenth century to move into all nature, even the wildest. They heard the call of the far-off. In the same way they wanted to go far back in time. They could not accept the restricted, over-rationalized, abstract and didactic views of man and of human affairs current in the eighteenth century, and by exploring both space and time they wanted to discover both the Total Man as the product of a flux and the *Urmensch* as its starting-point.

Basically, the Romantic Movement everywhere was a reassertion of the Germanic element in European civilization after its relative suppression in the Age of Enlightenment. Therefore the German Romantic Movement is *the* Romantic Movement, just as the Italian Renaissance is *the* Renaissance. But it was not only a reassertion of the Germanic element; it was also the most powerful and widest assertion of that element which gave the whole of European culture of the nineteenth century its particular expression. The post-Napoleonic era was the epoch of the ideological hegemony of Germany in Europe. This was in complete contrast to the political eclipse and even military decline of Germany in that age. For the Germans themselves German politics up to 1848 was an arena of futility and disappointment, and to the rest of Europe it was a spectacle of pitiful ineptitude. Even in the military sphere the prestige of Prussia created by Frederick the Great was wiped out by Jena. In fact, the regeneration of the Prussian army begun by Scharnhorst did not become evident to the world till after 1866 and 1870. But in the mental sphere the post-Napoleonic era was a period of the self-assertion of the Germans in Europe. 'What a change,' noted Treitschke, 'from the days of Louis XIV when our nation had been forced to go humbly to school to all other nations of the West.'

Neither Treitschke's German nationalism nor his unqualified championship of Prussia makes his summing-up of the spirit of the Romantic Movement and of its influence in Europe anything but an objective statement of historical facts, and it is as such that I quote the passage:

For the first time since the days of Martin Luther, the ideas of Germany once more made the round of the world, and now found a more willing acceptance than of old had the ideas of the Reformation. Germany alone had already got completely beyond the view of the world order characteristic of the eighteenth century. The sensualism of the days of Enlightenment had been long replaced by an idealist philosophy; the dominion of reason by a profound religious sentiment; cosmopolitanism by a delight in national peculiarity; natural rights by a recognition of the living growth of the nations; the rules of correct art by free poesy, bubbling up as by the natural energy from the depths of the soul; the preponderance of the exact sciences by a new historicoaesthetic culture. By the work of three generations, those of the classical and of the Romantic poets, this world of new ideas had slowly attained to maturity, whereas among the neighbouring nations it had hitherto secured no more than isolated disciples, and only now at length made its way victoriously through all the lands.

Such was the influence of this Germanic Renaissance that by the end of the nineteenth century it became impossible, as it still is today, to take any view even of the two most important non-Germanic elements in European civilization, the Graeco-Roman and the Christian, without taking account of the information and interpretation provided by the Germans. The foundations of modern classical and biblical scholarship were relaid by the intellectual effort set in motion by the Romantic Movement. Curiously enough, even the art of war as practised by the supreme Latin, Napoleon, became Germanized through the writings of Clausewitz. Max Müller's own contributions to linguistics, mythology and religion were an extension of the German influence in these special spheres, as they were also the products of the Romantic Movement.

The aspect of the Romantic Movement which is particularly relevant to Max Müller's mental formation is its impact on intellectual activities in Europe, and, more especially, the result of the impact in three directions: the creation of the historical attitude and the historiography of the nineteenth century, which made it *the century* for history; the appearance of a new motivation and spirit in scholarly pursuits; and, as an offshoot of these two, the exhibition of a deep and enthusiastic interest in the East and especially India. Of these, the third product will be dealt with in a later chapter. Here I shall briefly consider the other two.

The relation between the Romantic Movement and the historical output of the nineteenth century will be found set out and explained in every book on the history of historiography in that century, but what I would stress here is the fact that the historical attitude itself was a contribution of the Romantic Movement to the writing of history. Before that, history was of course written, but not in an historical spirit. To give only one example, that most outstanding historical work of the eighteenth century, Gibbon's *Decline and Fall* was a moral commentary in the spirit of eighteenth-century rationalism and on the events of an epoch of the past. Its spirit was didactic and not historical. The conception of history as a process through

4

which humanity has reached its present state, and which is continuously carrying it forward, came after the Romantic spirit and
was created by it. It was not only *post hoc*, but also *propter hoc*.

Nothing could be more natural. A new interest in history was
bound to be created by the Romantic's yearning and respect for the
past as a refuge from an unsatisfying present, and by his sheer
enjoyment of the Middle Ages and other periods of the past as
emotional experience. The claims of the past as consciously asserted
by the Romantic writers did not proceed from any *arrière-pensée*,
but were accepted as self-justified. But this interest had also behind
it a revolutionary philosophical assumption regarding the nature of
human phenomena of all kinds, the assumption being that these
were organic, that is to say, things which were always growing, and
were not finite wholes created at a particular point of time for all
time. This was bound to lead men to the past as the source of the
present, and to write history to explain its character. The apocalyptic attitude of the Romantics also helped history, for that attitude is
only the historical attitude projected forward into the future. But if
any apocalyptic vision is to be convincing, the eschatology it formulates has to be a logical extension of past history with intuitional
additions. In fact, the apocalyptic attitude and the historical are
closely connected in the psychology of a people, as was shown by
the Jews.

The impact of the Romantic Movement on the spirit of scholarship was equally decisive and fruitful, especially in Germany.
There the Reformation virtually destroyed humanism, and for
more than a century the religious wars hardly allowed the spirit of
scholarship to keep itself alive. Thus even the history of classical
scholarship in the seventeenth century, the great century of scholarship, was virtually a blank page in Germany. It was not till Leibnitz
re-created it that the spirit of scholarly inquiry became general again
in that country, and it was not till Gesner began to write and teach
that a new humanism appeared there.

By that time, however, European scholarship had become as
elaborate and as artistic an expression of the human mind as baroque
architecture. It had become a complex craft in the hands of Scaliger
and Casaubon, and had been given a new technique by Mabillon,
and also a new solidity by him and Tillemont, whose 'inimitable
accuracy', as Gibbon put it, 'almost assumes the character of
Genius'. But all this stupendous and meticulous scholarship, most

impressively represented in England by Bentley and Porson, was concentrated on books and not on life. The monastic scholars did indeed go beyond books, but their interest was to illustrate and justify a static Church and its doctrines. Basically, the object of both the secular and clerical scholarship of the pre-Romantic Age was collection of information, supplemented by exegesis. In its elegance and economy, in its sheer virtuosity, this scholarship was like the superb singing of the castrato Farinelli—but it did not help men to live, nor was it fecund in renovating the will to live. For that a different kind of scholarship was needed, which would be a voyage of discovery in space and time, and would discover ideas and facts to give a new meaning to life and lead to happiness. This impulse of scholarship to transform itself came from the Romantic Movement.

In all the ramifications of his scholarly interests and researches, and even more in the special field of language, religion, mythology, including Indian religion and philosophy, Max Müller remained within the framework of scholarship created by the Romantic Movement. He was historical as well as practical. In fact, he became so historical that in the end the prehistory of the human mind became a greater preoccupation with him than history. Almost at the end of his life, in a preface to the collected edition of his works (which began to be published early in 1898), he re-affirmed that the historical principle had been the essence of his method in all his inquiries.

> During the last fifty years [as he wrote] I have never lost sight of the pole-star that guided my course from the first. I wanted to show that, with the new materials placed at our disposal during the present century . . . it has become possible to discover what may be called historical evolution, in the earliest history of mankind . . . At the present moment it may truly be said that what is meant by evolution, or continuous development, has now been proved to exist in the historical growth of the human mind quite as clearly as in any of the realms of objective nature . . . Language, mythology, religion, nay, even philosophy can now be proved to be the outcome of a natural growth, or development, rather than of intentional efforts, or of individual genius.

In the previous year he had said the same thing in an interview given to a religious magazine: 'My interest in all religions is chiefly historical; I want to see what has been, in order to understand what is.' Nothing could be more unambiguous.

It was, again, his sense of historical continuity which made him justify his project of translating Kant's *Critique of Pure Reason*, which many of his friends disapproved of as wasting time on a mere translation, by setting down in the preface his feeling of a connexion between this book and the *Rig-Veda*.

The two friends, the *Rig-Veda*, and Kant's *Critique of Pure Reason*, may seem very different, and yet my life would have been incomplete without the one, as without the other. The bridge of thoughts and sighs that spans the whole history of the Aryan world has its first arch in the *Vedas*, its last in Kant's *Critique*. While in the *Veda* we may study the childhood, we may study in Kant's *Critique of Pure Reason* the perfect manhood of the Aryan mind.

On the other hand, the conviction that there must be a human motive even behind the most out-of-the-way inquiry into the past was also asserted by him in connexion with his edition of the *Rig-Veda*. As early as 1864 he wrote to his wife:

I feel convinced, though I shall not live to see, that this edition of mine and the translation of the *Veda* will hereafter tell to a great extent on the fate of India and on the growth of millions of souls in that country. It is the root of their religion, and to show what that root is, is, I feel sure, the only way of uprooting all that has sprung from it during the last 3,000 years.

It was this human approach to learning which made a parochial clergyman's wife in America write to Max Müller's wife after his death:

I feel almost as if I could burn incense daily to the memory of Professor Max Müller! To me he *lives*, and of late in all my spare time I am reading his books, and learning what it is to think of the greatness of the love of the Eternal One; and more than any of the devotional books I have read, Max Müller's teachings help me to understand what religion means. You know that in the rush and whirl of what is called Church life, one does not reach the highest. In my own little room, with Professor Max Müller I spend all my leisure moments. It is not his memory, but he himself, who in his strong, brave, beautiful life of searching for Truth, now helps me.

No scholar would have been read in this spirit if he had based his vocation only on the intellect. Something beside and beyond that was necessary, indeed by the time he settled at Oxford his intellectual quest had become part of his life of faith. This is revealed in a letter written in Oxford on his twenty-fifth birthday by Müller to Bunsen:

Twenty-five years of this life lie behind me today, and one feels involuntarily in a more earnest and solemn frame of mind at such a moment. I look back with gratitude on the first half of my life, which, notwithstanding many sad moments, leaves me with the memory of a happy youth, and what at the same time, after many struggles, has given me a firm faith in a Divine Providence, trust in mankind and peace in myself, and cheerful courage to begin the second half of my life.

Actually, fifty-two years lay in front of him.

Chapter 4

EARLY YEARS AT OXFORD

MAX MÜLLER came to Oxford in 1848, just in time to see the last years of the old, Laudian, Tory university, in which the part that was formally the university was a poor and almost unwanted relation of the colleges. The year 1854, which saw the Oxford University Act become law on August 7, was as great a landmark in the academic history of Oxford as 1832 (the year of the first Reform Act) was in the political history of the British people. Old Oxford did not disappear at once, but a process of transformation was set in motion, to continue for at least three decades until a new Oxford took a stable form.

The first two of the six pre-reform years which Max Müller spent at Oxford were an interlude of peace for the old order. The academic community had recovered from the stir and strife caused by the Tractarian Movement, and though its ideas were to be absorbed by the Anglican Church both in spirit and form, for the present they were discredited by Newman's going over to Rome in 1845. Some Oxford men still adhered to these ideas, but they talked about them in private. Müller, whose early friends belonged to the pro-Tractarian, as well as to the more emancipated anti-Tractarian side, could hardly perceive the opposition between them until initiated by Froude and Jowett, and even they spoke with great reticence.

So, in coming to settle at Oxford in 1848, Müller could say in the words of Pope:

> To happy convents, bosom'd deep in vines,
> Where slumber abbots purple as their wines.

The university was still a club—a religious, scholarly and epicurean club for its teaching members; a recreational, sporting and talking club for its student members; and a social club for both. It could serve as such because as a federation of colleges it was one of the greatest landowners of England, and supported its teachers on the income accruing from landed property. The students too were overwhelmingly supported by their fathers from the same kind of income, either secular or clerical.

Certainly Oxford also served the cause of education. In any case, the education of the dominant minority in England was the exclusive function of the two universities. It put the youth of that minority through the mental disciplines considered necessary for them, to profit or not to profit by them as they pleased. It also formed the manners of the young men, without as yet shaping their character—which was typical of a social class brought ready-made to the university. But it is quite inaccurate to say that the university created the great men of England simply because many of them passed through it. Where else could the poor devils go? In fact, Oxford did exactly for the young of the nobility, gentry and bourgeoisie of England what education in the convents did for girls belonging to the same classes in France. After passing through the convents they could become saints, bluestockings, social figures, leaders of fashion, frivolous gadabouts, *femmes galantes*, or even *demimondaines*. So with the English youth after passing through Oxford and Cambridge. If one Earl of Pembroke was a benefactor of Oxford, another figures in Casanova's memoirs.

When Müller went up Oxford was not a place which any great British mind had praised for about two hundred years. The pronouncement of Giordano Bruno that Oxford was 'the widow of true science' might be passed over as the opinion of a foreigner, but one cannot dismiss Milton, Gibbon, Adam Smith, Sir William Hamilton, or for that matter Jane Austen. Yet all of them speak of Oxford with either contempt or irony.

Derisive remarks, of course, are always made about persons and institutions which are too securely and solidly established. The most important thing was that Oxford could take itself for granted, and it could even make others take it for granted. Mud-slinging did no harm because the mud slipped down its granite face. Oxford would take no more notice of this than its heads of colleges would mind the pranks of their undergraduates at the Commemoration or Encaenia. The Monarchy, the Parliament before 1832, the Church, the aristocracy and the squirarchy all had similar status, and Oxford was only the clerical-pedagogic wing of a whole established order.

Max Müller soon became conscious of the educational shortcomings of Oxford. He wrote to his mother that it was more a high school than a university, and within a few months he wrote to Bunsen: 'Oxford is most beautiful, but one longs for German professors, for Greek societies, and seminars.' But at the same time his first and strongest impulse was to admire. He was overwhelmed by its grandeur, as well as the charm and sophistication of the academics. As he wrote in his autobiography: 'My first years at Oxford were spent in a perfect bewilderment of joy and admiration . . . To me it seemed a perfect paradise.'

What he felt most grateful for was the kindness shown to him by many of the heads of colleges. He was invited to their tables. At that time three venerable figures represented the gerontocracy of Oxford. The first of them was Dr Routh, President of Magdalen, who was ninety-three when Müller came to Oxford, and died in perfect possession of his senses in his hundredth year in 1854. In his best days he was a pillar of Anglicanism, and Newman dedicated his *Via Media* to him with the words: 'To M. J. Routh . . . who has been reserved to report to a forgetful generation what was the theology of their fathers.' But in Müller's time he was mostly seen at the window of his room in his wig and gown, and was heard only to talk of old times. He spoke about Dr Johnson, whom he had actually seen, and of King Charles I as if he had. A friend offered to take Max Müller to meet him, but Müller declined because he had learnt that the old man did not like to be shown as a curiosity.

After Routh came Dr Jenkyns, Master of Balliol, who began the rejuvenation of that college which Jowett was to complete. The Master's regard for his own dignity was very great. Once he slipped and fell as he was returning from a walk, and two undergraduates rushed to help him up. As they were laying their hands on him, he saw an M.A. coming and cried out: 'Stop, I see a Master of Arts coming down the street.' Helped on to his legs by the M.A., he dismissed the undergraduates with thanks. He rebuked young Jowett, whom he found standing in his dining-room in gown and cap: 'Do my eyes deceive me, or do I see a gentleman in my dining-room with gown and cap on?' But he also had a quiet sense of humour, and would say things without moving a muscle of his face which would make others laugh.

The third patriarch was Dean Gaisford, with whom Max Müller became more intimate than with the others, because he was made an M.A. of Christ Church. Gaisford never taught and was absorbed wholly in textual criticism, and he also held the opinion that Greek promoted emoluments. The report went about that he was unreasonable in everything except philology, and versifiers mocked him when he wooed his beautiful wife. But he himself said of his successor, Dean Liddell, who had also found that Greek helped emoluments, that Liddell 'had not found love and lexicography incompatible'. He was quickly put out if he sensed disrespect towards himself, and Müller found it easy to believe the story that he had once said to an undergraduate who had come too close to him: 'Get down from my hearthrug.'

But to Müller, a very young man, a stranger and a German, the Dean was uniformly kind. While many of the heads of houses invited him to dinner by sending a card, Dean Gaisford first called on him.

One morning at about eleven o'clock when Müller had gone into his bedroom to shave and had his face half-covered with lather, his landlady rushed into the room to announce that the Dean had come to see him and was being pulled to pieces by Müller's Scotch terrier and her puppies. Müller ran out to find the dogs tearing the sleeve of the Dean's gown and barking at him. As there was no time to change, Müller received the Dean in the state he was in. His guest did not mind, and listened as Müller told him what he was doing at Oxford. After that the Dean inquired about an Icelandic dictionary which was being offered to the University Press. 'Surely,' the Dean said, 'it is a small barbarous island, and how can it have any literature?' Icelandic studies had just begun, and Müller was able to explain to him the value of the literature of Iceland. The dictionary was accepted.

At a later date, when asked whether he would put Müller's name on the books of the house, the Dean at first hesitated, and asked him to come and see him. When Müller did, he got this reply: 'I have looked through the books, and I find two precedents of Germans being members of the house, one of the name of Wernerus and another of the name of Nitzschius, or some such name.' So the Dean was very happy to admit Müller, who was afraid that, without a precedent, he might not be taken in. But the Dean later told him that even if he had not found those names he would have acted as he did. People were astonished when they heard of the Dean's courtesy to Müller.

What overwhelmed Max Müller when he settled there was the magnificence of Oxford life. Soon after his arrival he had his first experience of Commemoration, and he described it to his mother:

There were great festivities for the end of the term. Guizot was here, two sons of Metternich, Baron von Hügel, and many of the best English families, and a crowd of such beautiful women as I have never before seen. The festivities lasted from early dawn till midnight; the gardens lighted up, with music and singing, were enchanting. There were good concerts, the *Messiah*, the *Creation*, in which Birch, Tadolinée, and Lablache sang; in fact it was magnificent, and champagne and hock flowed in streams.

It would seem from all this that Oxford in those days was nearer than it is today to what Matthew Arnold called the 'Centre' in regard to English social and cultural life, and its regular social life and entertainment impressed Müller. These struck him as very sumptuous. As a poor student in Germany and France he was accustomed to the Spartan diet of a German convictorium or a dinner *à deux francs* at the Palais Royal, and he was confounded by the plate, the furniture, the carpets, curtains and the whole style of living of the dons of Oxford when they asked him to dine with them. When invited to the houses of the heads of colleges, which he appreciated as a great honour, he found the company to consist of the other heads, canons, professors, and, at times, of distinguished persons from London, and even ladies of various ages and positions. As he sat among them Max Müller felt lost or, as he put it, *verrathen und verkauft*. He might well do so, for he was unused to this kind of life, and moreover, he was only twenty-five.

He saw other young men at these parties, in evening dress and the short gown of the undergraduate. They stood together on one side of the room. They were invited to join the company after dinner, and received a cup of tea. Beyond this they were not noticed, and they themselves called the ceremony 'doing the perpendicular'. Max Müller's position was different, but after the dismissal of the undergraduates at about ten o'clock he would go and join them in their rooms, and would talk or sing in a more comfortable posture.

At one of the earliest dinners, which was informal and private, Max Müller met Thackeray. A fellow of St John's had arranged it expressly for the great man. There were only four young men, all very much awed by him. No one ventured to say a word, and Thackeray maintained his silence till the soup was over, though the others were expecting a brilliant sally from him every minute. At last at the commencement of the second course he looked at the fine John Dory which was waiting to be splayed on the table, turned his large spectacled eyes on Müller, and said: 'Are you going to eat your own ancestor?' All of them stared, and Thackeray, looking very

grave and learned, said, 'Surely, you are the son of the Dorian Müller
—the Müller who wrote about the Dorians; and was not John Dory
the ancestor of all the Dorians?' There was general laughter, and
Müller explained that he was not the son of Otfried Müller who had
written about the Dorians, but of Wilhelm Müller who had written
Die Homerische Vorschule and *Die Schöne Müllerin*. Then he per-
petrated a joke as far-ranging as Thackeray's: 'How could John
Dory be their ancestor, because the original John Dory was *Il
Janitore*, that is, St Peter, who had no wife or would not acknowledge her in public, though he was kind to his mother-in-law.' This
wholly thawed Thackeray, who poured out his wit and sarcasm and
told anecdote after anecdote, helping himself meanwhile to plenty of
vinegar and cayenne pepper.

When Max Müller mixed with the undergraduates he felt as if he
was one with them, though he was already becoming recognized as
a scholar. He could not say which years he enjoyed more, those at
Leipzig and Berlin, or those at Oxford. Very early in his stay there
he even thought of formally enrolling himself as an undergraduate,
though he was a doctor of Leipzig University of five years' standing.
He wrote to Bunsen: 'I have an idea of entering one of the colleges
as an undergraduate, keeping my twelve terms, and then taking my
degree.' He also wanted to take riding lessons so as to be able to
join the crowds of students whom he saw pass by in their red coats
and riding hats going to the hunt. He had to give up the idea as it
was expensive. But as to the kind of life he led, he wrote in his
autobiography: 'In Paris I was already something of a scholar and
writer, at Oxford I became once more an undergraduate.'

He also wrote that it never struck him then that these young men
had within them the germs of future greatness. What struck him was
the general tone and level of conversation. There were many with
whom he lived on terms of great intimacy who afterwards became
bishops, ambassadors, judges, ministers. Thinking of them in later
life and remembering them as young men who were not so very
different from others who through life remained wholly unknown,
he wondered if he had slept through a number of years and suddenly
awoke to a new life. Some of his early friends he found to be the
same, whether in ermine or in lawn sleeves; others, however, became
different—the boy in them had vanished, and nothing was to be
seen except the bishop, the judge or the minister. But he was so
attached to them when he first met them at Oxford that he wrote

when they began to leave Oxford: 'My early Oxford friends, with whom I felt at home, leave one after another, and it is not worth while to make new acquaintances.' To become indifferent to new acquaintances at the age of twenty-seven showed a considerable capacity for attachment to people.

There is also no doubt that the young stranger from Germany had great attraction for the dons and undergraduates of Oxford. One of his early friends there wrote about him after his death:

> Max and I were nearly of the same age, and I am now seventy-eight, with a memory, alas! no longer quick and vivid. The figure of Max is, however, never dimmed in my vision. Though near my age, I never looked on him as less than ten years older than myself in wisdom, tact, experience of life, and knowledge of men. 'Klug' was the term Bunsen applied to him, and though he seems from the beginning to have lived with the Olympians, whether intellectual or social, it was they who sought him rather, I think, than he who climbed into their company.

A similar testimony comes from Canon Farrar, who wrote to Mrs Max Müller after his death about the occasion when he first met Müller.

> I was dining with Jowett, and Max Müller with Walrond. Though the talk during dinner was not strictly literary, some point of literature turned up, and Müller's opinion on it was asked by Walrond. Instantly, there was silence among the twenty men at table. All listened to the stripling as he appeared. Stanley who was sitting next to me, and who had been discussing the memoirs of Stirling, stopped and listened attentively. Müller replied to the question with great modesty, though with self-possession, and with a brevity which allowed the conversation to flow back soon to its previous course. I instantly asked Jowett who he was, and learned that he was a young German of great promise who had been at Oxford for about two years and was engaged in editing the oldest Sanskrit literature. I name this as a sign of the profound respect which at so early a period was shown to him in an élite society like that of Balliol.

But it was not solely his learning that attracted people to him. He had considerable social talent, and was a witty speaker and conversationalist. Unfortunately, no record of this survives. All the formal books by him are serious and solemn, because he did not like persiflage or even wit in serious discussion. He once said: 'People do not know what a dangerous game this French *persiflage* is, particularly in England, and how difficult it becomes to exchange it afterwards for real seriousness.' That prevented him from showing his humorous side in his writings. So there are only testimonies to his wit and humour, and virtually no examples.

But his greatest social qualification at Oxford in his early days was that he was musical, and a very fine player and singer himself. In those days he had the entrée to many Oxford drawing-rooms as a pianist, and chatter ceased at his brilliant touch. People who knew nothing about the *Rig-Veda* knew him as a pianist. In those days music was just beginning to be a part of Oxford life. No don dared play an instrument, and an undergraduate still less. The utmost length that the latter would go to would be to sing a song. Yet there was love of music, though hardly any execution. So Max Müller was much in demand. There was only one other person in Oxford's academic society who could play really well, and that was Professor Donkin. As he was an invalid and was always regarded as dying nobody minded his playing. So he and Müller were expected to make music at parties.

Müller hired a piano to keep up his practice, gave it up for want of time, and then had to hire one again because all his friends wanted him to play. In 1851 he actually bought an instrument, a grand square Collard, and through a friend got it for only £50. It was so large that it could not be carried up the stairs of his lodgings but had to be hoisted through a window. When his friend Victor Carus came to stay at Oxford for a short time Max Müller and he would play violin and piano sonatas and keep hearers spellbound, for under Müller's hands the sounds of the piano, as one of them said, became a poem in music.

So Müller's popularity grew. But there may have been another less consciously perceived factor which made for his popularity among the liberals of Oxford with whom he mostly associated. This was the fact of his being a German. Germans were not liked by the conservative Anglican churchmen, and were positively disliked by the High Church school created by the Oxford Movement whose leader, Newman, thought that Lutheranism and Calvinism were heresies.

But it was quite the opposite in liberal circles. For about a decade by the middle of the nineteenth century, Germanizing had become not only an intellectual trend but almost a fashion at Oxford. All the advocates of reform and of liberalism in theology and philosophy were called Germanizers by their opponents, and in a sense they were. Jowett, for instance, went to Germany, became familiar with Hegel's writings which were unknown at the time at Oxford, and came back determined to conquer this new world of thought. He became the pioneer in the naturalization of Hegel's thought which became the source of English philosophical speculation at the end of the nineteenth century.

The first step towards this end was a thorough mastery of the German language, which was rare in England at the time. But the trend grew, and in Balliol it became almost an affectation to employ German for saying things which could equally well be said in English. Max Müller's future wife acquired real proficiency in the language at this time. Even Pusey went to Germany in order to become familiar with the latest scholarship in theology and biblical studies, though only to become deeply distrustful of it. Among Müller's friends, Froude and Palgrave knew the language well. In 1849 he wrote to Palgrave that he wished he could read Goethe with him, and he added: 'For my own sake, not for yours, for you are not the man to misunderstand him.' This was a very handsome compliment to Palgrave's knowledge of German.

Palgrave was one of Müller's earliest friends at Oxford, and was of special help to him in guiding him in writing English. His English compositions were always revised by Palgrave in the kindest possible manner, and it was this help which enabled Müller to write the language so well and to use it for all his major works. When he left Oxford to join the Education Department in London, Müller missed him very much. None the less, he gave him news of Oxford:

> Oxford is flourishing again. Stanley, Jowett, etc., are up. Old Froude, however, has left a blank, and if you saw how they have pulled down your house, and how the fireplace where we smoked so many a jolly cigar is exposed to the eyes of the *vulgas profanum*, you would find it a subject not unworthy of an elegy . . . Bye-bye, old fellow. Don't forget Oxford and the old set, who send you their love.

Another still more famous figure was one of Müller's early Oxford friends. That was Matthew Arnold. He admired Arnold to the end of his life, and wrote in his reminiscences that he was beautiful, strong and manly as a young man, and yet full of dreams and schemes. Müller found it strange that nobody suspected his genius at the

time, and also that he never rose higher than an Inspector of
Schools while many of his contemporaries became great political or
ecclesiastical figures. Arnold, however, never gave any thought to
this. He never asked for anything, but Max Müller thought that his
friends should have done something for him to show that he had not
been left behind in the worldly race. Later in life, he wrote to influential friends urging public recognition for Arnold.

Some verses written by Palgrave in 1851 show at its best and most
touching the spirit of the friendship which sprang up between a
foreigner and some of the most brilliant English young men of the
day. Here are the lines:

> An English welcome to an English shore
> Such as we could, some four years since we gave thee,
> Not knowing what the Fates reserved in store
> Or that our land among our sons would have thee;
> But now thou art endenizen'd awhile
> Almost we fear our welcome to renew:
> Lest what we seemed to promise, should beguile,
> When all we are is open to thy view.
> But yet if aught of what we fondly boast—
> True-hearted warmth of Friendship, frank and free,
> Survive yet in this island-circling coast,
> We need not fear again to welcome thee:—
> So may we, blessing thee, ourselves be blest,
> And prove not all unworthy of our guest.

If the experiences described so far were making Müller's life
happy in England, there were other things which he could not understand. The first thing which surprised Müller at Oxford was the
absence of duels, whose prevalence in the German universities he
had defended. At Oxford a man either apologized, or proved himself a cad and was immediately dropped.

Another thing which almost shocked Müller was the disrespect
of the students towards their teachers. In the German universities
the students almost worshipped their professors, and never questioned their *ipse dixit*. At Oxford Max Müller found that it was the
common amusement of the undergraduates to make fun even of the
heads of houses, and the doctors of divinity in their red gowns and
black velvet sleeves were objects of the most outspoken disrespect.
The looseness of undergraduate tongues at the Encaenia he accepted

as the Saturnalia of their university life, and he could even enjoy some of the remarks he heard at the beginning. His first experience of this was when Dr F. Plumptree, as Vice-Chancellor, stood up to address the audience in the Sheldonian. His first words were not quite distinct, and the undergraduates shouted: 'Speak up, Old Stick.' Dr Plumptree was very tall and stately.

Max Müller himself was subject to some good-natured leg-pulling too on account of his ignorance. He had noticed the letters F.P. on boards at a height of about ten feet at many places in the streets. They stood for 'Fire Plug'. But when he inquired, his friends told him that they indicated the height of the very tall Dr Frederick Plumptree.

He also found the constitution of the university very puzzling. In Germany no university could do without a Minister of Education to appoint professors, or without a Royal Commissioner to look after the undergraduates and their moral and political sentiments. At Oxford he was told that the only ruling power consisted in the Statutes of the University. Professors and tutors were free so long as they conformed to these Statutes. 'If we want a thing done,' his friends told him, 'we do it ourselves, as long as it does not run counter to the Statutes.'

Then the practise and profession of religion at Oxford baffled Müller. When he came to Oxford he was strongly recommended to Dean Stanley on the one hand, and to Manuel Johnson the Observer (the University Astronomer) on the other. Johnson was in the High Church Movement, and in his house Müller met all its leaders. Stanley was a liberal, and received him very kindly as the friend of Bunsen, F. D. Maurice and Hare. At first Müller could not understand that he was dealing with two camps. At Johnson's as well as at other places he heard a kind of discussion he could not connect with the true religious spirit. He was puzzled to see men whose learning and character he sincerely admired, absorbed in subjects which, to his mind, seemed merely childish. He expected he would hear from them some new views on the date of the gospels, the meaning of revelation, the historical value of revelation, or the early history of the Church. But of all this he heard not a word. Nothing but discussions on the validity of the Anglican orders, on vestments, genuflexion and candles, on the altar being made of wood or stone, of consecrated wine being mixed with water, of the priest turning his back on the congregation, etc. Of the historical approach to Christianity with which he had become familiar in his country, there was no trace. In his bewilderment, he asked both Johnson and Stanley what all these things had to do with true religion, but was advised by them to keep aloof and say nothing.

Though Müller's simple Lutheran faith was bound to make him unsympathetic to ritualism, he could see where the desire for an elaborate ritual came from. His friend Johnson constantly complained about the monotonous and mechanical performances of the Anglican clergy. He had a strong feeling for all that was beautiful and impressive in art, and he wanted, as Müller perfectly understood, to see the service of God in church to be full of both reverence and beauty.

Max Müller also felt that Newmanism was a natural trend in the English Church, and he expressed the opinion to Bunsen that he was convinced that a regeneration of the English Church could only come from the High Church party. Even though inclining to Romanism, Müller felt that Newmanism could bring the English Church to a state of ferment out of which it was likely to emerge purified and reformed. What he saw of the practices and spirit of the official Anglican Church at Oxford was bound to confirm him in this view. It was lifeless.

But the ecclesiastical establishment, inert and somnolent as it was in many matters, could be extremely awake in detecting heresy and equally active in suppressing it. One of Müller's early and intimate friends at Oxford suffered from this. He was James Anthony Froude, the future historian, and at that time a fellow of Exeter College. He published his *Nemesis of Faith*, early in 1849, and at once there was a doctrinal storm. The scandal was such that Froude had to give up his fellowship, and lose his only means of livelihood. This was not, however, the worst of his punishments. His father, a well-to-do and well-known archdeacon, was so displeased that he stopped the allowance he was making to his son. Even when he secured the headmastership of a college in distant Tasmania, his enemies got the appointment cancelled. Froude, who was engaged to be married, was in great distress, and had to sell his books one by one. At that time a cheque from an undisclosed source came to Max Müller to be handed to him. Many years later Froude discovered the name of the donor, and returned the money which had saved him from insolvency.

Müller tried to help his friend by bringing him in contact with

Bunsen, who at once invited him to his house. Müller thought that it would be sad if a man of Froude's talents was to fall into the hands of the English Radicals, Chartists and Unitarians, and he thought if Bunsen could send him to Germany in some capacity he could perhaps serve religion better in his own country by transforming the results of German theological and historical investigations into a native product. But this came to nothing, and Froude had to leave Oxford. Before he did so even his friends and acquaintances avoided him. Many times, when walking in the streets with Müller, he would pass a former friend who took no notice of him, and say: 'That is another cut.'

Another discovery, of quite the opposite kind, pained Müller no less. He found that men who were considered quite orthodox were really without any belief. They spoke freely to him because they imagined that as a German he would share their scepticism. He saw that it was not simply honest doubt which was disturbing them. They had passed through that phase of disbelief, and had settled down to a Voltairian levity which scoffed at everything connected with religion. This was something which he never expected to find at Oxford. In writing of the prevalence of this kind of irreligiosity, Max Müller naturally did not mention names, but he thought it necessary to mention the fact as a part of the mosaic of religious thought and feeling which existed at Oxford when he went there.

While observing Oxford life as well as participating in it, Max Müller was, of course, carrying on his own highly specialized work of editing the *Rig-Veda*. It called for immense labour, but by the end of 1849 he had seen the first volume through the press. He had the German capacity for working on any project in hand without allowing his social life and recreations, his moods, or even his anxiety in respect of worldly prospects, to divert him from it. Nevertheless, he had his worries.

He was only a sojourner at Oxford, and had no connexion with the university. He did not know whether Oxford would have any permanent career to offer him, and he did not try to find any as yet. He did not know how long he would remain there, and had a vague notion that the stay would last until the whole of the *Rig-Veda* was published, which might take years. In fact, beyond the assurance that he was provided with an income which would enable him to live modestly as long as this commission continued and which would give him some freedom not to jump at any employment that might come in his way, everything about his future was undecided and unknown. However, within a month of coming to Oxford he discovered that 'I must find some further occupation here, for Sanskrit alone does not yield enough to live on'. As he extended his social life, he made the further discovery that to live in Oxford society was expensive. The question of a permanent career had to be considered, if not decided.

All this, together with a clash in his mind between his natural love for Germany and the growing liking for England, made him oscillate between the two countries when considering his future. At Oxford he was only a resident alien. As he wrote to his mother: 'Life is on the whole very pleasant, and yet one feels as if one hardly belonged to it; people are too polite for one to feel quite at ease.' He thought that if he could live at one of the universities on the Rhine, at Bonn or Heidelberg, one might enjoy life more. He hoped that would come some day so that he would be able to drink a good glass of Rhine wine with his family and friends. At the same time he also knew perfectly well that though his life in a foreign country often seemed tedious and made him wish to go back to his own country and people, 'one must work to live, and work where one finds work'. So he wrote to his mother on October 3, 1848: 'If I go to Germany next year, I must look about and see what can be done there, and if any prospects open for me; if not I must look out for some career that later on would settle me here.'

What made him yearn to go back to Germany in 1848 and 1849 was the turmoil produced by the revolutions of that period. 'It sometimes seems to me wrong', he wrote, 'to be sitting and working here so peacefully in Oxford, whilst so many in Germany are torn away from their scientific employments and must share all the dangers of war.' He was still more perturbed the next year when he learned about the disturbances at Dresden, and he wrote to his mother: 'If this goes on in Germany, I cannot leave you there without protection, and I am really thinking of giving up my work here, and going to you. In times like this all other considerations must give way, and many plans be given up.'

But this compulsion did not actually face him. So what he had to consider during these years was whether going to Germany would result in any good, given the kind of life he had chosen and the type of character that was his. He put his case to his mother quite clear-sightedly:

The revolutions in Germany have laid such hold on all circumstances of life, and have so undermined the foundations of society, that one loses all courage to build one's future on such a soil, unless one feels the strength and power to take an active part in initiating and settling matters. On the contrary, if one wishes to find one's ideal of life in the narrow quiet circle of science, one has the right, I think, to seek shelter there where science, if not patronized and aided, is at least tolerated and left alone.

He felt that, as he was, he would in Germany only be drawn into party conflicts without the power to effect any good. So he considered whether he would not do well to settle down in England entirely, and thought he might be quite at home and happy there. He put his state of mind even more positively: 'With all my love of the past, and with full belief in the future of Germany, I feel more drawn at present to English than to German soil.' But his ambivalence between the two countries was to continue for years.

The question was decided practically for him by external circumstances. He also found that he did not have full freedom to decide by himself. In the middle of 1849, when the first volume of his edition of the *Rig-Veda* was nearing completion, he thought that after it was published he would go back to Germany, take up any post he could find there, and continue editing and printing the work from there. He thought that would offer no practical difficulty, nor delay the final publication. So he put the idea to Professor Horace Hayman Wilson, who was supervising his work on behalf of the East India Company. At once there was an explosion. Wilson, a very self-willed and even irascible man, told him that he would never hear of it, and added sarcastically: 'It is no use talking about *Vaterland* and *Heimweh*. Why, all young men who go to India never see their fathers and mothers again. My father and mother died before I came back. That cannot be helped. But that is your lookout. You will never go to Germany with my permission.'

The next day Wilson relented a little, and Max Müller felt encouraged to toy with the idea of being able to edit the *Rig-Veda* from Germany. He was curiously unsettled in mind. Two weeks after the conversation with Wilson he informed his mother that, since he could not hope for a speedy settling down of Germany, he was going to look for a settled position in England. But in six weeks he wrote to her again that as he was to go on a holiday in Germany at the end

of the year, when the first volume of the *Rig-Veda* would be published, and spend the winter with her, he would try to find a place
in a German university, preferably Bonn, and see if it would be
possible to come over to England for a short period every year to
look after the printing of the *Rig-Veda*. The truth was that his
judgement told him that he was likely to remain in England for
many years, while his emotional preference was still for his own
country. He put that quite clearly to his mother: 'The longer one
lives in England, the more one longs to be back in Germany. A
stormy sea is better than a dead sea! The English grow more like
the Chinese with each year, and nature herself has built a Chinese
wall round their lovely country. But if one can make oneself into a
Chinaman, one gets on well with them.'

But as the long holiday in Germany was months away, and Max
Müller was ill and needed rest, his friend Morier carried him off
to the Lake District to join one of Jowett's reading parties and
also to meet Froude who was staying there. He felt well as soon as
he got there, and was enchanted by the beauty of the mountains
and lakes. He paid unstinted tribute to it in a letter to his mother.
'The beauty of England,' he said, 'is so great that one cannot understand why the English always go to the Continent in search of
beautiful scenery.'

At the end of October he went to Berlin. He paid visits to Dresden
and Leipzig, and then returned to Berlin bringing his mother with
him. But by January he was tired of his idleness and longing to be
back at Oxford. He had already met his old friend, Alexander von
Humboldt, and shortly before he was to leave, went to see him
again. Humboldt told him that King Frederick William IV had
expressed a wish to see him before he left Berlin, and brought him
an invitation to dinner. Müller had seen the King once and presented a copy of the first volume of the *Rig-Veda* to him in a private
audience. The King told him that he knew all about it, and had so
much to say himself about the book that Müller hardly got any
chance to give his own account of it.

But a strange thing happened on the morning of the dinner.
Müller was sitting in his lodgings with his mother, when a young
lieutenant of police entered and began an interrogation—why he
had come to Berlin, what was keeping him there, and when he was
to leave. Müller explained that he had come to collate manuscripts
in the Royal Library, but the officer informed him that the police

authorities wanted him to leave within twenty-four hours. At that Müller told him quietly: 'Of course, I shall obey orders and leave at once, but I must request the police authorities to inform His Majesty the King that I shall not be able to dine with him tonight.' When the officer saw that Müller was in earnest he looked thunder-struck and left with a bow. Soon after a senior official arrived at Müller's house to apologize.

In the afternoon Humboldt came to take him to Charlottenburg, and when told of the incident was extremely amused. Afterwards Müller found out the reason for his order of expulsion. In Berlin he had been seeing a fellow Sanskrit scholar, Goldstücker, almost every day, and Goldstücker had been mixed up with political acti-vities, was kept under surveillance, and was even looked upon as a dangerous revolutionary. Max Müller was taken as an emissary to him from England, then considered to be the focus of all political conspiracies.

Max Müller had arranged to leave immediately after this dinner, but his friend Morier, who was in Berlin, fell ill and he was obliged to stay on and nurse him. In the meanwhile, his long absence from Oxford and his work had angered Wilson, and on February 26 he wrote a peremptory letter to Max Müller saying that unless the work proceeded faster he himself would not live to see it finished. 'But seriously,' Wilson added, 'I wish you would soon resume your labours. It is high time to put a stop to all the wild fancies that a partial knowledge of the light and reliance upon such equivocal guides as the *Brahmanas* and *Sutras* seem likely to engender. I want you also to help in the distribution of copies.' So Müller had to return at once, and for the next few months he devoted himself to the *Veda*, and even spent the long vacation at Oxford, though he wrote to Palgrave to say that it was more like purgatory than any-thing else. 'Yet here I am,' he added, 'and I cannot get away on account of one miserable MS, which I must go and look at every day while I am carrying my *Rig-Veda* through the press.'

From this it could be anticipated that Müller would again be seized with a fit of weariness with England and his life there, and so he was. At the end of the year he thought he would write to Lassen, the great Sanskritist at Bonn, and in his desperation even contemplated that if nothing came out of Germany he would try India. He wrote to Bunsen, and spoke to Wilson about his inten-tions. Bunsen was frightened, and informed him that it was the very worst time to go to Bonn. Wilson advised him to remain in England or go to India.

Besides his love for and loyalty to Germany, it was the dichotomy in his character, divided between will and judgement on the one hand and passion and impulse on the other, which was causing him to waver in this fashion. But the immediate reason was the uncertainty of his prospects and the strain of living from hand to mouth. Even in his desperation Müller could summon philosophy to his aid: 'If Lassen makes difficulties,' he wrote, 'I must decide to stay in England, till a kindly fate leads me out of the Oxford hermit's cell, into free German air, or into a forest solitude in India.'

The fates decided for Oxford. At the end of the year (1850) there came an offer from the Taylorian Institution to lecture there on modern European languages. The Institution was an adjunct of the university, and it was governed by a body of curators. It was also housed in a building which in its style did not conform to Oxford architecture; in fact, it was the first Palladian building to be erected there with statues on its top. It is now the eastern wing of the Ashmolean, with its façade on St Giles. In 1848 the Institution had founded a professorship of modern European languages, to provide lectures from the point of view of comparative philology, and it appointed as its first holder a half-Russian, half-Swiss Orientalist and linguist, named Trithen, who was a friend of Müller. But soon after his appointment he began to go out of his mind, and could not deliver all the lectures. So Müller was asked if he would lecture in Trithen's absence on a part of his annual salary of £400. At first he hesitated, but afterwards accepted at Bunsen's insistence. He began his lectures from the Lent Term of 1851, and the subject of the first course was 'The History of Modern Languages'. The prospect of succeeding to the professorship also weighed with Müller, and as Trithen was found to be hopelessly ill and had to go into an asylum, Müller was appointed Deputy Professor.

In the courses of lectures which he delivered for three years in this post, Müller developed the ideas he was to set down more fully and formally as a pioneer in linguistics. But his unsettled mood continued, and he still longed to go back to Germany. 'If any sort of favourable prospect offered,' he wrote to his mother, 'I would willingly exchange my pleasant life in Oxford for a simple German *ménage*.' Again he wrote: 'I am nowhere so happy as in Dessau. You will laugh at this, but had you been living for six or seven years among strangers you would understand how delightful it is to see well-known faces and well-known streets and houses round one. If I had independent means, I would live in Dessau, and by choice in my grandfather's house with the garden, where I know every tree.'

The high grim busts of the Caesars on the railing of the Sheldonian must have smiled sardonically, for Oxford was soon to claim him permanently. And when in late life he went to his birthplace he did not meet one man or woman whose face or name he knew, and he had to go to the old cemetery outside the town to be greeted by old names, some very dear to him and others forgotten in his *wanderjahre*. However, he went for a holiday to Germany in the summer of 1852, and travelled as far afield as the Tyrol. But he returned to Oxford.

In 1853 Trithen died, and the Taylorian Professorship fell vacant. Max Müller immediately applied for it. He ran every chance of getting it, but the curators took a long time to decide, and again his temperament made him worry unduly. He wrote to Bunsen:

> It is a hard trial of one's patience . . . I really don't know what to do, and whether it is not best to return to Germany and finish up and publish what I have already done on the Rig-Veda . . . My friends advise me to stay on here, and they assure me Convocation would veto the election of anyone else, if the Curators attempted it. For myself, I am almost indifferent. I shall have another year of uncertainty, of which I have had enough in the past three years. However such is the world, says John Bull, and tries to console himself. I am doing my best to follow his good advice.

Bunsen gave him even more energetic admonition: 'It is a great trial of patience, but *be* patient, that is, *wise*. One must never allow the toilsome labour of years, of quiet reflexion, and of utmost exertion for the attainment of one's aim to be destroyed by an unpropitious event.' Max Müller obeyed.

But it did take nearly a year before, at the beginning of February 1854, the Professorship was at last decided in his favour. He wrote joyfully to his friend Palgrave:

> I cannot tell you how happy I feel, after the long suspense, to have at last a ποῦ στῶ for the rest of this life, and to be able to look on quietly till the moving panorama comes to an end. I feel now more than ever that it is owing to the kindness of those who first received me at Oxford

that I owe my further success and present position. *Ce n'est que le premier pas qui coûte*, and after I was once in the right boat I was sure to get into harbour sooner or later.

A month later he gave the news to his mother. After saying that he was tired of the endless parties that were being given him, he wrote: 'You can imagine I was not a little pleased when everything was definitely settled. But when one waits so long for a thing it does not give one the same pleasure as when it comes unexpectedly. But I heartily thank God that my future is now entirely secured, as far as food and raiment are concerned.'

Bunsen's congratulations were wholehearted. He had already told Müller that neither he himself nor Müller would ever again be quite at home in Germany, and he wrote: 'Your position in life now rests on a firm foundation . . . and that in this heaven-blest, secure, free island, and at a moment when it is hard to say whether the thrones of princes or the freedom of nations is in greatest danger.'

This appointment was not a professorship of the university, nor was his membership of Christ Church as an honorary M.A. since December 1851 a formal incorporation in it. But for all practical purposes he belonged to Oxford and his future was decided, though he would still think of going to Germany. He was to remain in England till his death, and even before the question of his selection as Taylorian Professor had been decided, another event had taken place which made it impossible for him to leave England. In November 1853 he had met the English girl who was to be his wife.

With his uncertain prospects he was not thinking of marrying at all. His mother often urged him, but he considered it would be madness to marry. Actually, in reply to one of her letters, he had written in the middle of 1853: 'I have not yet any plans of the sort. I think one has enough trouble in making one's way through the world. If such a thing presents itself—well; but I have no wish to take much trouble in looking about.' However, it did present itself. On November 26 of the same year he saw an English girl of nineteen, and at the age of thirty fell violently in love at first sight. This was going to be as great a combined romance and trial in his life as his career had been.

James Anthony Froude had married Charlotte Grenfell, while Charles Kingsley had married another sister, Fanny. The Grenfells were originally from Buckinghamshire, and had settled around

Taplow and Maidenhead. They had their money in banking and mining, and interests in sport. The brother of Charlotte and Fanny was Riversdale Grenfell, whose motherless and beautiful daughter Georgina was brought up by her maiden aunt, the eldest Miss Grenfell. The women of the family seem to have been different from the men, with stronger religious, intellectual and passionate inclinations. Froude had often talked of his clever young German friend to his relatives, and Riversdale Grenfell asked him to bring Max Müller to his house, Ray Lodge, near Maidenhead, for a Saturday to Monday visit. He came, and fascinated all present by his brilliant, lively conversation and exquisite music. Georgina Grenfell has described his appearance as it was then: 'He was very dark, with regular features, fine bright eyes, and a beautiful countenance full of animation, and it was difficult to reconcile his youthful appearance with his already great reputation.'

On Max Müller the impression was decisive. Years after he told his wife that as soon as he saw her he felt: 'That is my fate.' I have seen the journal which Georgina Grenfell kept for three years to set down her agony of mind at not being allowed by her father to marry him. I read the following in his own handwriting: 'I loved you from the first day I saw you, and wherever you are my soul will always cling to yours . . . I never loved any one, till I saw you, and I never shall love any one else.' Underneath were pressed three pansies with some leaves, and they still retain some of their colours.

This passionate commitment at first sight is in the line of direct descent from Dante, who wrote about his first vision of Beatrice: 'At that moment, I say most truly that the spirit of life, which hath its dwelling in the secretest character of the heart, began to tremble so violently that the least pulses of my body shook therewith; and in trembling said these words: *Ecce deus fortior me, qui veniens dominibatur mihi* [Here is a deity stronger than I, who, loving, shall rule over me].'

But Dante's poetic idealization of love needs a good deal of explanation, especially to those who have come to employ the word 'Victorian' as a pejorative. Even less clever people smile at the mention of love at first sight. This is natural. For one thing, neither love nor death seem quite real when they strike down others. And, being supra-rational, love is never wholly accessible to the intellect. This makes ordinary minds admit its existence but without understanding its nature.

In an age which is weary and blasé it needs a renaissance of wonder to understand love. As soon as one pauses to think about it, love takes on the appearance of a mystery or even a miracle. This is of course more true of love at first sight. It is not created by any attraction set going by the mind. Far less is it the product of sexual desire. If Max Müller was transfixed by the very first sight of Georgina Grenfell, it could not have been through the rousing of such an urge. Nor had he any knowledge of her mind. What was it in her then that had brought this about?

The question really cannot be answered. If Max Müller recognized his 'fate' in Georgina, it was the kind of fatalism which makes a wireless set tuned to a particular wavelength receive only the messages transmitted to it through that wavelength. In short, love at first sight is ineluctable and beyond reason, and it has nothing to do with the mind. That also makes it very dangerous. Perhaps that is why love has been called blind, which is only a crude way of saying that it is abstract and yet compulsive. Max Müller found it to be so.

Two days after his visit to Ray Lodge, the Grenfells went to Oxford for a meeting of the leading church choirs of the diocese, and there he was their constant guide in sightseeing. When they left they invited him to spend Christmas with them. He could not go, and gave engagements with Bunsen and his own work as reasons. But something else had happened in the meanwhile to make him shy. Müller had not lost time, and had written to Froude about his wish to marry Georgina. The latter replied on December 19, saying that he was not altogether surprised, for he had had a full account of what had taken place at Oxford. He had to say something, but also felt that it was hard indeed to know what to say when the means of coming to a right judgement were so small, and a mistake could be dangerous.

He could not hold out any immediate hope for his friend, and felt unhappy. 'I am writing like an icicle,' he said, 'as if the east wind had got into my ink and chilled it. But what I want you to see is that they have not yet had time to form such a judgement upon you as would allow them in common prudence to give a favourable answer at present.' As to going to Ray Lodge, his advice was wise: 'If you feel,' he said, 'that you can control yourself I believe I may advise you to go as you will to Ray Lodge; if not, I should say certainly do not go. But I do not know whether I have a right to say "go" under any circumstances, and her happiness may be at stake; I do not mean now. But if she sees much of you it might become so.'

The immediate obstacle, as Froude saw it, was insufficient acquaintance. The girl, he said, 'is only nineteen and there would be a natural desire that she should not so early in life be allowed to come to a hasty decision'. So he advised Max Müller to go on gently, to let acquaintance ripen into intimacy. He spoke to his wife, and she wished that Müller would come and see her. Froude strongly urged his friend to come, saying: 'It will be worth your while even for your dearest purpose, as you will be gaining acquaintance among the other members of the family.'

But the most serious difficulty was money, without a sufficient amount of which according to his own ideas Riversdale Grenfell was never likely to give his consent to any proposal of marriage for his daughter. On this score Froude gave information about his relations which showed how much trust he had in his foreign friend. Though Riversdale Grenfell lived in great comfort and was bringing up his daughter almost in luxury, Froude thought he could not leave her much money. As he explained:

> Riversdale married secretly, the match not being approved by his family, and therefore there was no marriage settlement . . . no one in consequence can tell what his children's fortunes will be. He has been extravagant and is not likely to have saved, and my impression is that he has insured his life largely, but that in his life he will not be able to give very much to them. You would not mind this in itself, but you are aware that it will make him feel it the more necessary that by an insurance if not by other means a provision of some sort must be made by whoever marries Georgina, though on the other hand he would probably make her a liberal allowance . . . I speak of these things because it will be on them, if anywhere, that the difficulty will arise.

Nothing could be more realistic and frank. But Froude saw the want of money only as a temporary obstacle, though Max Müller as lover was inclined to look on it as the blasting of his hopes for ever. So he was reminded of his prospects, both near and distant. Froude said that the Grenfells were fully sensible of the high and distinguished position which he occupied, and in actual fact his prospects were as good as any professional person could wish for. He told Müller that in January the question of his professorship was to be settled, and then the salary might be raised, and the Sanskrit professorship held by H. H. Wilson might also become vacant. 'At any rate,' Froude observed, 'the more they see and hear you the more good they will see and hear . . . the more they will be assured that even in a worldly point of view you have a clear and prosperous future before you, and I do not pretend to say that considerations of this kind will not be of weight . . . God bless you, my dear fellow, I wish I could say more.'

Froude conveyed to his friend some idea of the dramatis personae who were to have a voice, direct or indirect, in this matter. Of his wife, the girl's aunt, he said that she entirely and heartily sympathized with him and wished him success. She even proposed to speak to her eldest sister privately, so that the matter might not go any further. Froude particularly asked Max Müller to take Miss Grenfell into his confidence, and assured him of her sympathy in all circumstances, though not of her consent at this stage. Müller, he said, could depend upon receiving the wisest and kindest advice from her. On this point he was insistent. He wrote: 'If I were you I would implicitly trust Miss Grenfell. I would go to Ray Lodge, see her, talk to her, and ask her indirectly as you easily may. She will understand you and you will understand her without any painful explicitness . . . You may count on the utmost goodwill from everyone.'

But it was the father who was going to be the uncertain factor. Not that he disliked Max Müller. On the contrary, even on that short acquaintance he had taken a fancy to him. One of the Grenfell ladies said laughing that if Mr Müller were a lady Riversdale would want to marry him himself. But Froude pointed out that he was a very odd person, and neither his wife nor he could answer for him. 'Words,' he went on to say, 'which would bear the best interpretation with a man of a more normal kind, cannot be interpreted with equal certainty in him. He likes you exceedingly as a personal friend. He has taken a fancy to you and will in all probability continue and like you better. But the likelihood of an affection springing up between you and his daughter has probably never occurred to him as it would with any other father.'

All this advice and other admonitions were addressed to Müller by Froude between the end of December 1853 and the beginning of February 1854. One thing he specially warned Müller against, and that was precipitancy, haste and impulsiveness. But, characteristically, Müller could not bear the uncertainty, and he asked his friend to broach the question with Miss Grenfell. So Froude wrote to her, and on February 9 he informed his friend: 'I have written . . . I shall get an answer on Saturday and you will perhaps therefore on Sunday learn all you desire. You know my heart is with you. God bless you, dear fellow, in your future whatever it is to be.' Then he gave a very curious warning, and that about his brother-in-law Charles Kingsley: 'Avoid Kingsley in this matter, Don't breathe it to him.'

Miss Grenfell's reply to Froude is of such quality that I quote it in full:

RAY LODGE, Feb. 10 (1854)

My dear Anthony,

I do not wish to lose any time in answering your letter—which I do with a feeling of great regret at the idea that we may unconsciously have occasioned suffering to a person we all feel as much regard for as it is possible to do on so short an acquaintance as ours is with Mr Müller. It certainly had not occurred to *any of us* to view him in the light of anything but a most agreeable and improving friend—and surrounded as we are—and as Georgy especially is, with frivolous and far inferior men, I have been glad to indulge my own taste for what is better and to give her when the opportunity occurred the benefit of such good society—I am truly grieved if in so doing we have led Mr Müller into any false views or expectations, but, after all, our meetings with him have been only *three* since the time you first brought him among us—at Oxford for two days—and one visit here of two hours before the last when he remained from Saturday till Monday. On all these occasions there has only been general conversation and I am quite sure he has never had ten minutes' real intercourse with G. during the whole time. Nothing in his manner has been the least marked or peculiar and I am sure she is quite ignorant of his feelings—being quite convinced that she likes his society as a most superior, agreeable man from whom there is always something to be learned and *nothing more*—I felt that the pleasure we all take in his visits might be safely indulged and when he came in on Saturday invited him to remain—this you will observe is the first invitation since Christmas—and the other in prospect is the London Madrigal Meeting to which my brother asked him. Perhaps I am dwelling too long on all this, but I am anxious to prove that the degree of intercourse there has been *could not* have prepared us for this result.

To turn to the specific part of the subject—you must tell Mr Müller what I fear will be painful—that my brother considers G. too young to wish to have anything of the kind seriously proposed to her—that without an adequate provision for the *future* as well as the present he could not, however high a person's character might be, listen to anything of the kind—that we know far too little of Mr Müller, however that little may be appreciated by us all, to enter on such a question with him—and that I have not the least doubt if it was put before G. herself she would at once desire it might go no further. I have not mentioned the subject to her, nor shall I do so unless it would be a satisfaction to Mr Müller to have my words confirmed by her. I think it may save awkwardness and discomfort in future if she is not told this —and I must add my sincere regret that under the circumstances I shall feel it right and wise not to ask him to our home again for his own sake and that it will be a loss and privation to us all. My brother has an especial enjoyment in his society—and so I need not say have I—and I fear G.'s pleasure in listening to him and her interest in his conversation must have misled him for she has this in common with us all—but nothing beyond it.

I shall feel more sorry for all this if I could reproach myself with throwing them often together but both his visits lately paid were quite unexpected tho' very welcome—and *when* here I know they had very little intercourse and that only with all the rest of the party—I cannot help wishing you had not been quite so discreet, for if I had the least idea of Mr M.'s feelings I should never have exposed him to having them strengthened and I wonder he could suppose that I understood these when I gave him on his going away the last time such a cordial invitation to return often. It would have been strange to do so if I had had anything of the kind in view, supposing that I had quite approved of it—I can truly say I have seldom met anyone I liked so much and I have no doubt that my manner has—*if he could suppose I understood him*—helped to encourage his feeling, for it has expressed quite what I feel—as much regard and interest as on such a recent acquaintance I could feel. I think it must be flattering to any young person to be preferred by such a Man, but it would be more so if it had been the result of a longer and more intimate acquaintance. It is quite painful to me to have one agreeable—I would say valuable friendship broken up, and I trust nothing I have said will unnecessarily wound him. As I shall tell G. nothing I cannot help hoping at some future time when it is not painful to his feelings our intercourse may be renewed. I will just add that I was obliged to mention the subject in a very hurried way to Riversdale this morning as he was going from home—but what I have said are his sentiments as well as mine.

I have written a long letter, but found it difficult to say all I wished in fewer words. Pray let me know what you hear further of Mr Müller and give him my kindest regards.

Yours affectionately,

G. M. Grenfell

The letter *was* long, just short of one thousand words in length. It would certainly not have been expected from a Victorian old maid by anyone who had taken the anti-Victorian fripperies of writers like Lytton Strachey seriously.

On February 13 Froude sent the letter to Max Müller and felt sure that on reflection Müller would see how reasonable much of what she said really was. He himself felt that 'it would have been wrong on so slight and brief an acquaintance to have written with decided encouragement'. His advice about the future was manly and sensible:

> You will see [he wrote] that at present the very question will not be entertained. If in our point of view it seems hard, on the other hand you have reason to be grateful for it, for when the question is not entertained there is no refusal. The future is before you to make your way. Let me entreat you to look at it in this way. Take no steps which may force them to speak decidedly. Above all, do not now think of going to Ray Lodge or of asking to be allowed to do so. My dear Müller, everybody knows what your talents are. Show now what your character is.

It seems Max Müller was not quite persuaded. Therefore Froude wrote again on the 15th:

> My dear Müller, I cannot see why because you cannot have what you wish at first asking for it, you should assume that it is beyond your reach for ever . . . I have read in books, I have witnessed in life years of warm and loving devotion without hope, almost without desire of return, cheerfully and nobly offered. It is beautiful to love and to be loved. It is noble to love for true love's sake what is truly and really lovely.

Then he disclosed a secret about Miss Grenfell herself. 'Do you know,' he wrote, 'that Miss Grenfell herself has carried with her out of her young years the scars of a disappointment which will go with her into her grave? When we meet people whom we admire how little do we guess the school in which they have been training.' Froude could match his knowledge of the world with sensibility.

The Grenfell family, on its part, did not judge Müller harshly. 'On the contrary,' Froude assured his friend, 'she speaks of you with the very warmest affection and cannot find words to express the sorrow that both she and Riversdale feel at the interruption of the intercourse between you . . . I would advise you to smother your feelings . . . I tell you to hope gallantly.'

But even the intercourse was not to be interrupted. In May the Grenfells were going again to Oxford, and Miss Grenfell wrote to Froude to tell Müller that as Georgina knew nothing of the past there was not the slightest unwillingness on their part to meet him, on the other hand there was every desire.

This closes the first stage of Max Müller's courting of Georgina, when she knew nothing of what was going on. The episode shows how superficial, untrue and malicious was the later running-down of the Victorians as stodgy, insensitive and snobbish people. On the contrary, they had not undergone that erosion of the passionate side of the human personality which has certainly come about today, passion and sensuality not being exchangeable terms. Only, the great Victorians knew that passion brought in its wake suffering just as it also did exultant happiness. The suffering they tried to bear with stoicism and in silence, a type of behaviour not accessible to cleverness. But even worldly Victorians could sense the stoicism and respect it. The Grenfells did not sneer at Müller because without possessing money he had aspired after their daughter. Their worldliness could go with an appreciation of unworldliness.

PART TWO

BLESSED IS HE WHO HAS FOUND HIS WORK

THE *RIG-VEDA*

IT took Max Müller five years of continuous labour, which was partly mechanical drudgery, to complete the editing and printing of only the first volume of his edition of the *Rig-Veda*. To understand the spirit and motivation of this project as well as his interest in the wider field of Sanskrit literature as a whole, it is necessary to take note of a basic contrast; that which existed between the German and English attitudes towards India in his young days. This is essential because in his own position there was an amalgamation of the two. He began as a purely German Indophile and Indologist, and soon assumed the roles in their British form, without however losing his original affiliation and inspiration.

Generally speaking India attracted Continental Europeans, especially the Germans, and repelled the British. This difference persisted even down to the last quarter of the nineteenth century. For instance, when Sir Henry Maine in 1875 delivered the Rede Lecture before the University of Cambridge on 'The Effects of Observation of India on Modern European Thought', he began by remarking that in speaking on a subject connected with India he would under ordinary circumstances preface what he had to say with an apology. But the proverbial dullness attributed to Indian topics by Englishmen, he continued, did not reflect any particular credit on the latter, nor was it felt by the learned classes in any other country. Then he described the situation on the Continent:

> No one can observe the course of modern thought and enquiry on the Continent, and especially Germany, without seeing that India, so far from being regarded as the least attractive of subjects, is rather looked upon as the most exciting, as the freshest, as the fullest of new problems and of the promise of new discoveries. The fervour of enthusiasm which glows in the lines written by the greatest of German poets when the dramatic genius of the Hindoos first became known to him through the translation of *Sakuntala*, seems to have scarcely abated in the scholars of our day who follow philological studies and devote themselves to the new branches of investigation constantly thrown out by the sciences of Comparative Philology and Comparative Mythology. No

one can avoid seeing that their view of India affects in some degree their view of England; and the community, which is stigmatised more systematically on the Continent than it is perhaps aware, as a nation of shopkeepers, is thought to have had a halo of romance spread around it by its great possession.

Seven years later, in 1882, Max Müller said the same thing, again at Cambridge, when delivering a course of lectures on India. In England, he told his audience, a study of Sanskrit, and of the ancient poetry, the philosophy, the laws and the art of India was

सायणाचार्यविरचितमाधवीयवेदार्थप्रकाशनामकभाष्यसहिता

शर्मण्यदेशोत्पन्नेनंगलण्डदेशनिवासिना भट्टमोक्षमूलरेण संशोधिता

श्रीमङ्गारतवर्षाधिपतीनामनुमत्याच

उक्षतरणाभिधाननगरे

विद्यामंदिरसंस्थानमुद्रायंत्रालये मुद्रिता

संवत् १९०६ वर्षे

॥ प्रथमाष्टकः ॥

The Sanskrit Title-page of Volume I
of the First Edition of the *Rig-Veda* edited by Max Müller (1849).
(See page 140)

looked upon at best as curious, but was considered by most people as useless and tedious, if not absurd. Then he drew the contrast:

In France, Germany and Italy, even in Denmark, Sweden and Russia, there is a vague charm connected with the name of India. One of the most beautiful poems in the German language is the *Weisheit des Brahmanen*, the 'Wisdom of the Brahman', by Rückert, to my mind more rich in thought and more perfect in form than even Goethe's *West-östlicher Divan*. A scholar who studies Sanskrit in Germany is supposed to be initiated in the deep and dark mysteries of ancient wisdom, and a man who has travelled in India, even if he has only discovered Calcutta, or Bombay, or Madras, is listened to like another Marco Polo. In England a student of Sanskrit is generally considered a bore, and an old Indian Civil Servant, if he begins to describe the marvels of Elephanta or the Towers of Silence, runs the risk of producing a count-out.

This was in every way natural, for the German and British involvements in India were of wholly different kinds. The German interest was spontaneous, the product of a combined emotional and intellectual urge created by the Romantic Movement, whereas the British was forced, a by-product of the establishment of British political power. In other words, the German interest was ideological and imaginative, the British practical and objective. For the Germans the knowledge of India was an ingredient in a process of *becoming*, by the acquisition of which they wanted to make their European personality deeper and fuller. They felt that India had thoughts and feelings which were different as well as complementary to theirs. The Englishman would not even consider the possibility that anything from India could enrich his English personality. His problem was what to do with India, an unwanted, troublesome and largely unintelligible possession for which his country was becoming politically responsible.

The Romantic *Drang nach Osten*, with India as its particular goal, refurbished the old Graeco-Roman notion of *ex Oriente lux*, which tempted even Plotinus to think of going to India, and this urge proclaimed its faith quite early and explicitly. Friedrich Schlegel declared, even before he knew Sanskrit himself, that it was in the East that the Europeans must look for the highest Romanticism. After he had learnt the language—he could not have learnt much— he stated his conviction even more emphatically. In his famous

Über die Sprache und Weisheit der Indier (On the Language and Wisdom of the Hindus), which he published in 1808, he issued what might be called the manifesto of a new Renaissance for Europe from India.

> If the study of the Indian language [he wrote] were able to find only a few men to pursue it! Thus in Italy and in Germany in the fifteenth and sixteenth centuries was seen a sudden outburst of an ardent love for Greek and Latin literature within a very short period of time, so that through a rediscovered knowledge of antiquity the whole aspect of science or to be more exact that of the world came to be changed and as it were renovated. Not less sweeping, not less general, we venture to say, will be the result of Indian studies, if they are undertaken with equal ardour and if they are introduced into the classical circle of learning in Europe. And why should it not be so?

Though this fervent expectation from India had come into existence without any worthwhile acquaintance with Indian literature and history among the German pre-Romantics and Romantics, it was actually sustained and developed by the objective and painstaking work in India of a number of English Orientalists who, in whatever leisure they could secure from their administrative work, tried to collect as much reliable information about the history and civilization of their Hindu subjects as they could; men like Sir William Jones, Wilkins, Colebrooke, Halhed, to mention only the more important figures. They were aided and encouraged in this work by the policy of Warren Hastings, who believed in and patronized Oriental learning both from intellectual curiosity and a realization of its importance for the rightful governing of India which, according to his own conviction, could be done only in the Indian way. These scholars founded the Asiatic Society of Bengal in 1784, began to publish their work in its journal, *Asiatic Researches*, and within ten years a number of important Sanskrit works in translation made it possible for men of letters in Europe to form some adequate idea of what Sanskrit literature was like. The key works and dates of this early phase were as follows: *Bhagavad-Gita* by Wilkins in 1785; his *Hitopadesa* in 1787; *Sakuntala* by Sir William Jones in 1789; *Gita-Govinda* by Jones in 1792.

None of these men, with the exception of Sir William Jones, had enthusiasm in the slightly pejorative connotation of the age, and even Jones did not allow his enthusiasm for ancient India to suppress his scientific spirit. On the other hand Colebrooke, who made the most substantial contributions to the extant body of information about the Hindu past, was the coolest and the most rigorous of them all. As a young official in India he at first even resisted the enthusiasm of the local Orientalists, considering it facile and superficial. But his accuracy and industry made him the foremost scholar among them when he applied himself to Indian subjects.

But their work had a sensational effect in Germany, where the *Asiatic Researches* were read, along with the other books, with an almost delirious interest. Of all the early books it was Jones's translation of Kalidasa's *Sakuntala* which produced the most powerful impression. He published it from Calcutta under the title of *Sacontala or The Fatal Ring: An Indian Drama*, and it went into five impressions immediately and made Jones famous all over Europe. Herder wrote to one of his friends:

> Do you not wish with me that instead of these endless religious books of the *Vedas*, *Upavedas*, and *Upangas*, they would give us the more useful and more agreeable works of the Indians, and especially their best poetry of every kind? It is here that the mind and character of a nation is best brought to life before us, and I gladly admit that I have received a truer and more real notion of the manner of thinking among the ancient Indians from this one *Sakuntala*, than from all their *Upangas* and *Bagavedams*.

Goethe's apostrophe to *Sakuntala* is, of course, famous:

> Willte Du die Blüthe des frühnen, die Früchte des späteren Jahres,
> Willt Du, was reizt und entzückt, willt Du was sättigt und nährt,
> Willt Du den Himmel, die Erde mit einem Namen begreifen,
> Nenn ich, *Sacontala*, Dich, und so ist Alles gesagt.

> (Wilt Thou the blossom of spring and the fruits that are later in season, Wilt Thou have charms and delights, wilt Thou have strength and support, Wilt Thou with one short word encompass the earth and heaven, All is said if I name only, *Sacontala*, Thee.)

Goethe wrote this when he was getting tired of the intellectual Charlotte von Stein and finding a different kind of happiness in the arms of his *bettschatz* (treasure of the bed), Christiane Vulpius, whom the proud Weimar ladies called his 'Fatter Half'. Perhaps he saw in the unsophisticated hermitage girl that Sakuntala was, an etherealized Christiane.

5*

Goethe's admiration of *Sakuntala* is however just symbolic, and it is referred to only because of his great name. He was not in the main stream of Orientalism in Germany, literary or speculative. He was not interested either in Hindu religion or in Hindu philosophy, and felt a kinship solely with such Sanskrit poetry as he could read in translation. Hindu art repelled him, the worshipper of the Apollo Belvedere, and he wrote: 'The tiresome trunks of elephants, the coiling nests of crawling snakes, the age-old tortoise in its cosmic swamp, those kingly heads on a single trunk—such things will turn us mad.' And he cried: 'I should like to live in India, if only there had been no stone-masons there.'

The typical impact of ancient Hindu India on the German mind was seen in the true Romantics who came later—the two Schlegels, Novalis, Tieck, Jean-Paul Richter, Rückert and the like; and among philosophers in Schopenhauer above all, but in Hegel and Schelling too. The first contacts with the authentic literature from India produced the most uncritically enthusiastic notions about the significance of Hindu civilization. Sanskrit was represented as the mother of all languages. The beginnings of all language, of all thought and of all religion were traced back to India. F. Schlegel even thought that the architectural monuments of Hindu India were as old as the Egyptian!

Bearing this attitude in mind, in 1840 H. H. Wilson, the leading English Sanskritist of his time, who distrusted the German school of Sanskrit, wrote in the preface to his translation of the *Vishnu Purana*:

It is the boast of inductive philosophy that it draws its conclusions from the careful observation and accumulation of facts; and it is equally the business of all philosophical research to determine facts before it ventures upon speculation. This procedure has not been observed in the investigation of the mythology and traditions of the Hindus. Impatience to generalize has availed itself greedily of whatever promised to afford materials for generalization; and the most erroneous views have been confidently advocated, because the guides to which their authors trusted were ignorant or insufficient.

In the first thirty years of the nineteenth century, following some twenty of the eighteenth, as A. W. Schlegel said, Europe had acquired more knowledge about India, both ancient and modern, than she had obtained in the twenty-one centuries since Alexander the Great. This knowledge was assimilated in Germany in two ways. First India, or whatever the Germans of that age looked upon as India, was absorbed as an element in the German selfhood, poetical as well as philosophical, which was expanding under the many-sided influence of the Romantic Movement, and in that absorption there was no India *per se* but only India as a colouring material of the stuff of German thought and feeling. In the second approach India was treated as the primary object of investigation. This activity manifested itself in the growth of a definite German school of Sanskrit and of Indology in a number of universities, and this school built up through erudition a German image or idea in the Platonic sense of India. But though not unscientific, that image too was very characteristically German—a projection of the German *Weltanschauung* on India. It was based wholly on an exegesis of books, and was an intellectual and imaginative but also a very selective reconstruction of the Hindu civilization and mind. The length to which German speculation could go in pursuing its quest of India is very forcefully illustrated in Hegel, who wrote in his *Philosophy of History*:

India has always been the land of imaginative inspiration, and appears to us still as a fairy region, an enchanted world. In contrast with the Chinese state which presents only the most prosaic understanding, India is the region of phantasy and sensibility . . . It is in the interest of spirit that external conditions should become internal ones; and that the natural and the spiritual world should be recognized in the subjective aspect as belonging to intelligence; by which process the unity of subjectivity and being generally—or the idealism of existence—is established. This idealism is found in India, but only as an idealism of imagination . . . In India the state of absolute being is presented as in the ecstatic state of a dreaming condition, and therefore in India was to be found, not the dreaming of an actual individual, but the dreaming of the absolute spirit.

The German historical reconstruction of India was not quite this castle in the very rarefied air of German philosophy. Its feet at least, if not the head as well, was in touch with the Indian soil. Even so, it was also a German structure built on concrete piles driven into the very treacherous morass of dependable knowledge about ancient India. It created the myth of Indian spirituality, which still haunts the world as part of two modern phenomena: the Hindu chauvinism of our day, and the spiritual degeneracy of the contemporary West.

Gradually however the absorption of India into the German personality stopped, and the foundation of the German Empire in 1870 is the key event in this eclipse. On the other hand, the intellectual and scholarly interest too lost its pioneering spirit and its initial fervour. The urge to discover a new world of thought and feeling in India weakened, and Indology became an established academic discipline concerned with filling out the gaps and correcting the details of the structure already created.

As early as 1859, when Max Müller published his first book on ancient Sanskrit literature, he had become conscious of this drift towards ossification. He remarked that the progress of Sanskrit philology was being retarded by an affectation of learned pedantry, which had done so much mischief to Greek and Latin scholarship and which he had resented in his university days. He admitted that the specialist in Sanskrit had much to learn from the methods of a Bentley or a Hermann, but he also observed:

> But in Greek and Latin scholarship the distinction between useful and useless knowledge has almost disappeared, and the real objects of the study of these ancient languages have been wellnigh forgotten. More than half of the publications of classical scholars have tended only to impede our access to the master-works of the ancients; and a sanction has been given to a kind of learning, which, however creditable to the individual, is of no benefit to the public at large. A similar spirit has infected Sanskrit philology. Sanskrit texts have been edited, on which no rational man ought to waste his time. Essays have been written on subjects on which it is folly to be wise.

In England, too, the great exploratory and garnering adventure of the early English Orientalists finally became a specialized academic discipline. But before they converged on that ground, the British and German learning of Sanskrit and ancient Hindu India ran along different, though parallel, courses. The very first difference was that even to the end of the nineteenth century the British learning never wholly lost its utilitarian object of being an aid and instrument in governing India. But this help was sought by the British political authorities in the form of information, and never as an ideology to shape policies or even outlooks. This attitude influenced even those who officially represented Christianity and

Christian morals in India, namely, the ecclesiastical establishment of the Government of India. With a few distinguished exceptions the regular clergy in India left the cultivation of Sanskrit and the languages derived from it to the missionaries. This, H. H. Wilson wrote in 1830, had had the harmful consequence of depriving the Christian presence in India of the means of exercising its proper religious and moral influence on Indians. As he put it:

They have been unable to communicate freely with the Hindus, and have consequently failed to exercise that influence over them which it is likely they might enjoy to a much greater extent than the Missionaries. In Bengal the better order of Hindus regard the Missionaries with feelings of inveterate animosity, whilst they invariably express a high respect for the clergymen of the Established Church. They cannot avoid seeing that the latter are held in higher estimation by the European society, and that they cannot be reproached with practices which not infrequently degrade the Missionary character in the eyes of the Natives. Did the regular clergy add to their personal respectability a reputation for scholarship in Indian literature, particularly the literature which the Hindus themselves consider as classical and sacred, consequences of the most important and beneficial nature might be confidently predicted.

This of course did not happen, and could hardly be expected to happen, on account of the very narrow and severely practical view of the place of Sanskrit learning held by the British authorities.

The second important difference between the British and German schools of Sanskrit learning was that the British throughout remained in touch with the indigenous tradition of Sanskrit learning continued by the pandits in their time, which the Germans deprecated when they did not wholly reject it as obsolete or dead. If this prevented the British Orientalists from building castles in the air, it also made them infuse some of the decadence, artificiality and fossilization present in the survival of Hindu culture among the pandits into their conception of Hindu civilization. They could not reconstruct an ancient India which was independent of the India of their age. In other words, their account of ancient India never became so genuinely historical as was the reconstruction in the nineteenth century of classical antiquity by European historians of Greece and Rome.

The third difference between Germany and Britain in respect of

Hindu civilization was that the English people did not accept it as an element in their mental formation and their cultural activity. This result could never be expected from them when they were not ready to accept the Hindu heritage even for governing India. There were a number of basic reasons for this rejection, the most important being their first-hand knowledge of living Hindus and of their ways. The British in India found them to be so crude and ignorant and even degenerate that they could hardly believe that they had been highly civilized at any time. Secondly, the positive and active ideology for the government of India, which developed after Warren Hastings and which admitted any possibility of progress on the part of the Indian people, was based on three schools of English political thinking: Utilitarianism, Evangelism and Whig Liberalism. All these were hostile to the beliefs and customs of the Hindus which they regarded as stagnant and obscurantist. Lastly, the idea of ancient India which the British Orientalists were putting forward appeared to all progressive Englishmen as archaistic and retrogressive. So all those who represented the progressive or liberal side of British rule in India discounted the value, and partly even the existence, of the Hindu civilization.

No one was more forthright in holding and expressing such a view than James Mill, the Utilitarian, who held an influential position in India House in London. In his *History of British India*, which was published in 1817 and immediately became a classic, he attacked the idea that the Hindus were in any sense highly civilized at any period. The whole of his second book is a coldly contemptuous dismissal and denunciation of the Hindus as creators and products of a high culture. In later editions of the book H. H. Wilson tried to correct Mill's bias in running footnotes disputing all his generalizations. Even so Max Müller thought that the book was responsible for some of the greatest misfortunes that had happened to India. Every aspect of Hindu life and culture was taken up by Mill and described from a standpoint opposite to that of the Orientalists, and the garment made by them was turned inside out. It was in demolishing their idea of Sanskrit literature that Mill was most ruthless. Among peoples who were just entering a civilized state, Mill said, all literary expression was in verse. The literature of the Hindus had always remained in this first state.

Mill more specifically made both the book which established the idea of a great literature in Sanskrit, and the man who was responsible for presenting it to Europe, the objects of his criticism. Of *Sacontala* he said that though it had some pretty passages, as a whole it was not a 'story which was above the powers of imagination in an uncultivated age' and there was nothing in it 'which either accorded with the understanding or could gratify the fancy of an instructed people'. Of Sir William Jones he spoke with regret and even some disapproval: 'It was unfortunate that a mind so pure, so warm in the pursuit of truth, and so devoted to oriental learning, as that of Sir William Jones, should have adopted the hypothesis of a high state of civilization in the principal countries of Asia.'

Nevertheless Mill succeeded in spreading a view which became influential and determined policy. In Macaulay his disparagement of Sanskrit literature became a cool appraisal, and the basis for the support given to English as the medium of education in India. In his famous minute on education in India written on February 2, 1835, he wrote about Sanskrit literature:

I have no knowledge of either Sanscrit or Arabic. But I have done what I could to form a correct estimate of their value. I have read translations of the most celebrated Arabic and Sanscrit works. I have conversed both here and at home with men distinguished by their proficiency in the Eastern tongues. I am quite ready to take the Oriental learning at the valuation of the Orientalists themselves. I have never found one among them who could deny that a single shelf of a good European library was worth the whole native literature of India and Arabia. The intrinsic superiority of Western literature is, indeed, fully admitted by those members of the Committee who support the Oriental plan of education . . . It is, I believe, no exaggeration to say that all the historical information which has been collected from all the books written in the Sanscrit language is less valuable than what may be found in the most paltry abridgements used at preparatory schools in England. In every branch of physical or moral philosophy the relative position of the two nations is nearly the same.

The disparaging thesis, promulgated by two men who were regarded as the greatest authorities on India of their age, persisted and was not wholly discredited even in the twentieth century. In 1917 William Archer, the dramatic critic, published a book entitled *India and the Future*, in which he denied that India was civilized in the accepted European sense. I myself remember the scandal it raised, and its refutation came, among others from Aravinda Ghosh, more famous under the name of Shri Aurobindo.

Of course, in spite of the detractors, the English Orientalists carried on their researches as scholars and their propaganda as apologists. But their discoveries and views as well as their defence built up only a counter-thesis for those who were seriously interested in ancient India. As for the educated British public, at their most understanding and sympathetic they recognized ancient Indian culture as a civilization in being at one time, but which was also for them a thing apart. The majority were indifferent, except when they looked at things Indian as curiosities. Outside a circle of more or less charlatanesque dabblers and pedlars of Indian spirituality, there was no disposition to assign any universal human value to the religion, philosophy, literature and art of the Hindus.

Max Müller avoided both extremes, the callow German enthusiasm and the hardboiled English contempt. He adopted and retained in his attitude to India the strongest and the most sympathetic features of the interest in that country of both Englishmen and Germans. He never shed the enthusiasm he had imbibed from the Romantic Movement, nor the pioneering spirit of the early days of Sanskritic studies. Driven by the ideological motivation of the German Indophiles, he continued to seek the origins of religion and thought through a study of ancient Indian literature. He also believed that it had a value for all men and for all time. But he derived from the English Orientalists his conviction of the practical importance of Sanskrit for British administrators as well as for contemporary Hindus. He thought and said that British rule would be more understanding and sympathetic, and therefore more productive of good for the Indian people if the ruling order became familiar with their culture. On the other hand, he expected a regeneration of the life of the Hindus by bringing their own cultural heritage to their knowledge. Lastly, he showed the most humane side of the English scholarly interest in India by becoming not only an apologist but a very vigorous champion of Hindu culture, and telling Englishmen how much they had to learn from India. By combining all these positions in his function of Indologist, he maintained the primacy of England in Sanskritic studies in the Western world.

He proclaimed the larger purpose of Sanskrit philology quite emphatically in the introduction to the first book he wrote on Sanskrit literature: *A History of Ancient Sanskrit Literature*, published in 1859. He wrote:

The object and aim of philology, in its highest sense, is but one, to learn what man is, by learning what man has been. With this principle for our pole-star, we shall never lose ourselves, though engaged in the most minute and abstruse inquiries. Our own studies may seemingly refer to matters that are but secondary and preparatory, to the clearance, so to say, of the rubbish which passing ages have left on the monuments of the human mind. But we shall never mistake that rubbish for the monuments which it covers . . . If, then, it is the aim of Sanskrit philology to supply one of the earliest and most important links in the history of mankind, we must go to work historically; that is we must begin, as far as we can, with the beginning, and then trace gradually the growth of the Indian mind, in its various manifestations, as far as the remaining monuments allow us to follow this course.

The primary object of Müller's Sanskrit studies was thus neither philology nor literature as such, but the evolution of religious and philosophical thought. Indeed, to his history of ancient Sanskrit literature he added the qualification 'so far as it illustrates the primitive religion of the Brahmans'. Therefore he was bound to specialize in Vedic literature. Mentioning the fact that all later Sanskrit books on religion, law and philosophy refer back to one early and unique authority called by the comprehensive name of the *Veda*, he wrote:

It is with the *Veda*, therefore, that Indian philosophy ought to begin if it is to follow a natural and historical course. So great an influence has the Vedic age (the historical period to which we are justified in referring the formation of the sacred texts) exercised upon all succeeding periods of Indian history, so closely in every branch of literature connected with Vedic traditions, so deeply have the religious and moral ideas of that primitive era taken root in the mind of the Indian nation, so minutely has almost every private and public act of Indian life been regulated by old traditionary precepts, that it is impossible to find the right point of view for judging of Indian religion, morals, and literature without a knowledge of the literary remains of the Vedic age.

But in actual fact, Müller's study of Sanskrit literature did not begin at its starting point, and in the circumstances it could not. The early European Orientalists could not begin the study of Sanskrit and Sanskrit literature with the earliest books in the language. As Max Müller pointed out, the Hellenists began where they ought to begin, namely, with Homer, Herodotus and Thucydides, and not with Anacreontic poetry or Neo-Platonist philosophy. But the Orientalists concerned with ancient India had to begin with later books, like the code of *Manu*, the *Gita*, the *Hitopadesa*, *Sakuntala* and such works in classical Sanskrit. At that stage of Sanskritic studies no authentic text of the *Vedas* was available, nor was Vedic Sanskrit known.

So Max Müller also began with classical Sanskrit literature, and he also shared the current admiration for it. His first work in Sanskrit scholarship was a translation of the *Hitopadesa*. But from the beginning his main interest was in ideas, and therefore he had been drawn towards the *Upanishads*, though he had also read a little of the *Rig-Veda*.

In later life, in a letter to Gladstone (January 18, 1883), Max Müller described this backward progression of Sanskritic research from classical Sanskrit literature to early Vedic literature, and also explained its significance. In presenting Gladstone with a copy of his lectures on India delivered at Cambridge in 1882 he tried to interest the great statesman, and he wrote:

> I must confess I have long wished for an opportunity of engaging your interest in behalf of India; I do not mean the mere surface India, with its grotesque religion, its pretty poetry, and its fabulous antiquity, but the real India that is only slowly emerging before our eyes; a whole, almost forgotten act in the great drama of humanity, very different from Greece, from Rome, from modern Europe, and yet not so different that in studying it we cannot feel that *mutato nomine de nobis fabula narratur*. The discovery of that real India, of that new intellectual hemisphere, is to my mind a far greater discovery than that of Vasco da Gama's.

Then he described the manner in which this India of his was recovered and studied:

> It was a misfortune [he observed] that all early publications of Sanskrit texts belonged really to the Renaissance of Sanskrit literature. Kalidasa's plays, which were supposed to be contemporaneous with Virgil, belong to the sixth century; the Laws of Manu, which Sir William Jones placed 1280 B.C., cannot be older than 300 A.D. But there was an older literature in India, the Vedic and the Buddhistic, which are only now being slowly disinterred, and it is here that we can watch a real growth from the simplest beginnings to the highest concepts which the

human mind is capable of, it is there that we can learn what man is, by seeing once more what man has been.

As an old admirer of Gladstone, Max Müller hoped that he would look at the work the Sanskrit scholars had been doing recently, but he was also realistic enough to see that the fulfilment of his desire was not to be expected. However, the letter very clearly explained the beginning of Vedic studies.

As has been mentioned in a previous chapter, it was after going to Paris and meeting Burnouf that, following the old scholar's advice, Müller decided to make the *Rig-Veda* the main subject of his researches. When he saw Burnouf the latter told him: 'We know what is in the *Upanishads*, but we want the hymns and their native comments.'

Burnouf made his advice even more explicit. 'Either one thing or the other. Either study Indian philosophy and begin with the *Upanishads* and Sankara's commentary, or study Indian religion and keep to the *Rig-Veda*, and copy the hymns and Sayana's commentary, and then you will be our great benefactor.' He insisted more particularly on publishing the commentary on the *Rig-Veda* by Sayanacharya, which dates from the fourteenth century. 'Don't publish the extracts from the commentary only,' he added. 'If you do, you will publish what is easy to read, and leave out what is difficult.' Max Müller thought that it would be very difficult to find a publisher for so large a work, but when he confided his fear, said: 'The Commentary must be published, depend on it, and it will be.' So Max Müller was launched on the project which kept him engaged for thirty years.

At this time the study of the Vedic literature was in a very rudimentary state. The legend of the *Veda* as the 'Aryan Bible' had been created long before the true text of the *Rig-Veda* was known. The earliest authentic account of Vedic literature was given by Colebrooke in his paper 'On the *Vedas* or Sacred Writings of the Hindus', published in the *Asiatic Researches*, vol. VIII, printed in Calcutta in 1805, and for decades this essay remained the basis of all serious and scholarly discussion on the subject. The only printed text available was that of the first book of the *Rig-Veda*, edited with a Latin translation and incomplete notes (also in Latin) by Rosen, and published in 1838 in London by the Oriental Translation Fund of Great Britain and Ireland. It was by basing himself on this text supplemented by the manuscripts in the Bibliothèque Royale that Burnouf lectured on the *Rig-Veda*. But he never published any extensive work on it. His incidental comments are embodied in his commentary on the *Yaçna*.

Burnouf not only told Müller what Vedic MSS were to be found in the Bibliothèque Royale, but lent him his own MSS. Müller then began to copy and collate all the manuscripts he could use, but he found to his astonishment that he was making many mistakes. Therefore, in order to avoid the extra labour of comparing his own copies with the originals, he devised a method of using transparent paper and tracing every letter. At first his progress was slow, but with practice he increased his speed, and his materials grew in extent and value.

Max Müller trod a lonely path, and worked independently of the other Sanskritists in the field, though he was engaged on a task which was most important and urgent in connexion with the *Rig-Veda*, namely, the publication of a full text with the commentary of Sayana. Rudolph Roth, who with Müller, became the most notable scholar on the *Rig-Veda*, was several years his senior. But they never got on well together, though they were fellow-pupils of Burnouf.

It has already been related how Muller came to England to carry on his work and secured the patronage of the East India Company, and how at last he settled at Oxford because the printing was being done by the University Press. The work had begun in the early part of 1847 as soon as the question of financing it had been decided. At first progress was slow because many of the types had to be manufactured, and printing Sanskrit needed 300 types. What surprised Müller when he was superintending the printing from London was that on the proofs many of his own mistakes on the copy were either corrected or queried. At last he asked if there was a Sanskrit scholar at Oxford who was doing this. He was told that there was none, but that it was the compositor himself, who did not know a word of Sanskrit, who was responsible for both. When at Oxford he asked the man how he came to make the corrections. 'Well, sir, my arm gets into a regular swing from one compartment of types to another, and there are certain movements which never occur. So, if I suddenly have to take up types which entail a new movement I feel it, and I put a query.' Of course, this was due to the fact that in all languages certain combinations (like *s* following an *h* in English) can never occur, and these impossibilities are numerous in Sanskrit.

But by July 1847 the first two sheets of the text of the *Rig-Veda* were printed off, and on July 13, he sent them to Burnouf in Paris, followed by the first sheet of the commentary by Sayana on October 8. His object in doing so was to obtain Burnouf's opinion on the soundness of the general principle of printing and style that he had adopted. The old scholar sent his enthusiastic approval in a letter written on November 9, 1847, writing: 'I thank you for having sent me the sheets of your grand edition of the *Rig-Veda*. I use the word grand, not to avoid saying excellent, for I consider it both grand and excellent, but because I must express my admiration of Professor Wilson's fine and vigorous Devanagari type.'

As to the quality of the editing, Burnouf said: 'I must own that I am astonished that in so short a time you have been able to master the mass of materials in hand.' Then the old scholar and pioneer in France of Vedic studies, concluded with a generosity which is not common among specialists. He wrote:

I congratulate you with all my heart on your début, and I venture to say on your success, for your success is secured . . . It is a great delight to do it for a man whose knowledge I admire and whose character I love. And I think I may be allowed to reflect with pleasure on any effort I may have made to encourage you to march on in entire independence, avoiding all collaborations. This is the only thing on which I can pride myself, and again it is entirely to your honour, because it only proves that I recognized all that science might expect from you.

Anything nobler from an old scholar to a scholar of twenty-six can hardly be imagined.

Max Müller steadily produced the sheets, and in two years finished the editing and printing of the first volume, which was published at the end of 1849. The Oxford University Press must be given the credit for producing a volume which in its beauty of typography and layout recalled to me some of the early *incunabula* from the presses of Aldus and Jenson. The volume, a heavy quarto, was presented to the British Museum by the Court of Directors of the East India Company. It is in mint condition, and on its flyleaf is pasted a letter in the beautiful handwriting of the day, forwarding it and explaining the scope of the work:

Sir,

The Court of Directors of the East India Company impressed with a sense of the great Literary and Antiquarian Value of the 'Rig-Veda Sanhita' or Sacred Hymns of the Brahmans as containing important facts relating to the early Religion, History, and Language of the Hindoos, and actuated by a desire to perpetuate and render the Work accessible to the World of Letters, have authorized the publication at the Company's expense of an Edition of the Manuscript, together with its Sanskrit Commentary by Sayanacharya; and the First Volume of the Work, which it is expected will be comprized in four volumes has now issued from the Press, Edited by Dr Max Müller of Berlin, under the general superintendence of Professor H. H. Wilson, the Company's Librarian.

The Work is intended for sale to those who may desire to possess it, but it is the intention of the Court to make gratuitous distribution of Copies to certain Public Institutions, and to a few distinguished individuals, and the Court have commanded me to state that they have much pleasure in presenting a Copy of the first Volume, which is herewith forwarded for deposit in the Library of the British Museum.

The remaining volumes will be forwarded in like manner as they successively appear.

They were, and the six volumes of the first edition in the Department of Oriental Printed Books and Manuscripts of the British Museum are this presentation set bound in morocco.

One particular feature of bibliographical interest in this volume might be mentioned. It had a second title-page in Sanskrit, in which Max Müller Sanskritized the names of Germany, Oxford and himself respectively as Sharmanya Desha (the Brahminic country), Ukshatarana (ford of the Ox), and Bhatta Moksha Mulara (the learned Moksha Mulara, the nearest Sanskrit-sounding equivalent to his name, but later translated by the pandits of India as the 'giver of the root of salvation' by means of an etymological flight worthy of Sayanacharya himself). Since, in boyhood, I often saw him mentioned as Moksha Mulara in Bengali magazines and books, I assumed that we in India had transformed his name into an Indian form. But from the first volume of his edition I discovered that it was Müller himself who was responsible for this.

After the publication of the first volume Müller proceeded with the preparation of the second volume, but his appointment as Deputy Taylorian Professor of Modern Languages prevented his giving full attention to the Rig-Veda. Still he carried on for more than two years, and finished the preparation of the greater part of volume two. But towards the end of 1852 he fell ill, and found it advisable to follow the advice Bunsen had long been giving him, to engage an assistant for the *Rig-Veda*. Bunsen also seems to have suggested the name of a Sanskrit scholar in Berlin, Dr Aufrecht. Müller entered into negotiations with him, and Aufrecht arrived at Oxford in the middle of December 1852. As this step was to produce a very unpleasant sequel for Max Müller, and after his death for his wife, it is necessary to describe his relations with his assistant in some detail. Early in December Müller wrote to Bunsen: 'I expect Aufrecht daily. You have always advised me to seek help, and I could no longer get through my work alone, with the many interruptions caused by my health. Aufrecht is a very conscientious scholar, and as far as the rest goes that will be all right.'

After that Müller reported to his mother on December 19: 'Dr Aufrecht is a very clever man, a Sanskritist, etc. We work together, and he helps me with my *Veda*, for which I pay him enough to live here. We shall try the plan at first for six months, and I hope it will go well.'

Aufrecht as a scholar seems to have been of the type which made Mock Turtle describe his classical master as an old crab. Besides, he had not been baptized, and that caused him mental unsettlement. So after a few weeks' association with him Müller again wrote to his mother, on February 2, 1853:

I get on better with Aufrecht, but not so very well yet. He decidedly desires to be baptized, but he does not feel inclined to talk to others on this point or anything connected with it. It is possible that when he has once taken this step he may get to feel more inner satisfaction and confidence in friends . . . But there can be no question about working *together*, for as soon as one presses him a little hard he draws his head into a shell like a tortoise . . . But I still hope that in time things will take a better shape.

Seventeen days later Müller writes to his mother again, and says: 'I am very well and happy. Aufrecht begins to "thaw".' During the Easter holidays of 1853 Aufrecht, according to his own wishes, was baptized by Bunsen's son, Henry, who was an Anglican clergyman and Rector of Lilleshall.

The second volume of the *Rig-Veda* was published early in 1854, and in its preface, dated Christmas, 1853, Max Müller formally acknowledged Aufrecht's help for the first time in these words: 'In the latter portion of this volume I have been able to avail myself of the assistance and active co-operation of my learned friend Dr Aufrecht of Berlin, and the benefit hence derived cannot be too highly valued.'

On March 10 he wrote to his mother: 'Aufrecht is still working for me, but he lives in another house for himself, and gives private lessons. He is happy here, and very useful to me, but it is rather expensive.'

At the beginning of 1855 Aufrecht decided to leave Max Müller and Oxford, and to go to London, So Müller wrote to Bunsen: 'Aufrecht has at last made up his mind to go to London. I have written to Dr Jelf, who may probably secure for him the Sanskrit Professorship at King's College . . . Aufrecht was too good for this mechanical work.'

In the preface to the third volume, published in 1856, Müller acknowledged Aufrecht's assistance as follows: 'I have had again for this volume the valuable assistance of my learned friend Dr Aufrecht, and I sincerely regret that I shall no longer enjoy this advantage.'

Finally, in the preface to the fourth volume published in 1862, Müller wrote:

I have stated on former occasions how much I owed to the assistance of my learned friend Professor Aufrecht, and I am glad to say that in the present volume also I have to a considerable extent had the benefit of his co-operation. Though I regret his departure from Oxford, nothing could have been more beneficial to the interests of sound Sanskrit scholarship in this country than his appointment to the Chair of Sanskrit at Edinburgh.

After the departure of Aufrecht Müller secured the help of other young Sanskrit scholars, and carried through the work to its completion by publishing the fifth volume in 1872 and the sixth in 1874. On July 1 Max Müller wrote the last lines of his text of the *Rig-Veda*, and only the preface remained to be written.

The first International Congress of Orientalists was held in London from September 14 to 21, 1874. To it came all the distinguished Oriental scholars of the day, including Max Müller's first teacher of Sanskrit, Brockhaus. Müller presided over the Aryan section and delivered a very eloquent address on the importance of

Oriental studies and learning. At the end of the address he presented the last sheet of the last volume of the *Rig-Veda* to the Congress. The volume was published at the end of the year, and in its preface he took leave of the work in the style of Gibbon: 'When I had written the last line of the *Rig-Veda* and Sayana's commentary, and put down my pen, I felt as if I had parted with an old, old friend.'

In the preface Müller also clearly explained how he had worked with his assistants and acknowledged their help:

> I believe I have acknowledged, without stint, whatever assistance I have received from other scholars during the progress of my work. They themselves have assured me, that I have said more than they deserved or expected. I have never liked the rule, followed by nearly all scholars, of not acknowledging services for which payment has been accepted. But as it has been broadly hinted, that for certain portions of Sayana's commentary, I had parted with my editorial responsibility, I take this opportunity of stating, once for all, that there is no page, no line, no word, no letter, no accent, in the whole commentary, for which I am not personally responsible.

At this point I must go back to Max Müller's first detailed examination and description of the *Rig-Veda* and the whole of Vedic literature, which was published in 1859. Already, when he was completing the first volume of his presentation of the text of the *Rig-Veda*, Müller had written a long explanatory essay, both descriptive and historical, on Vedic literature, and he wished to print it as a preface to the volume. With the approval of Bunsen he wrote a letter to the Court of Directors of the East India Company seeking permission to do so.

The Directors agreed to his petition, which was a great surprise to Müller. This happened through Bunsen's intervention. Max Müller thought he would print and publish it in England, and a note was inserted in the first volume announcing that an introductory memoir on the literature of the Vedas was ready for publication. Ten sheets of the essay were printed by 1851, when he was appointed Deputy Taylorian Professor and had to give up the project for want of time. However, he adapted parts of the intended prolegomena into an essay for the Prix Volney awarded by the Institute of France. The competition was hard, but Burnouf and other friends worked for him, and early in October 1849 Burnouf gave him the glad news that he had got the prize, which was 1,200 francs.

For ten years Müller could do nothing further with the essay, but in 1859 he brought it out as his first full-length book, *A History of Ancient Sanskrit Literature*, and dedicated it to Horace Hayman Wilson, as 'a token of admiration and gratitude by his pupil and friend, Max Müller'. In the meanwhile, a good deal of work had been done by other scholars who had concerned themselves with the Vedas. In the preface to his book Müller mentioned the names of Wilson, Burnouf, Lassen, Benfey, Roth, Boehtlingk, Kuhn, Regnier, Weber, Aufrecht, Whitney, among the most notable workers. He himself had also published a short essay on the Vedas in 1853. He regretted that owing to external circumstances he had been anticipated by others in producing a general account of Vedic literature, but that regret was balanced by his satisfaction in finding that in the main his original views had not been shaken either by his own further researches or by those of others. Quite deliberately the preface of the book was dated August 3, 1859, the day of his wedding.

Like his marriage, the book was a great success. It is surprising to note that this highly specialized book of 607 pages, containing in its index of 19 pages more than 1,500 Sanskrit words and names, and also Sanskrit citations in the text in Deva Nagari type, was completely sold out in its first edition in less than five months, and a second edition had to be brought out in 1860. There were also long and appreciative reviews not only in the learned journals but also in the newspapers. *The Times* published a flattering review on December 30, 1859. Two of the scholarly reviews were by Wilson himself in the *Edinburgh Review* for October, 1860 (the last thing he wrote, but published after his death), and by the great French Orientalist Barthélemy St Hilaire, in five articles in the *Journal des Savants*, the famous journal of scholarship.

The French scholar said that Müller's book showed considerable progress in Vedic studies and answered a number of questions, and, above all, it brought order and light into the huge and confused treasure-house of the primitive monuments of Brahmanic religion. According to him the book was of so high an order that it was not likely to be surpassed or even equalled for a long time. Wilson wrote: 'It is not possible in a brief survey like the present to render justice to a work every page of which teems with information that no other scholar ever has, or could have, placed before the public.'

A third edition of the book was also called for. But Max Müller thought that Vedic studies were making such rapid progress that with the time he could give to the subject he could not keep abreast of it. His failure to get the Boden Professorship of Sanskrit at Oxford at the end of 1860 made it impossible for him to devote himself exclusively to Sanskrit literature. To carry on the publication of the text of the *Veda* was in itself a task heavy enough. So he never re-published this pioneering book.

But he did not feel happy about it. In a letter to his wife written on December 7, 1864, he said: 'I still have a great work to do, and I often feel that I might have done a great deal more, if I kept the one object of my life more steadily in view. I sometimes wish you would help me more in doing that, and insist on my working harder at the *Veda* and nothing else. I hope I shall finish that work.' Then he explained to her how his edition and translation of the *Veda* was likely to help the Hindus in recovering the original spirit of their religion (see p. 90) and observed: 'If those thoughts pass through one's mind, one does grudge the hours and days and weeks that are spent in staying in people's houses, and one feels that with the many blessings showered on one, one ought to be up and doing what may be God's work.'

Notwithstanding his self-accusation, he continued to work on both the text and translation of the *Rig-Veda*. Moreover, till almost the end of his life he never neglected any opportunity to explain the meaning and importance of the *Vedas* to a larger public. He delivered a long lecture at Leeds in March, 1865, before its Philosophical Institution, devoted five of his seven lectures at Cambridge in 1882 to the *Vedas*, and, last of all, summed up his views on them in the second volume of *Auld Lang Syne*, containing recollections of his Indian friends, among whom he counted the *Rig-Veda*. That was in 1898, two years before his death.

He even made use of social occasions to promote knowledge and respect for Vedic literature. When the phonograph was invented one of its first appearances in England was at a party at the house of J. Fletcher Moulton, Q.C., and afterwards M.P. There was a fashionable company, with some eminent men of letters and men of science. Among them was also the American journalist, a friend of Max Müller's, Moncure D. Conway, who in his long notice on Müller after his death, published in the *North American Review*, described the incident. I shall quote his account:

Max Müller was first called on to utter something in the phonograph. We presently heard issuing from it these sounds: *Agnim ile purohitam Yajnasya devam ritvijam—hotaram ratnadhatamam.*

There was a burst of merriment when these queer sounds came from the machine, but a deep silence when Max Müller explained that we had heard words from the oldest hymn in the world—the first (if I remember rightly*) in the *Vedas*: 'Agni I worship—the chief priest of the sacrifice—the divine priest—the invoker—conferring great wealth.'

And then young people gathered round the smiling scholar to ask questions. Moncure Conway did not hear exactly what Müller said to them because he:

stood apart observing the picturesqueness of the scene, and finding in it something symbolical of the whole career of the polite scholar. He had evoked from the oral Sanskrit phonograph the ancient Aryan literature and mythology; the thin, metallic voices became real and cast their poetic spell not merely on the learned, but on fashionable young ladies and gentlemen in drawing-rooms, throughout Europe and America, adding vast estates to their minds, delivering them from the mere pinhole views of humanity and of the universe to which our ancestors were limited.

I shall end this chapter by adding to Conway's vivid account of the impact of his work on the *Vedas*, the observation on it of one of the leading Sanskrit and Vedic scholars of our times, M. Louis Renou. *'Nul n'a contribué davantage,'* he says in a monograph entitled *Les Maîtres de la Philologie Védique*, *'à créer le miracle védique, consacré par une revelation surnaturelle, entretenu par d'exceptionelles circonstances; il a apporté au service de cette cause le tribut d'un art et d'une science égales.'*

* It is the first verse of the *Rig-Veda*.

Chapter 2

BEATA GEORGINA

THERE is a gap of two years in the story of Max Müller's love for Georgina Grenfell, between the spring of 1854 when his proposal for marriage was rejected by her family, and the spring of 1856 when a love affair acknowledged and accepted by Georgina but without any hope of marriage began for them. What happened in the intervening years is unrecorded both in the published biography and unpublished papers. All that can be said is that Müller did not forget his love, and remained dejected. But since he did not meet Georgina his suffering was not such that he could not put on a brave face to his mother, as he felt he must, because he knew that nothing would distress her more than the knowledge of his being unhappy in love. So, to one of her letters written in 1855, in which there was the usual insistence on his marrying and even a suggestion as to a possible wife, he replied with humour: 'That you are so anxious to find me a wife is very good of you! . . . Elise who delighted you so much in Carlsbad, seemed to me pleasant enough; but as I had no opportunity of knowing her better, I have never thought more about her. If you are writing greet her kindly, but don't make any proposal for her hand!' The future Mrs Müller, on the other hand, knew nothing of Max Müller's love and was not herself consciously in love. But the whole aspect of their relations changed dramatically in the early summer of 1856.

In her biography of her husband Mrs Max Müller was naturally very reserved about her marriage. She briefly described his first visit to her father in November 1853, and also set down what Müller had told her later about his final commitment to her from that very meeting. As regards the second meeting from which a two-sided love affair started, she only wrote: 'In April of this year Max Müller had again met his future wife, and during six weeks they saw each other constantly at her home, and in London, and at the Grand Commemoration and Peace festivities in Oxford; little foreseeing the painful three years of total silence and separation that they had to go through before their marriage was allowed.' But her own journal and Max Müller's letters reveal a tragic experience of suffering. It is a story of romantic love without a ray of hope, until it ended suddenly and unexpectedly in happiness.

It has to be told at some length not only as an essential part of Max Müller's life, or as a romance which no one would expect to be experienced by a scholar, but also for its historical interest as a part of the attitude to love in nineteenth-century England. The idea of love which finds permanence in marriage without losing its intensity has become very distant in this age. What has taken its place is the concept on which polygamy is based, with the difference that while the Hindu or the Muslim polygamist uses a number of women as notes in a simultaneously sounded chord, the modern Western polygamists play them *arpeggio*, making marriage very much a matter of sexual convenience; and their love life is an alternation of crests of infatuation with troughs of disillusionment, except for those who are too humdrum to enjoy that game of chance.

Vanitas vanitatum, omnia vanitas, and nobody saw the vanity more clearly than the great Christian Pascal, who said: 'A sense of the hollowness of present pleasures and failure to perceive the hollowness of absent pleasures cause inconstancy.' The Victorians, on the contrary, succeeded in a very great measure in reconciling the intensity of love with its concentration on one object. This is most strikingly illustrated in a letter which Sir George Otto Trevelyan wrote to his daughter-in-law in 1908 at the age of seventy, when his wife was away from home for a few days: 'I am never unhappy for a few days with work and solitude; for that amount of solitude, brief, and at long intervals, introduces an element of contemplation and recognition into one's feelings about the person whose presence makes one's life.' Of course, many such examples can be given.

That does not mean, however, that at any level love between man and woman is free of the sexual urge. Only a fool or a hypocrite will deny that this love originates in sexual desire and seeks its rhythmic fulfilment in physical union. But only a fool will say that it is all sexual desire or lust, finding its ultimate satisfaction in a tactile sensation. We Hindus committed that mistake and have paid the price. So will the Western people if they go our way. From the beginning of time men have been adding values and colours to this primordial urge until fully evolved love has become as differentiated from basic lust, as old port is different from absinthe, though both contain alcohol. Indeed, the sublimation has gone further, and it

has made many ardent lovers feel that it is not of the order of the
flesh, being a human replica of the love of and for God. Max Müller
held this view, or, to be more accurate, had this sort of feeling about
love. On the page of the journal of his future wife on which I read
his confession of love at first sight, I also read: 'There can be no
true and lasting love that has not its spring and life in God'; also this:
'I felt we had this in common—our love to the same God, our faith
in the same saviour, and our will to make our life on earth a sacrifice
to him.' His future wife, as I shall show presently, also held the
same quasi-religious view of love.

In feeling in this way about love neither Max Müller nor Georgina
were taking up any position which could be called individual. We are
hardly aware that what we call individual choice is normally nothing
more than a particular adaptation to the general historical situation
in which a person is placed. In this case both the lovers stood at the
convergence, in mid-nineteenth century England, of three historical
trends, and therefore their love has to be placed in its historical
setting. These trends were—the Protestant rehabilitation of marriage; the romantic glorification of sexual love; and the Victorian
transformation of the love of the Romantic Movement into married
love. Each of these has to be considered by itself.

The Protestant rehabilitation of marriage was a revolt against the
Catholic Church's prohibition of marriage for the clergy, and the
corresponding attitude which regarded marriage only as a *pis aller*
for those who remained in the world. Sexual relations had the taint
of original sin even in wedlock, and it was to rescue them from this
taint that the Catholic Church made marriage a sacrament. All these
stemmed from the Pauline view that it was better to marry than to
burn. Luther fiercely rejected both celibacy of the clergy and the
sacramental character of marriage. But he asserted unambiguously
that God himself had instituted marriage, and thus the Roman
Church's prohibition of marriage for the clergy was no better than
Antichrist's mounting himself to a place above God. In his *De
Captivitate Babylonica Ecclesiae* he stressed the sacred and mysterious nature of marriage among believers and unbelievers alike.

This position was refurbished by a section of the Anglican clergy
out of their revulsion from the unnatural emphasis placed on
asceticism and virginity by the leaders of the Oxford Movement.
Mr Svaglic in his fine edition of Newman's *Apologia* has pointed
out that there was a passionate urge behind Kingsley's attack on

him. Kingsley had found peace and had been able to reconcile the world and the spirit through his love for and marriage with Fanny Grenfell, and he revolted against the Catholic view which made such a pure bliss (derived as he thought from God) a sin. Mr Svaglic also draws attention to the fact that Kingsley belonged to the circle of Carlyle, Froude, Tennyson, Shaftesbury and Bunsen, and shared their Germanic Protestant view of history, one of whose particular expressions was that the Reformation had reasserted the sanctity of marriage and the family, and revived the Teutonic virtues which had been suppressed by the Roman Church. Max Müller belonged to the same circle.

There is direct evidence that Kingsley held this view of sexual love and marriage. In one of his letters to Max Müller he said he would fully decide in Müller's favour if he were in Riversdale Grenfell's place by saying to himself: 'The thing is of God, and I dare not fight against it.' Furthermore, advising him to remain patient in his present disappointment, Kingsley wrote: 'It would be a great experiment; my comfort is, that it would be a great experiment in the highest sense of the word; a committing, as thousands have done, of true love into the hands of Him who inspired it, and saying, "God, Thou hast made this, surely Thou wilt also water and prune it till it bear fruit to everlasting life."'

This will show to what school Müller's love belonged. But it belonged too at one remove to the romantic love of the early nineteenth century, especially in its German expression. The Romantic revolt against the rationalism of the eighteenth century also impinged on the man-woman relationship. The rationalistic attitude tended to ignore the differences between the sexes, to favour their equality in respect of position, interests, activities and opportunities, to emancipate women, and to create the *femme forte*. Its impact on the physical relations between men and women attenuated passion and fostered sensuality. To the pure rationalist the urge for sexual satisfaction is only a refined form of the urge to defecate, as was felt by Montaigne, the pioneer rationalist. You should not for your health's sake resist it, but do not try to glorify it.

The Romantic Movement rejected all this, lock, stock and barrel. It proclaimed the particularity of man as well as woman, recognized the special genius and function of each, and thought that human life was made whole by a combination of the two. As the Austrian Romantic, Lenau, put it: 'Who has genius? Can woman have it?

Max Müller and his wife, Georgina, in 1865 by Edmund Havell

Fatuous question. Man and woman have it conjointly.' With this there was bound to go a glorification of the basic element in the man-woman relationship, sexual love. This Romantic view of love treated marriage as an institution largely irrelevant to love. In fact, it depicted love at its most intense outside wedlock. There were two natural if not good reasons for doing so: first, marriage was almost wholly subject to worldly considerations in that age, and the Romantic, who thought this degrading, wanted to make love independent of the world; second, sexual satisfaction in wedlock was also the assertion of a legal right, and that made the ardent Romantic have the same feeling for it as we have for income-tax. Moreover, they had no revulsion from the physical expression of love. But that was wholly different from the nonchalance about sexual intercourse of men and women of our days, who have made the act as amoral and neuro-muscular as playing tennis. To the Romantics, in contrast, the physical union was the climax of a passionate union.

The Germans took over the concept of Romantic love and practised it with traditional German thoroughness, and the Germans who did so most thoroughly were also the most solid Germans, the philosophers and scholars. As I have discovered, it is very unsafe and unsound to try to appraise a German of the Romantic Age by his books. These give a wholly wrong idea of his personality, passionate power and motives of action. I have arrived at a more adequate image for the German scholar-philosopher: he is the volcano which sends up hot, molten lava from his blazing depths, and that lava solidifies on the earth's surface to become the hard basalt of his books.

Max Müller as lover was affiliated to that tradition. Without assuming that, it is impossible to explain his equal devotion to the *Rig-Veda* and to Georgina. But living in England in the middle of the nineteenth century he could not be entirely a Romantic lover, not because Victorian England was cold and respectable but because that England had gone one step further in romanticism by bringing the illicit and burning love of the Romantic Age into married life. It had carried out a revolution through which the wife became a greater idol than the mistress, and so no husband could say of her, like La Rochefoucauld: *Il ne faut pas parler de sa femme.* To put it briefly, love retained all the strength and lure it had as sin, and yet became sanctified in wedlock. The Victorians were stodgy in their moralizing but not in their love-making.

6

Since the words of love which Robert spoke to Elizabeth were heard and sanctioned by God, not all the Barretts of Wimpole Street could prevent her from becoming Mrs Browning. Coventry Patmore defined love in marriage more directly:

The love of marriage, above
All other kinds, the name of love,
As perfectest, though not so high
As love which Heaven with single eye
Considers, Equal and entire,
Therein benevolence, desire,
Elsewhere ill-joined or found apart,
Which now contracts, and now dilates,
And both to the height exalting, mates
Self-seeking to self-sacrifice.

These men and women, living in a profoundly religious age, had no streak of asceticism. Far from it, they even obliterated the distinction which the early Christians, horrified by the Pagan lusts of the flesh, had drawn between *Agape* and *Eros*. Max Müller moved naturally into this world of love. What his love for Georgina was before his marriage I shall presently describe, but its character is even more intensely and truly revealed in a letter he wrote to her a year after his marriage.

I went under the old Ilex tree and there I sat down and read it [her letter], and thought for a long time about my darling, and my happiness, and my unworthiness, and God's unbounded mercy! And then I heard the words within me, 'Be not afraid!' Yes, my darling, there must be no fear. When there is fear, then there is no perfect love. Our happiness here is but a foretaste of our blessed life hereafter, we must never forget that. We shall be called away, my darling, but we shall meet again . . . My darling Georgina, you would sleep quietly and peacefully in the arms of your husband—but our Father in Heaven loves us more than any husband can love his wife, or any mother her child. His hand will never hurt us . . . So let us hope and trust always.

I cannot say that all this was typical of the academic life of Oxford. Its monastic past, together with the obligation of celibacy for the fellows, made the dons either suspicious or incapable of love, and to this suspicion and incapacity a man, regarded as the incarnation of the Oxford spirit and who was also a friend of Max Müller, bears witness. He is no less a person than Benjamin Jowett. His preoccupation was purity of life, and he set it down in his notebook that a man was not a man who did not control his passions. He uses the word 'passion' in a bad sense. But he was also aware how difficult it was for Oxford dons to master their passions, because their marriage was deferred generally for fifteen or twenty years after the passions were strongest, and was sometimes impossible without loss of rank. The social downgrading through marriage was described by a Highland girl who saw Oxford just before Max Müller's time, and she wrote that many heads of colleges, constant to the loves of their youth, brought ladies of inferior manners to grace what was so dignified a station in life.

But even Oxford dons could love. The lecturer in mathematics at Christ Church, Dodgson, better known as Lewis Carroll, fell in love with his Alice when she grew into a beautiful girl of sixteen, and had to be tacitly forbidden the house by Mrs Liddell, the famous Dean's wife. Mark Pattison, the most desiccated and calcinated of Oxford dons, married a very young girl probably out of love. Even the great Benjamin Jowett had a romance with the even greater Florence Nightingale. But all these men outgrew and survived their love, though not the spleen which is a by-product of unrequited love. Lewis Carroll nursed a life-long spite against the Liddells, and even against their friends, one of whom was Max Müller; and Mark Pattison drove his wife into the arms of Sir Charles Dilke.

But the German Max Müller would certainly not have survived his love, if denied. Actually, he once wrote to Miss Grenfell: 'I am a German, full of foolish romantic ideas, which give me happiness where no Englishman or woman would find it.' But, as it happened, even in Victorian England his love did not end in tragedy, because he was not being slain by a cruel fair maid; on the contrary, Georgina herself was on the point of pining away. It was an English father, insisting on a proper settlement for his daughter, who was putting impediment in the way of true love, and Max Müller could not employ the method by means of which in that age lovers of equal social and economic status could make the best of both worlds: that is, by keeping the love-making to themselves and leaving the settlement to their solicitors.

The new act opened in April, 1856, with a letter from Max Müller to Miss Grenfell telling her about the accommodation he

had arranged for the Ray Lodge party at Oxford for the grand cele-
bration there of the close of the Crimean War, at which Jenny Lind
was to sing at two concerts. 'The arrangements,' he wrote, 'will be
somewhat Crimean, I fear, yet I have no doubt that the battle will
be won. There is one large bedroom and two small ones, so your
maid will have to sleep in a neighbouring house. If I had known
yesterday I could have offered a bed to Mr Grenfell in my house
. . . I have secured carriage room and stalls for two horses, and beds
for two servants, and by a most fortunate accident I got a ticket for
the first concert.' Then he gave details of the programme he had
arranged and this included lunches and dinners and balls at many
colleges, outings, and even visits to the Observatory where they
were to see the Observer's Heliometer and the stars generally. The
whole visit was most gay and festive.

It was at the end of the visit that Max Müller and Georgina
Grenfell declared their love for each other, probably on June 5, one
day before the Grenfells returned to Ray Lodge. Müller's inscription on his future wife's journal: '*Zur Erinnerung an den 5 en : Juni,
1856, Oxford*' bears testimony to the date. But the episode is described with anguish by Georgina Grenfell in the very first entry of
her journal kept from the middle of 1856 onwards. She writes:

Ray Lodge, June 7. Returned from Oxford yesterday—I had such a
sad ending to our gay week. My poor little Müller. I cannot bear to
think of his grief. In an agony he told me of his faithful love, and how
for ever he should love me—and though I feel Papa is right, with his
little income, in now saying *No*, yet I cannot but think of him. What
can it be in me that could win such intense love from him? He in such
real grief. To hear such a man say that he felt that for two years his
powers had been going, and to know that one word would make him
happy, and that one might not, could not say that word, yes, it was
trying indeed. My poor Müller. But there are years before us and they
all say some day he must hold a very high position and then perhaps.
Meantime, should not the love of such a man raise one? I felt humbled
by his fixing on me. What am I compared to him? Let me try in every
way to raise my mind and be more fit to become the wife of one with
such a mind.

This journal, kept over three years, is an extraordinary document.
It was as if the intensity of the love set down seemed to burn the
very pages, and it would seem nobody but Max Müller and his wife

had read it before me. Of its eighty pages, sixty-eight describe her suffering over the three years during which her father would not hear of her marriage with Max Müller, and this suffering is borne with such tenderness, stoicism and religious fervour that the pages read like a *Magnificat* in sorrow. The rest of the pages, only twelve, record her joy and gratitude at being permitted to accept him, and they utter a *Gloria in excelsis* in happiness.

What strikes the reader in the first instance in this journal is the extraordinary frankness and honesty of the record. On September 20, 1857, she asked herself: 'Is it wise to write down all the thoughts that course thro' the mind?' and answers herself: 'Yes, I think it does good if they are true ones.' I quote some passages to show that there can be no doubt about the frankness and truthfulness, and also to establish the key, and sound the leit-motives, of her love. She writes on July 10, 1859, when she and Max Müller were meeting as affianced lovers: 'In the evening we stayed from Church and after sitting with Gommy [Miss Grenfell] sat together under the Ilex tree and then late at night we went to Charlotte's arbour, and sat there heart to heart, till our souls seemed one, the mere bodily covering seemed too full of love and joy. There are not many such hours in this workaday world, but they are pricelessly precious.'

The next day brought a different kind of experience, and it is described in the next entry: 'Max and I sat in the boat together. It was very hot, and I was very cross, because he would kiss me. I have since been very unhappy about it, for there was a grieved look in his eyes at my childish behaviour, which I could not bear to see again. We sat and looked in each other's eyes. I often can hardly bear to meet his eyes. I feel I am not worthy of all that God has given me, and then I shut my eyes or look into the far blue sky, and pray to be worthy of my own Max.'

She also makes no secret of her love affairs before she had finally fixed her love on him, and even of her waverings after she had. She wrote on May 31, 1857:

I did not think I could so deeply and truly love anyone. Before a year had passed from Captain H.G.W. I was flirting most violently with Colonel Vyse . . . I had all along thought in spite of myself that I had wasted a great deal of feeling on him, indeed I told Max so . . . Charlotte tells me on good authority that he did really care for me, but that Papa would not hear of it, and hinted so to H.G.W., and this stopped all his attentions in that sudden way. Somehow I am glad to hear this, for tho' I own it would have been a poor life with him and that I soon got over the feeling and that my love to Max is real and true, yet I did care for H.G.W. very much and with all a girl's eager feeling, and therefore I am glad to hear that he was not a mere flirt, attracted for a time by my lovely face.

She prays that she may not give in to coquetry, and at the very beginning of her passionate surrender to Max Müller sets down this prayer: 'Oh God, help me watch myself very carefully that womanity may [not?] draw me from him.' Even in 1857, when she was in deep despair and distress of mind, she wrote: 'If anyone were ever to see this book what would they think of me. I had my whole time passed in *affaires de cœur!* Why am I allowed to make so many unhappy? Am I really careful enough or do I not like incense, and thus encourage these poor men? I will be far more circumspect. Loving another as I do, I ought to be as indifferent as possible to everyone.' Furthermore, she does not suppress the natural envy that she feels and the sense of injustice that she has, when she sees others happy in their love, even her younger sister Charlotte. 'I have been staying with Mary Goodlake, seeing and enjoying her little home—I often wonder why such discipline is needed by Müller and me. I am so down tonight. I could cry for hours. Ah! why cannot I find rest in God.' After this entry comes another: 'There is Mabel Irby, who from the way she has gone on, cannot be capable of a deep true feeling, about to marry that clever Augustus Vansittart, and there are no difficulties of any kind. Such is life—One glad and another miserable! Oh! Lord my God, keep my own dear Müller, in body, soul, and spirit as Thine . . .'

Last of all, she was capable of being extraordinarily realistic about money, the cause of her suffering. On October 10, 1856, she wrote:

Gommy went to Eversley [Kingsley's living] and saw Müller and, of course, they talked long of the subject. His love for me is unchanged, and mine for him is as strong as ever. Only I see now clearly all the difficulties. He has £500 from his Professorship and makes nearly £300 more by his writings, and my fortune could ensure the sum Papa demands. This is small, but next year he will have £100 more. I have thought it all over deeply, and I think I shall wait till next year, as I am now, and then see if in any way the thing is settled either way by external influences, if not I will try again to get Papa's consent.

But the next year only brought new difficulties, and she wrote on April 18: 'All this week I have been tried by feeling that perhaps I ought to give up Müller! Papa seems as determined as ever against it—and my friends even think would, if dead, leave some clause leaving away my fortune if I married Max, and I know no one could live on Max's income alone and make any provision for the future.' As a matter of fact, she came to know later that he had altered his will, so that if his daughter had married Max Müller she would have had nothing.

But with all her honesty and realism she knew equally well that she could not give up Max, even if she would. So, on the very day on which she set down her sensible view about money, she also wrote: 'I know many would say "Give him up", but it is like cutting away the ground under my feet. I think I shall put it all before Uncle C.K.'

These samples should be enough to convince anybody of the honesty and frankness of an English girl of the Victorian Age, brought up in typical squirarchal surroundings, and also to give glimpses of her capacity for love. I shall now set forth the story of her love in her own words, which will fully reveal her passionate intensity. This should go to show that the idea that the Victorians were given to suppressing their passion is a myth. There is no evidence for it in fact or fiction; rather, the evidence to the contrary is decisive. The Victorians had no sense of guilt even about their libertinism, and seduced or committed adultery with as light a heart as anybody could do today, only perhaps with greater elegance and dignity. The Victorian rake was as thoroughbred as his hunter, and the virtuous Victorians on their part had no sense of guilt about their virtue.

Georgina Grenfell was a modern Heloïse in that her love was inseparable from her religion and morality. There is not one sentence in her whole confession in which her love is not placed under the eyes and in the hands of her God. The whole journal is written in this spirit, and since it is not possible to reproduce the whole of it I shall give a selection of characteristic passages.

June 8, 1856: The Sacrament today such a real help. Long and deeply did I pray for dear Müller, that whatever was for our good might be done, and that in 'silence and prayer' we might bear all that God sends.

June 28, 1856: Thank God after three weeks of sad anxiety and earnest prayer for him I have today heard that my dear Müller is more peaceful and enjoying the idea of his mother coming. Ah! were it not for deep earnest prayer, how could one bear it? I cannot think of his grief. Such a man. Why, why am I allowed to cause sorrow to such a mind? God keep me true to him. Every day I think more of him and feel if for our good God will order it all and allow it—But if it may never be, Oh! my God teach him to forget, lay not deep sorrow on him.

August 2, 1857: 'Take from us all things hurtful and give us those things which be profitable for us.' How very difficult to put up this prayer in faith and resignation—Yet God knows all and we can by no effort of ours make or mar His plans. If He sees this right for us, then no power on earth can prevent it. Shall we not wait on him then, and strive to possess our souls in patience?

After considering the financial situation of Müller, Georgina Grenfell had decided that for the present she would say goodbye to the subject and prayed to God to keep her true to Müller and herself. But only a few days later she had to write:

October 19, 1857: 'Thou knowest not what a day may bring forth'— 'Man proposes, but God disposes'—How easy to say and write this, but how hard to really believe and acquiesce in it. I resolved when I closed this book ten days ago it should not be opened again for many months and yet in these ten days the story of my life has been decided.

On the 14th she got a letter from Max Müller begging her to settle the question in one way or another. She at once wrote to her father entreating him to allow their marriage, and telling him how her whole heart was Müller's, but he would not. So, 'feeling that my first duty was to my father', she wrote to Müller on the 17th to tell him that all was over and to say farewell. Then she set down her feelings in her journal:

Thus the whole joy of my life is gone and his. Ah! I cannot face his sorrow and I write this calmly, but Oh! the storm within. It is hard to submit to duty. It is bitter to give up all the happiness of life at twenty-two. It is wrong to say this: for may not God have other joy in store for me and for him?—but I cannot bear the idea of joy now.

On the last day of 1857 she steels herself to bear her sorrow, reminding herself of the greater suffering of her people in India during the Mutiny:

Dec. 31, 1857: Nearly gone and with it my hope? No, I cling to him. I cannot yet give him up! My Max who loves me with the tenderness of a woman, and the strength of a man. Oh! Lord may Thy richest blessing be with him now and ever, and grant me grace to see Thy hand in every event, and bow before Thee. How many have lost relatives this year or suffered agonies for them, how many have endured mutilation and worse and shall I murmur at a grief which more or less seems to fall to nearly everyone?

She puts up this prayer at the beginning of 1858:

At sacrament today I prayed earnestly for grace to watch against and overcome the cross and bitter feelings that I know are in my heart. My love for Müller should not have this effect on me. No! God grant me strength to feel more for others, to mix more in their pursuits, and to quell the angry feelings that rise in my heart. Doubt and disappointment are difficult to bear. But am I doing myself and Müller justice by giving way to angry, even peevish feelings? No, with God's help they shall be conquered.

To illustrate her faith in God in her suffering I shall quote only one other entry, set down on May 1, 1859, and only twelve days before the event which was to make her father agree to her marriage with Müller: 'What would life be', she writes, 'if one could not take every care to God—little cares or worries which can be breathed to no human ear, but which one may lay before our heavenly Father, the gracious God to "whom all hearts be open, all desires known," even when hardly known to oneself.'

This mingling of intense religious feeling with love shown by Georgina could be expected in mid-Victorian England, where faith was becoming more assertive and active than in the age immediately previous because of the growth of philosophic doubt and scientific disbelief. But the devout high-seriousness which it generated was still exceptional in the upper classes, for whom worldliness was an inheritance in entail.

The menfolk of the Grenfell family were of the normal type, and so Kingsley, Georgina's uncle, was very glad to see that she and his friend were drawn to each other by a common spirituality, and he wrote to Max Müller:

You are one of the few men to whom I have been drawn passionately at first sight. When I found out that you loved her, my affection for you

6*

deepened. I should have liked any man the better for loving her: but that *you* did so, was quite a triumph to me, because I knew that it was not [her] face merely which would attract you: but that you had seen the inward spiritual grace which I had always known was there, dormant chiefly, but only waiting to be called out.

He also loved Georgina the better for being attracted to Müller. He had always thought well of her character and pictured her to himself, as he put it, 'as the model lady-of-the-manor in a large estate'. But this showed her wisdom, in that brought up as she was, she should see 'how much better a noble human soul was for her than wealth or rank'.

But even this did not reassure Kingsley that Georgina would be happy on the £750 that Max Müller had, and he wrote:

No doubt that people could be as happy as angels, even in this expensive England, on that. But when children come, and come they will, fast enough and too fast—you would find that very little indeed. True, hundreds of thousands of educated people will be rich on that, but you must remember what her bringing up has been—she never has had a physical want, or a fancy, unsatisfied since she was born—She would give up these and 'rough it', for herself, easily enough if she is a true woman, and find a joy and an honour in sacrificing herself for her children, and in that fact lies the danger . . . Don't tell me of *not letting* her make sacrifices. She will never let you find her out—Oh my dear Max, you don't know the diabolical cunning of women when they intend to be angels.

Kingsley also warned Müller against an alternative evil which was worse:

Her family see what her husband cannot, and then come endless presents. You cannot refuse them, ought not: but they are most galling to all valiant men. She cannot refuse them because they will go to her children or enable her to save for her children, and so is established a habit of aristocratic pauperism which does no soul good. And worse, it tempts her to get into the chronic habit of pleading poverty, giving hints, all but begging.

This would not have happened, Kingsley added, if she had no rich relations, but since she had, Kingsley concluded with a final word of advice: 'Oh, Max, keep your feet and hers out of the net, and wait a while and all will go as God wills.'

Max Müller thanked Kingsley for his advice, saying: 'Your clear and decisive words have brought me more comfort than pain—they have driven away a swarm of vain hopes and plans, and the sooner they are scattered the better.' But, as lover, he wholly rejected one part of the warning: 'Only one thing I must say. If she is what I believe, and what you know her to be, all you write about aristocratic pauperism—true as it is and as I know it to be—applies as little to her as to Mrs. Kingsley. I share all your other fears, but this one I cannot share.'

Whether Kingsley or Max Müller was right about Georgina on this score was never proved, because her father would not agree to the marriage even when in 1858 the emoluments of a Fellow of All Souls was added to Müller's £750 or so. But if she were put to the test she would have fully justified her lover's confidence by never becoming an aristocratic pauper. The stoicism with which she was bearing her sorrow at being forced to kill love for the sake of money, would not have left her if she had had love and little money. She did not think it right even to indulge the sorrow. Throughout the journal she tells herself that she must mope less, keep herself less aloof, and mix more with others in all their pleasures:

I have many many blessings—the love and approbation of so very many—a happy home, every temporal luxury and indulgence, so many dear ones round me. I have many duties to perform, Father, aunt; brother, sister, servants and poor to comfort and influence. I have great responsibilities—money, time and beauty to be well employed. I have temptations—the peculiar foibles and sins of my own character, vanity, indolence, selfishness, the difficulties of my position—admired and spoilt; the little peculiarities of others to bear with quietly and kindly. I have sorrows—one great, absorbing grief. God grant I may read *all* its lessons aright. When I look back I see such wasted time and talents, such forgetfulness of God. When I look forward much seems dark and sad. Let me cling to the 'Now the present and the seen'. And here I would desire to live for others this year, help or comfort others. I must strive that my own grief may not entirely *engross* me. I must be often sad, for I would not leave Müller. No! I am too weak to resist the reaction. I should then very likely make some foolish marriage, but I would be more alive for the sake of others to the duties, interests, and even pleasures of each day. The *poor and my own family* must be my objects this year.

Like a true moralist she knows that in such situations as hers what a person *does* always matters more than what he merely *thinks*. So she goes on to write: 'I would lay down a few rules for my guidance in the use of my time.' In doing so she could not be more severe if she had been a nun.

I must never be in bed more than 6 hours at the outside, in summer it might be 5. That leaves me 18 hours—Of these 5 at least are spent at meals and in the drawing room, 2½ more in dressing. Then I have 10½ to spend. Of these but few go in outing. How much is left. I would be always busy and able to feel each day 'my time has been entirely employed this day'. I pray God that I may be able each week to feel increasingly that I do everything 'with all my might'. *Living for others and redeeming the time*, shall, with God's help, be my *earnest, constant, hourly* objects.—G.A.G.

But there lurked a great danger to Max Müller in the very fervent religious sensibility of the women of the Grenfell family. He could be attacked through it, and attacked he was, though not by his rivals in love. The attack came from Oxford. The dons there always thought that the deeds of God were manifest in their worldly advancement, and they were given to making a ruthless use of the *odium theologicum* to strike down competitors. Two of the greatest figures of nineteenth-century Oxford, Pattison and Jowett, were both harmed in their careers by this, and Max Müller was to be also. He was rejected for a professorship. To begin with, however, someone tried to spoil his prospects in marriage, and complained to Miss Grenfell that he was an unbeliever. How serious the consequences of such a charge could be can be gusssed from the entry which Georgina Grenfell set down in her diary on October 8, 1856: 'Dear Müller! I know God will bless him. I saw on Sunday night some reports that Gommy had received as to his religious opinions, in which he was called an unbeliever. These deeply grieved me, and I felt, intense as the struggle would be, I must give him up, if he could not refute such reports.'

Fortunately, Max Müller came to know about it, probably through Kingsley, and though he was busy with his mother who was ill and needed to be attended by him because she did not know English, he at once wrote to Miss Grenfell:

I feel I ought to write to you, if it were only to say, *Do not* believe uncharitable reports. You know that in England more than anywhere

else, and in Oxford again, more than anywhere in England, religion
has been dragged into party struggles, and many persons think it
neither uncharitable nor sinful to call a man a heretic or unbeliever
who differ from them on matters, concerning not so much the doctrine,
as the discipline and policy of the Church. Though I have abstained
as much as possible from mixing myself up with any party, yet I know
that the very fact of my being made Professor at Oxford,* has roused
some angry feelings against me.

But he also honestly admitted that when he first came to Oxford
he had spoken 'rather strongly against those who, while they professed their faith so very loudly, seemed to be guided in their actions
by principles so very different from those of Christianity'. Then he
concluded with the words:

Nothing is more dangerous, and nothing more apt to bring out the
worst features of a man's character, than religious controversy. The
more we can avoid it, the better for ourselves and for others. Faith,
Love and Honour, as the old knights used to say, are treasures of
which those speak least who profess them. And does it not seem to you,
that, as our love to our neighbours has its springs in our love to God,
so where there is faith in God, there is also faith in man? I can say no
more today.

It would seem that Miss Grenfell was not wholly satisfied by this,
for in his second letter on this subject he quotes a passage from her
reply in which she said: 'I could not consent to the union of her
whom I had above all things desired to train as a Christian, with
one who would lead her away from faith in the Scriptures, and
dependence on the Divine Teacher and Redeemer.' This language
hurt Müller very much, and he wrote an elaborate and almost
panic-stricken *apologia pro fidem suam* to convince Miss Grenfell.
He began by telling her that it was impossible for him to defend
himself if she did not believe him when he asked her not to believe
in the accusation, and after that he dealt with his un-named
accuser:

If I have said or written anything that has given offence to your friend,
let me know it, and I shall then be able to defend myself. But if someone, without giving any proof, without giving even his name, tells you

---

* Taylorian Professorship of Modern European Languages on £500 a year in
which he was confirmed by the Convocation on February 21, 1854.

that I am an unbeliever, that I do not believe in the Bible, that I do not believe in Christ, our Lord and Saviour, I need not fear him . . . I have many friends who know me and know my religious convictions, and though I have always avoided theological controversy, I have never avoided to express my faith in the doctrines of Christianity where I felt called upon to do so.

Continuing, Max Müller said:

If you read the history of the Church you will find that . . . all divisions and persecutions in the Church have arisen from the attempts of theologians to substitute their own thoughts and their own expressions for the simple language in which Christianity has been revealed to us in the Bible. And if we know the dangers of religious controversy, if we see how it is opposed to the very spirit of Christianity and how it appeals to the worst passions, and destroys every feeling of charity, we ought to pity the priest or theologian who, like a physician, must enter into this pest house.

Max Müller's plight was worse than that of Jowett when he was made to sign the Thirty-nine Articles. Jowett was unrepentant and cynical. As he wrote to Stanley, 'I have taken the meaner part and signed. It seemed to me that I could not do otherwise without giving up my post as a clergyman.' Müller could not afford such a mere formality. It was bad enough to be rejected by the father for want of money; it would have been much worse to be rejected by the aunt for want of faith. If he had known of Georgina's attitude he would probably have been even more elaborate and earnest. But as it was Georgina was wholly satisfied, and wrote in her diary after setting down her insistence on a refutation:

This he did in a letter that deepened my love to him, and made me feel more than ever that he would make me happy. At the same time he said he had given up all hope of ever having me, and this made me feel *I* could not give him up! Therefore I have written and would wait in faith, prayer, and patience. However it is, God will be with such a man, whose religious views are so deep and true, and in heaven if not on earth we may meet. Dear Müller, I cannot cease to pray for him.

This true story of love is an example, among many others which may be found in the biographies of notable Europeans, of a relationship of which we Hindus can learn nothing at first hand—

namely, the relationship that exists between love in life and love in literature. But a full documentation illustrating it can be found in Europe. Georgina Grenfell's journal, for instance, has shown me the counterpart in life of the confrontation between love and morality or society and also of the combination of love with stoicism which is found in all the novels of Charlotte Brontë. Take *Jane Eyre*, for example. Loving Rochester passionately, she ran away from him and set down her judgement even when she was suffering:

> Which is better? To have surrendered to temptation; listened to passion; made no painful effort—no struggle; but to have sunk down in the silken snare; fallen asleep on the flowers covering it; weakened in southern climate, amongst the luxuries of a pleasure villa: to have been now living in France, Mr. Rochester's mistress . . . Whether it is better, I ask, to be a slave in a fool's paradise at Marseilles—fevered delusive bliss one hour—suffocating with bitter tears of remorse and shame the next—or to be a village school mistress, free and honest, in a breezy mountain nook in the healthy heart of England?

In all this Madame de Staël is not dead, she is simply reborn in Yorkshire.

But stoicism, efficacious as it is in helping a man to suffer without cowardly wailing, is still a philosophy of defeat in life, in fact, the grandest philosophy of defeat. It cannot prevent those who are young from suffering because their flesh remains quick and has not yet been tempered or annealed to endure the pain, so that young stoics feel as if they had chosen to have a surgical operation without anaesthetic. Georgina was resolved to be heroic but felt in the same way. At the end of 1857 she writes: 'The year nearly gone, and though the summer was bright and gay, yet all the year there has been a deep slow undercurrent of sorrow and anxiety . . . I am so weary. I long often for rest from it all like a tired child. How will it end?' Again she writes early in 1858: 'All this tries me very much, and the spring time of life gone, and autumn seems gathering over without any summer. I am very worn and weary, and long for rest.' At the beginning of 1859, only a few months before the sudden happy turn in her life she sets down—'My twenty-third year gone. We bring our years to an end—so quickly they move from us and so fast does eternity draw on. I thank God for the *Past*, and trust Him for the *Future*, only praying to serve Him in the *Present*.' It is harrowing to read all this from a young girl of twenty-three, but it is also chastening to do so in an age given over to peevish self-pity and boastful self-indulgence.

What adds to her sorrow is her knowledge that Müller also loves her and is suffering as much as she is. She felt too that all his suffering was due to his love for a girl not wholly worthy of him. She set down that conviction a few days after his declaration of love to her, and she reverts to the theme again and again: 'Except through deep love to him, I can never be fully, really worthy of him! Are my worldly advantages to be for a moment considered as equivalent to his mind and character? The hollow, vain world may think them so, I never can.'

Another thing which was causing sorrow to her was the thought of the unhappiness of the other young men who were falling in love with her. 'I am worried,' she writes, 'about C.S. I do hope he is not to be made unhappy by me—he is too nice, for me to suspect a feeling in him I cannot return, without being sorry and vexed about it.' In about ten days she feels more positive and writes: 'I have begged papa not to ask C.S. here so often, as it is very evident what his feelings are.' Six months later she felt that she could not allow this to go on, and she gave Charles Scrobold his *congé* in very great sorrow. 'Poor Charles Scrobold,' she wrote on August 11, 'will have received the blow to all his hopes today. I sent a message yesterday by Gommy to his mother, to say it was hopeless.'

There are references to other suitors, who were found on discreet inquiry by the aunt to be far far too poor to think of marrying. Georgina often thought over in her mind if it would not be better under the circumstances to give up Müller and seek peace if not happiness in marriage. In February 1858 she wrote in her diary: 'I feel sometimes that if some clever good man, whom I could respect, were to like me that would settle it. But it would be a dreadful undertaking, and yet unless Papa consented to my union with Max I must either make that sort of marriage or remain single all my life—for my heart and youth and soul are with Max.' Meanwhile, Max Müller had been suffering no less. Actually, from the very morrow of his open declaration of love to Georgina he had ceased to hope. For instance on July 3, 1856, less than a month from the declaration, he wrote to Miss Grenfell: 'How right you were when you said, Oh foolish man! Yes, I have been extremely foolish, and I feel I have fully deserved the penalty which I pay. But it is too late to lament over it now.'

He concluded the letter by giving his promise that she would hear no more complaints, and by even setting down his appreciation of Riversdale Grenfell: 'I wish I could tell Mr Grenfell how fully I appreciate his motives, and how much I value the kindness and forbearance which he has shown to me on all occasions.'

But the extraordinary thing was that though everybody said that the matter was ended, nobody brought it to a conclusion. For three years Müller and Miss Grenfell kept up this intimate and confidential exchange of letters, and Georgina saw some of them. It was at the beginning of this correspondence that Miss Grenfell called for a vindication of Müller's faith. But why? The Grenfells could have got rid of him finally by accepting the accusation at its face value without giving him any opportunity to justify himself, which, as has been seen, only deepened Georgina's love for him. But the mid-Victorian old maid continued to show affection and sympathy to Müller, and even consented to serve as an intermediary between him and her niece. This would remain a puzzle unless one could revise one's notion of a Victorian old maid.

Max Müller was equally despondent with others. He confided in his intimate friend, Charles Kingsley, to whom he wrote on August 10, 1857, from Leipzig:

I can wait and work—and sooner or later all this waiting and working will come to an end, for this life cannot last for ever and it will last no longer than we can bear it. I have no right to complain. I have all I wanted—more than I ever hoped for, more than I deserved. A disappointment in love is hard to bear because it destroys our faith in ourselves and in everything else—a disappointment in marriage may be a life-long trial, but it need not destroy our faith in our own nature, in the truth of others, or in the wisdom of God. I should like to see her once more before I go—but God knows best his season of blessings—and if I should never meet her again in this life, I feel that I owe to her more than I can tell you. To say that it would have been better for me if I had never seen her, seems to be as foolish as to say, it would have been better for me if I had never been born. No, no. Life may grow more strange and awful every day—but the more it reveals to us its truest meaning and reality, and the deepest depth of its divinity. 'And God saw everything that He had made, and behold it was very good.'

He kept Miss Grenfell informed about his work, his literary projects and campaigns, and told her on one occasion:

So you see I am in harness again, and I shall try to make up for the three years that I wasted in despair and misery. Life was then a riddle, a foolish dream—I did not know for what purpose I should live and work. It is so no longer, and the burden I shall have to bear, perhaps through the whole of my life, has become light and even dear to me since I know who wishes me to carry it.

But he can bear it only by thinking of the transcience of life: 'I feel', he says, 'that much more than half of this earthly journey is finished—year after year seems to go more rapidly, and we shall have arrived sooner perhaps than we expect.' He was then only thirty-five years of age.

In reply to another letter of Miss Grenfell's in which she had mentioned that it was being written while the Septet of Beethoven was being played in another room, he wrote:

Your letter written with the accompaniment of Beethoven's Septet was all music to me. What is time and space, and earth and life, and all that people call stern reality? While I was reading your letter I was sitting in a quiet corner of your room—watching the dark cedar tree that stretches out its broad branches to bless you and your house, and I listened to every note.

But to write in this way to the aunt of the girl whom one wants to forget was not the best means of ensuring that result. Nor was it better to discuss lost love with her. A small novel called *The Lost Love* had just been published and was very popular, and Max Müller sent it to Miss Grenfell, who read a personal note in it. He replied at once, not unwilling to discuss the subject:

You cannot possibly allude to me when you say in your last letter speaking of a little book I sent you, that you hope there are not many such cases! ... But is there such a thing as a lost love? I do not believe it. Nothing that is true and good is ever lost on earth though its fulfilment may be deferred beyond this short life. Marriage is meant for this life only, but love is eternal, and all the more so, if it does meet with its fulfilment on earth.

Max Müller did not take long to pass from the general to the concrete and in doing so wrote as the typical disinterested lover:

As long as I imagined that the happiness of your dear niece depended on her marriage with one so unworthy of her as myself, I sometimes feared that my mind would break down under the burden which God had placed on me. As it is now, I feel relieved, because I know that she is happy and there may yet be greater happiness in store for her than she could have found as the wife of a poor man.

He even thought that Kingsley was wrong in assuring him that Georgina still loved him, as he wrote: 'Though Mr. Kingsley no doubt meant very well in all he did, it was a mistake of his to imagine that it could be any consolation to me to be told that your niece, although she wished everything to be over, still entertained her deep affection. This *ought not* to be. It is different with a man whose heart is strong, and who can shape his life as he likes.'

After that the formal gesture of renunciation was bound to come, and it did in a postscript to this very letter, in which Müller wrote: 'Whenever you write to me again please to tell me distinctly that you have burnt all my letters. I know they are safe with you, but those eyes for which alone they were written may be closed by the hand of God, and there is something sacred in the intimacy of friendship that ought to be protected against profane eyes.'

In his very next letter, written nine days later, he informs Miss Grenfell: 'I have just burnt the last letters which I had kept—it was painful to read then again for the last time.' But he is not sure that Miss Grenfell has done the same thing.

Miss Grenfell had certainly left the subject *intentionally* vague, having her own mind about the matter, and that has enabled me to document this part of Müller's biography. Müller convinced himself that he had found a compensation. He wrote to Miss Grenfell: 'I hope you will some day come to All Souls and see me in my little cell. I think you would agree with me that one may be very happy here—perhaps too happy . . . I have found a home, a very pleasant home, as you will see when you come to Oxford.' This exchange of letters continued. She never withdrew her sympathy and good will from him, and Max Müller never ceased to be grateful. Perhaps he would have been still more grateful if he had known that at one stage she had come forward with an offer to remove the money difficulty out of her own income. There is no doubt that even if the marriage had not taken place Miss Grenfell would never have ceased to hold her place in his heart.

But it was neither Georgina's love nor her faith which was to bring about her own and Müller's release from suffering. It was her body which did that at last, by failing to bear the agony. Some two months after she had set down her view of the tranquillizing effect of a loveless marriage, she saw Müller at a concert from a distance and fainted away. Instead of feeling ashamed about this melodramatic weakness she gloried in it, and wrote in her diary as soon as she was strong enough to attend to it:

Last Thursday the 12th May I saw Müller at a concert. It was agony. I saw him come in, he only saw me at the end. I always knew it would harrow up the very core of my heart whenever it happened and so it did. So near, and yet so far off—no word, no sign between us, whose very souls cling so together. Yet thank God it has happened, for it has undeceived myself and others, who fancied it was all over. I have submitted so quietly, so cheerfully to my father's stern will that many think that the sacrifice was light. Few know how my whole life's joy is gone . . . He looked well and at peace. God grant that it may really be so and give me grace to trust on. 'A little longer' and he and I shall meet where none can part us.

But that was not to be. The doctor who was called in said that Georgina's will to live was gone, and she would just fade away. Both Kingsley and Froude advised Riversdale Grenfell to give his consent, and the father, who had never paid any heed to the mental suffering of his daughter, was frightened by the failure of her body. He gave his consent.

So the trials of both Max and Georgina were drawing to a close. On June 8, 1859, when on her way to Ray Lodge from Scotland she had reached Lichfield, Miss Grenfell wrote to Max Müller, apparently resolved not to lose a minute to give him the happy news:

My dear friend, This day three years you were very sad, and so were others, but there is a great change in the aspect of your lives—and I am allowed by my Brother to say that you will be welcome at Ray Lodge again, and that we shall expect you there on *Saturday* next—your long patience and submission to what was hard to bear is to be rewarded, and it seems to be all like a dream. Perhaps you have heard of my Brother having been in Oxford, or may have seen him there. He does not tell me if this is so—but in a letter just arrived he says he withdraws his objection to your union with his beloved Georgie, and now I may say that I hope and trust it will be the object of you *both* to contribute in every way to his happiness—for he is (I may say it to you without the fear of offending you) making a sacrifice of his own views and feelings in thus consenting to what he opposed so long . . . But so it is—whatever has brought it about, and now my dear friend you have a great treasure to take care of. Oh may you guide and help her in all that is good, and holy, and in a word Christianlike.

You know my regard and affection for you, but you do not know what a difficult path I have had to walk in, so as to be kind and yet upright with everyone. But all this is over now—May God realize all your happy expectations and give me the great blessing of seeing both *these dear children* happy for life. Theodore and Charlotte are all joy. Georgie is feeling rather stunned by the suddenness of the change. After Saturday we shall feel quieter. Let me have a line to say what time you are likely to arrive. We are here on our way home from Scotland, and little thought what was awaiting us. May God bless you.

She adds in a postscript: 'Remember you will have to take some care of me in my old age.' Max Müller got the letter on the 9th and replied immediately:

My dear friend, Here I have been sitting for hours, but I cannot collect my thoughts, much less can I write them down. You must have patience with me, but such a sudden burst of light dazzles my poor eyes, and I hardly dare to trust them when I look at your letter. I cannot understand it, I did not see Mr. Grenfell when he was at Oxford. I knew of his being here, and I felt keenly that he evidently did not wish to see me . . . In moments like these we must be alone, quite alone with God. I shall be more collected when I see you on Saturday; today I feel broken down in mind and body. Do you know that so much happiness is very hard to bear? Do help me to bear it by sharing it with me!

Then after signing his name he remembered that he had not told her the time of his arrival. So he wrote a postscript like Miss Grenfell, but with a more immediate application: 'May I come by the train that arrives at Maidenhead at 11.25?'

On the same day after arriving at Ray Lodge, Georgina set down in her journal: '"Thou dost all things well!" Great joy given me. God help me to bear it. Papa removes his veto and Max and I meet the day after tomorrow. "Tarry thou the Lord's leisure, be strong and He shall comfort thine heart."'

At 11.25 Max Müller was going to arrive at Maidenhead station. Georgina was sitting in her room expecting him and she set down

in her diary: 'June 11, 11.4 a.m.—I am waiting for my great joy.
God give me grace to bear it rightly.'

The next entry for the same day:

Max arrived at 2, and then we were together, really together, and the
long three years since he put me into the carriage at Oxford rolled
away like a dark dream. All the others were out, and we sat together
under the ilex tree and began to know each other and see how those
three years had taught us and fitted us for our life together, how even
in absence our souls had grown together, and I thanked God for His
great love and mercy and for giving me such a soul to love and live for,
to call mine for time and eternity. In the evening he played to me—
those sounds I had never thought to hear again. We walked round by
the river and stood long together at the gate at the back. How happy!

The next day, Sunday, Max Müller wrote to Kingsley:

My dear Kingsley, Can you believe it? I cannot, though I see her with
my eyes. I knew not that the world contained such happiness. You
know her, you know what treasure she is. You know also what we have
suffered, and now think of us, and pray for us to God that He may help
us and teach us how to bear such joy and blessing. You are not angry
with me? Do not let us think of the past, it was so dark and awful, and
the world around us is so happy and bright, there must be no cloud
anywhere. We shall meet on Tuesday. I long to see my new dear aunt,
—my old dear friend, Mrs Kingsley. Oh this world of God is full of
wonders, but the greatest wonder of all wonders is Love.

On this letter there is a short note in Kingsley's hand: 'For
Georgie.' And without a doubt Georgie saw it.

The wedding was to take place on August 3, nearly seven weeks
later. But the days passed almost in a delirium of joy for both, talking to each other, listening to Beethoven's and Handel's music,
walking, attending church together, reading F. D. Maurice and
Keble and even the marriage service in advance. I have already
quoted some entries from Georgina Grenfell's diary during this
period which illustrate her ecstasy. But I would still quote three
typical ones. The first of these describes how she took Max Müller
to the grave of her long-dead mother at Taplow. She writes: 'I took
him to my mother's grave. That fair young mother but little older
than I am—could she but see us, she would be *satisfied*. Yes, that is

the word—it is not mere bright happiness, but such entirely, utterly satisfied feeling. This grows every day.'

The following entry was the last one before her wedding day:

Thursday 12 p.m.—Just in from the garden. Oh! how happy we have been; sitting under our own ilex, and next time we are together it will be as husband and wife. What solemn words, yet how blessed. 'Oh! God our Heavenly Father, Thou hast led us hitherto and ordered everything to this end. Do thou still lead and guide us and enable us to offer ourselves our souls & bodies as a sacrifice to Thee, so that after training here on earth together, we may together dwell for ever with Thee, in a brighter world where nothing changes or passes. Amen.'

And on the morning of her wedding day she wrote: 'My wedding Day. "Bless the Lord, oh my soul." I go with perfect confidence and trust. May God bless us both and may our lives be devoted to Him. Amen!'

After the wedding at Bray Church the newly married couple spent a week at Eversley Rectory lent by Kingsley, and then they went on a Continental tour, meeting Bunsen at Heidelberg, Max Müller's mother at Dresden, his sister at Chemnitz, and visiting Bohemia, Switzerland and western Germany on their way back to Oxford, which they reached on October 24. Two months later she set down the last entry in her diary about her love affair and marriage:

Ray Lodge—X'mas Day, 1859: I have not written anything in this book in the last four bright months. My life seemed too bright for words. I am not disappointed. Much as I had expected from my long-loved Max I had no idea of half his value. I cannot express his deep love, his tenderness, his forbearance. Our three months abroad were indeed happy and there began the hope of even greater joy for the future and tho' God has destroyed that hope for a time, still intense happiness is showered on us. Our joy is *awful*. I can but pray that our good and gracious Father will bless our happy life now, to our real eternal good as I feel he did the years of sorrow that preceded it. And here we are assembled, our whole party, well, bright, and with every blessing showered on us. Gracious God, teach us all to remember Thee, as the author of all our blessings, and may we so pass through things temporal as finally to lose not the things eternal. Bless us for time and eternity.

How poor words seem. How can they describe such joy as mine and

Max's, how can they fitly express the hourly prayer, that I can truly say my grateful heart is always offering up, that we may both be God's true servants and training together for an ever brighter higher life hereafter—'Thou God seest us.' Thou dost know the thoughts, no need of our faltering words, when we approach Thee, our omniscient Father.

This fusion of human and divine love was one of the finest achievements of the Christian civilization of Europe, and it resulted in an exultant mysticism of the sex relationship. Both have become things of the past in the world in which they were once created. But even when this kind of love was a force in the life of European men and women, it could hardly be expected to be found in the lives of a German specialist on Sanskrit and comparative philology and an English girl belonging to fashionable society. Appraisal of personal life is always baffling, because one can never discover fully what happens in its hinterland.

At this point I must describe a by-product of Max Müller's disappointment in love. It was a short novel or long story in German to which he gave the title *Deutsche Liebe, German Love*. He wrote it in the autumn of 1856 when his mother was with him at Oxford, and it was published anonymously by Brockhaus of Leipzig in February 1857. It became very popular there, and before Max Müller's death in 1900 went through twelve editions. An English translation by one Miss Winkworth was immediately published, and it was widely read. There was also an unauthorized American translation which was very free, but it sold in very large numbers. Georgina Grenfell, who knew and spoke German very well even before her marriage with Müller, made her own translation but it was not published for twenty years. Then it was allowed to supersede the older translation because Max Müller thought that his wife's translation more nearly gave the exact tone and colouring of the original and was more literal. It was also translated into many other European languages. A pocket edition was issued as late as 1913.

The book seems to have appealed to some deep-seated and universal human mood and, as Mrs Max Müller wrote in 1909, it had been dearly loved by many in many lands. Max Müller himself was particularly pleased that his novel had succeeded in winning friends among the hard-headed readers of the United States. There is striking evidence of its appeal in a letter which he received from a total stranger in California in 1899, more than forty years after its publication. This American informed him that his wife had just died, and added: 'I want to tell you that your *Deutsche Liebe* lies upon her breast, in accordance with her wish. I want to thank you on her behalf and my own, for that most beautiful story of spiritual affinity.'

It is a story of love between a crippled German princess and a young commoner in a small German principality, and can be called a Ruritanian idyll except for its deep pathos. I do not characterize the book as a tragedy because it is so instinct with the spirit of the Christian mystic and Quietist that no sense of any tragic catastrophe is created.

Max Müller himself explained why he had written it in a letter to Baron Bunsen:

> What I wished to make clear to myself and others was, why with the inborn love to our fellow creatures, we could show that love to so very few of them only; why love had to be confined almost entirely to the members of our family, to our parents, our wife, our children, and why any attempt to go beyond generally ended in sorrow. It is so, and we know not why, except again to show us that this life was not meant to be perfect, but only to give us by its very imperfections a faith in and a longing for a better life.

Froude in reviewing the book for the *Saturday Review* pointed out the historical position of this novel as another depiction of love.

> One of our first impulses on seeing the general character of this work was to turn to the *Bekenntnisse einer schönen Seele* in *Wilhem Meister*, and to refresh our recollection of that remarkable production. It was not without feelings of satisfaction that we laid down the volume of the great master and took up the one before us, reflecting how much half a century had done to elevate and purify the tone of society.

Max Müller himself had another contrast to Goethe in his mind. To his mother, to whom he had not disclosed his authorship, he wrote: 'He [the author] only published the book because he thought that here and there it might do some good, and might cure young people of the epidemic of so-called unfortunate love. The book contains the antidote to *Werthers Leiden*, and in so far is interesting.' But he also adds: 'But it ought to have been more fully worked out to have much influence.'

The anonymity of the book was preserved for three or four editions, and then Müller came to be known as its author. Bunsen was informed, and Froude suspected the authorship.

The object of all this evasion seems to have been to avoid speculation as to whether the book contained a real personal story, and that story concerned the handsome young German don at Oxford. But as soon as the fact of his authorship became known that was the very attribution which continued to be made. So, in the preface to the sixth English edition published in 1898, Müller wrote: 'I have received during the last forty years ever so many inquiries whether the book was autobiographical, and I have had to explain again and again that it was not, and why it was not.' He explained that it was only the idea of love with which he was concerned, and the story was no more than the frame in which it had to be set. Love was a word, he added, 'which has had many and often very conflicting meanings assigned to it, and which, I thought and still think, each man and woman has a right to define after his or her own heart.'

Mrs Max Müller, too, in her biography of her husband published in 1902, set down a final contradiction. 'So much has been written and said about this prose idyll, so many people have declared it to be autobiographical, that it is perhaps well once for all to say that it is pure fiction as far as the characters and circumstances are concerned.' One wonders whether as she was writing this she recalled what she herself had set down in her diary on May 31, 1857:

> I have read *Deutsche Liebe* and know who it is by. [She had assumed as a matter of course that the story was autobiographical.] I cannot feel anything but pleasure that Max should have loved that pure holy Gräfin—it is like having loved and been loved by an Angel, and I feel that the sort of love he had for her, cannot, has not, lessened his power of loving me. How after intercourse with her he could see anything in me to attract, I cannot guess . . . When I think of Maria [the Princess in the story] I quite shrink at thought of my own weakness and nothingness. But I can never doubt Max's real love to me!

Chapter 3

LANGUAGE

To Max Müller the *Rig-Veda*, which kept him occupied fully or partly for thirty years, was only a means to an end. Not that he ever underrated the value of the means, absolute or relative; on the contrary, he emphasized its importance so much that people might justifiably have thought of him as a man who was riding a hobby-horse. Conscious of this, he again and again made out a case for studying the *Rig-Veda*. Nevertheless, the establishment of its text and that of Sayana's commentary, followed by an attempt to understand its meaning, was to him the preliminary investigation in a wider quest—the examination, in a particular field, of phenomena he was primarily interested in and wanted to understand. In short, his work on the *Rig-Veda* could be compared to the experiments carried out by a theoretical physicist or, better still, to the investigations of Darwin.

The cast of his mind was speculative, philosophical, or even metaphysical, and its natural inclination was towards generalization. This grew stronger in him as he became older, and towards the end of his life he gave expression to his respect for generalization by quoting a sentence of Emerson and providing his own gloss on it.

Let us take such a sentence as 'Generalization is always a new influx of divinity into the mind—hence the thrill that attends'. To the ordinary reader such a sentence can convey very little; it might seem, in fact, a mere exaggeration. But to those who know the long history of thought connected with the question of the origin of conceptual thought as the result of ceaseless generalizations, Emerson's words convey the outcome of profound thought. They show that he had recognized in general ideas, which are to us merely the result of a never-ceasing synthesis, the original thoughts or *logoi* underlying the immense variety of created things; that he had traced them back to their only possible source, the Divine Mind, and that he saw how the human mind, by rising from particulars to the general, was in reality only approaching the source of those divine thoughts, and thus becoming conscious, as it were, of the influx of divinity.

As was natural, this bent found its concentrated application in his basic intellectual interest—human thought, its origin and development. Actually, as it progressed, his intellectual activity became more and more concerned with what I have called the prehistory of the human mind, on which he showed himself to be a pioneer. This was pointed out in a French book, *L'Origin de la Pensée et de la Parole*, published from Paris in 1900, a few months before his death and recommended by him in his autobiography 'as giving a clear and complete abstract of my writings'.*

The name of the author was given as M. Moncalm, but it was the pseudonym for a woman, Madame de Wagner, who lived in Rome. She wrote to him in 1895 asking permission to quote from his works in a book which she said was being written by a friend. Leave was granted, and when passing through Rome in 1897 he met the lady, he found that she herself was the author. When the book was sent to him after publication Müller was recovering from his severe illness of the previous year, and he could only write: 'Many thanks for your present. Today I can only say, *Brava! Brava!* But I hope to say something more as soon as I can shake off my weakness.' But he could not.

In the introduction Madame de Wagner said that till recently those who were interested in the origins of life or of man could hardly get beyond the account in the Bible, or imagine that there were documents to illustrate the unexplored regions of the physical and mental world which were much more ancient. But, she went on:

> Two enterprising men, Darwin and Max Müller, visited and studied them. Darwin sought to explain what the origin of organic beings might have been, and in what way they passed through a series of evolutions, from one form to another of great dissimilarity . . . The development of human reason has been one of the objects of Max Müller's researches. This great thinker, who is at the same time the first philologist of our time, has sought in the Science of Language for the origin of thinking man.

Here the whole connexion between Max Müller's basic intellectual propensity and his philological work was indicated. If his end was to understand the beginnings of mental activity in man, whose first notional products were about religion and mythology, he had to

---

* Translated into English by G. S. Whitmarsh under the title of *The Origin of Thought and Speech* (London, 1905).

understand the emergence and employment of language at the very outset. So his philological inquiries would have been another means to an end for him. But, in actual fact, it was much more than that—a merging of his interest in thought as well as in language. This was due to a theory of his which held that thought and language were inseparable and co-existent. To use a theological phrase: there was a consubstantiality between the two. *Ratio et Oratio*, he said, were one, and he referred to the fact that the Greeks designated both by the same word, *Logos*. Therefore, one is not surprised to find Müller saying: 'Language is the autobiography of the human mind.'

Max Müller's conclusions about language will be summarized later in this chapter, but before this is done it is necessary to describe his work on language in general. I have already mentioned that his first public utterance was on a problem of language, when he appeared before the British Association for the Advancement of Science at its meeting at Oxford in 1847, and that foreshadowed his matured ideas about philology. His next contribution was an article in the October 1851 issue of the *Edinburgh Review*. It was nominally a review of the English translation by Lieutenant Eastwick of Franz Bopp's *Comparative Grammar*, but it was also an essay summing up the results achieved to date by the new science of Comparative Philology. Müller concluded the article with the words: 'It may be seen from this single instance that *Comparative Grammar* addresses itself not only to the Grammarian, but to the Philosopher and the Historian also.' He never forgot this comprehensive ambiance of philology in his treatment of language.

It was, however, as deputy and full Taylorian Professor of Modern European Languages that Max Müller developed his linguistic ideas over a number of years. This professorship was intended not only to advance the study of the languages and their contents, but also to deal with them in the light of the new science of Comparative Philology. Speaking as Trithen's substitute, he devoted his first lecture to the history and origins of modern European languages. His second lecture was on the *Niebelunglied*, and the third on the origins of the Romance languages. These lectures foreshadowed the ideas which he finally embodied in two courses of lectures delivered in 1861 and 1863 on the science of language.

These roused not mere interest, but enthusiasm. After reading the 1861 lectures when they were published in book form, Dean

Liddell wrote to Müller on November 16, 1861: 'It is humiliating to learn that the lectures have been delivered to the heedless ears of Oxford hearers.' He was unfair to Max Müller's audience, for the hearers, so far from being heedless, remembered their thrill even as old men. Cowell, who went to Calcutta as principal of the Sanskrit College and afterwards became Professor of Sanskrit at Cambridge, was then an undergraduate. He wrote: 'The lecture was a written one, and was delivered to a large and attentive audience, and to most of those present, as well as myself, it was an introduction to the new world of Comparative Philology. It was the first of a series of such lectures, all of which I attended.'

Tuckwell, author of a volume of delightful Oxford reminiscences, also went to the lectures with Dr (afterwards Sir Thomas) Acland, the physician. Acland, he said, was disturbed, fidgeted, bit his nails, and remarked: 'It frightens one!' Tuckwell wrote that these lectures taught him the novel doctrine of Aryan migrations, and the rationale of Greek myths. Story-Maskelyne, another Oxford figure and Professor of Mineralogy, also attended, and after Müller's death described the impression the lectures had made on him fifty years before:

> Well do I remember his lectures. It was a new star in the Oxford firmament . . . I do not think any Oxford man—unless it was Church of Oriel [afterwards Dean of St Paul's]—could have given such a course of lectures. It was a new light, a new idea of literature and lecture, that Max imported into the grey old walls of beautiful Oxford.

Story-Maskelyne added that Philip Pusey, son of the great Doctor, rode over with his boy-son all the way from his place near Faringdon sixteen miles away to hear each lecture: 'An early homage to the rising fame of the redactor of the *Rig-Veda*.' Finally Story-Maskelyne wrote:

> Natural science was not in high vogue then at Oxford, but the leaves on the trees were beginning to stir, so that when Max proclaimed his thesis that Comparative Philology and the historical development of language should rank with the Natural Sciences, there was a little rustle of scepticism, though in fact he was anticipating the assertion of evolution being the key to Natural Science.

Max Müller's next philological excursion was an essay on the

Turanian languages contributed to Bunsen's *Christianity and Mankind,* and published in 1854, though written almost entirely in 1853. This led to a controversy with Renan, which to the credit of both was ended quickly. Renan found Müller's views unacceptable, and in his *Histoire générale des langue sémitiques,* published in 1855, made a sharp attack on Müller's views on the Turanian languages.

Müller became very angry, and wrote a long and fierce review of Renan's book and had it printed as a pamphlet. Renan then wrote to Müller: '*Pardonnez-moi, je n'ai pas compris ce que vous vouliez dire.*' Upon this Müller suppressed the pamphlet, though its printing must have cost him some money, and afterwards he and Renan became intimate friends. Later in his life Müller gave up all the views on the Turanian languages expressed in the essay, as they were disproved by subsequent researches.

In carrying on his linguistic studies and researches for their own sake, Max Müller never forgot that they had a bearing on practical affairs. So it is not surprising to find him drawn, as soon as his standing as a linguist became known, into linguistic discussions arising out of cultural, administrative and even military activities.

In March 1853 the Crimean War began and, as the British army despatched there had to be familiar with the languages of the region, Sir Charles Trevelyan asked Müller for information about the languages of the northern part of the Turkish Empire and the adjoining Russian provinces, with which the officers serving in the war should become acquainted. Max Müller at once wrote a long pamphlet on *Languages of the Seat of War.* The corner of Europe from north Italy to the Danube, he said, was a real linguistic rookery, in which all the lost daughters of the European family of languages had taken refuge. This book needed a second edition in a year.

At the end of 1854 Macaulay invited Max Müller to his rooms in the Albany to discuss with him the new regulations for the Indian Civil Service, so far as they related to the teaching of Oriental subjects and languages. During his membership of the Council of the Governor-General of India twenty years before, Macaulay had shown himself to be the most vigorous and effectual supporter of English as the medium for the education of Indians, and had imposed his views on the Indian Government. It was also well known that he was no admirer of Oriental learning and literature. But Müller thought that he would perhaps be open to conversion, and went to the great man armed with facts and arguments to counter Macaulay's. As he wrote in his autobiography at the end of his life, he went back to Oxford a sadder, and—he hoped—a wiser man, for Macaulay never gave him a chance to put in a word.

Macaulay said that he knew nothing of Indian languages and literature, and wanted to know all that Müller had to say about the advantages to be derived by young civilians from a study of Sanskrit. He put some questions, but before Müller had a chance to answer any one of them, he began to relate his experiences in India, ending up with the usual diatribes against the natives of India on the score of their untruthfulness and untrustworthiness in a court of law.

Müller soon engaged himself in another linguistic campaign which was more ambitious, and which he sustained in one form or another throughout his life. It was for establishing schools for the study of Oriental languages, either in the universities or as independent public institutions. He had written about it to Sir Charles Trevelyan at the time of the Crimean War, when sending his report on *Languages of the Seat of War*. In it he pointed out the connexion between the political role of England in India and a competent knowledge of Oriental languages.

> It is undoubtedly high time [he wrote] that something should be done to encourage the study of Oriental languages in England . . . In all other countries which have any political, commercial, and religious connexion with the East, provision has been made, by Government or otherwise, to encourage young men to devote themselves to this branch of studies. Russia has always been a most liberal patron of Oriental philology . . . The French Government has founded a school. At Vienna there is an Oriental seminary. Prussia finds it expedient to give encouragement to young Oriental scholars, employed afterwards with advantage as consuls and interpreters. In England alone, where the most vital interests are involved in a free intercourse with the East, hardly anything is done to foster Oriental studies.

The Indian Mutiny of 1857 filled Müller with an even greater sense of urgency in pressing the matter on the public and the government. At the end of the year this thread was taken up, and there began the publication of a series of letters discussing the linguistic aspect of the Mutiny and making proposals for establishing a school for the study of Oriental languages. The first letter which had the heading, *On the Neglect of the Study of the Indian Languages considered as a Cause of the Indian Rebellion,* was dated December 30, and was written by Max Müller under the name of Philindus. The point he made was that it was the ignorance of the language of northern India which prevented the officers of the East India Company, who were taken completely by surprise by the rebellion, from having any real intercourse with the natives, and it was the same ignorance which created a feeling of estrangement, mistrust and contempt on both sides. He observed that 'a man need not have been in India to see that in order to govern a people, and to gain the confidence and goodwill of a conquered race, it is necessary to know their language', and then he put forward the operative part of his argument:

> It ought to be, and no doubt will be, one of the first things for Parliament to declare that a study of the native dialects shall be obligatory on every candidate for the Indian civil and military services . . . In the examinations for India . . . it will . . . be the duty of Government to provide candidates with the means of learning the Indian languages in this country, by establishing an Oriental college.

This letter was followed by six others, two from Max Müller writing as Philindus, two from Sir Charles Trevelyan, one from Professor Monier Williams of the East India College of Haileybury and one from an Indian Muslim, Professor Syed Abdoolah.

In his advocacy of Indian languages Max Müller naturally stressed the importance of Sanskrit as well. One part of his reasoning, as set forth in his letter of January 4, 1858, is worth quoting:

> But there are other considerations of a more subtle nature perhaps [he wrote], yet of considerable weight for making an elementary knowledge of Sanskrit an essential part of a civilian's previous education in England. It has been said that Sanskrit is a dead language; but, although Sanskrit is no longer spoken by the people, it is still the very life-spring of their thoughts, their faith, their feelings, and prejudices. In most countries the spoken language would at once be the key to the literature, and through it to the social, moral, and religious character of a nation. It is not so in India. There the state of literature at the present day is about the same as that of Italy at, or rather before, the time of Dante. The spoken language, *il volgare,* is Hindustani, Bengali, or Guzerathi; but the language of literature, law, and religion is still the classical Sanskrit.

7

He also expressed a definite view as to the method which should be adopted to teach Sanskrit to young civilians. He wrote:

> To learn Sanskrit from a pandit in India, according to the native system of grammar, must be a most tedious process; and this is the very reason why this part of a civilian's education should be finished in England with the assistance of grammars, dictionaries, and reading books, composed on a more rational system than the grammar of Panini, the Mahabhashya, and the Amara-kosha.

But nothing was done at that time, though Prince Albert took a lively interest in the scheme after the publication of the letters in *The Times*. The Prince saw clearly the disadvantage for England of not having such an institution, and spoke to Lord Granville, the Foreign Secretary, who wrote to Müller asking him to make further proposals. This Müller did, but he would not go further, because at that time there was such a feeling against Germans that the association of the name of Prince Albert and of a German scholar with the scheme would have been enough to wreck it.

More than thirty years later the idea was again taken up, and then successfully. A School of Modern Oriental Studies was established by the Imperial Institute in co-operation with University College and King's College, London, and Max Müller was asked to deliver the inaugural address. He did so on January 14, 1890, at the Royal Institution, with the Prince of Wales in the chair. He recalled his plea for teaching Oriental languages and said that it had fallen on deaf ears. When imperial interests were at stake, he declared, the country had a right to expect imperial, that is, concentrated action, such as had been taken in Russia, France, Austria and Germany. He dwelt on the commercial and political importance of the languages, and also explained how the task of governing India would be simplified if the governing race were able, by knowledge of their languages, to enter more readily into the thoughts, lives and aspirations of those they governed. The newspapers took up the subject warmly, but Müller heard from the Chairman of the Committee of Management that there was little prospect of getting any assistance from the government; and in fact the government did not contribute anything to the maintenance of the School established by the Imperial Institute.

Though Max Müller was writing and speaking on languages for many years, he did not make his formal appearance as a Comparative Philologist until 1861. In April of that year he began a course of lectures at the Royal Institution in London, which, followed by a second series in 1863, established him as the foremost authority on philology in Britain. The original lectures were published under the title of *Lectures on the Science of Language*, and the book was his second full-length contribution to scholarship.

Before the lectures Müller was very nervous at the prospect of having to address a select audience of not only the intellectual but also the social élite of London. Among the distinguished hearers were the Duke of Argyll, Connop Thirwall, Milman, Stanley, F. D. Maurice, Faraday and John Stuart Mill. As the lectures proceeded the lecture-room became more and more crowded and Albemarle Street more and more blocked by the fine carriages of people who came to hear about Aryan roots, Aryan ancestors and the common Aryan home in Asia.

'It is,' said a contemporary notice, 'a fact of no ordinary significance that, in the height of the London season, an enthusiastic audience of both sexes crowded the benches and endured the heat of a popular lecture-room, not to witness the brilliant experiments, or be fascinated by the revelations of a Faraday or an Owen, but to listen to a philosophical exposition of the inner mysteries of language.' Max Müller's reputation now had a solid aspect, which was fully proved when the lectures came out in book form. By 1886, that is, in twenty-five years, fourteen editions were printed.

The second course of lectures was delivered by Müller from February to May 1863. There were twelve in this series, and they were more technical than the first lectures. They were even better attended than the first ones, and were published in book form in the middle of 1864. Before that Müller was invited to Osborne House on the Isle of Wight, where Queen Victoria was residing, to speak on language before the royal family and suite. He gave the lectures in January in the Council Chamber, and for the first one the entire company were assembled, except the Queen and her children. After a while they too came in. The Queen had not attended a lecture for more than ten years. Max Müller proudly reported to his wife: 'She [the Queen] listened very attentively, and did not knit at all, though her work was brought.' He was informed by the Queen's Private Secretary how pleased she was with the lectures.

Three more expositions of Comparative Philology given by Müller in the next few years have to be noted in this chapter. The first of these was the Rede Lecture at Cambridge in 1868. He was invited in January to deliver it, and at the end of May went with his wife to Cambridge. It was proposed to confer the degree of LL.D. on him on this occasion, and also on the Arabic scholar Dr Wright and the American hydrographer Commodore Maury.

He delivered the lecture, which was entitled *On the Stratification of Language*, on May 29. The main thesis was the idea that in philology, as in geology, there were stratifications which, though forming a chronological series, were exposed to simultaneous observation in their distribution, and thus enabled philologists to deduce the early development of language from the isolating stage to the agglutinative, and again from the agglutinative to the inflective.

Müller's next address was his inaugural lecture after being appointed to the chair of Comparative Philology created expressly for him at Oxford, and this was delivered on October 27, 1868. His third was also an inaugural lecture, delivered on May 23, 1872, before the Imperial University of Strassburg created after Alsace had become part of the German Empire.

By that time, largely through Müller's own writings and speeches, the claims and value of the science of Comparative Philology had been established and its far-ranging importance recognized. To sum up the stage reached at that date in the words Müller himself used in his Strassburg address: 'This short survey must suffice to show you how omnipresent the Science of Language has become in all spheres of human knowledge, and how far its limits have been extended, so that it often seems impossible for one man to embrace the whole of its vast domain.' Henceforward Müller's purely philological interests were never merely linguistic; on the one hand they merged in his wider interest in the origin and nature of thought, mythology and religion, and on the other involved him in some very acrimonious controversy. Therefore 1872 is a convenient date at which to summarize Müller's purely linguistic ideas and define his role as a philologist.

In the most popular and easily recognized aspect of his activity as such, Max Müller is comparable to two of his famous contemporaries, T. H. Huxley and Matthew Arnold. Just as Huxley carried on propaganda for evolution and Arnold for criticism, Müller also preached the cause of philology for its indispensability to the mental effort summed up in the age-old saying: Know thyself. His skill in presenting ideas and success in the propaganda into which he put his heart, were shown by the number and quality of the audiences he attracted. This power to interest and hold attention even for the most abstruse matters he retained till the end of his life.

When he delivered the first course of his Gifford Lectures in Glasgow in November 1889, it was followed by all the distinguished Scottish intellectuals in the city. Principal Caird attended the lectures, as did Dr Dickson, the Divinity Professor and Professor Edward Caird. Most significant of all, it was the undergraduates who paid unqualified tribute to Müller's power of holding attention. Describing their attendance, a Glasgow paper wrote:

> Your university student is generally thought to be a very rowdy individual, and yet it must be confessed that no one listens to a good lecture with closer attention than he. The whistling of *Two Lovely Black Eyes* by the students of Glasgow University did not promise well for the attention Professor Max Müller would receive in delivering the first of his Gifford Lectures in the Bute Hall on Wednesday; but when the famous scholar plunged into his subject he could not have wished for a more attentive audience.

From the 1,400 on the first day, Müller's audience settled down to a steady 1,000 throughout the course, which compared with the fifty an Oxford professor could get as a fair number, spoke well not only for Müller but also for the Scots.

Müller appealed also to people in whom one would not assume the existence of any active intellectual interest. For instance, as a man in the Cab Office, Edinburgh, wrote to him: 'I am all the poorer today in that I missed hearing you when you were lecturing in Edinburgh, but I shall deem it a misfortune indeed if I am not present at your concluding lecture.' On a previous occasion, when travelling with his whole family from South Wales, he was greatly helped by the guard, and he offered him a tip. But the guard said: 'Oh, sir, would you send me instead one of your books? I have read some of them.'

This appeal was created by Max Müller in the first instance by the clarity of his style. He was an admirer of clear writing, and he tried to be as clear as possible himself. In 1861 he wrote to Renan: 'There is that charm about your views and opinions, that they are carved out of marble and not out of plaster . . . I cannot help thinking that there is nothing that cannot be made clear, and bright, and simple, and that obscurity arises in all cases from slovenly thinking and lazy writing.'

In advising Taine how to speak when he was invited to lecture at Oxford in 1871, he wrote:

> Oxford is an extremely difficult place to lecture in, because all audiences are very mixed . . . It is difficult to hit where there are so many targets . . . I should lecture as if I were addressing a highly educated lady, not taking much for granted, making everything clear by a full statement of facts, but then drawing out the very best lessons that the facts will yield.

This in a nutshell was a complete theory of employing language to communicate ideas, but not one expected from a philologist. There was general recognition of the skill which Müller displayed in presenting his ideas. For instance, in the obituary published the day after his death, *The Times* wrote:

> Some contemporaries questioned the accuracy of his verbal scholarship. No one could question his gifts as a man of letters . . . Renan and Darmesteter—to mention two Oriental scholars—writing in their own tongues, were perhaps greater masters of making Science speak gracefully; but in lucidity of arranging the most imposing matters, in power of generalization, in a certain large charity of spirit he had no superior.

This, however, lowered Müller in the eyes of specialists and academic scholars, among whom there is a deep suspicion of both popular fame and clarity of literary style. Bergson was called 'a philosopher of the drawing-rooms' on account of this by the German admirers of Rudolph Eucken.

But no writer can be effective, that is to say, proselytize others with his ideas by being only a stylist. In fact, he cannot even acquire style, for style is the man himself, and the man himself has to possess the charity of which *The Times* spoke, which is the same charity of which St Paul spoke. Not only great thoughts, but also the power to preach thoughts, come from the heart. It was by speaking from his heart that Max Müller touched the hearts of his hearers and readers. Mere scholarship would not have given him that power. He was very eloquent in expounding even dry linguistic ideas. That came from his faith in his ideas. He publicly stated his credo in the concluding words of his address at Strassburg, from which I shall quote the passage in which he himself cited Niebuhr:

Allow me in conclusion, to recall to your remembrance another passage from Niebuhr. He belongs to the good old race of German scholars. 'Above all things,' he writes, 'we must in all scientific pursuits preserve our truthfulness so pure that we thoroughly eschew every false appearance; that we represent not even the smallest thing as certain of which we are not completely convinced; that if we have to propose a conjecture, we spare no effort in representing the exact degree of its probability. If we do not ourselves, when it is possible, indicate our errors, even such as no one else is likely to discover; if, in laying down our pen, we cannot say in the sight of God, upon strict examination, I have knowingly written nothing that is not true; and if without deceiving either ourselves or others, we have not presented even our most odious opponents in such a light only that we could justify it upon our death-beds—if we cannot do this, study and literature serve only to make us unrighteous and sinful.'

'All of us,' Max Müller added, 'young as well as old, should keep these words before our eyes and in our hearts. Thus and thus only, will our studies not miss their highest goal: thus and thus only, may we hope to become true etymologists—i.e., true lovers, seekers, and, I trust, finders of truth.' Throughout his life, both in writing and in dealing with other scholars, he followed these principles.

Turning now to Max Müller's views and theories about language, it is not easy to give a brief summary of them, for they had a very wide range, covering everything concerning language from a methodology to study it to what might be called its metaphysics. Besides, he went on re-stating them in the light of the work of other philologists and their criticism of his own work, which was very vocal. However, as he never abandoned any position though he amplified or explained it in different words, it is not necessary to take a historical view of his linguistic work.

From the very first he maintained that the science of language was one of the physical (or natural) sciences. This was the theme of his first lecture in 1861, and in later life he became involved in some very unpleasant controversy over this. But in thinking of his own subject in this way he did not have in mind the distinction between philosophy and science which was a matter of discussion for many philosophical writers. This distinction hardly existed for him, for he passed quite naturally from a strictly scientific study of language to sweeping philosophical speculations about its nature and origin.

The distinction which he kept in view when he called linguistics one of the physical sciences was a different one, and in his view more basic. This was the distinction which, according to him, existed between the physical or natural sciences and the historical or moral sciences. The former, he said, dealt with the creations of God (by which he meant what we would call creations of Nature) and the latter with the creations of man, such as his tools, crafts, arts or literature. In support of this view he first of all pointed out that the science of language had developed in three stages, as all the physical sciences had. These were, first, the empirical stage concerned with the collection and examination of facts, then the classificatory stage in which the inter-relation of the facts was studied, and the third was the theoretical stage, which he also called the metaphysical, in which the student searched for the origin and meaning of all the facts which the classificatory stage had shown to belong to one or many systems. In the development of all the physical sciences these stages followed one another in a chronological order, except for rare departures from the sequence. The science of language, too, was developing in that order.

But, basically, his concept of the science of language was the product of a concept of the nature of language, and not merely derived from methodology. He could not regard language as a creation of man, and went even further in holding that man could not modify language by an exercise of conscious will. He put that view quite strongly:

> Although there is a continuous change in language, it is not in the power of man either to produce or to prevent it. We might think as well of changing the laws which control circulation of our blood, or of adding an inch to our height, as of altering the laws of speech, or inventing new words according to our pleasure. As man is the lord of nature only if he knows her laws and submits to them, the poet and the philosopher become the lords of language only if they know its laws and obey them.

Max Müller had to emphasize the powerlessness of the human will in respect of language in order to counteract the theological view derived from the Book of Genesis, which was still current in his time. Perhaps the idea has to be kept in mind today too, on account of the growing habit of using language very carelessly. All illiterate ages and men look upon grammar as a tyrannical imposition

on language, instead of regarding it as the anatomy and physiology
of language which can be discovered but not invented by man.

But of course Müller was perfectly aware that language was not
wholly a natural production, and that the conception of it as a
natural phenomenon had to be qualified by recognizing that it also
arose from the human mind, both in its conscious and unconscious
workings. The role of the human mind in shaping language he
defined in the second edition of his lectures on *The Science of
Language* published in 1862, in the following words:

> The process through which language is settled and unsettled, combines
> in one the two opposite elements of necessity and free-will. Though the
> individual seems to be the prime mover in producing new words and
> new grammatical forms, he is so only after his individuality has been
> merged in the common action of the family, tribe, or nation to which he
> belongs. He can do nothing by himself, and the first impulse to a new
> formation in language, *though given by an individual*, is mostly given
> without premeditation, nay, unconsciously. The individual as such is
> powerless, and the results apparently produced by him, depend on
> laws beyond his control, and on the co-operation of all those who form
> together with him one class, one body, or one organic whole. But
> though it is easy to show that language cannot be changed or moulded
> by the taste, the fancy, or genius of man, it is nevertheless through the
> instrumentality of man alone that language can be changed.

Language, he said by way of summing up the case he was making,
reflects the double nature of man, half animal and half a sentient
being: 'With one foot language stands, no doubt, in the realm of
nature, but with the other in the realm of the spirit.' This naturally
led him to raise the question which he himself put in these words:
'Every language has to be learnt, but who made the language that
was to be learnt?' But this question, he said, could not be answered
by simply recounting its history, for that history did not seem to
have any beginning.

> The history of language [he wrote] opens a vista which makes one feel
> almost giddy if one tries to see the end of it, but the measuring-rod of
> the chronologist seems to me entirely out of place. Those who have
> eyes to see will see the immeasurable distance between the first his-
> torical appearance of language and the real beginnings of human speech:
> those who cannot see will oscillate between the wildly large figures of
> the Buddhists or the wildly small figures of the Rabbis, but they will
> never lay hold of what by its very nature is indefinite.

Max Müller stated quite definitely that there was no means of solving the problem of language *historically*, that is to say, by describing what happened in a certain locality and at a certain time, because history did not begin till long after mankind had acquired language. Nothing, he declared, would be more interesting than to be able to say from historical records by what exact process man began to use words, and to be rid for ever of all the theories about the origin of language. But this knowledge was denied to historians and scientists. Indeed, the problem appeared so insoluble in his time that the *Société de Linguistique* of Paris, founded shortly before he delivered his first lectures and composed of the most distinguished scholars of France, laid down in its rules that it would not receive any communication on the question of the origin of languages.

However, there was a second-best. If nobody could trace the events through which any language was produced, perhaps it might not be impossible to infer the process through which languages might have been formed. This, it may be recalled, was what Darwin sought to do about the origin of species, because in his time the palaeontological evidence of the appearance of animals in a sequence of more and more complex forms was not exhaustive, and even if it were it would not have established evolution, but only the appearance of species at successive points of time, which might have been particular creations without being simultaneous. Darwin was therefore more concerned with the process by means of which evolution might have taken place, than with merely establishing evolution as the successive appearance of animals of different species on earth. Max Müller also applied himself to lay bare the linguistic processes, including both structural and functional changes.

What, however, he could not accept, even after considering linguistic processes exhaustively, was an extension of the Darwinian theory of evolution to the origin of language. Although he was ready to admit the evolution of man from pre-existing species in his bodily attributes, he could not do so in regard to language. This puzzled the Duke of Argyll, who wrote to him on February 2, 1872: 'In fact, I am quite unable to understand why you oppose Darwinism so much as applied to *language*—when your views as to *religion* seem to me essentially Darwinian.' Müller replied to this question on the 4th:

Where I differ from Darwin is when he does not see that nothing can become actual but what was potential; that mere environment explains nothing, because what surrounds and determines is as much given as what is surrounded and determined; that both presuppose each other and are meant for each other. Now I take my stand against Darwin on language, because language is the necessary condition of every other mental activity, religion not excluded, and I am able to prove that this indispensable condition of all mental growth is entirely absent in animals. This is my palpable argument.

There is, however, another argument, based on the nature of all known languages, viz., that they presuppose the faculty of numbering, an argument somewhat Pythagorean, but not therefore the less true.

Even if it could be proved that man was the lineal descendant of an ape, that would not upset my argument. The ape who could become the ancestor of man, would be a totally different being from the ape that remained for ever the ancestor of apes. That ape would be simply an embryonic man, and we have no ground to be very proud of our own embryonic phases.

He said that nobody could doubt that certain animals possess all the physical requirements of articulate speech. For instance, there was no letter of the alphabet which a parrot would not learn to pronounce. Therefore the fact that the parrot was without a language of its own had to be explained by a difference between the mental and not the physical faculties of animals and men. Next, the higher animals had a share of the mental faculties of man. Nobody, he said, could dispute that the higher animals had *sensation, perception, memory, will* and also *intellect* if it was restricted to the correlation of single perceptions. What then, he asked, was the fundamental difference between man and the brute world? He answered without hesitation: 'The one great barrier between the brute and man is *Language*. Man speaks, and no brute has ever uttered a word. Language is our Rubicon, and no brute will dare to cross it.'

He went on repeating this idea, and the impossibility of man's ever developing his faculty of speech from the animal stage by any process of natural selection similar to the mode of creation of species assumed by the Darwinian theory of evolution, and most emphatically he did so in his book *The Science of Thought*, published in 1887:

By no effort of understanding, by no stretch of imagination, can I explain to myself how language could have grown out of anything which animals possess, even if we granted them millions of years for that purpose. If anything has a right to the name of specific difference, it is language, as we find it in man, and in man only. Even if we removed the name of specific difference from our philosophic dictionaries, I should still hold that nothing deserves the name of man except what is able to speak.

Of course, Max Müller was thinking of evolution in terms of Darwin's natural selection, when the idea of mutation had not been advanced and anything like creative evolution as distinct from adaptive evolution had not been thought of.

Max Müller took the view that the results of the science of language did not tally with the results of evolutionism up to his time, and words could not be derived directly from the imitative and emotive sounds made by animals. A barrier had been raised between the two kinds of sounds by the very nature of the symbolic sounds to which the science of language had traced back the origins of true language, and which the philologists called roots. These roots, from which with certain exceptions all words were derived, were expressions of general concepts, and unless animals were capable of arriving at general concepts language could only have originated with man. On this point Müller argued as follows:

We do not know anything and cannot possibly know anything of the mind of animals: therefore, the proper attitude of the philosopher with regard to the mental capacities of animals is one of complete neutrality. For all we know, the mental capacities of animals may be of a higher order than our own, as their sensuous capacities certainly are in many cases. All this, however, is guesswork; one thing only is certain. If we are right that man realizes his conceptual thought by means of words, derived from roots, and that no animal possesses words derived from roots, it follows, not indeed that animals have no conceptual thought, but that their conceptual thought is different in its realized shape from our own.

Taking this position, Max Müller was bound to hold that the origin of language and the origin of thought were coeval and connected, though it was impossible to ascertain when they came into existence. What was fully established in his view was that the two were inseparable. He could conceive of a stage of human development when man had neither language nor thought, but he could not admit that one of these could exist without the other. In all his pronouncements and writings he repeated the idea. In the second course of lectures on *The Science of Language*, delivered in 1863, he said that 'to treat of sound as independent of meaning, of thought as independent of words, seems to defy one of the best principles of the science of language'.

In his very much later book (1887), in which he tried to understand thought and its processes for himself rather than for others, and to which he gave the title *Science of Thought*, he put the argument for taking language and thought as being inseparable much more strongly. 'It is possible,' he said, 'to distinguish in our knowledge four things: Sensations *(Empfindungen)*, Percepts *(Vorstellungen)*, Concepts *(Begriffe)* and names *(Namen)*. But though we can distinguish them, we must not imagine that these four ever exist as separate entities. No words are possible without concepts, no concepts without percepts, no percepts without sensations.' Since sensations preceded the other three, he was ready to admit as a matter of argument that they could exist independently of the others. But as a matter of fact, he said, thought was utterly impossible without the simultaneous working of sensation, percepts, concepts and names, and in reality the four were inseparable.

In a letter to the Duke of Argyll, written on April 14, 1888, he explained his position in a less formal manner:

It requires an effort to see the inseparableness of language and thought. It has taken me a whole life to perceive it. People imagine that I hold that language and thought are identical. There is no sense in that. No two things can be identical. But they can be inseparable—neither can exist without the other, that is what I mean. We imagine that we can think without words, because we can distinguish between the sound and the meaning. So we can between an orange and its skin, but in *rerum natura* there is no skin without an orange nor orange without a skin. You were one of the few men in England who I thought would see what I meant. But it requires an effort, and it is only an historical study of language in all its phases that has at last led me to the conviction that the Greeks were right, and that what really makes us men and distinguishes us from the animal, is the Logos, i.e., the gathering or, as Hobbes said, addition and subtraction.

Considering language in its next stage, that is, after it had come into existence, Max Müller held that language had *growth*, but not *history*. The second of his first series of lectures was devoted to explaining the growth of language in contradistinction to the history of language. 'We must distinguish,' he said, 'between historical change and natural growth. Art, science, philosophy, and religion all have a history; language, or any other production of nature, admits only of growth.' But the term 'growth', he explained, must be taken, if it is applied to language, in a sense which is wholly different from what it has when employed in connexion with the natural unfolding of organic beings. The idea of growth in respect of language was like the idea of growth of the crust of the earth, i.e., a process comparable to geological formations, by means of which continuous new combinations were formed out of given elements without the control of free agents. It was not surprising therefore that he should apply the term stratification to the process of linguistic evolution.

He illustrated this by giving the example of the relationship of Italian to Latin, and observed that:

> If we call Italian the daughter of Latin, we do not mean to ascribe to Italian a new vital principle. Not a single radical element was newly created for the formation of Italian. Italian is modern Latin, or Latin ancient Italian. The names *mother* and *daughter* only mark different periods in the growth of a language substantially the same. To speak of Latin dying in giving birth to her offspring is again pure mythology, and it would be easy to prove that Latin was a living language long after Italian had learnt to run alone.

Growth of language so defined comprised two processes which had to be carefully distinguished though they might be at work simultaneously. Max Müller called these processes: *Dialectal Regeneration* and *Phonetic Decay*.

By 'phonetic decay' he understood a very special aspect of the continuous phonetic changes in any language by means of which it passed from the 'isolatory' stage to the 'inflectionary' stage—that is to say, from the stage in which the relations of words or the various extensions and modifications of their denotations were expressed by employing two or more words with independent meaning, to the stage in which the modifying independent words lost their independence and became vestigial sounds like inflections and constituted in their totality the whole range of the accidence of a language. In simple words, Max Müller said, it was phonetic decay which created truly grammatical forms.

He illustrated the process by taking the word 'twenty'—20. In Greek, Latin, Sanskrit, English and French the word for this number was originally composed of two elements—*ten* and *two*: so that in its formation the word stands for 'two tens', but through phonetic decay the two words together have come to stand for one concept. In Chinese, however, twenty had remained two tens = *eul-shi* without any phonetic decay. It was Chinese and the monosyllabic languages related to it which, Max Müller observed, had remained immune to the disease of phonetic decay.

On the other hand, by 'dialectal regeneration' he understood not only the creation of a new language through the break-up of the sounds of a language which had ceased to grow by becoming written and literary, but also the entire existence of spoken words as a language unembodied in literature and writing. It was only as dialects that language had growth, which always stopped when they were written down in a standard form. What people were accustomed to call languages, such as the literary idioms of Greece, Rome, ancient India or modern Europe must be considered, he said, as artificial, and the real and natural life of languages was to be found only in the dialects.

According to him it was a mistake to imagine that dialects everywhere were corruptions of the literary language. Even in England, he observed, the local dialects had many forms which were more primitive than the language of Shakespeare, and the richness of their vocabulary surpassed on many points that of the classical writers of English of any period. Dialects had always been the feeders rather than the channels of a literary language. They were parallel streams which existed long before one of them was raised to that temporary eminence which was the result of literary cultivation.

Whatever the origin of language among men its first tendency, he said, must have been towards an unbounded variety. To this there was a natural check in a parallel development towards forming a national and literary language. Before there can be a national language there must be hundreds of dialects in districts, towns, villages, clans and families, and though the progress of civilization and centralization tended to reduce their number and to soften their features, it had not yet annihilated them.

Max Müller described this process of continuous break-up and reformation of language in a passage of extraordinary vividness in his first series of lectures. I shall give it almost wholly in his words. Literary dialects pay for their temporary greatness by inevitable decay and they are haunted by their own ghost. They are like stagnant lakes at the side of great rivers. They form reservoirs of what was once living and running speech, but they are no longer carried on by the main current. At times it may seem as if the whole stream of language was absorbed by these lakes, and we can hardly trace the small rivulets which run on in the main bed.

Or, he said, it may be more accurate to compare a classical or literary idiom with the frozen surface of a river, brilliant and smooth, but stiff and cold. It is mostly by political commotions that this surface of more polite and cultivated speech is broken and carried away by the waters rising from underneath. It is during times when the higher classes are either crushed in religious or social struggles, or mix again with the lower classes to repel foreign invasion; when literary occupations are discouraged, palaces burnt, monasteries pillaged and seats of learning destroyed; it is then that the popular dialects, which had formed a kind of undercurrent, rise beneath the crystal surface of the literary language and sweep away, like the waters in spring, the cumbrous formations of a bygone age.

In more peaceful times, a new and popular literature springs up in a language which seems to have been formed by conquest and revolutions, but which in reality had been growing up long before, and was only brought out, ready-made, by historical events. From this point of view, we can see that no literary language can ever be said to have been the mother of another language. As soon as a language loses its undoubted capacity for change, its carelessness about what it throws away, and its readiness in always supplying the wants of mind and heart instantaneously, its natural life is changed into a merely artificial existence. It may still live on for a long time, but while it seems to be the leading shoot, it is in reality but a broken and withering branch, slowly falling from the stock from which it sprang.

These are a few of Max Müller's ideas about language which I have selected for their general interest out of an immense number which were always coming out of his active and fertile mind. It will however be noticed that all of these ideas relate to that stage of the science of language which he called the theoretical. That was the field in which lay his deepest and most active interest. But these conclusions, philosophical rather than strictly linguistic as they were, had their basis on a very solid knowledge of linguistic facts in the other two stages of the science, namely, the empirical and the classificatory. His mastery of these facts was certainly greater than that which Spengler had of historical facts in presenting his philosophy of history, and would seem to be more complete than the knowledge of the past of different human groups which Toynbee had when he wrote his *Study of History*. The dislike which contemporary specialists feel for sweeping generalizations is only a narrow intellectual pose, or rather a fashion. It is not intellectually justifiable. Generalization and detailed study of facts are only two sides of the same process of knowing. They may alternate cyclically, or they may be taken up by persons of different but complementary temperaments at the same time, or even by the same person to satisfy two sides of his yearning for knowledge. No one could say that Eddington, Jeans, or in these times Hoyle or Heisenberg, as mathematicians or physicists, had no right to their cosmological speculations.

In regard to the empirical stage of the science of language, Max Müller was one of the great authorities of his age. He was a pioneer in Sankritic studies both as an explorer and as an exploiter. And since it was the discovery and knowledge of Sanskrit which had created the science of Comparative Philology, the empirical foundations of his theories cannot be said to have been inadequate. Max Müller himself knew this very well, and wrote:

> Sanskrit certainly forms the only foundation of Comparative Philology, and it will always remain the only safe guide through all its intricacies. A comparative philologist without a knowledge of Sanskrit is like an astronomer without a knowledge of mathematics. He may admire, he may observe, he may discover, but he will never feel satisfied, he will never feel certain, he will never feel quite at home.

Perhaps there was a certain amount of exaggeration in this statement, but that was not unnatural in an age (1868) when Sanskrit was still the main element in the growing science of linguistics.

In the classificatory stage of the science Max Müller's writings not only established the concept of an Indo-European family of languages more firmly, but they also popularized it in a manner nobody else rivalled. But his own special contribution in the field of classification or taxonomy of language was not purely philological: it extended to the social and cultural spheres. He spread the idea of a common Aryan family and culture, from which a number of related societies and cultures had evolved. It had important social, cultural and even political consequences in many countries. So its character and validity will have to be examined later.

What remains to be done here is only to place Max Müller's linguistic work in its proper perspective in the history of the science of linguistics. Long before his death, in fact even from the middle of the seventies, his ideas on language began to be challenged, and many later workers in the field thought that they were being superseded. But hardly any pioneer worker in any science would expect or even wish it to be otherwise, although he might have made a fundamental contribution to its creation. But such a statement about Max Müller's work would apply only to the more technical part of his contribution. His speculations covered the origin and nature of language, about which the present age, in spite of all the research which has followed, is no more certain than was Max Müller's age. In the very nature of things there can be no finality on such questions.

In any case, Max Müller was perfectly aware of his position, and if he was being left behind he showed himself to be perfectly reconciled to the possibility. He knew very well that it was the inevitable fate of all investigators. He noted this in the case of Professor H. H. Wilson, who was really the first genuine English Sanskritist on the strength of his own knowledge of the language. Of him Müller said that he had done nothing but original work, but was abused for not always having found at the first trial what others discovered when standing on his shoulders. In his posthumous autobiography he said the same thing about himself in connexion with an essay of his on the Turanian languages. 'It was published', he wrote, 'in 1854, but it still continues to be criticized as if it had been published last year.' Then he commented wisely, though also sadly: 'No astronomer is blamed for not having known the planet Neptune before its discovery in 1846, or having been wrong in accounting for the irregularities of Saturn. But let that pass. I only share the fate of others who have lived too long.'

But there was more to it. By living as long as he did, Max Müller passed from one age of learning to another, not only in respect of his own subject but of all subjects: that is to say, from the age of exploration to that of intensive cultivation. By the end of the nineteenth century the age of specialization was already in full stride.

But to say that for this reason all that had preceded was obsolete, is like saying that it is only reaping that matters, and not sowing. Max Müller began his linguistic work in the full age of wonder of his science, and he was perfectly aware of the function of wonder in the progress of human knowledge. 'Wonder,' he observed in his Rede Lecture delivered before the University of Cambridge in 1868, 'no doubt rises from ignorance, but from a peculiar kind of ignorance; from what might be called a fertile ignorance; an ignorance which, if we look back at the history of most of our sciences, will be found to have been the mother of all human knowledge.'

But what he noted with surprise was that the wonder that was incentive to knowledge was not present in respect of all subjects in any particular age. For ages, he said, men had looked at the earth with its stratifications and at the embedded petrifications of organic creatures, and yet they looked and passed on, thinking no more of it, and without wondering. Not even an Aristotle had eyes to see, so that the conception of a science of earth was reserved for the eighteenth century.

In the same way, he added, men regarded language without wonder. Centuries had elapsed since the first names were given to all cattle, to the fowls of the air, and to all beasts—here, too, the clearly marked lines of different strata seemed almost to challenge attention, but still the conception of a science of language was reserved for the nineteenth century.

In all his work on language Max Müller continued the age of wonder of linguistics both for himself and his readers and hearers. He made a wide circle of men and women aware of the romance of language, as he was himself attracted by the romance. He could say:

> Bliss was it in that dawn to be alive,
> But to be young was very heaven!

Chapter 4

OXFORD—DARK AND BRIGHT

By the time Max Müller, as Taylorian Professor, had become an associate member, so to speak, of the academic club of Oxford—the date being February 1854—the university had ceased to be the happy convent it was even in 1848. The *Pax Oxoniana* was shattered at one stroke by the appointment of the Royal Commission of 1850. As Mark Pattison said, if a man had fallen asleep in 1846 and woken up again in 1850 he would have found himself in a different world. It was torn into two factions, the opponents and the supporters of reform. The old guard was in power, and feeling ran so high against the renegades that one of them asked a junior professor to invite him to dinner because the heads of colleges would no longer admit him to their table. Actually, the Commission made a difference to the social habits of Oxford. Before its appointment there were hardly any private dinners besides those in the halls. But the Commission broke up the academic society into sets, and private dinners had to keep up the social life of those who were excluded from the high table on account of their support for reform.

The university as an official body refused to co-operate with the Commission. It questioned not only the kind of reform that was proposed, but also the power of Parliament to legislate for Oxford. 'The Government did not know Oxford, nor Oxford the Government,' was the accepted formula, and men who were thoroughgoing Erastians in always submitting to the supremacy of the State over the Anglican Church, now opposed the intervention of the State in the affairs of an organ of the same Church—the University of Oxford. As Max Müller found, even those who thought reform necessary were afraid of calling in the government. Some of them told him that if they once let in the government, it would interfere too much.

The case of the opponents of reform, a majority of whom certainly put the vested interests of a closed corporation before education, was stated at its most idealistic and disinterested by Dr Pusey. He was never in doubt about the basic issue, which in his eyes was clear: should Oxford continue to be a religious body in obedience to the intentions of the founders, or was it to become merely a secular educational institution? He had only one answer to the question. He did not object to improvements, but declared firmly: 'Only let it be really solid, and, above all, under the control of a firm, unwavering faith, to the glory of God. It will yet be well with Oxford if she forget not her own motto—*Dominus illuminatio mea.*' None the less, the Commission reported, and the reform bill was passed. What shocked the anti-reform men most was that Gladstone, the member for Oxford and at first an opponent of State interference, became a convert himself and carried through the reforming measures in Parliament. For this he was to lose his seat later. But reform was set in motion, and Dr Pusey, who was to fight the rearguard action against it to the last, could only lament: *Fuit Ilium, fuit Ilium!*—We were Trojans once, but Troy is gone!

Of course, old Oxford did not die at once. For at least two decades it kicked very hard, and even after that a core of anti-reform opinion remained there, just as Jacobitism survived into the Hanoverian age. The most characteristic expression of the conservative attitude is to be found in seven volumes of reproductions of Oxford caricatures preserved in the Bodleian. Satire is always conservative, as the whole tradition from Aristophanes to *Punch* proves. So were these caricatures, and even more so their captions, in many instances in faultless Greek or Latin, which showed that reform had served even the satirists by raising the level of classical education at Oxford.

As was to be expected, all the champions of reform came in for their share of ridicule or censure, and most of all Jowett, who was not only a very active reformer, but was also suspected of having a good deal of *arrière-pensée* in his reforming zeal.

Academic reform at Oxford in the second half of the nineteenth century, like parliamentary reform, was carried out in three stages: before and after 1854 by a commission of inquiry, an Act of Parliament and an executive commission. There was in 1872 another commission of inquiry, and an Act of 1877. This was followed by an executive commission from 1877 to 1881. As a result, there was substantial improvement in details of organization as well as teaching. But there was no revolutionary change in the university's formal structure and functioning. For instance, the very basic issues which the reformers had raised, such as the relation between the university and the colleges, the imbalance between professorial and tutorial teaching, of the extension of research, were dealt with superficially and remained open even till after the First World War, when they had to be examined again.

Nevertheless, a great change certainly came over the spirit in which Oxford carried on its work. This was due far less to the specific measures of reform than to the *Zeitgeist*, illustrating the invariable principle that it is the society which shapes the educational system, and not the system the society.

Once anybody wanted to see it, the basic transformation was all too obvious. As an institution, from having been an educational monastery run by a clerical oligarchy deriving its authority from an overwhelmingly clerical franchise of Masters of Art, the university became for all practical purposes a secular body. In function, it ceased to be primarily a clerical seminary, and though it did not lose its novices, it became the educational centre of a modern bureaucratic State and a worldwide Imperial polity. In putting their classical disciplines to this extended use, the dons of Oxford took a great deal of pride as the teachers of senators, consuls and proconsuls. But in reality it was the British Imperial State which made the university serve it, in the same way as the schools of rhetoric and law in Rome and the schools of philosophy in Athens served the Roman Empire.

Naturally schooling, widened and immensely improved, remained the main function of Oxford, and the dominance of the colleges and the tutorial system continued. Among the students the crammers more or less balanced the idlers. Despite all that, the outstanding feature of the reformed Oxford was not that it became a better university, but that it was converted into a very advanced public school. For its students Greek and Latin meant what they did at Eton, Harrow or Rugby, and by an unwritten convention sport and games became a part of the academic curriculum. As a result, they lost their free and personal character, and became organized, obligatory, strenuous and honoured disciplines. Those who regarded boat-racing as being as much a part of Oxford education as were the Greats, did not always recollect, even if they were dons instead of undergraduates, how recent this was. Muscular Christianity preached by some Oxford men never became a force in English life, but muscular university education did.

With this transformation Oxford ceased to be the home of dreams and lost causes, and offered a complete contrast to its past by becoming a participant in British success and by affiliating itself to the imperial greatness of Britain. Gladstone, who set the reforming movement going, did not seem to be wholly satisfied with what he had sponsored; and on his deathbed he could only recall the Oxford dedicated to the glory of God which he had known in his student days. Thus to a message sent to him by the Hebdomadal Council in 1898 he replied: 'There is no expression of Christian sympathy that I value more than that of the ancient university of Oxford, the God-fearing and God-sustaining university of Oxford. I served her, perhaps mistakenly, but to the best of my ability.' But that Oxford of his was as dead as that of Newman. By the end of the century Oxford had transferred its allegiance from God to Caesar.

The imperialistic re-orientation of Oxford quite naturally brought into existence a worship and awareness of Oxford education such as had not existed before. The men who passed out from unreformed Oxford took their association with it for granted, as they did their parentage and their ancestral homes. But the products of reformed Oxford began to look upon themselves as members of a *corps d'élite*, and acquired a feeling for it which was similar to conscious family pride. In the normal English Oxonian, this pride remained unassertive and reticent, though at times very studiedly so and therefore not quite convincing in its modesty. But among those Englishmen who went out from Oxford to the colonies and dependencies, and among the White colonials and the Orientals who came to Oxford, the cult of Oxford became meretricious, and even dubious.

The worship of Oxford as exported was of a piece with the English imperialistic sentiment of the late nineteenth century, which was self-conscious, intellectually shoddy, and wholly unworthy of the historic phenomenon that the British Empire in its practical existence really was. Thus it was natural that Cecil Rhodes, the most counterfeit of English imperialists, who thought that spectacular financial success in a colony (and of all places on the Rand), gave him a right to patronize the British Empire, should become a benefactor of Oxford. And the callowness of the imperialism of Oxford was shown by its grateful acceptance of his bounty. Even Oriel accepted it, and allowed Rhodes Gaudens to look down on the university church of St Mary the Virgin from his niche in the pediment opposite.

But the most baneful impact of imperialistic Oxford was seen on the Indians who came there. The English civil servants and educationalists in India were mostly from one or other of the two ancient universities, and they buttressed their prestige there by fostering an abject worship of Oxford and Cambridge among Indians. So the more ambitious and wealthy among them came over for their higher education, which was really a pursuit of career and prestige, and even with a third-class degree they could ensure both. If they were clever enough they could make an *aegrotat* degree do as well. But they also showed what a *femme fatale* Oxford or Cambridge could be for them.

Max Müller at Oxford saw many of them, and in spite of being a champion of India and Indians he has not left a favourable account of them. As he put it:

The manners of young Indians when they arrive at Oxford are generally excellent, but they soon acquire what they consider English manners, rough and ready, bluff and blunt, and by no means an improvement on their own. The same young man who at first enters your room with folded hands and a graceful salaam, will after a very short time walk in, sit down, stretch out his legs, and address you in the most familiar terms. They imagine this is English.

He continued:

Even if they pass their examinations, I am afraid that some of them return to India not much improved by their English exile. The worst of it is that they often return *désillusionné*. At first everything English is grand and perfect in their eyes, an Oxford degree is the highest goal of their ambition. But when they have obtained it, chiefly by learning by heart, they make very light of it. And this making light of it is soon applied to other things English also, which they hear constantly criticized or abused, particularly in the newspapers and parliament, so that they often leave England better informed, it may be, but hardly better affected towards the Government which they are meant to serve.

Max Müller had some understanding of what rankled in the minds of these Indian students. It was the absence of personal relations with their English fellow-students.

At Oxford [he wrote] they find it very hard to make friends among the better class of undergraduates. Most of our undergraduates come from public schools, and have plenty of friends of their own. If they are asked to be kind to any of the Indian students, all they can do, or really be expected to do, is to invite them once or twice to a breakfast party. They have hardly any interests in common with them, and anything like friendship is out of the question.

He continued sadly: 'The present state of things is certainly discouraging, particularly as it seems impossible to suggest any real remedy.' The Indians themselves made it worse by setting down this natural canalization of social intercourse to racial and political pride and treating it as conscious apartheid. Moreover, they themselves had a sense of guilt. They felt keenly that they had come to promote their own worldly interests by serving a foreign government, and therefore the more thoroughgoing their interested association, the more rancorous was their vicarious disaffection.

Yet the same men, when they went back to India and enjoyed their prosperity and prestige, showed an arrogance to their own countrymen which was not less than that of the English rulers. This internal dichotomy almost predetermined that Indians from Oxford and Cambridge should be sterile adventurers incapable of exercising any influence on the life and culture of their own people. In fact, some of the most brilliant Indian students of Oxford turned out to be the worst careerists in their country. Even Nehru failed to impinge on Indian life and behaviour with his ideas.

Max Müller also had a concept of a possible Imperial role for Oxford and Cambridge, but in its combination of vision with realism it was in complete contrast to the pretentious and artificial idea which lay behind the Rhodes Scholarships. He did not believe that the peculiarly English traits and outlooks could be imposed on aliens simply by giving them an opportunity to pass through the two universities. In fact, in a letter written to the Duke of Argyll when he became Secretary of State for India in 1868, Müller said:

India can never be anglicized, but it can be reinvigorated. By encouraging a study of their own ancient literature, as part of their education, a national feeling of pride and self-respect will be reawakened among those who influence large masses of the people. A new national literature may spring up, impregnated with Western ideas, yet retaining its native spirit and character . . . A new national literature will bring with it a new national and a new moral vigour.

Historically, this was exactly what happened in the second half of the nineteenth century in Bengal, but it did not come about by bringing Indians to Oxford and Cambridge. Max Müller's prescription was to give the desired education in India by training Englishmen at Oxford to play their educational role there effectively. He saw the fulfilment of British rule in India in this educational mission, which was really a task of cultural proselytization. He had put forward the idea as early as 1856, in a letter written to Bunsen in which he said: 'After the last annexation the territorial conquest of India ceases—what follows next is the struggle in the realm of religion and of the spirit, in which, of course, centres the interests of the nations.' He repeated the idea in different words to the Duke of Argyll: 'India has been conquered once, but India must be conquered again, and that second conquest should be a conquest by education.'

He added in the same letter that as a result of Western education a class of young Indians had already risen in Bengal, who were known as Young Bengal and who were ready to play their part in this movement of cultural proselytization, because they were the 'product of English ideas grafted on the native mind'. He informed the Duke that Englishmen in India were always finding fault with this Young Bengal, but set down his view that in spite of their faults they had promise, observing shrewdly that 'their faults were apparent everywhere, but their good qualities were naturally hidden from the eyes of careless observers'. Then he gave the example of a young Bengali who had just published a book on his travels in Europe, in which he said that 'if it was the will of Providence that a nation would have a yoke on its neck the yoke of the English was the least galling'. Max Müller also quoted to the Duke the words in which this young man summed up the achievement of the English people in India, and at the same time put his finger on the weak spot of the British attitude towards Indians:

Nothing less than British phlegm, and imperturbability, and constancy, and untiring energy could have steadily prosecuted the task of consolidating the disjointed masses of India, and casting her into the mould of one compact nation. They want but 'high thoughts seated in a heart of courtesy' to attach us to their rule, with a feeling of loyalty that, not merely playing round the head, should come near to the heart.

On this Müller commented: 'A society leavened by such men will make it possible for the Government to save hundreds and thou-

sands in soldiers and policemen, and millions in wars and suppression of rebellions.'

Müller had also thought out how the emergence of such a class
of Indians could be promoted. It was that young Englishmen
should have the kind of education in English universities which
would make them capable of playing their cultural role by giving
them on the one hand intellectual competence and knowledge and,
on the other, sympathy and understanding for the Indian people.
The very first step which had to be taken to realize this purpose was
to create a school of Indian languages in the universities. His long
campaign to establish such an institution and to introduce the study
of Oriental languages in England, has been described in the previous
chapter.

But Max Müller's concept of a cultural mission in India was
never taken seriously in England, either in its doctrinal or in its
practical aspect. On the contrary, young Englishmen went to serve
in India in ignorance of the country and with contempt for the
people. The only corrective to that situation, which was provided
more by the circumstances than by any conscious perception of the
problem, was to bring young Indians over to Oxford or Cambridge,
give them an English veneer, and sterilize them. It was an application of the idea which afterwards Rhodes consecrated with his
money. This was a negation of true imperialism, and it is no wonder
that the country named after Rhodes and the country where he
achieved his spectacular success have both become the most unequi-
vocal symbols of the failure of British imperialism.

However, one must not judge the imperial aspect of reformed
Oxford by its expression among the colonial British and the Indians
educated at Oxford and Cambridge. It had a higher and more imposing aspect, as shown by men such as Curzon and Milner who
were more authentic Oxford men than Rhodes. Long before either
of them Max Müller had found himself wishing that the lure of the
Indian Civil Service had not brought Indians to Oxford, and that
they had remained in their own country to serve it as scholars and
thinkers.

In spite of all this an Oxford Magna did emerge out of the reforms, between which and the larger political and imperial existence
of the English people there was a very close nexus. Oxford, too,
became proudly conscious of the relationship. In the earlier stages
of reform the most majestic political personality moulded by

Oxford, Gladstone, was hounded out, but with the completion of reform the university took pride in noting the fact that in the last year of the nineteenth century there were ten Oxford men in a Cabinet presided over by its Chancellor.

Along with this however the old Oxford Parva was not only allowed to survive, but was even infused with a new vitality. Its scholarship, speculations and art of living were made more active and fervid. All activities of the mind were recreations pursued and valued more for the sense of self-realization than for the contribution they made to knowledge or thought. Nowhere was the Latin saying *Abeunt studia in mores* (study fulfils itself in a manner of living) better illustrated than in this little Oxford, Oxford *Parva sed Apta*. There settled on its grey stones some light from far away Fiesole and Sienna. The men who represented this Oxford were figures like T. H. Greene, F. H. Bradley, Walter Pater, to mention only a typical few.

The scholarly and speculative creations of this Oxford enlivened, enriched, and sustained mental life in the outside world, even including India. But in its own existence they were only *parerga academica*, incidental music at a banquet. The value of the education which Oxford gave was frankly recognized by all; but anyone who knew anything about scholarship, learning, science and speculative thought, also knew that love of knowledge for its own sake was the last thing fostered by new Oxford among its students. On this point foreigners, natives and domiciled foreigners were all agreed. Renan observed that a minor German university with its poor and uncouth professors did more for the human spirit than the aristocratic university of Oxford with its princely revenues, its magnificent buildings, its opulent style of living and its idle fellows.

Pattison, whose one positive passion in life was the pursuit of learning and who as reformer had before his eyes the vision of Oxford as a home of higher research and advanced learning, became a confirmed misanthrope when reform was at last fully under way. He did not deny that Oxford efficiently performed its function as a great national *lycée*. But this was precisely the Oxford he disliked and disapproved of. To him this function showed a preference for the 'lower states of education of which all men do or can partake', as against the superior education which a university professes to administer. In his exasperated moments he called this Oxford a cramming shop.

Max Müller, who was associated with the reformers from the beginning but would not take any active part in the movement because he was a foreigner, very soon became disappointed with the outcome of the reforms. Even in 1855 he wrote: 'Oxford is in a sad condition; the reform has done nothing, and we are worse off than before . . . Gladstone's Bill has introduced a complicated and impractical system, which suffocates all proposals for the better . . . What remains therefore is nothing but the coffee-grounds which nobody desires to have—clergymen without a parish and scholars without scholarship!'

Thirteen years later, on October 27, 1868, he spoke no less emphatically in his inaugural lecture delivered as the new Professor of Comparative Philology:

Noblesse oblige [he declared] applies to Oxford at the present moment more than ever, when knowledge for its own sake and a chivalrous devotion to studies which command no price in the fair of the world, and lead to no place of emolument in Church or State, are looked down upon and ridiculed by almost everybody.

There is no career in England at the present time for scholars and students. No father could honestly advise his son, whatever talent he might display, to devote himself exclusively to classical, historical, or physical studies. The few men who still keep up the fair name of England by independent research and new discoveries in the fields of political and natural history, do not always come from our universities; and unless they possess independent means, they cannot devote more than their leisure hours, left by their official duties in Church or State, to the prosecution of their favourite studies.

This, he declared, neither ought to be nor need be, for if only twenty men at Oxford and Cambridge had the will everything was ready for reform and the restoration of the ancient glory of Oxford.

In 1878, a writer giving a portrait of Max Müller in *Contemporary Portraits*, New Series, No. 10, quoted the passage from his inaugural lecture and explained why it was so, as he saw it. 'The reason,' he said, 'that meets these pertinent queries is the shameful one that Oxford is of the world and that in the world's ways the ideally best must hide its shamefaced beauty before the power of position, the scorn of vested interests, the laziness of the luxurious, the intrigues of self-seekers, the worshippers of material *prestige.*'

Strong as this was, it was also the view of the life and aspirations

of the Oxford dons held by the town, which had very little respect
for the gown. As it happened, the university and the colleges were
themselves responsible for creating such notions. They had refused
to disclose the facts about their revenues to the Commission of 1850,
and, as a result, speculation was rife about their hidden and hoarded
wealth. It was the Cleveland Commission of 1872, which, in its
report published in 1874, for the first time fully revealed the extent
of the wealth and properties of the university and the colleges, and
showed that they were neither as wealthy as many had supposed,
nor careless as landowners. But great landowners they still were, the
university being the junior partner and the colleges collectively the
senior. The income of the two was classified under six heads:
(1) Lands; (2) house property; (3) tithe rent charges; (4) other rent
charges, such as free farm rents and fixed charges; (5) stocks,
shares, and other securities; (6) receipts from fines, tuition, minerals,
etc. Overwhelmingly, the money came from landed property, of
which the university had 7,684 acres, and the colleges jointly
184,764 acres. The total income of the university was £47,000, of
which £29,000 came from property. The total income of the
colleges was £363,000, of which £280,000 came from the same
source.

The authorities of the university and the colleges showed themselves as very competent managers, and never buried their material
talents. Mark Pattison, with all his love of learning and absorption
in mental life, was not less attentive to the properties of Lincoln.
Jowett, for all his cherubic looks, was an astute business man both
as master and as Vice-Chancellor. Max Müller has left a most illu-
minating account of the business flair of an Oxford don and clergyman, Dr Bull, Canon and Bursar of Christ Church.

A well-known banker had for years been handling the money of
Christ Church, and no one suspected him. One day, however,
Dr Bull invited him to dinner, and he was struck by the very pious
and orthodox remarks the banker made, which he thought suited a
Canon of Christ Church more than a wealthy and worldly banker
from London. Without saying a word Dr Bull went to London the
next day, drew out all the money of the college, and the day after,
to the dismay of all London, the bank failed. All the other depositors
lost their money, but not Christ Church.

But in the pre-reform days, that is, in the days of the Don Logs,
the scramble was not indecorous, for the distribution of patronage

and preferment was controlled by a fixed procedure and confined
to an oligarchy without reference to merit. But the reforms which
dragged merit into the question of preferment, at once promoted
the scramble by bringing into existence a class of pushing Don
Storks and giving respectability to their monetary ambitions. The
first appearances of the factionalism were seen in the rejection of
Pattison's claim to the Rectorship of Lincoln in 1851 and of Jowett's
to the Mastership of Balliol in 1854. Max Müller was also to suffer
from it, as will be related later. For a decade or so the tactics for denying money to a person not acceptable to the dominating caucus was
to fasten the *odium theologicum* on him. But as time passed the religious or dogmatic narrowness declined, and the scramble became
a tussle for money pure and simple.

Two men, above everybody else, stood out among the leading
personalities of the reforming Oxford in the latter half of the nineteenth century, and they represented both its bright and dark sides.
They were, of course, Jowett and Pattison. No one living at Oxford
in those days could be unaware of their overwhelming presence.
Jowett provided its *son et lumière*, and Pattison its thunder and
lightning. Moreover no one, judging them contemporaneously or in
historical retrospect, could deny that they had their unquestionable,
though particular, greatness and genius. But no one could also fail
to be conscious that both had traits of character which repelled or
alienated. No theologian to my knowledge has described what the
fallen angels were like when they had rebelled and been thrown out
of heaven. Jowett and Pattison could give a very good idea of them,
the first as Belial and the second as Moloch. Both showed themselves at Oxford as seraphim who had qualified for hell.

It is curious that of the two Pattison should, in the final summing-
up, turn out to be the better scholar. Jowett was the best boy at
St Paul's, won the Balliol scholarship, was elected fellow as an
undergraduate and took a first. Pattison, on the contrary, never
went to school and was taught by his father at home, got a second
class at Oxford, and after failing to be elected fellow at Oriel,
University and Balliol, got a Lincoln fellowship as a sort of consolation prize. Yet he could despise Jowett's scholarship. But Mark
Pattison's poor opinion of Jowett's scholarship was both unfair
and irrelevant. Scholarship is a matter of temperament. Pattison had
that, while Jowett did not. Jowett was essentially and above all a
pedagogue and a moralist. What Jowett sought to do was to pour

on to the three main interests of nineteenth-century Englishmen, politics, money and religion, the spikenard of a refurbished Hellenism, which might be called Victorian neo-Platonism, but which was of course very much more superficial. Jowett was called 'Master' by men and women of fashion, and the Master he remained.

Pattison could see with perfect clearness where he and Jowett differed as to the end of university education. 'The separation between Jowett and myself', he wrote, 'consists in a difference upon the fundamental question of university politics—viz., Science and Learning *v.* School keeping.'

Pattison's defects of character were obvious, and therefore clever novelists could satirize him easily. Swinburne broke out with the epigram that Pattison was a 'morally and spiritually typical and unmistakable ape of the Dead Sea'. Jowett's failings, on the other hand, were extremely insidious, and could hardly be perceived by outsiders unless they were almost cynically percipient. Also, he had the intelligence and moderation to utilize them for advancing his career rather than letting them damage it. He was a flatterer of the aristocracy and of people of fashion.

There could be no doubt whatever but that Pattison was the greater man. He achieved at its highest level the personality of a man endowed with great intellectual power and with a demoniac passional potential, but without the faculty of positive and disinterested love which is the Christian *caritas*. In its default, he was bound to arrive at the state of mind which proclaimed itself in an invincible repugnance for all action. He feared moral and religious enthusiasm, for he knew not where it might lead. He distrusted religion, and set down in his memoirs that 'religion is a good servant, but a bad master'.

In nothing else was the desiccation of Mark Pattison shown more characteristically than in his intense desire for love and his failure to get it, with one exception. He wanted love, but never realized that love cannot be had without loving, without shedding all egoism. Pattison in everything was an uninhibited egoist, and even his affection for Meta Bradley was a projection of his self-love flattered by the adoration of a weak woman. His wife described her horror of his last days in the following words: 'Let not my last days be like his! The moral ruin is awful.'

Jowett was the opposite. He inspired affection and could also show affection. But the interchange was superficial, for he distrusted passion and always employed that word in a bad sense. Therefore, over his puritanism, which was both fierce and narrow, he succeeded in laying a coat of unctuousness, which made worldlings look up to him for moral inspiration and guidance. But there was also no doubt that his moral sense was fundamentally right. His intellectual capacity and moral sensitiveness were such that one could not easily perceive that he was an adventurer. Very few adventurers in the world have taken an adventurer's life to a higher level, morally and intellectually.

There is one test which is dependable in judging the personality of any Oxford man in the latter half of the nineteenth century, and that is his attitude to John Henry Newman, the disinherited among the great sons of Oxford. Jowett and Pattison agreed in substance over him, but in a wholly different spirit. After reading the life of Newman, in 1891 Jowett wrote to Margot Tennant (later Asquith):

> Considering what he really was, it is wonderful what a space he has filled in the eyes of mankind. In speculation he was habitually untruthful and not much better in practice. His conscience had been taken out, and the Church put in its place. Yet he was a man of genius, and a good man in the sense of being disinterested. Truth is very often troublesome, but neither the world nor the individual can get on without it.

Mark Pattison also believed, like Jowett, that Newman did not care for truth apart from dogma, but he showed no personal disrespect for him. He had called Newman 'Master', and to the end he called him that. When Pattison was dying, Newman wrote to him expressing a wish to see him. He at once agreed, though his antireligious cynicism attributed a motive to the visit. After it was over Pattison wrote: 'It was not all personal regard, but the hope, however slight, that I might still be got over in my last moments.' Though cynical, the comment was not disrespectful to Newman personally. Newman did have that hope, but it could not be dishonourable in a man of faith to hope to bring back to the fold a follower who had strayed from it.

The truth of the matter is that in the unfolding of their careers both the men remained true to their origins, commercial and clerical. Jowett remained throughout the successful businessman, and Pattison the unsuccessful cleric.

8

Between them they represented the new Oxford in its personal ambitions and in its consciously adopted educational role, though one gloated on success and the other almost exulted in failure. There were, however, two others who kept up the spirit of old Oxford through the changing times, here again with contrasted results for themselves. These men were Dr Pusey and Dean Liddell. Pusey died fighting to the last for an Oxford in the service of religion. Liddell adapted himself to the reformed Oxford very successfully, and even helped further reforms, but in spirit he remained true to old times.

A very mistaken idea of Dr Pusey as an intolerant bigot was current among his latter-day contemporaries, and still survives. Actually, in spite of his failure and indeed owing to that very defeat —for at Oxford only defeat could canonize a man to greatness—he was the only saint and hero in the Oxford of the late nineteenth century. He was indeed uncompromising in what he regarded as true doctrine and its application. To give only one instance of his intolerance, which came within Max Müller's personal knowledge: he refused to administer the Holy Communion to Müller because he had not been confirmed by a bishop. But he also helped Müller in his efforts to get the Boden Professorship of Sanskrit, and no one canvassed more energetically for him. He met the Hindu reformer Keshub Chunder Sen, and though they had a long argument, they also parted as friends. He also had the warmest sympathy for students in every branch of Oriental philology. After Pusey's death in 1882 Max Müller, who had considered him dangerous in early life, paid the most unqualified tribute to his greatness of character in a letter to *The Times*.

In fact, Pusey was a true Christian in the very combination of intolerance and understanding. There is no greater misrepresentation of Christianity than to call it a religion of strength made perfect in weakness. The modern conception of Christianity as a religion of degenerate compassion which enjoins tolerance for all human failings, crimes and perversions, is a grotesque distortion. On the contrary, Christianity was merciful to the weak because it was so strong. Pusey was a true Christian in that he condemned himself (not merely others) as a sinner.

Pusey's excessive sense of his own sinfulness may now seem horribly unnatural, but Christianity was never a religion for the natural man, whom it regarded as unregenerate man living in original sin. A conviction of sinfulness, however unfounded, was of the very essence of Christian faith and morality, and, as the biographers of Pusey point out, self-condemnation has come from St Augustine, St Francis of Assisi, St Vincent de Paul, John Bunyan, St François de Sales and John Wesley. Pusey only continued that tradition. It was strange that a man who was really angelic should consign himself to hell with only a slender hope that, justified by faith alone, he would be allowed to redeem himself there; whereas the two fallen angels, Pattison and Jowett, continued to strut and bask in the heaven that was Oxford. But certainly Pusey's self-torture was preferable to the moral complacence of Jowett, purred out to fashionable men and women, who saw in it a gilding of their worldly hedonism.

It was in such a setting that Max Müller had to live his life at Oxford. His reaction was a strange dichotomy of attraction and repulsion, as was perhaps unavoidable from the dual nature of Oxford. The whole relationship can be illustrated by Müller's relations with Jowett, which were symbolic. They became friends very early, and in all the vicissitudes of Jowett's career Müller sided with him. He was on Jowett's side when the latter brought theological troubles on himself, and by that association Müller also got into trouble. And he expressed himself even more strongly when at one stage the proposal to increase Jowett's salary as Regius Professor of Greek fell through.

Yet there rankled in Müller's mind some sense of grievance against Jowett, some dark suspicion of duplicity or disloyalty. This came to a head early in 1876, at the time of the reconstitution of the terms of the Professorship of Comparative Philology. Müller suspected Jowett of sitting on the fence, if not actually opposing the proposal. After the matter had been settled in Müller's favour and Jowett had supported him strongly, Müller wrote to Stanley that though he admitted Jowett had 'behaved well, he still could not quite forgive him. He observed: 'I cannot understand him. Perhaps we make idols of our friends, and if they break we cannot bear it.'

There is finally the cool statement about Jowett in Müller's autobiography, published after his death:

Jowett knew quite well, and he did not hesitate to say so, that to do much good in this world, you must be a very able and honest man, thinking of nothing else day and night; and he adds, 'You must also be

a considerable piece of a rogue, having many reticences and conceal-
ments . . .' Now Professor Jowett has certainly done some good work
at Oxford, but if any one were to say that he also was a considerable
piece of a rogue, what an outcry there would be among the sons of
Balliol.

The fact was that Max Müller by nature and upbringing was too
simple a character to be quite at home at Oxford with all its com-
plexity and sophistication. He was uncomfortable with its subtle
and often casuistical ethics, and on his part he repelled the more
typically Oxford characters. Mark Pattison, without knowing him
intimately, gave the following psychological explanation of the
failure of Müller to get the Boden Professorship: 'It was due,' he
said, 'first and chiefly, to his own unpopular manners and to the
experience his own friends (including myself among the number)
have had of his inability for real attachment. We all knew that he
only valued us so far as we could be of use to him.'
For Pattison to say that of Müller was almost scandalous. Müller
never came to know of Pattison's opinion, but he knew his man. He
looked upon Pattison as the best-read man at Oxford, and added:
'Anywhere but at Oxford he would have grown into a Lessing.'
None the less he also wrote to Bunsen: 'Pattison is as reserved as
ever, and trusts no one.'
Moreover, on account of his German-trained mind he yearned
for a kind of intellectual communication at Oxford which its society
regarded as 'shop-talk'. Even at the age of forty-three Max Müller
showed a metaphysical proclivity which Oxford, with all its Hegeli-
zation, had no taste for. Thus in 1867 Müller was complaining to
Professor Bernays:

What I miss most here in Oxford is stimulating intercourse in literary
and scientific circles. That is entirely wanting, especially in my special
branch of study. Altogether the Englishman seems to me to have no
interest for the 'becoming' or 'growing'; it is all to be tangible and
ready-made. All dialectic is wanting in the true sense of the word.
However, there are deep shadows everywhere, and I do not want to
forget the bright sides of English life, and I am afraid that I should
find it somewhat difficult to get accustomed again to the rather narrow
German trousers.

He was however very grateful to Oxford, and added in the same letter that 'here in Oxford, I must say, everything is done to make up for what has been done amiss'.

Max Müller decided to solve the social problem of remaining at Oxford by following St Paul's dictum about the world: Thou shalt be in it, but not of it. He tried to keep aloof from the incessant movement of wheels within wheels at Oxford for monetary and other worldly advantages. Nor would he join the reforming movement actively, because he felt that his open participation in it would do harm because he was a foreigner, and of all foreigners a German. For this he suffered personally. However, remaining dependent on the academic community of Oxford for money and position he could not hope to be entirely free of its intrigues, rivalries, antipathies and partisanships.

It is Muller's involvement in the life that was the most typically Oxonian of all Oxford life which now has to be described. It has already been seen how the delay in appointing him to the Taylorian Professorship had irked him. But this post was not a university preferment, and in any case the appointment of a European as a lecturer on European languages was not likely to be resented. So Max Müller had the Professorship easily. The Greek language, however, was looked upon as a special prerogative of the Oxford dons. After Liddell came to Christ Church as Dean in 1855, Müller discussed with him the Greek lexicon, the famous Liddell and Scott, and observed that, good as the dictionary was, its etymologies were mostly inaccurate. Though Liddell was no student of comparative philology, he was broadminded enough to ask Müller to undertake the task of revising them. All seemed settled between the two, when one day the Dean came to him, shrugged his shoulders, and said that the proposal had to be given up. He did not explain the reason, though evidently he was very displeased.

It was only in 1898, two years before his death, that Müller learned from an anonymous review that Scott was the man who had obstructed the proposal for revision. Even then Max Müller would not believe it, because in his early years at Oxford Scott has shown great kindness and courtesy to him. He had heard also that Scott was associated with those who were against him in connexion with the Boden Professorship. But it is quite possible that Scott had lost all friendly feeling for Müller because he was a friend of Jowett, to whom Scott had been preferred as Master of Balliol. Privately, Max Müller held a poor opinion of Scott, and in 1870 he wrote to his wife: 'I consider Scott as a thoroughly dishonest man, and yet he is respected by many people. Who knows who is right?'

The next step in the advancement of Max Müller at Oxford was, however, a most gratifying experience for him. In 1858 he was elected a Fellow of All Souls, an unprecedented honour for a foreigner at that time. This was done at the instance of Henry Coxe, Librarian of the Bodleian and known as Bodley Coxe. Coxe entertained a very warm friendship for Müller and, realizing that the status and home offered by the college would be a great help to him, discussed it with another friend, Sir Robert Herbert, and they joined in pressing upon the Fellows of All Souls the advisability of electing him under the special powers conferred by the Act of 1854. This was done, and Müller's delight knew no bounds.

A writer, after his death recalling Müller's life at Oxford, observed that he never ceased to find an exquisite kind of amusement in his own position as a Fellow of All Souls: 'For him, the self-devoted *Stubengelehrte*, the youth of austere training and unworldly ideals, to have drifted into that fat paradise of the voluptuaries of learning struck him as a delightful joke on the part of Fate, and one which he frankly enjoyed seeing appreciated by others.' To his mother Müller wrote: 'The bells have been rung again for me in Oxford, for I have, quite unexpectedly, received a fellowship in All Souls College . . . I had no idea of it, and the thing has excited great surprise. A fortnight ago I was asked if I should have any objection if I were elected, and the next day I was elected. Why they elected me I have no idea; it is a great distinction.'

This unsolicited distinction and kindness evoked a sneaking kindness in Max Müller for the old unreformed All Souls which elected its Fellows as if they were members of a social club. But he himself was elected under the new Ordinance which required that the Fellows should be chosen according to their merits.

At all events, he showed very little of the don as a new Fellow. At the annual Gaudy on All Souls' Day he would become the German student again, and join with the somewhat tumultuous merriment of the younger fellows, and be induced to sing *Gaudeamus igitur*.

Max Müller's next attempt to secure a higher income and position at Oxford, by obtaining the Boden Professorship of Sanskrit, ended in a complete failure. This was a decisive turning point in his scholarly and intellectual life, and for this reason the episode has to be narrated fully. But the story also illustrates the dark and bright Oxford which had become the setting of his life. The election to this Professorship of Monier Williams instead of Max Müller in December 1860 was an incident in the long struggle between the academic reformers and conservatives, in which the latter, after being defeated over the wider question of remodelling the university, won a startling incidental victory.

The Professorship was endowed by Lieut-Colonel Joseph Boden of the East India Company's service, who had retired in 1807 and died in 1811. He bequeathed all his property, valued roundly at £25,000, ultimately to Oxford to found a Professorship of the Sanskrit Language, 'being of opinion that a more general knowledge and critical knowledge of the Sanskrit language will be a means of enabling his countrymen to proceed in the conversion of the Natives of India to the Christian Religion, by disseminating a knowledge of the sacred scriptures amongst them, more effectually than all other means whatever'.

The legacy came finally to Oxford at the death of Boden's daughter at the age of nineteen, and after some litigation. In 1832 one of the distinguished early English Sanskritists, Horace Hayman Wilson, was appointed to the post. As its salary was between £900 to £1,000 a year and as it was tenable for life, it was looked upon as a very lucrative living at the disposal of the university. Certainly competition for it would have been much more severe if it had not been reserved for a scholar in Sanskrit. Thus it happened that over about a century the post had only three incumbents: Wilson from 1832 to 1860; Monier Williams from 1860 to 1899; and Macdonnel from 1899 to 1927. Appointment to it was in the hands of the Convocation, which was to choose the candidate most fitted in its judgement to fulfil the post. In January 1861 the Convocation had 3,786 members. Thus the election to the Professorship had the character of a parliamentary election, and the candidates followed the same methods in contesting for the post.

Wilson died on May 8, 1860, and the notice of an election to be 'holden' on December 7 next was issued on May 16. Max Müller immediately sent in his application with numerous testimonials, and so did Monier Williams. Among those who recommended Müller were all the noted Orientalists of Europe of the age, dignitaries like the Bishop of Calcutta and Raja Radharanta Deb in India, and many leading English ecclesiastical figures, including

Pusey, Keble, Church and Stanley. The supporters of Monier Williams equalled in number those of Müller, and included many Bengali pundits, but they were not so distinguished. For six months and more a vigorous election campaign was carried on, with mani-festoes, handbills, letters to newspapers and, above all, personal canvassing by means of letters and word of mouth. Müller had his committee, and Monier Williams had two, one at Oxford and the other in London. In less than a month Müller was sick of the business.

There is no doubt that, in a more or less conscious way, Max Müller had had his eyes on this post as the culmination of his career at Oxford and also as a secure means of pursuing his vocation of studying Sanskrit. In any case, his friends and fellow-scholars had always expected that it would come to him in time.

Before the election took place a supporter of Müller wrote to *The Times* that the difference between the two candidates was the 'difference between respectable and honourable proficiency, and the complete and masterful knowledge of the subject possessed by a rare genius and profound scholar, from whose authority on the subjects of Indian philology and philosophy there was no appeal in Europe'. This was perfectly true in the light of contemporary repu-tation. A French Sanskritist kept on declaring, in spite of what others were saying, that Müller's defeat was impossible.

But all this was irrelevant to the question of Müller's election, which was to be swayed by a different consideration—the intention of the Founder. The paradoxical aspect of the matter was that after the rejection of the intentions of the Founders in respect of the working of the whole university, the Convocation was being asked to respect the intention of a Founder in regard to one Professorship. The question was thoroughly discussed. During the election cam-pain both Max Müller and Monier Williams circulated manifestoes explaining their respective views on the nature of the Professorship.

Of these, Müller's was the first and was dated September 3, 1860. He said that if elected it would be his most obvious duty to give practical and daily teaching to those who wanted to learn or study Sanskrit, but he also pointed out that this alone would be 'but a mean return for the liberality of the Founder of the Chair of San-skrit'. He added that a Professor of Sanskrit at Oxford ought to lecture on (1) the history and literature of India; (2) the religion and philosophy of the Hindus; and (3) Comparative Philology. He thought that the Boden Professor should create a school of Sanskrit Scholarship and Comparative Philology at Oxford.

On the basis of such a definition of the functions of the Professorship, Monier Williams was ready to concede Müller's superior claim unreservedly. But was the definition right? Williams began by saying that before applying for the post he had taken the first step of ascertaining what the requirements were for the Professorship in the exact words of the Founder, and he declared:

Had I found plain instructions that the electors of the University were to search throughout Europe for the man most likely to secure a worldwide reputation for the Sanskrit Chair, I confess that I should have hesitated to prosecute my design. But Colonel Boden thought more of aiding, by means of Sanskrit, the diffusion of Christianity in India than of promoting in all parts of the globe the fame of the Professorship . . . The establishment of a school of European comparative philology and Indian history, mythology, and philosophy, would doubtless be attractive; but such a departure from the one object of the Founder and strict province of the Professorship would not, in my opinion, be justifiable.

Then he went on to give an analysis of the contents and character of Sanskrit literature in order to show which branch of it was most important from the Founder's point of view, and if in so doing he also showed that Max Müller's special studies were irrelevant he was not to be blamed, for in what he said he was right.

Williams pointed out that Sanskrit literature could be classified under three distinct periods and categories. Of these the most ancient and the first was the Vedic literature; the second was made up of the six systems of Hindu philosophy and the entire collection of philosophical writings; and the third comprised the mass of the later literature, including the epics, secular poetry and prose, and sacred law. The Vedic literature, he observed, was not the sacred writings used and studied by the contemporary Hindus, and did not constitute their scriptures in the sense that the Bible and the Koran were Christian and Muslim scriptures. Thus the *Rig-Veda* (Max Müller's speciality)—which, Williams said, was being published at an expenditure of time, labour, money and erudition far greater than was ever bestowed on any edition of the Bible—was 'a curious monument of a bygone worship, at which the missionary, more usefully engaged in studying the present condition of the Hindu mind, would content himself with a rapid glance.'

8*

The second class of books, the philosophical texts which Monier Williams did not know as well as Max Müller, were according to Williams writings of a very abstruse and mystical nature, which very few learned natives understood, and which a missionary needed to know nothing about beyond their leading principles.

In contrast, it was the third class of Sanskrit books (of which he had better knowledge than Müller and on which he had done more work), which were the real Sanskrit scriptures, which every missionary must study if he wished to understand the natives of India and be understood by them. Moreover, classical Sanskrit, in which these books were written and to which Monier Williams had devoted his linguistic studies, 'really lived and breathed in the current speech of the people', though nominally dead. So, if the missionary had to translate the Christian scriptures into the modern Indian languages, it was this classical Sanskrit which they had to know, and not Vedic Sanskrit, on which Max Müller was the leading authority of the age.

Finally, Monier Williams pointed out, Max Müller's Sanskrit scholarship was of the Continental type, and not attractive to the English mind. He had felt that until the study of Sanskrit was in a manner anglicized, it would always be nauseous to the English palate. 'Englishmen,' he explained, 'are too practical to study a language very philosophically.' All these arguments, besides being patriotic, were also legitimate from the standpoint of the Boden Professorship as envisaged by Boden, a pious Colonel of the Indian Army.

If the contest between Max Müller and Monier Williams were confined to the airing of antithetical conceptions of the Professorship, it would have been a sharp academic competition, but not an election campaign of the parliamentary type, which is what it became. From the beginning all the spices which make the curry that is a parliamentary election were put in it. At the end of the campaign even the ideology of the Professorship was highly emotionalized, and the religious stake involved was explained to the electors in the following handbill distributed on behalf of Monier Williams:

BODEN SANSKRIT PROFESSORSHIP
A Sacred Trust has been committed to the University of Oxford by the late COLONEL BODEN.
Members of the Convocation in voting for a Boden Professor must not overlook their obligation to use his Endowment *primarily* to carry out his expressed intentions.

What then is this primary object?

It is 'to enable his *Countrymen* to proceed in the conversion of the Natives of India to the Christian Religion, by disseminating a knowledge of the Sacred Scriptures among them'.

There are Two Candidates, with ample Testimonials.

The Organs of Public Opinion have thought the contest not unworthy of their notice.

What then is the result?

By common consent both are pronounced scholars of world-wide reputation.

But one of them is specially and earnestly recommended to Convocation by a great number of our *Countrymen* in *India itself*.

These *Englishmen,* educated by him, grateful for his instruction, and personally attached to him, are a machinery existing ready to hand for the great work to be done.

They have no Votes to give, but their voice from that distant land should ring in our ears and hearts.

They know their man, they know the Natives, they are in daily communication with them. Is it wise to disregard their opinion?

The Professorship is not for Oxford alone.

It is not for 'The Continent and America'.

It is for India.

It is for Christianity.

Let us then Vote for the man who is well-known and loved in India, and who, even by the voice of his opponents, is declared to be a trustworthy depositary of the Christian interests of a Christian Foundation.

M.A.

At once Max Müller's supporters issued a counterblast in almost the same words, but with tell-tale modifications, such as: 'By general consent one is pronounced a Scholar of world-wide reputation, the other a Scholar well known to his Friends and Pupils.'

But even from the missionary point of view, both Dr Pusey and the Bishop of Calcutta wrote in favour of Müller. Pusey informed Müller that at the time of the first appointment to the Professorship in 1832 the question of giving a direct missionary turn to the appointment had arisen, and as a voter he had then given weight to it. On the final notices of the election which he forwarded, he wrote in his own hand: 'Max Müller has already done more for the Gospel in India than any other Sanskrit scholar, by opening to the missionaries their [the Hindus'] sacred books.'

The Bishop of Calcutta wrote among other things that 'it would be more fitting in my opinion for a great Christian University to place in its Sanskrit Chair the scholar who has made the Sanskrit scriptures accessible to the Christian missionary'. He gave leave to Müller to use his letter in any way he considered fit.

After the question of the intention of the Founder, there also arose the question of the wishes of the previous holder of the Professorship, as if the principle of apostolic succession was involved in the appointment. Monier Williams had no difficulty in producing decisive proof of his testamentary right. With his application he submitted the following letter written by Wilson shortly before his death:

14 Upper Wimpole Street, April 21, 1860.
My dear Williams, I am quite incompetent to give you any hints for your industry, for I have been and am suffering dreadfully. I am about to undergo an operation; and, as there is always a certain amount of risk in such an operation at my age, I recommend your being alive to the chance of a vacancy. I always have looked to you as my successor; but you will have a formidable competitor in M. Müller, not only for his celebrity, but personal influence. However, if God be pleased, I may get over the trial, and for a few years more keep you in expectancy.
Yours ever affectionately,
H. H. Wilson.

Though this was explicit, a friend of Max Müller's, W. S. W. Vaux of the British Museum, at once raised the question whether Wilson could have meant what he said. Vaux wrote:

My dear Müller, I was a little surprised to read among Williams's testimonials the short note from our late friend, in which he states that he had always looked forward to his succeeding him in the Boden Professorship, whenever he should make a vacancy. On many occasions —and especially on the last time (about two months since, in the East India House Library) when I had the pleasure of seeing him—he stated that, in his judgement, you were the first Sanskrit scholar in Europe. I remarked that I was glad to hear him give so decided an opinion, as I and several others were naturally anxious that his successor at Oxford should be the fittest man we could procure. To this he said, 'You will be quite right if your choice should fall on Max Müller.'

But on balance it appeared that Wilson was for Williams. Even as far back as 1830 Wilson had expressed his low opinion of German Sanskrit scholars and provoked a controversy with A. W. Schlegel.

The campaign also made full use of personal arguments in the manner of parliamentary elections, and in respect of them Müller was an easier target than Williams. He was accused of intending to hold two professorships (the Taylorian and the Boden) at the same time; of not being an Englishman; of not being able to write English well; and of being irreligious. To one of these alone he pleaded guilty, 'that of not having been born in England, and having no right to the name of an Englishman'. But he added, 'If, however, residence and work in the University give a right to the name of Oxfordman, I may, without presumption, be thought to have acquired some claim to that title.' All the other charges he rejected totally, and especially the charge of being irreligious.

As to his English, a friend (who remained unknown) wrote to *The Times*: 'Mr Max Müller's English is perfect. Many who have not heard the wonderful force and clearness of his public lectures must have read, without knowing it, some of his many contributions to periodical literature.'

At the very height of the campaign Müller was accused of misrepresenting Williams in his reply in *The Times* to the latter's manifesto by misquoting 'some of his statements in a manner prejudicial to his interests'. Max Müller, who was very sensitive to any charge of dishonesty, immediately submitted the matter to four distinguished members of the university, who reported as follows:

> We the undersigned, having examined Mr. Monier Williams's Circular of October 12, and Mr. Max Müller's Letter of October 23, beg leave to state that we consider the charge brought against Mr. Max Müller, in Mr. Monier Williams's Circular just issued, of having 'misquoted' Mr. Monier Williams in a manner prejudicial to his interests, to be wholly unfounded.
>
> William Thomson, Provost of Queen's,
> E. B. Pusey, Regius Professor of Hebrew,
> William Jacobson, Regius Professor of Divinity,
> Mountague Bernard, Chichele Professor of
> International Law and Diplomacy.

But the game was not all one-sided, and at some moments Williams too must have felt both awkward and stung.

There was for instance an attack on Monier Williams on the score of his incompetence on the external side of Sanskrit scholarship. It was put about that he could not read a Sanskrit manuscript.

To disprove that some evidence was produced, and to this Max
Müller's supporters replied as follows:

> The extracts given by the Master of University and Mr Medd merely
> prove that Mr. Williams is able to recognize the letters of a Sanskrit
> MS when he can compare it with an existing text. This is a kind of
> mechanical labour which is paid for at the public libraries at Paris and
> Berlin at the rate of half-a-crown an hour. Mr. Williams has yet to prove
> that he can take a Sanskrit author *existing in MS* only and give him to
> the world for the first time.

From Williams's side a complaint came that some of Müller's
supporters had improved on this charge in one of the circulars by
putting this comment on a circular: 'The eyes of Europe are on our
election. Shall we elect a man who is great as a Sanskrit scholar,
philologist, and teacher, or one who cannot read a Sanskrit MS?'

It was in this atmosphere of hustings that the election for the
Professorship was held on December 7, 1860. The voting was 833
for Monier Williams and 610 for Max Müller. The defeat was a
severe disappointment to Müller and his friends, and they all held
that the scales were tipped against him on irrelevant personal,
religious and political grounds. Müller himself wrote to his mother:
'The opposite party made it a political and religious question, and
nothing could be done against them. All the best people voted for
me, the Professors almost unanimously, but the *vulgus profanum*
made the majority.' His father-in-law expressed himself very
strongly: 'I know not when I have felt more deeply for the trials of
others or had more reason to admire patience and resignation to
God's will than in the spirit you have shown, in what I know to be
a most severe trial and bitter disappointment. But now that all is
over, and I have time to think, I am inclined to believe that with
such unscrupulous opponents we could not have won.'

But the noblest comfort for him came from Stanley:

> I have never experienced [he wrote] the peculiar trial under which you
> are suffering, but I believe, from my own bitter disappointment on
> your behalf, I can feel what it is for you. You will have many consola-
> tions, I need not dwell upon them. But *you* must also give *us* the best
> consolation that we can have, and that is the assurance that we have not
> been mistaken in the high expectations we had formed of you . . . You
> can still show that, although not Boden Professor, you are and will

remain the oracle of all who wish to know the secrets of Indian literature and religion.

Stanley, through sheer spiritual sympathy, had already anticipated
the course Müller's intellectual efforts were to take.

After Max Müller's death two friends wrote to his wife explaining
the reason for his failure to get the Professorship. One of them was
Canon Farrar, who was a member of his committee. He said that he
was inclined to think that the opposition to him was not strictly
religious or political, but it sprang from 'the Englishman's dislike
to an adopted son'. He added that Müller did 'not realize the stub-
born fixedness of English and Oxford preference for an old Oxford
man'. But the other informant, W. B. Gamlen, told Mrs Max
Müller that on the strength of the version of the affair given to him
by 'Tommy' Sheppard of Exeter, who was one of the leaders of the
Oxford Tories, the verdict was entirely political. As he put it: 'I
should judge that the same opposition would have been offered to
any candidate, whether an Englishman or foreigner, who could have
been identified with the liberal, or Gladstonian party.'

There can be no doubt that both personal and public reasons lay
behind Max Müller's defeat.

His next move to have a share in the flesh-pots of Oxford succeeded, though not without some characteristically Oxonian opposition. In October 1865 Max Müller applied for the post of the
Oriental Sub-Librarian at the Bodleian, finding that his friend
Coxe, who was the Librarian, could not secure the services of any
other Orientalist. With the unanimous consent of the curators his
name was forwarded for consideration by the Convocation, and the
date of the election was announced. At once letters began to appear
in the press against him and for another aspirant.

A formal contradiction to some of the statements made was
issued by Coxe himself as the Bodleian's Librarian. He asserted
that 'it may be as well to correct three mis-statements which appear
in the first of the letters now under circulation: Professor Müller's
salary as Taylorian Professor is £500, not "more than £600". He has
resigned the Examinership for the Indian Civil Service. His labours
in editing the *Vedas*, so far from being "well paid", entail on him a
considerable pecuniary sacrifice.'

However, this time Müller was elected, and he enjoyed the work
very much. But the double work proved too much for his health,

and he resigned the sub-librarianship after about a year and a half, In 1868 the university on its own initiative recognized the merits of Max Müller in a striking manner. It abolished the Taylorian Professorship of Modern European Languages, and created in its place expressly for him a new chair of Comparative Philology on a higher salary. This was the first professorship created by the university itself. All the previous professorships were established either by royal benefactions or private endowments. This relieved Müller of the duty of lecturing on the European languages, and left him free to pursue his own subject.

For the next eight years Max Müller's life and career at Oxford ran smoothly. But at the end of 1875 he himself raised a storm about his career at Oxford, and on December 1 sent in his resignation of the Professorship of Comparative Philology to the Vice-Chancellor. At the same time he also printed the letter of resignation in a circular, and distributed it so that his friends, both inside and outside the university, might know why after long consideration he had taken the step. His main and declared reason was that he wanted leisure to pursue his Indian and Sanskritic studies. In his letter of resignation he said that he had to choose between Sanskrit and Comparative Philology, and he repeated that explanation in a personal letter to the Duke of Albany, one of Queen Victoria's sons:

> If I had continued to discharge my duties as Professor of Comparative Philology, I should have had to surrender my Sanskrit studies altogether. Were I Professor of Sanskrit at Oxford, nothing would have drawn me away from this, in many respects, delightful place; but in order to concentrate my powers, and to do something at least before it is too late, I see no choice but to give up my pleasant position here, and retire to some quiet town in Germany.

None of his friends questioned the reasonableness of his decision on this ground, though all of them regretted it.

As soon as the news spread, letters began to pour in from all parts of the world, and even from India.

There was no doubt that Müller was sincere in giving this reason for his resignation. But there was much more behind it than was publicly stated. For some years he had been feeling a very strong emotional revulsion from Oxford, and for a few months before he had actually decided to leave it he had written quite frankly to his intimate friends about his dissatisfaction. For instance, on August 22 he wrote to Stanley:

> I think my time in England is nearly up. I doubt whether I ought to stay longer. I am only tolerated at Oxford, allowed to help when I am wanted, but never helped myself when I want help. If I had worked in Germany as I have worked for twenty-five years in England, my position would be very different. Here I am nobody in the University; and when I see how I am treated, I really feel sometimes ashamed of myself, not for my own, but for my wife's sake.

He felt he was at Oxford only on sufferance. That this mood was also behind his resignation he admitted to his friend George von Bunsen, son of his old patron and helper, in a letter written in January 1876, in which he said: 'I will tell you viva voce why I have finally made up my mind to leave Oxford. Clerical intrigues and petty jealousies, alas! were partly the reason.'

Even this was not the whole story. What brought his sense of grievance against Oxford to a head and finally induced him to act was a particular personal matter—the decision of the Hebdomedal Council to put up the name of Monier Williams to the Convocation for the honorary degree of D.C.L. This was the only time in his whole career that Max Müller acted from personal pique, which showed that though intellectually he had outgrown his disappointment over the Boden Professorship, it still rankled in his mind emotionally.

The decision to give the degree to Monier Williams was in itself an exhibition of the *mores* of academic Oxford. Towards the end of the summer term of 1875 the friends of Williams in the Council applied to it to propose a decree which would enable him to have the formal degree of D.C.L. without passing the examination for it. The Council agreed and put forward a draft decree of exoneration. As soon as it was published in the University Gazette the University Professor of Law made a solemn remonstrance that such a step would overthrow the whole fabric of legal studies which had been laboriously erected and by which an Oxford degree in law had been recognized by the Inns of Court. If, he said, this degree was now conferred without an examination on a person ignorant of law the university would stultify itself. But this argument, the Law Faculty added, did not apply to an honorary D.C.L., because it was well known that the honour was conferred annually on all sorts of persons and implied no legal qualifications in the recipient.

The Council admitted the force of the argument and cancelled the session of the Convocation. Williams's friends at once declared that this would be regarded as a stigma on him, for all the world had come to know that a degree was intended, and they even said that the stigma would be out of all proportion to the distinction which the degree would have given him. Then the Council decided to propose the honorary degree of D.C.L., and proceeded with the matter. This was regarded as a personal slight by Max Müller, and at the beginning of November he told his friends that he was going to resign.

At this juncture his friends to a man showed themselves to be his real friends. All of them disapproved of his decision, though they were ready to consider his other and main motive, securing greater leisure for his work. His brother-in-law Walrond wrote strongly to him: 'I don't think you have any idea what a bad effect it would have. For one man who would give you credit for indignation in a sacred cause, the cause of real learning against the shallow pretence of it, a hundred would accuse you of petty personal jealousy. And what a triumph your enemies will have then!'

Stanley wrote: 'If you have on general grounds determined that you ought to pass your remaining years (and, oh! may they be many!) in Germany, much as I shall regret it I shall have nothing to say against it. But that you should leave Oxford on the ground that an undeserved honour has been bestowed on Monier Williams seems to be both insufficient in itself and unjust to yourself.' Dean Liddell, as soon as he heard about Max Müller's intention from Rolleston, wrote to him:

It grieves me much to hear you say that M.M. really contemplates resignation . . . It appears to me that he, at once, greatly overrates the importance of the thing itself and greatly underrates his own position and character . . . I am as sure . . . that it will not occur to anyone . . . that any slur will be cast on M.M. because the Council has rashly and undeservedly lavished an empty honour on M.W. M.M. stands far too high . . . If, on the other hand, he should resign, I know my countrymen well enough to feel sure that he will be generally blamed and that his conduct will be set down to . . . petulance. You and I would feel too much interested in him not to dread this for his sake and to wish it averted, if averted it can be.

A few days later Liddell wrote to Müller himself in the same vein, and urged him to put off the resignation even if it were on general grounds. Other friends also wrote to him. All this showed that Müller's fancy that he was only tolerated at Oxford was due to his own temperament which created these passing fits of impatience.

Anyhow, when he did resign on the general ground of work, they all set about doing something for him which would enable him to pursue his vocation without being encumbered by the duties of the Professorship. The idea was to relieve him of the burden of lecturing on Comparative Philology by giving him a Deputy who would do that work, and to give him the status of a Professor Emeritus. Even Lord Salisbury, as Secretary of State for India, took up the matter, and on January 27 Liddell wrote to Müller: 'I have just received a "private" letter from Lord Salisbury, in which he expresses a warm desire on the part both of himself and of the India Council that you may be induced to remain at Oxford and in which he says that there "seems to be no objection in principle to the India Council co-operating with the University to incur the cost of publishing the 'Indian Works' which are mentioned in your list".' He also informed Müller that on Monday next he hoped to bring forward a proposal which might not be unsatisfactory to him. This proposal was put into the form of a decree to be approved by the Convocation on February 15 and circulated by the Vice-Chancellor on January 31, 1876. It ran as follows:

> Whereas it is expedient to allow Professor M. Müller to devote himself without interruption to the studies on the Ancient Literature of India which he has hitherto prosecuted with so much success and with so much honour to the University; In a CONVOCATION to be holden on Tuesday, February 15, at Two o'clock, the following form of Decree will be submitted to the House:—'That the provisions of Statt. Tit. IV, Sect. 1, 37, cl. 3 be suspended, and that the Electors proceed to the nomination of A Deputy to be approved by the Vice-Chancellor, and the Deputy shall receive one half of the salary of the present Professor.'

Even so the author of *Alice in Wonderland* brought into play against the proposal the devastating logic exhibited in his fantasy. He said that the deputy would be the real professor, and the retiring Professor would really get a pension; that the two were wholly independent questions; that the university should be able to provide the pension without mulcting the real professor of half of his

income. All this, he said, he was writing in the interest of the unknown future holder of the Chair, though also in the interest of
Max Müller, 'for surely the very proposal to invite the new Professor to do the work for half the present salary, is to say, by implication, that the work has been hitherto overpaid—against which
suspicion I, for one, desire to record my protest'.

But the Convocation found the logic—sound as it was—unper-
suasive, and the decree was carried, Jowett spoke in favour of it,
and Liddell made a reasoned appeal in a long speech, with an
eloquent peroration:

> Other Governments have acknowledged Professor Max Müller's great
> achievements; the French Institute several years ago elected him a
> Foreign Member, the Royal Academy of Turin paid him the same
> honour, and made him one of a distinguished six, the others being
> Cousin, Thiers, Böckh, Mommsen, and Grote. He received the Cross
> of the Order of Merit from the German Emperor two years ago, along
> with von Moltke. England has been behindhand. Let Oxford by a
> unanimous vote today do something to repair this backwardness; not
> for his sake, but for our own, I ask it. Let us keep him if we can, how
> we can, while we can.

Max Müller was informed of the decision and wrote to the Vice-
Chancellor in the most grateful terms, saying that he looked forward with great satisfaction to spending the remaining years of his
life at Oxford.*

On hearing of it Froude wrote gladly: 'My dear Max,

Two words only to express my hearty delight that all is well
settled and that we are to be spared the dishonour of losing you.'

And just as Molière said that *la comédie finit par un petit ballet
qui avoit été préparé*, the University Musical Club sent Max Müller
the following invitation and message:

> The President ventures to invite Professor Max Müller's attention to
> this evening's programme, and to express to him the very great
> pleasure it would give the Club if he were able to be present this
> evening.

---

* The post of Deputy Professor went to Archibald Henry Sayce, M.A., at the
time Fellow of Queen's, an Orientalist and philologist, who became a leading
Assyriologist later. The salary of the Professorship was £600 a year. So the
Deputy got £300.

At the same time he wishes to congratulate the Professor most heartily on the result of yesterday's Convocation, and to express his great regret that anyone should have thought it their duty to oppose the proposition of the Council.

The programme will include
Mozart's Clarinet Quintet,
Beethoven's Trio for Clarinet, piano, and violoncello,
Beethoven's Sonata (G min.) for piano and violoncello,
Beethoven's arrangements of Scotch songs with string accompaniment.
(Violoncello, Herr Daubart.)

PART THREE

'I gave my heart to seek and search out by wisdom concerning all *things* that are done under heaven: this sore travail hath God given to the sons of man to be exercised therewith.'

Chapter 1

POLEMICS: POLITICAL AND SCHOLARLY

In his conscious formulation of an ideal of life Max Müller wanted to be a studious recluse, seeking knowledge and truth for their own sake, and believing that there must be a division of labour in human activities.

None the less, all through life he was involving himself in political controversies, and showing himself eager to fight the opinions of majorities when they were baying in a pack out of nationalistic passions. This was due to his interest in politics. As a student in Germany he was a liberal nationalist. As an adult scholar in England he remained the same liberal, and associated with the English Liberals. At no age did he shrink from expressing his opinions in conversation or correspondence. Though the realization of German unity and the creation of the German Empire in 1870 satisfied his nationalism, he never ceased to take an interest in Anglo-German friendship in the international field. Even in his letters to his young son he set down his political views very freely.

But his interest in politics did not remain confined to private expression. As soon as he had acquired sufficient standing in the scholarly world he began to intervene in the public discussion of all the burning political questions of his times. He was also given a hearing, for celebrity flows out through all sorts of outlets. But it was not the desire for personal publicity which made him do so. He felt that it was his duty to support the side which he believed to be right, and in committing himself to a cause he showed neither timidity nor half-heartedness, though this brought him more than a controversialist's share of abuse.

But in the first instance he was only the typical German scholar of the nineteenth century. After the French Revolution and the Romantic Movement, which between them created a new form of nationalism, a life like that of Kant became impossible for a European philosopher or scholar, because this nationalism put an end to the specialized, restricted and calculating manifestation of politics, and based it on the passion for selfhood of a whole people. Moreover, there stood behind that a far older Western tradition of involvement in public affairs. Plato created the political function, both theoretical and practical, of the thinker. Before him the Athenians had begun to think that a man who took no interest in the affairs of the *polis* was not just a harmless man, but a useless man. Since that time nobody in the West has disputed that the scholar and also the poet, the philosopher and the historian, have their practical role in politics. But till the end of the nineteenth century the political intervention of the writer was almost without exception on the side of right, and never on the side of might, whereas from the end of the nineteenth century onwards the perversion of the political function of the intellectual was an accompaniment of the perversion of its driving force, nationalism.

Max Müller's interventions in politics conformed to the older tradition in Europe. Even so he seemed to think that a justification for them was called for, and once he wrote: 'If you want to be at peace with yourself, do not mind being at war with the world.'

In the course of his life Müller was drawn into public controversy by three wars: the Schleswig-Holstein War of 1864 between Denmark and the German Confederation, but fought on its behalf by Austria and Prussia; the Franco-Prussian War of 1870; and the Boer War of 1899.

As a German nationalist he held that the two Duchies of Schleswig and Holstein were German. So, when they were annexed by Denmark in 1850 and Prussia did nothing to prevent that, he wrote to Bunsen: 'God help Schleswig-Holstein, and not punish Prussia in His wrath . . . But if a power, to which all Europe has offered the leading position, allows itself to be intimidated by the threats of the Danes and Russians, and withdraws a given promise, that is worse than a retreat before a battle.'

The status of the two Duchies became an issue of war again when King Frederick VII of Denmark died at the end of 1863. The new king laid claim to them, but the German Confederation rejected his claim and called upon Austria and Prussia to take military action against Denmark. They did, and of course the defeat of the Danes was inevitable.

In England feeling ran high against Germany. The Queen herself was pro-German, but her ministers and people were inflamed against Austria and Prussia. There was even talk of war, and Palmerston himself would have liked it. Almost all the newspapers were wholly on the side of Denmark. At this juncture Max Müller thought he would explain the German case, and try to remove the grave misunderstanding between the German and the English people.

On February 15, 1864, he sent a long letter to *The Times* from Oxford. The editor, Delane, wrote to inform him that he would publish it, though he and his paper supported Denmark. The communication was published on February 18, accompanied by an editorial which expressed lack of conviction. Müller feared that public clamour might at any moment carry England into a war with Germany, and that, he said, would be the most terrible misfortune. As for the English attitude, he understood it. 'The sympathy felt for Denmark as the weaker Power,' he said, 'is both natural and honourable. But weakness, as has been well said, does not confer the divine right of doing wrong, and in this conflict between Denmark and Germany, Denmark has been in the wrong from beginning to end.'

Then followed what Delane described as Müller's elaborate defence of the conduct of Germany towards Denmark. But on the larger public in England it fell flat.

Yet his views were moderate. He upheld the right to independence of the Duchies, and disapproved of the highhandedness of Bismarck. He said: 'They are sovereign and independent states and are indissolubly united.' But this question was not as simple as he made it out to be. In fact, it was discussed *in law* for a long time and was set as a question in examination papers. His advocacy of the German claim pursued him not only to the end of his life, but even after his death.

He himself revived it in an article published in the *Nineteenth Century* in its May 1897 issue. In substance he made it a restatement of the German case. The Editor of the review published it with the following note: 'The subjoined article has been submitted to and approved by the highest possible authority upon the facts, who vouches for the correctness of this version of them.'

The challenge was at once taken up by a Danish historian, A. D. Jörgensen, who was also Keeper of the State Archives of Denmark. He flatly denied the impartiality of Müller and observed that Müller had derived most of his information from the University of Kiel, 'the headquarters', as he put it, 'of all the seditious writings against Denmark.' The Editor of the *Nineteenth Century* published this rejoinder in the December number of his review, and to it also

he added an explanatory note: 'The following reply to Professor
Max Müller's article in the May number of this Review is published
at the desire of an exalted Personage in this country, interested in
the Danish side of the question, who considers that Professor Max
Müller's views are incorrect and inconsistent with historic truth.'
The Personage could only have been Alexandra, Princess of Wales,
or her husband the future Edward VII.

Even this was not the end of the matter. In November 1915,
both the articles were republished as a pamphlet in London, with a
preface by K. Lindblom. It was a piece of war propaganda against
Germany, but the moral drawn in the preface was incontrovertible.

The Powers [Lindblom wrote] who acted neither honourably nor
wisely—the same thing if people only had knowledge to see it—have
since had cause bitterly to regret their passivity. Some may look on
what the Great Powers have suffered since in the light of retribution
. . . 1864 shows what could well have been realized in 1914, namely,
that a war in Europe, however small, is not merely somebody's but
everybody's concern.

1864 shows that it is easy to see injustice done and difficult to re-
dress it . . . Knowledge of injustice in the past and its consequences
may help to the avoidance of injustice in the future. Hence the repub-
lication of the following articles, of which the net proceeds of sales
will go to the Red Cross societies of the Allies.

The long-drawn-out causality hinted at by the writer is indisputable if the fundamental cause of the First World War is assumed to
be the very foundation of the German Empire. To Bismarck the
Schleswig War was the first trial of a method which he was to use
with ever greater confidence and thoroughness in order to unite
Germany under the hegemony of Prussia. Eventually Max Müller
recognized it himself, although during the war he condemned the
action of Bismarck and the annexation of Schleswig-Holstein to
Germany. As his wife related in her biography: 'In later years he
saw that Bismarck's policy with regard to the Duchies was the first
link in the chain that led to the unity of Germany.' And Müller
himself explained the connexion very clearly in his article published in 1897:

There can be no doubt [he wrote] that without the initiative taken by
Duke Frederick and the people of Schleswig-Holstein in resisting the
Danish claim the great events of the second half of our century, the

war between Prussia and Austria, and the subsequent war between Germany and France, would never have taken place, at all events not under the very peculiar circumstances in which they actually took place. The name of *Zündhölzchen*, lucifer match, given at the time to Schleswig-Holstein, has proved very true, though the conflagration which it caused has been far greater than could have been foreseen at the time.

But the end of this war, which left the Duchies divided in control between Austria and Prussia, did not set at rest Müller's anxiety about them. He still awaited a final settlement, and tried to interest Gladstone in it. Thus on April 2, 1865, he wrote to that statesman. But obviously nothing came out of it. The next year the status of the Duchies was finally decided by force by Bismarck, and that led to the war between Prussia on the one hand and Austria and the South German States on the other. This was the second step in the process of realizing German unity under Prussia.

In this conflict Müller's convictions and sympathies were wholly with Prussia. But he refrained from giving public expression to them. He did not think it binding on him to declare himself publicly as a partisan of one of the two German States which were at war with each other. Nevertheless, he wrote frankly to his mother and, while offering his view of the conflict, he also set down his anticipations for Germany. In both he was remarkably correct. On June 17, one day before the formal declaration of war by Prussia on Austria, he wrote to her:

> Sooner or later a war between Austria and Prussia was unavoidable, and if it is decisive, it will lead to what all true Germans have desired for years, a united Germany. Prussia and Austria are merely names, and stand for no more than Anhalt and Reuss. The great thing is that the dualism of Prussia and Austria should be ended. Who conquers, or is conquered, is of little consequence. Germany remains Germany, and cannot be governed, even by a Roman Catholic Emperor, otherwise than she allows herself to be governed. If Prussia wins, she must cease to be Prussia; Austria the same. So wait quietly, no excitement, no partisanship.

He reassured his mother about the practical consequences of the war for her. Her investments were in Austrian stocks, and they had fallen. So he told her that she must not scruple to ask him for money, for, as he put it, 'if I don't give you, I give to others'.

After the battle of Königgratz he wrote again:

All good Germans have long desired what is now happening. The methods employed might have been better, here and there, but Prussia staked her existence to make Germany united and strong, and though I thoroughly doubt whether the motives were throughout honest and pure yet I rejoice over the results. Prussia will have a yet harder war to wage, for a war with France can hardly be avoided. But in spite of all that, Germany will at last take her right place in Europe, and that she never could have done with the Bundestag and thirty princes.

This war made him forget a good deal of the dislike which as a German liberal he felt for Bismarck's authoritarianism, and even made him regard that statesman as a possible benefactor of Germany. He wrote to his mother on July 16: 'You can well imagine I am no admirer of Bismarck, but I am convinced that his policy is the only one to make Germany strong and respected by other nations.'

About the final outcome for Austria Max Müller offered to his mother consolation in a fatalistic vein: 'One cannot alter matters, and when you think that Babylon and Nineveh, and Athens and Rome, have passed away in the course of time, you cannot wonder so much at the Hapsburg catastrophe.' One wonders, however, if instead of Austria Prussia had suffered a resounding defeat, whether he would have been so philosophical.

Max Müller's next involvement in current politics was over the Franco-Prussian War. It moved him heart and soul. This war roused the German nationalist that lay dormant in his scholar's personality. Being divided between Germany and England also he could not forget the issue of Anglo-German understanding, and this gave him as much concern during the war as the cause of German unity.

On July 17, 1870, even before the formal declaration of war by France, he wrote to his mother: 'I do not for a moment doubt the result. Germany may lose some battles, but Germany cannot be killed. The present devil's brood in France will fall after one lost battle. There is perhaps nothing better for the ultimate consolidation of Germany than this war . . . Who knows how long this war may last? I should like to live to see its end!' He was only forty-seven!

He wrote to Stanley:

My heart is too full to say anything about this terrible war. I believe it is a cup that could not pass. France cannot break a united and strong Germany, and the reckless gambler who usurps the throne of France took advantage of this national jealousy to save himself from his inevitable end for a few years longer. But the misery it brings to thousands of happy homes passes all description! This war can only end either in the destruction of Germany, or in a revenge without parallel in history.

He rebutted in advance any plea that might come from Stanley to show no vindictiveness to a beaten enemy: 'War in Germany is different from war in England. It was easy for the Duke of Wellington to preach moderation at Paris. He had to avenge defeat, but no outrages, whilst every German soldier that marches into Paris (and I trust I shall live to see it!) has to avenge the blood of brothers, and tears such as only a mother can shed.'

That reveals nationalism as an amoral biological phenomenon, which can make nations faced with a threat to their independent existence as blindly fierce as a wild beast at bay. But in Max Müller's age this ferocity burst out in periodical crises. It had not solidified into a persistent human hatred (called 'cold war' in modern jargon) which can contemplate and plan in cold blood the annihilation of a rival human group. Thus, as soon as the tide of war turned, Müller's tone became different. On August 14, even before the battles of Vionville, Mars-la-Tour, St Privat and Gravelotte were fought—and these French defeats decided the war—he wrote to his mother: 'You can fancy all our thoughts are with Germany, and I wish I were there. Such a triumph of a good cause has seldom been seen in history.' On the same day, he wrote to his historian friend Freeman: 'Though I never doubted of ultimate success, I was afraid of reverses in the beginning. Now I expect the war will be over soon, and what I looked forward to for the last eighteen years almost everyday as I opened the paper—the downfall of the Empire —has come to pass at last . . . Peace will be easy, for Germany wants no conquests, not even Alsace and Lorraine; the land is fine enough, but the people are not worth having.' He was soon to form different views about these provinces.

Even then his mood was not wholly one of triumph. The following passage from his letter to Stanley written just on the eve of

Sedan, on August 30, reveal the mingling of nationalism and humanitarianism in him: 'I cannot tell you how this war crushes me. I sometimes feel as I could bear it no longer and must be off. What savages we are in spite of all these centuries! But surely the Teutonic race is better than the Latin and the Slavonic, and the Protestants better Christians than the Romans; and the Germanic cause is surely thoroughly righteous, and the French thoroughly unrighteous.'

It would be easy to label Müller as a German chauvinist. But it was not in Müller's nature to be partisan, though he always chose what in his lights was right. So he wrote to his mother after the defeat of France: 'I cannot agree with the German abuse of the French nation. The French as a nation fight bravely, and show that they are by no means so depraved and perishing as the writers in the German papers think.'

Soon after he also wrote to Gladstone: 'I feel quite ashamed when I see German writers speak of the whole of France as one vast Babylon, implying at the same time that Heaven has granted to us the exclusive privilege of all virtue and godliness.'

In spite of being a German and his complete identification with the German cause, Müller showed himself to be less of a partisan than Carlyle, who concluded a long letter to *The Times* (November 11, 1870) with the words: 'That noble, patient, deep, pious, and solid Germany should at length be welded into a nation and become Queen of the Continent, instead of vapouring, vainglorious, gesticulating, quarrelsome, restless, and over-sensitive France, seems to me the hopefullest public fact that has occurred in my time.'

In a letter to his friend Professor Bernays, Max Müller even spoke regretfully of the respect with which the world was now treating victorious Germany. 'I feel with you,' he wrote, 'the horrors of this time, and though I am so proud of the heroism of the German nation, I am nevertheless ashamed to think how often the world looked upon the great spiritual victories of the Fatherland with scorn and indifference, and now is on her knees because we have learnt to aim our bullets with accuracy and skill. However, I trust that the wild beast will soon retire, and that the *spirit* in Germany will attain the upper hand.'

For the sake of the mental sanity of the German people he wished France to remain strong, and not to be permanently weakened. He wrote on September 16, 1870, to his American friend Moncure be intolerant of the successes, especially military, of other nations.

Soon the disapproval of Prussia became quite vocal. The idea gained ground that France, instead of being the aggressor without qualification, might have been manœuvred into that role by the astuteness of Bismarck, for whom there was great dislike in English political circles. This found its first public and very strong expression in a letter to *The Times* written by Sir Harry Verney and published on August 29, 1870. In it the writer accused Bismarck of complicity in a design put forward by France to partition Holland, Belgium and Switzerland between the two as a *quid pro quo* for a French acceptance of the unity of Germany under Prussian hegemony. Sir Harry Verney charged Prussia and Bismarck with entertaining this scheme, and said that 'an English Minister who could dishonour his country by listening for a moment to such proposals, would be driven from office by an indignant people'.

Max Müller at once replied, denying that the acceptance of the document by Bismarck in any way implied his agreement with the proposals. But on the very next day (July 26) he wrote to Stanley: 'I feel by no means quite happy about the *Traité de paix entre la France et la Prusse*. If it is genuine, however, then neutrality on the part of England would be criminal.' Afterwards he contended that though Bismarck kept the document he was not in collusion with France. But the main contention of Sir Harry Verney was that Prussia and Bismarck had aggressive designs already prepared and so were responsible for the war. This Müller disputed, and declared that Prussia was only fighting a purely defensive war.

But Max Müller's task became more difficult when Prussia disclosed the obvious intention of taking Alsace and Lorraine from France. British opinion, and still more that of Gladstone, turned sharply against Germany. At the beginning of October Gladstone, then Prime Minister, himself wrote to Müller conveying his strong view that he could not approve of the annexation of Alsace-Lorraine by Germany, and seeking more information on its possibility. But it was not easy to justify the German intention, and Müller had to admit that 'the conquest of territory inhabited by people that are not German in national sentiment is an idea repugnant to the German mind'. He himself had at first thought that Prussia would make no such demand. But he could see that it would be made and the cession exacted. So he had to justify the step on the ground of military security.

He also knew, however, that there was more in the German claim on Alsace-Lorraine than military security. He informed Gladstone that these provinces once belonged to Germany, and that had never been forgotten by the German people. But he added that any offensive war to recover the lost patrimony was impossible. Only the action of France had provided the opportunity. He now supported the claim, and in his letter even went to the length of saying that 'if there are people in the annexed portions of Alsace and Lorraine who cannot bear the idea of belonging to Germany, surely it is not too much to expect from their patriotism that they should follow the example of thousands of German families which emigrated to Philadelphia when Alsace was annexed to France'.

The correspondence with Gladstone continued, and Müller even had one prolonged meeting with him at Hawarden. But in the meanwhile he involved himself in a controversy in *The Times* on the whole subject.

A long letter, his second on the war, was called forth by an appeal made to England by a French merchant-politician, Arlès-Dufour, to save Alsace-Lorraine for France. Max Müller recognized Arlès-Dufour's sincerity, but restated the case with the same arguments he had employed with Gladstone, and set forth more elaborately. This led to a lengthy and sharp controversy in *The Times* between him and a writer who signed himself Scrutator. Müller did not underrate either the knowledge or the controversial ability of Scrutator. Indeed, he wrote at the beginning of his fifth letter, 'When I ventured to accept the first challenge of Scrutator, it was not from any presumptuous confidence that I should be able to withstand the arguments of one of the most powerful athletes of our time.' This statement was made under the belief that Gladstone was the inspirer of Scrutator.

After Max Müller's death, Mrs Max Müller in her biography repeated all this, and in a letter to *The Times*, published on February 3, 1903, Scrutator revealed himself to be the Rev. Malcolm McColl; and also said that long after the controversy both he and Gladstone had informed Müller about this. To clear up the matter, he wrote: 'Will you kindly allow me to say emphatically, and once for all, that Mr. Gladstone was as ignorant as the rest of the world of the identity of Scrutator.' Mr McColl repeated his view that Prussia had brought about the war deliberately from aggressive designs against France. After praising the Berlin correspondent who at that time was warning England against the similar designs of Germany against England, he hoped that these warnings would be heeded.

Even without knowing the real identity of Scrutator, Max Müller was pleased to find that the controversy had not lessened Gladstone's friendly feelings towards himself. In fact, Müller was invited to Hawarden expressly to discuss the war and the prospective peace. He arrived there on December 9, and stayed till the afternoon of the 12th. There he found the American General Burnside as well. He was one of the commanders of the Unionist armies in the Civil War, and it was from his ample side whiskers that the word side-burns has come to us. He, as Müller reported to his wife, 'told Gladstone some useful truths'.

Müller was fully aware of the sympathies and attitude of Gladstone. Even in October he had written to Abeken that Gladstone's sympathies were more Latin than Teutonic.

In his letter of the 13th he elaborated the theme further: 'As I told you before, Gladstone's sympathies are by no means for Germany, neither is he familiar with the German language or literature, or the German character or ways; also the French refugees have taken great hold on him. He distrusts Germany, especially Prussia.' Still Max Müller thought that he could be persuaded, once the justice of the German claims could be brought home to him. Then, Müller thought, Gladstone would be loyal to his perceptions.

But Gladstone put Müller on the most unfavourable ground. The conversation turned mainly on the future of Alsace-Lorraine. Here Müller himself had private mental reservations. He had informed Stanley in his letter of August 30 that he felt it was a misfortune that the provinces should be demanded by Germany. But he added sadly: 'The so-called logic of facts makes it almost impossible not to demand them.' It was on this 'logic of facts' that he now took his stand when answering Gladstone, putting forward the plea of strategical necessity.

Gladstone at once replied that the greatest mistakes of the statesmen of his time lay in giving greater consideration to physical than to moral powers, and that the realization of German wishes would become a misfortune for Germany. Max Müller could only reply that Germany had the right to decide, and would have to bear the responsibility and the consequences. In his anticipation Gladstone was certainly right. On the other hand, Müller showed himself to be prescient on the practical plane. He threw in the hint that hostile relations between Germany and England would force the former to found a formidable navy. As Müller admitted, the discussion accomplished nothing, but the participants certainly parted friends.

Between the two peoples, on the contrary, unfriendliness grew. German public opinion and the German press were very hostile and at times abusive towards England. Gladstone's attitude was well known there, and the British policy in the war was attributed largely to his influence.

For his efforts to make the British people understand the German case, Bismarck himself thanked Müller through Abeken, who wrote: 'First my thanks for what you have done and are doing for Germany, for our holy cause! This expression of gratitude is not from me alone. I write in the name of Count Bismarck, who spoke to me only yesterday with a full and thankful recognition of your great and influential activity during this time, which he has heard through newspapers. He rejoiced to have such an ally.' Georgina Müller got the Cross of Merit for Ladies from the German Emperor for her work for the wounded.

Looking back on Max Müller's involvement in the Franco-Prussian War, one finds it unnecessary to pronounce a judgement on his view that Germany was fighting an unprovoked defensive war. Even now historians are not in agreement either about the immediate or the basic responsibility, and the more cautious of them apportion the blame evenly. Bismarck himself spoilt the case for German innocence by taking credit in later years for having 'played the part of a toreador and trailed his coat to make the French bull charge'.

What is forgotten is that there are basic political situations which make wars inevitable between certain nations, and the immediate occasions are like the windings of a river flowing into the sea. The plain fact was that France had held a dominant position in Europe since the seventeenth century, and Germany was now trying to acquire this for herself. In a poultry run the pecking order is established easily and almost instinctively. But men do not have that good sense, either individually or collectively.

If this fundamental aspiration of Germany, which was consistent with her new power, had brought her into conflict with France, the same basic situation promised a prospective conflict with Great Britain, whose traditional policy was to keep the first power in Europe in check. It has now to be recognized that the Franco-Prussian War was the watershed across which the British people moved from their opposition to one Continental Power to their opposition to another. The causes of the First World War, and *a fortiori* of the Second, have to be traced back to the situation created by the war between Germany and France in 1870. So Max Muller's anxieties about the consequences of the Anglo-German misunderstanding that was arising out of this war were fully justified.

The same passionate eagerness for maintaining or resuscitating Anglo-German friendship, which was already gone, made Max Müller join in his last political controversy only a few months before his death, when his physical strength was reduced to its lowest. It was over the Boer War, during which the whole Continent and more especially Germany displayed a fierce emotional hostility towards Great Britain. On this occasion Germany could take up the moral position of Great Britain in 1870 with greater plausibility, and represent her as a Great Power which was brutally suppressing the independence of two small and weak republics.

This Müller would not admit, and he thought it was his duty to demonstrate the rightness of the British action in the same way as he had tried to show that of Germany in 1870. In the summer of 1899 he fell very ill, and the illness continued well into the autumn. Even so he followed the course of events with attention, and by the beginning of September had become convinced that a conflict was unavoidable. On September 8, when his doctors had given up all hope for him, he wrote to his son that he had a voice in the matter too, and drew his attention to the possibility of war: 'Today is an ominous day, war or peace, and I am afraid it must be war, and all about the definition of a word, sovereignty.' Then he added: 'I want rest, but must take care not to indulge too much in it. In fact . . . I do not mean to lay down my arms as yet. True, I am growing thin, and very yellow. Many things are wrong, yet every morning after a good night I feel as if nothing was the matter with me.'

A few days after the war had begun, on October 29, he wrote again to his son: 'That horrible war makes me feel very unhappy— but now it cannot be helped, and the more it is fought out, the better. I still hope that before the appearance of England's real power, the Boers and South Africa may collapse. Is it not a mistake that England has now no foreign newspapers in her pay? She had formerly, but not now. They do little good, but they can prevent mischief.'

He thought too that British generalship was poor, and the soldiers would not fight well under such leadership. That was before Lord Roberts and Lord Kitchener had gone to South Africa. It must not be imagined from all this that Max Müller was a warmonger. Even when he was trying to prove that Great Britain had the right to subjugate the Boer republics, he raised the question: 'Was the war justified? I, in my own heart, am convinced that no war is ever justified, even when it seems inevitable.'

He had no fear that Britain would not win the war. But the aggravation of the already existing Anglo-German misunderstanding was causing him great worry. He wrote to his friend Prince Christian on January 2, 1900: 'The Germans do not indeed think of sending any Pomeranians to help Kruger, but the entire misunderstanding of the position of England is very grievous. It was different in the old times, but even England's old friends in Germany are misled. How much I should like to step in, but my bodily strength fails me.'

The Prince suggested that he should write in some serious German magazine, and Max Müller sent an article to the *Deutsche Rundschau* of which he was an old contributor. But the Editor could not publish the article. However, afterwards another German paper, *Deutsche Revue*, published the piece. At once there was an outcry against Müller in Germany, and the really solid attack on his position being made by the German historian Mommsen, who was a friend of his. Müller wrote a second article as answer to Mommsen's rejoinder, and Mommsen again replied. This controversy ended in April 1900. In addition Max Müller contributed an article to the American magazine *Forum* explaining the causes of the anti-English feeling in Germany.

In England Müller's articles were very much appreciated, and Lord Salisbury wrote the following note in his own hand:

20 Arlington Street.
S.W.

Mr. Barrington,
This is an excellent statement. Please tell the Professor how much I was impressed by it.

S. Ap. 1. 1900

But in Germany there was fury, and it was only from the fury that

Max Müller could guess that his arguments had gone home. In one letter he was even threatened with the gallows should he venture to show himself in Germany. But even apart from such extreme outbursts, it would seem that sober opinion in Germany regretted Max Müller's advocacy of the British cause. After his death a German scholar and publicist, Karl Blind, a friend of his too, wrote in the May (1901) number of the *Westminster Review* that deep regret was universally felt in Germany when Müller set his face against the cause of the South African Republics: 'It is a pity that the cloud of obloquy which thus suddenly overshadowed his name should have dimmed the lustre of his renown near the very end of his laborious life.'

This may be one of the reasons why his name was forgotten in Germany. But if Max Müller courted all this unpopularity, it was in obedience to his conviction that peace in the world could be maintained in the future only through friendship between Great Britain, Germany and America. However, it must be recognized that in regard to the true character of the Boer War Mommsen was more correct. He observed in his reply to Müller:

> The Transvaal war is one of the strangest, as well as one of the saddest, known to history. The old, obstinate, religious-political fanaticism is struggling, in this forgotten and lost remnant of the Cape-Dutch, with modern civilization, based on a not less fanatical desire of exploiting the whole world . . . Two views of the world are here in conflict—the battle is being waged, so to speak, between the 16th and 20th centuries.

What Mommsen regarded as unconvincing was the legalistic justification of the war, about which there was no disagreement between him and Müller. The final outcome has also shown that Max Müller's arguments did not touch the heart of the matter. The position of Great Britain in relation to the European colonists in South Africa could not be worse today if the Boer War had not been fought. It is Krugerism which has won, and all the optimism created by the reconciliatory measures taken from 1908 onwards has been proved to be unfounded. The Dutch have even won over the British in the Cape Province and Natal. That has happened because the Dutch clung to a living idea with faith. The British standpoint was merely well intentioned, and had no genuine ideological strength behind it. That is not realized even now by the British people in their thinking about South Africa.

Nevertheless, Max Müller clung to his idea till the very end of his life in spite of all the signs against him. In his article in the *Deutsche Revue* he wrote: 'Germans, instead of looking for true blood relations and allies for the future in England and America, have sought for them in France and Russia. They may look for a long time. I hope they will discover, before it is too late, that blood is thicker than ink, and that the Saxons of Germany, England and America are the true, manly and faithful allies in all struggles for freedom in the future as in the past.'

In the American magazine *Forum* also he wrote:

The German and English characters form complements of each other. Why not admire what is good in Germany and what is good in England? . . . If Germany, wherever she turns in her colonial expansion, finds ground occupied by England this is, no doubt, provoking, but it cannot be helped now. Property is property . . . A war of words between the two countries seems harmless enough, but a real war would be so terrible that humanity shudders at the very mention of it.

Fortunately, he did not live to see that war.

Though Max Müller found any opening for joining in a political discussion irresistible, he seems always to have had a feeling that such controversies were almost futile. During the Franco-Prussian War he had written to Gladstone: 'We must take men as they are, and we must take nations as they are; a nation flushed with victory and crushed by grief is not like a nation in its right mind. It is with nations as with individuals.'

All that can be said in explanation of the intellectual who involves himself with political matters is that in the first place he is driven by the innate impulse of man the political animal; and in so far as he is a sentient being, it becomes a case of conscience with him.

Not even this tenuous plea can be put forward to justify scholarly controversies. They are always barren and futile, often ill-tempered and unmannerly, at times scurrilous. Only those who do not follow such controversies and their results can imagine that knowledge is advanced by them. Max Müller wrote in 1875, when he opened the only scholarly duel of his life: 'I am not one of those who believe that truth is much advanced by public controversy, and I have carefully eschewed it during the whole of my literary career.'

There can be no doubt that he was right in this view. Scholars are scarcely ever convinced by the opinions of other scholars working

9*

in their field. Max Müller himself wrote that he had considered
the objections of his critics but had been confirmed by them in his
conclusions. At all events he said to some of his distinguished
opponents, as he did to Mommsen: 'Let us agree to differ.' So he
wrote to Romanes in 1891: 'I believe we both care far more for
what is right, than for *who* is right . . . Facts and correct deductions
from facts, are all we ought to care for; who discovered them and
who made them is of very little consequence. Yet I know from
experience that there are but few who would be so completely above
all personal feelings as you have shown yourself to be.'

He knew it only too well, and was taking the most charitable view
of scholarly disagreements. These are due in the first instance to
dogmatism, which will ignore facts deliberately when they are not
consistent with the dogmatic view; and beyond dogmatism stands
self-conceit and jealousy, which make the disputants descend to
personalities. When a scholar gets hardened in his animosities he
behaves like a gladiator or a prize-fighter, or rather worse because
he is not exposed to any physical punishment. But Max Müller,
even when he had to be severe on the arguments of his opponents,
never indulged in discourtesy, far less abuse. He even scrupulously
avoided expressing an opinion when it might be attributed to personal motives.

It was not however Max Müller's fate to be spared scholarly
attacks, and some of the worst kind, in spite of his disapproval of
them. These continued over more than thirty years during his life,
and were carried on even after his death. They came from a single
source, partly inspired from another. The direct source was the
American Sanskritist, William Dwight Whitney of Yale, and behind him stood a clique of German Sanskritists. Scholars who do
not agree in their positive views generally agree in their animosities.
The feud of Whitney against Max Müller was almost like an in-
herited Corsican vendetta.

But the immediate occasion of this disagreeable controversy was
furnished by a very pleasant expression of difference between two
learned men. They were Darwin and Max Müller. An account has
been given in a previous chapter of Max Müller's view that Darwin's theory of evolution could not be extended to explain the
origin of language. The *pooh-pooh theory*, as it was popularly called,
which Darwin had originated under the influence of his friend
H. Wedgwood, the author of the *Etymological Dictionary of the*

English Language, could not, according to Müller, account for human speech.

Early in 1873 Max Müller decided publicly to express his dissent to Darwin's theory, and in March he gave a series of lectures at the Royal Institution entitled *Mr Darwin's Philosophy of Language*. These were printed in the May, June and July issues of *Fraser's Magazine*. Max Müller sent the pamphlet to Darwin on June 29 and expressed the hope that he would accept the remarks in it 'as what they were intended to be—an open statement of the difficulties which a student of language feels when called upon to explain the languages of man, such as he finds them, as the possible development of what has been called the language of animals'. He also assured Darwin that he was one of his diligent readers and sincere admirers.

On July 3 Darwin replied with equal courtesy and frankness:

> As far as language is concerned, I am not worthy to be your adversary, as I know extremely little about it, and that little learnt from very few books. I should have been glad to have avoided the whole subject, but was compelled to take it up as well as I could. He who is fully convinced, as I am, that man is descended from some lower animal, is almost forced to believe *a priori* that articulate language has been developed from inarticulate cries; and he is therefore hardly a fair judge of the arguments opposed to this belief.

Later Müller and Darwin met. He was taken to Down, Darwin's house in Kent, by Sir John Lubbock, later Lord Avebury, and in his autobiographical reminiscences Müller said that there were few episodes in his life which he valued more. I shall quote the whole account from *Auld Lang Syne*, vol. I, which in the copy of the book I am using bears corrections in his own hand. He wrote:

> I need not describe the simplicity of his house and the grandeur of the man who had lived and worked in it for so many years. Darwin gave me a hearty welcome, showed me his garden and his flowers, and then took me into his study, and standing leaning against his desk began to examine me. He said at once that personally he was quite ignorant of the science of language, and had taken his facts and opinions chiefly from his friend, Mr Wedgwood. I had been warned that Darwin could not carry on a serious discussion for more than about ten minutes or a quarter of an hour, as it always brought on his life-long complaint of sickness. I therefore put before him in the shortest way possible the

difficulties which prevented me from accepting the theory of animals forming a language out of interjections and sounds of nature. I laid stress on the fact that no animal, except the human animal, had ever made a step towards generalization of percepts, and I gave him a few illustrations of how our words for one to ten, for father, mother, sun and moon had really and historically been evolved. That man thus formed a real anomaly in the growth of the animal kingdom, as conceived by him, I fully admitted; but it was impossible for me to ignore facts, and language in its true meaning has always been to my mind a fact that could not be wiped away by argument, as little as the Himalayas could be wiped away with a silk handkerchief even in millions of years. He listened most attentively, he asked questions, but raised no serious objections. Before he shook hands and left me, he said in the kindest way, 'You are a dangerous man.' I ventured to reply, 'There can be no danger in our search for truth,' and he left the room.

Max Müller also sent to Darwin his subsequent controversial pieces, and though in them there were strong criticisms of Darwin's theory the latter never took offence. To the last pamphlet that Müller sent him, Darwin sent the following characteristic reply:

'Down, Beckenham, Kent
15th October, 1875

My dear Sir,
    I am greatly obliged to you for so kindly sending me your essay *In Self-defence*, which I am sure will interest me much. With respect to our differences, though some of your remarks have been rather stinging, they have all been made so gracefully, I declare that I am like the man in the story who boasted that he had been soundly horsewhipped by a Duke.

Pray believe me,
Yours very sincerely,
CHARLES DARWIN

Anything more to the credit of two great minds in their disagreement over a scientific question cannot be imagined. Yet this balance of mind was completely absent in its offshoot; in the course of which Darwin's son George forced Müller into his only open controversy with another scholar, Whitney.

George Darwin was not very straightforward in defending his father in the *Contemporary Review*, for instead of calling his article a reply to Müller and relying on his own arguments he gave it the deceptive title of 'Professor Whitney on the *Origin of Language*', and leaned heavily on the American scholar. The article was substantially a dishing out in England of Whitney's attacks on Max Müller in America. So Müller did not read the piece until a friend told him about it.

Max Müller in his reply to George Darwin in the *Contemporary Review* (November 1874) was very severe on Whitney, and Whitney then published another intemperate attack. This provoked Müller so much that he gave up his wise resolution to take no notice of Whitney's attacks (which had been going on for more than a decade), nor to take up any of his frequent challenges, and came out with a long pamphlet of seventy-seven pages, to which he gave the title *In Self-defence.*

However, Müller put forward a practical suggestion, which was to place the differences before a panel of three scholars who were to be chosen by Whitney from his best friends who were also *Professores ordinarii* in any English, German, French or Italian university. He also promised to abide by their judgement unreservedly. He then set forth twenty points as to simple matters of fact which he regarded as the principal bones of contention between himself and Whitney. They were indeed bones, and very bare ones too, as will be seen from the selection of five that I give. The numbers are Müller's.

1. Whether the Latin of the inscription on the Duilian Column represents the Latin as spoken in 263 B.C.
2. Whether *Ahura-Mazda* can be rendered by 'the mighty spirit'.
3. Whether *sarvanama* in Sanskrit means 'name of everything'.
14. Whether in saying that the soft consonants can be intonated, I could have meant that they may or may not be intonated.
18. Whether E. Burnouf has written two or three bulky volumes on the *Avesta*, or only one.

Publicly Whitney took no notice of the proposal for arbitration. It is impossible to explain the ferocity of Whitney on any scholarly grounds. The American journalist Moncure Conway, who was a friend of both, felt very distressed by this misunderstanding. He tried to mediate and bring about a reconciliation. He said that when leaving England to visit the United States for a few months he met Max Müller and discussed his intention with him. Müller authorized him to put the proposal for arbitration personally to Whitney, which Conway did. But Whitney was not willing, and Conway was not able to discover exactly why. Nothing further came out of his efforts.

Whitney took his revenge on Max Müller in a review of Müller's edition of the *Rig-Veda*, which had been completed in 1874. This review, published in *The New Englander* for October, 1876, proclaimed Aufrecht's edition as the real publication of the *Veda* and added that 'nothing can take away from this scholar the chief honour of being the editor of the *Veda*'. As to Max Müller, he observed, apart from what he had done in publishing the commentary of Sayana, 'he has yet to link his name with the *Rig-Veda* itself by any special tie which will bear testing'. Then he concluded:

> He has had his reward. No man was ever before so lavishly paid, in money and in fame, for even the most unexceptionable performance of such a task. For personal gratitude in addition, there is not the slightest call. If Müller had never put hand to the *Veda*, his fellow-students would have had the material they needed perhaps ten years earlier, and Vedic study would be at the present moment proportionately advanced.

Not satisfied with this, Whitney added a footnote which ran: 'The original honorarium, of about £500 a volume, is well-nigh or quite unprecedented in the history of purely scholarly enterprises; and the grounds on which the final additional gift of £2,000 was bestowed have never been made public.'

One wonders whether Whitney was conscious that in all this he was providing a self-revelation not less frank than Rousseau's deliberate *Confessions*.

He continued his attacks, and in 1892 published a violent one on a new edition of Max Müller's *Science of Language*. Upon this Max Müller wrote to a friend who had criticized Whitney:

> I feel very grateful for what you said about Whitney. I do not know whether you have followed his raids from the first. I thought at first he was honest and sincere, and took the trouble to answer him in a long paper, *In Self-Defence* . . . He went on sending me articles, anonymous or signed; in fact, he placed himself outside the pale of literary criticism. As without losing all self-respect, I could not answer him, I have made it a rule for at least fifteen years never to read his invectives.

Whitney died in 1894, and Max Müller had a respite for a few years before his own death.

But Whitney bequeathed his vendetta. When Max Müller died, in its obituary notice the New York *Nation* revived Whitney's rejection of the claim of Max Müller to be the editor of the *Rig-Veda*, and wrote: 'What Max Müller constantly proclaimed to be his own great work, the edition of the *Rig-Veda*, was in reality not his at all . . . A German scholar did the work, and Müller appropriated the credit for it.'

In great distress Mrs Müller wrote to the well-known Sanskrit scholars who had known her husband or collaborated with him, and after obtaining their opinion set down their version of the matter. 'Had there been any truth in the accusation its discovery would not have been left to an anonymous accuser in America, nor its exposure reserved until after Max Müller's death.'

This so infuriated the writer in the *Nation* that when reviewing Mrs Müller's biography of her husband he repeated the statements in a more offensive and cruel manner. He said that there was no due acknowledgement from Max Müller of the help received from his assistants, and gave his version of the facts in the following words:

> Müller was hired to bring out the *Rig-Veda*. A part of the work had already been done by Rosen. This part of the text, together with the commentary, Müller brought out without Aufrecht's assistance. But Müller had already grown weary of the scholarly toil. He spoke of it as slavery, and said that, in his opinion, life was meant for more than the drudgery of collating manuscripts. So, for part of the next volume and for all of the third volume, he hired Aufrecht to do his work for him, though it was just the work he himself had been hired to do.

There was more in this vein.

How Max Müller worked on the *Rig-Veda* and what help he received, as well as his acknowledgements to Aufrecht and his other helpers, has been described in a previous chapter.

Perhaps from the point of view of a specialist in Sanskrit scholarship the opinion which Cowell expressed to Mrs Müller was the most balanced. Cowell knew Max Müller well, and was then Professor of Sanskrit at Cambridge. He wrote:

> My dear Mrs Max Müller,
> I sympathize with you most sincerely in what you say—my doubt is whether it would be well to rouse up again old feelings of animosity

which the lapse of years has very much thrown into oblivion. Professor Whitney was the main leader in those attacks; and since he passed away we have heard hardly any allusion to them. I hardly think it is right to consider the edition of *Rig-Veda* your husband's pre-eminent work, surely such books as his *History of Ancient Sanskrit Literature* and other similar, works show more clearly his real genius and original powers. The text of the *Rig-Veda* has been kept so religiously in the MSS that it was a very easy task to edit it. The Commentary which fills so much of Max Muller's edition and which I and many Sanskritists prize so highly, was an especial object of attack to Whitney and most of the representatives of his school. Max Müller proved that he thoroughly understood that difficult commentary by the masterly way in which he edited alone the whole of Vol. I and the great part of Vol. II. After that he left part of the labour of collation etc. to his younger co-adjutors, while he himself thus gained some leisure for researches into other fields of Sanskrit literature. He was doing far better service to the Sanskrit cause by interesting such a wide circle of readers by his enthusiastic lectures and disquisitions, expressed in his singularly beautiful English style, than he would have done if he had spent the years in toiling alone to complete the text of Sayana's Commentary.

You will thus see that I look on the great edition of the *Rig-Veda* as only one part of the wide field of Max Müller's energy, and by no means the part which showed his powers at their highest point . . .

I hope this letter will not grieve you. I hope you will think it quietly over.

Nothing could be more sensible, if Max Müller's work on the *Rig-Veda* were only for fellow-scholars. But it was not. He edited it to make it widely known both in the West and the East, and with the more practical motive of influencing the religious life of contemporary Hindus. So far as popularization was concerned he fully succeeded, and he also did for Hindus what no other scholar had ever accomplished. From the very first the value of his edition was recognized in India. Among the notable Hindus to do so was Raja Radhakanta Deb, a Bengali nobleman, patron of Sanskrit scholarship and himself the editor of a new Sanskrit encyclopaedia and dictionary, and a leader of orthodox Hindus in Bengal. On receiving the first volume, he wrote a long letter of appreciation to Max Müller in which among many other things he said: 'Your labours will furnish the Vaidik Pandits with a complete collection of the holy *Samhita* of the first *Veda* only detached portions of which are to be found in the possession of a few of them.'

He wrote again when the second volume was also sent to him: 'By successfully embarking on such an arduous undertaking, you have done to the Hindus an inestimable benefit, supplying them with a correct and superb edition of their Holy scriptures. Accept therefore my most grateful and sincere thanks, which, in common with my countrymen, I owe to you.'

After the publication of the first three volumes Dr Martin Haug, who was at Poona, informed Müller how a great assembly of Brahmin pundits there had made use of them to correct their own MSS. They would not themselves touch the volumes, because the idea had got abroad in India that the ink used in printing them had cow's blood in it and so had become impure. They had Müller's text read to them, and pronounced the judgement: 'This edition must be written by a great Pundit versed in the *Vedas* and Sastras.'

Finally, when the whole work was published, one of the associations of the new monotheistic Hindus formally thanked Müller and wrote: 'By publishing the *Rig-Veda* at a time when Vedic learning has, by some sad fatality, become almost extinct in the land of its birth, you have conferred a boon upon us Hindus, for which we cannot but be eternally grateful.' Last of all I shall translate from Bengali the public tribute which Swami Vivekananda, leader of the new Hindu revivalist movement in Bengal, paid to Max Müller in one of his books. He wrote: 'Professor Max Müller is the leading figure among Western Sanskrit scholars. The *Rig-Veda*, upon which nobody could set his eyes as a whole, has now been beautifully printed, and can be read by the general public, as a result of an enormous expenditure on the part of the East India Company and years of labour on the part of the Professor.'

The fact remains that Max Müller's text was the only one for decades in which modern Indians could read or see their oldest scripture. That was why, after the exhaustion of the first volume and expected exhaustion of the others of the first edition, when the Secretary of State for India would not sanction the money for reprinting the whole work, an Indian Prince came forward to contribute more than £4,000 for a complete and revised second edition.

In his preface to the first volume of this second edition, Max Müller wrote:

The Members of the India Council, however, took a different view from that taken by their predecessors, the Directors of the old East

India Company. While the Directors on the advice of the greatest Sanskrit scholar of the time, Professor H. H. Wilson, their illustrious Librarian, declared that 'the publication of so important and interesting a work as the *editio princeps* of the *Rig-Veda* was in a peculiar manner deserving of the patronage of the East India Company, connected as it is with the early religion, history, and language of the great body of their Indian subjects', the Literary Committee of the India Council, acting on somewhat different advice, declined my offer of publishing a new edition of the *Rig-Veda*, though a strong desire for it had been expressed by scholars both in India and Europe, and though my gratuitous services were placed at their disposal.

Even this involved Müller in an unpleasant controversy with a fellow-Sanskritist, Professor Boehtlingk of St Petersburg, who had never forgiven him for refusing to go to that city to work under him. In 1891, in a pamphlet attacking him as a mythologist, he said that what Müller had written about the refusal of the India Office to bear the cost of the second edition was *pure invention*.

A general moral seems to be justified by all scholarly controversies: scholars themselves should avoid them, and the layman should ignore them.

Chapter 2

LIFE, LOVE AND DEATH

FROM all the accounts that Max Müller gave of his intellectual aims, methods and work it could be seen that he was less a scholar in the strict sense of the word than an intellectual, and the difference is basic. It is that which distinguishes a painter or sculptor from a craftsman. What then is an intellectual? An intellectual is a man or woman who applies his intellectual faculties to understanding and interpreting the world around him in any or all its aspects. As a result of study, observation or experiment, he formulates conclusions which he believes to be true and communicates his ideas to his fellow-men with a view to influencing their minds, lives and actions.

But within this definition, broadly speaking, intellectuals fall into two classes. The first type is *des cérébraux pur sang*; and the second, those whose intellectual activity is driven by an emotional motive power, principally love, but at times even by its opposite, hatred.

'Great thoughts come from the heart,' said Vauvenargues, and even impersonal scientific thought dealing with the world of matter does not furnish any exception. Pasteur's scientific researches were inspired by compassion.

Max Müller belonged to this type, just as his respected and elder contemporary, Darwin, belonged to the other type. Müller was naturally endowed with an immense zest for life, and also with an overmastering impulse to love. He believed the two to be connected in some way, and at the very end of his life wrote to his son:

You certainly have grown older and more serious—no wonder, considering what you have had to go through. You'll understand now my old motto, *Das Leben ist ernst* [Life is earnest], though that does not prevent us from enjoying what can be enjoyed. I hope you would grow very fond of somebody or something—that is after all the secret of enjoying life, call it a hobby or some passion, even a passion for statistics or something of the kind, but a passion, Otherwise, life becomes humdrum. Dressing and washing in the morning and undressing at night—one gets so tired of it.

What suffering Max Müller inflicted on himself by falling in love at first sight has already been described. But when at last he got married he could have been expected to live happily ever afterwards. He could not and did not, however, for love brings the idea of death ever near to life, and even when it is not expected it seems to lie in ambush everywhere.

'All men are under a sentence of death, with indefinite reprieves', said Victor Hugo. As a rule, however, men are able to forget that this sentence is the most certain thing in life. The spectacle of death always carries this anaesthetic with it. There is nothing wrong in this reaction so long as men live and die like animals, which basically they are. But it becomes contemptible when it is aired as a superior moral attitude.

As soon as man became conscious of his existence and capable of evaluating it, he also felt that living was meaningless unless he could reconcile it with death. One of the oldest and most sublime of the Hindu religious utterances is that which says: 'What should I do with anything which does not make me indestructible?' The answer given so far has been an amazing illusion: belief in the continuation of individual life after death.

This consolation has been enough in most circumstances, for basically men live on by virtue of a biological impulse. But when one human being has loved another so much that he or she has ceased to be self-reliant in living, the death of the loved one mortally wounds that biological urge to live. And that wound is most grievous when a child dies, for here two biological forces clash, the one which makes us cling to our own life and the other which makes us love our children. When this happens even the strong and the brave can only limp through life. They are never able to recover their faith in earthly life. Even when they have an unwavering faith in an afterlife, they cannot explain why they should have received this blow.

This terrible calamity of living on, crippled by death, befell Max Müller when he lost his eldest daughter in 1876 when she was only sixteen years old. In her biography Mrs Max Müller wrote: 'He never entirely recovered from this loss: the spring, the joy of life was gone. He suffered severely, and it was months before he could at all rouse himself and take up work again.' But she did not describe what his suffering really was. He set that down in a diary, kept over seven years on 486 folios. To read this volume among the papers left by Max Müller is a harrowing experience.

However, he was familiar with the idea of death from his child-hood on account of the early death of his father. After that he also saw many relatives die, and on many occasions recorded his thoughts and feelings about death. More intimately the idea of death came home to him when a year after his marriage his wife lay very near to death for some days after the birth of her first child. On December 20 the child was born, and for two days the doctors were without any hope of saving the mother. Even before this she was very unwell, causing Müller very great anxiety. So on December 10 he wrote to Miss Grenfell: 'If anything should happen to her now, our Christmas will be a very sad time! I try to keep up my spirits, but it is hard work: yet I feel that suffering with her is worth more than all the happiness of the world with others. I pray to God that it may all pass over, but if it must be, we both feel that it is meant as a whole-some trial, and that we must thank God for what He gives and what He takes from us.'

He described his state of mind when his wife was sufficiently recovered, and wrote on February 6, 1861:

Darling baby . . . I hardly dare to call her ours as yet, and yet what can we call ours if God did not vouchsafe it to us from day to day? And yet it is so difficult to give oneself up entirely to Him, to trust everything to His Love and Wisdom. I thought I could say 'Thy will be done', but when you were so ill I found I could not—my own will struggled against His will—I prayed as we ought not to pray—and yet He heard me. My darling, it is so difficult not to grow very fond of this life and all its happiness—but the more we love it, the more we suffer, for we know we must leave it and it must all pass away. Does love pass away, too? I cannot believe it.

Some months later he also wrote to Palgrave about his rebellious mood. Palgrave's father had died, and he wrote:

I know from experience that in the presence of great grief I have nothing to say, and for a loss like yours there is no comfort till we can say by ourselves, 'Thy will be done'. I remember but one time in my whole life when I could not say that . . . when my wife, whom I had loved for six years without the faintest hope of ever calling her my wife, when she, after one year of a blessed life, was for two days given up as hope-less by the doctors, then I broke down, and I could not say, 'Thy will be done'.

Whenever Max Müller heard of the death of someone who was a friend or relative, and more especially when parents lost a child, he tried, in offering his consolation, to understand or rather come to terms with death. But he could only fall back on faith. So, when he heard of the death of his sister Auguste's little son, who was his godson, he wrote to his mother:

> Sorrow is necessary and good for men; one learns to understand that each joy must be indemnified by suffering, that each new tie which knits our hearts to this life must be loosed again, and the tighter and the closer it was knit, the keener the pain of loosening it. Should we then attach our hearts to nothing, and pass quietly and unsympathetically through this world, as if we had nothing to do with it? We neither could nor ought to act so. Nature itself knits the first tie between parents and children, and new ties through our whole life. We are not here for reward, for the enjoyment of undisturbed peace, or from mere accident, but for trial, for improvement, perhaps for punishment; for the only union which can ensure the happiness of men, the union between our self and God's self, is broken, or at least obscured, by our birth, and the highest object of our life is to find this bond again, to remain ever conscious of it, and hold fast to it in life and death.

Müller wrote this when he was only twenty-five.

At the age of forty-three when he was the father of four children, three daughters and one son, he wrote in a reconciled vein on the occasion of another bereavement of his sister, the death this time of a daughter. He observed to his wife: 'Krug [his brother-in-law] speaks so freely about those who are no more; I can only listen, for what can one say? Our view of death is wrong, no doubt, because our view of life is wrong.'

He thought his happiness in his family was so great that he could neither wish nor ask for more. Then he remarked: 'I should like to sit quiet, to rest and be thankful, not to move, lest something should move and fall.'

Early in 1868 he lost his only sister Auguste, and after getting a letter from his mother wrote to his wife: 'Now that she is gone, all those pleasant recollections ... which constantly pass through one's mind are altogether changed, all life and reality taken out of them; one's own life brought more clearly before one's mind, as what it really is, a short stay in a foreign land.'

Again he reverts to their own life with the same premonition:

'There is still so much left us, so much to be happy and thankful
for; and yet here, too, the thought always rushes across one's
brightest hours, it cannot last.' A fear of happiness seems to have
been growing on him, for a month later he again wrote to his wife:
'It is true that I have plenty of happiness, but great happiness makes
one think so often that it cannot last, and that one will some day
have to give up all to which one's heart clings . . . But at the same
time we can thankfully enjoy all that God gives, and few have more
reason to say this than I.'

Six years later, after visiting the grave of his sister-in-law
Charlotte, he wrote to his wife: 'By a grave one learns what life
really is, that it is not here but elsewhere; that this is the exile, and
there is our home. As we grow older the train of life goes faster and
faster, those with whom we travelled together step out from station
to station, and our own station, too, will soon be reached.'

These are only a few of the reflections on death which Max
Müller set down even before he suffered any bereavement in his
own immediate family. He could never forget death. None the less,
his natural vitality enabled him to carry on a post-marital love
affair with almost childlike gusto, in which he could be as playful
as he was passionate. For instance, three years after his marriage,
when he was conducting an examination for the Civil Service Com-
missioners in London, he wrote to his wife:

> I have not much time, my dear wifey, and I am sitting surrounded by
> sixty candidates, all writing Sanskrit as hard as ever they can—but I
> can send you a few lines just to shake hands with you or to send you a
> loving kiss. It is quite miserable to be away from you, and I feel hardly
> myself when I am away from you. We have grown into one as much as
> two souls ever can, and I feel when I am with you that there is nothing
> more to wish for, that life is perfect. May God let us enjoy His happi-
> ness for many years.

He also showed his capacity for love by being willing to spend
money on her without being compelled to do so by being black-
mailed by the turning of her back on him in bed, in the manner of
the normal Hindu wife who believes that in married life money or
gold, silk, and fine cotton, are the outward signs of an inward grace.
A Maltese lace shawl for the 'dear wifey' at ten pounds, a satin gown,
pins and jewellery are mentioned in Müller's letters. There are also
two unusual communications after more than nine years of marriage.

'I have ordered for you,' he writes on January 31, 1869, '24 pint bottles of champagne from London. I thought small bottles would be better for your small meals—they will arrive tomorrow afternoon or Tuesday morning. Is there anything else I can send you, for with all your hard work, I feel sure that you want support?'

He wrote again three days later: 'I am so glad to hear that you are better. Would it not be better to ask Seymour to let you have a dozen of his port and pay him for it? I have no port here, and if I write to London it will take several days before it settled again and is fit to drink. If you cannot get any port, the best thing would be to write to the Civil Service.'

Two days later he tells about a different kind of order: 'I also want to order a carpet for your bedroom. The green carpet turned out very bad, it is tapestry, not Brussels—so I had one of those put down in the nursery, and the other put away. I have had all the boards taken up and relaid . . . The curtains will look very well, but the old chintz would not do.'

Mrs Max Müller liked the social life of the class from which she came, and at times she appears to have been away from home. These absences, as well as Max Müller's when he travelled abroad, gave him the opportunity to write letters to his wife, which are pre-served in five volumes. They give a picture of the sunshine and showers in their married life, the sadness being as tender as the gaiety, with the religious note always coming up to the dominant level, as when he wrote: 'I am yours as you are mine. It is not that you own me or I own you—we were given to each other by Him who made all things—you are mine by Divine right as I am yours. Though many people talk of Divine right and know not what they mean, My own beloved Soul, I know it, and sometimes feel as if I live with you in heaven and in full eternity.'

Müller on his part hated social life as conventionally understood, especially in London. So he wrote to his wife on July 16, 1864: 'I should not like to live in London, no, not for much money,—this noise, this skirmish, this dining out and gossiping, this trying to out-do each other in pretence and conceit, is quite sickening.'

Again, learning of the death of Dickens, he wrote: 'Poor Charles Dickens! It is a great loss—but I believe his life was not happy in spite of all his brilliant success. They call him vulgar, but in his abstaining from mixing in what people call good society, I think he showed the true nobility of his soul. I confess I never see so much vulgarity of soul as among that good society with its insolence of wealth and pride of millinery.'

And in 1890 he wrote: 'It is the most horrible invention, what is called Society, and is really no society at all, but simply make-believe, stupidity, and vanity. Life is one thing, society another—but society eats up life.'

He particularly disliked the large dinner parties in London, and preferred a small party of four to six guests. To the end of his life he received many distinguished guests in his own house at Oxford, and from all parts of the world. Even when he was only a young married man the great Tennyson came and stayed one night in his house in High Street. His wife, a young housekeeper, did her best for the honoured guest, but at dinner Tennyson was rather put out to find that the sauce with the salmon was not the one he preferred. He was pleased however with the wing of a chicken, and said that the only advantage he got from being Poet Laureate was that he generally received the liver-wing of a chicken. The next morning at breakfast the young people rather plumed themselves on having been able to get a dish of cutlets, but Tennyson whipped off the cover of the hot dish and seeing them cried out: 'Mutton chops! the staple of every bad inn in England!' But otherwise he was delight-ful, and asked many questions about Indian poetry. Max Müller knew Ruskin very well, and could not help comparing the two. He wrote: 'It is difficult to define the difference between an Oxford man and a Cambridge man; but if Ruskin was decidedly a repre-sentative of Oxford, Tennyson was a true son of the sister univer-sity.' That was not on the score of manners, for Ruskin could be very ill-mannered in writing as well as in speaking.

When children came Max Müller's happiness brimmed over. There were three daughters, the first Ada, born in December 1860; the second Mary, born February 1862; and the third Beatrice, born August 1864. Then arrived the only son, on June 9, 1867. Max Müller had professed to be quite satisfied with his three little girls, but he also rejoiced in the birth of what in Germany was called a *Stammhalter*. Giving the news to his cousin, Captain Adolph von Basedow, he wrote: 'I wish to ask you to be one of his godfathers. Both G. and I wish the boy not to be exclusively English, and, like his name, Wilhelm Grenfell, so his godfathers should be of both countries. He can then later on choose his own home, and like the old proverb, *ubi bene, ibi patria*.'

Of course, to all responsible and affectionate parents children are a constant trial, but the really important thing in the parent-child relationship is the question whether under these eddies of anxiety and even irritation there runs a deep current of happiness. In Max Müller's case there could be no doubt about that. After his death a companion of his daughters, who was then Mrs Boas, wrote a description of Müller as a father. 'The memory I have of him will always be chiefly that of the loving father of our dear child-friends, Ada, Mary, and Beatrice. No doubt you will have quite forgotten the way in which he would join, with bright unfeigned sympathy, in our plays and projects on the happy Saturday half-holiday after-noons we spent together; but we—the children—will never for-get it.'

But even then Max Müller's distrust of life in this world, his sense of the evanescence of human happiness, would not leave him, as will be seen from the following letter to his wife written on March 13, 1869:

> I long to have my two chicks here again—it seems so incomplete without them. How hard it must be to give up one of one's own children —and yet there was a time when we had not got them and we seemed quite satisfied with life then. So it goes on—more and more ties with every year—happiness that binds us to this life, while we ought really to try to get freer and freer from what binds us here, and more ready to leave it all when the time comes to part.

The blow fell, and he was not ready. In the summer of 1876 the whole family went to Germany, and settled for the time being at Dresden. There the son Wilhelm went to a German Gymnasium, and the girls studied under masters and made good progress in their studies. There he heard of the death of Edith, Dean Liddell's daughter, and wrote to Stanley: 'Poor Liddell, I think of him every day, and I fear that he will never recover from that blow. That daughter of his was a most charming, lovable creature, so natural, so beautiful, and he so fond, so proud of her! "Let us die, in order," says a poet in the *Veda*, "that the old may not weep for the young." It was then, as it is now, inscrutable; and I doubt whether we have learnt to be more patient, and to wait for our time more cheerfully, than the old worshipper of the Vedic gods.'

'Darkness and light divide the course of time', said an old English mystic. In the *Veda*, too, the night and day are called sisters. That the young do not weep for the old belongs to the day, and that is natural; but when the old weep for the young that belongs to the everlasting night out of which they never come. In just over six months from the day he wrote about the death of Liddell's daughter, Max Müller was to pass into that night.

His eldest daughter Ada began to feel ill from the end of November, and was seriously ill in the second week of December. It was meningitis. She died at 6 a.m. on the morning of the 16th. Mrs Max Müller had left a day-to-day account of her illness, death and burial in fifteen pages, and this is her account of the last moments:

I remember when watching her that hour, I prayed that God's Will might be ours. We sent for Dr Oehme, but I saw what was at hand, the breath grew quieter and slower. I threw myself on my knees by her and said aloud—'Lord into Thy hands we commend her spirit.' Then came three deep sighs, and the shoulders moved a little, and all was still. Max poured down some strong wine and we heard it swallowed. I never heard any breath after that, and I turned to Max and cried, 'It is over.' I thought I felt a little fluttering of the heart, and we continued to fan her—but I believe now it was my own pulse, and when Dr Oehme came he said it was all over. It was 6 a.m. that her sweet spirit must have passed away. No struggle or spasm. There could not have been anything more gentle and blessed. Max told the other poor children and his old mother, and it was heart-breaking to hear their cries as I stood over the still form that should never hear cry or know sorrow again.

She was buried on the 19th, a day before her sixteenth birthday, in the graveyard of the beautiful church at Dresden. Max Müller remained there till April 1877 with his mother. Then the family returned to England.

The loss of his daughter completely broke Max Müller, and made him incapable of relying on his own mental resources in order to live. So within a few days of his bereavement he wrote to his friends and relatives in identical language: 'My whole life now belongs to her and her memory, till our long journey is over.' It was not said under the immediate shock of grief. This became his settled mood. A year later he wrote to his wife: 'One can never believe in life again. One does what is one's duty, but the joy of life of which we had so much, is all gone. It is not that one does not feel grateful for what life is,—but one always asks—For how long? This has ceased to be our home, though it was such a happy home—one feels now, it is a mere waiting room where one is hustled about.'

This leitmotive recurs in successive letters. Some may be quoted. January 8, 1878: 'I hope I shall have a little rest now—I cannot do without it—it is only when I am alone, and can be together with our darling child that I feel able to endure this life, and can go on with my work.' August 23, 1878: 'It is strange being here alone—I feel as if I had no business to be here at all—I only live for you and with you. My own life seems finished here on earth. I have had that feeling ever since our darling left us—I ought to have gone first, not she.' He wrote this from Whitby, where he had gone to have a change. January 13, 1879: 'I find it so hard to be idle, still harder to smile and look happy, and talk about everything except what is in one's heart. When I saw all the children together, I looked for one face only which was not there. You know what it is. I can bear it all when I am alone.' April 20, 1879: 'I sometimes think I can go on no longer—what should I not give for my quiet study! I begin to feel the wear and tear of life much more than formerly—everything is a real effort—one can just do it and that is all.'

Again as late as December 14, 1881, on the eve of the fifth anniversary of his daughter's death: 'My darling Georgie—If you were here, what could one say—it is always the same weight that crushes all thoughts and all words. Ever since our dear Ada was taken from us, this life has become a mere waiting—one goes on as if it were the same as before, but one always feels it is not: part of oneself is no longer here—and what is here, can only be for a short time . . . Let us work on and love on to the last, as our own dear Ada did—happy child—that is what I always say when I think of her.'

It must have been a sore trial for Mrs Max Müller, strong-minded woman that she was, to see her husband in this state of mind for the rest of his life. I am not surprised that in her biography she did not give any description of it, and embodied her comment in just one sentence. But without disclosing his state of mind there can be no full understanding of Max Müller's personality.

Another decisive effect on Max Müller of his daughter's death was his persistent distrust of happiness. His third daughter Beatrice was happily married to Thomas Colyer-Fergusson, and had two children. After staying with them in their house, Ightham Mote, in 1893 he wrote to his son: 'They all seem so happy here that one trembles.' A year later he made the same kind of observation to his friend Madame Butenschön: 'My daughter also, and her husband, and her three children, often come to stay with us. I ought to feel happy, *mais la joie fait peur!*'

The fact was that he had lost his faith in life, and when his first grandson was born he could not repress his pessimism, though he only gave it a playful form because a new-born child always brings with it a rejuvenation of life. So he wrote to his new-born grandson:

> I am glad you like your Grandmama; I like her too, and I know she will be very kind to you, and she will not mind your crying. I do not wonder at your crying; it is a hard world you enter, as you will find out by and by. Many people would cry all their lives, if they were not ashamed of it . . . And now when you have cried yourself out, try to sleep, and forget the beginning troubles of your life. Your grandfather is trying to do the same, but he does not always succeed.

Not finding it satisfying enough to dwell on his lost daughter in thought alone, he began to keep a diary which over the years ran to nearly one thousand pages of close handwriting. In it he set down not only his feelings about her, and expressions of inconsolable grief, but also his thoughts on all his interests, including even politics, as if he could give utterance to them only in her imagined presence. There is something infinitely pathetic to find a man of his intellect and at the age of fifty-seven addressing an analysis of his political opinions and comments to a dead daughter.

> I feel more and more as I grow older, how blessed your little life has been [he wrote on May 2, 1881]. Have you lost more than you have been spared? It is difficult sometimes to have patience with this life. I feel more and more solitary—frightened almost when I see how I stand alone in my opinions and judgements. I try my best to be true— I have no interests that draw me away right or left—and yet I arrive at conclusions far away from those of my friends.
>
> The whole country [he continued by way of illustrating the difference] rings with the praise of Disraeli and abuse of Carlyle. Now, I have watched Disraeli's career—and I have always felt that he has lowered through life the standard of political morality in England. Expediency was his guiding star through life—nor did he make any secret of it—which is a kind of tribute which selfishness, as a hypocrite, it is true, but yet as recognizing the existence of higher natures, pays to unselfishness. Never has there been, even by accident, a spark of generosity from that block of brass, never even an appeal to the nobler

instincts of those whom he addressed, and excited. Now, other statesmen, however discouraging their experience of men may be, have not
lost all faith in true nobility. Gladstone has that redeeming feature in
him that he believes in ideals, in duty, in unselfishness, in generosity.
I know he has not always been true to himself, but he has tried, and
those who look at history as it passes before their eyes have again and
again seen him struggling to be true to his better self. To see this keeps
a belief in morality alive among the people, but to watch a career like
D's, destroys all faith in public virtue. I know nothing against D's
private life, and it speaks well for him that he had had so many private
friends. But a man may have too many friends. Woe to you, if all the
world speaks well of you! G. Smith once wrote of him that he was a
valet in the guise of a statesman—hard words, no doubt, but do they
not express some truth?

England mourns over Disraeli and has forgotten Carlyle—it is difficult to hold to one's convictions, but one must.

All this seems morbid. I have seen Hindu women nursing their
grief, or rather their self-pity, over years with a persistence which
I have always regarded as perverse, almost unclean. So I was
grieved to see something similar in Max Müller. But an introspective
and analytical mind like his could not be unaware of the moral
aspect of his grief and fail to put forward a justification for what he
was doing. He gave one explanation long before his bereavement.
He had gone on a visit to Queen Victoria at Osborne House, where
he found the rooms full of recollections of Prince Albert and everyone talking about him as if he were still among them. Mentioning
this in a letter to his wife, he also offered his explanation. 'This,' he
wrote, 'is thoroughly German, and it always struck me in England
how carefully all conversation on those who have gone before us is
avoided, and how much of comfort and good influence derived from
the memory of those we loved is thereby lost.'

Three years after the death of Ada he wrote to his son, who at
that time was only twelve.

Young as you are [he wrote] you have felt what it is to have one whom
we love dearly taken from us. We do not mourn for her—she is happy,
and she has been spared many of the hard struggles of this life. We
mourn for ourselves, because we miss her so much, and we know she
would have made our life so bright and happy. But we must learn to be
ready to give up everything, however dearly we love it, when God bids
us to do so. Sooner or later we know we shall have to leave all those

whom we love on earth, till we meet again as God's love and wisdom may order it . . . Think always what those whom you loved and who loved you on earth, would think of you, and then you will never never go far wrong.

Of course, behind all this lay the Christian view of life and death, and above all its central doctrine of resurrection. In his childhood Max Müller had read and pondered the inscription over the gateway of the God's Acre at Dessau where his father was buried: 'Death is not death, it is but the ennobling of man's nature.'

Anyhow, Müller kept his diary for many years. I shall give some quotations from it. He began to write in it from December 1876, and called the reflective chapters *Paroksha* in Sanskrit, which can be translated as *Out of Sight*. In the third *Paroksha*, under the date February 8, 1877, occurs this cry of agony, at the thought of another blow.

Since yesterday morning Wilhelm is ill with scarlet fever. I cannot gather my thoughts—I cannot. I feel after God, that He may help. I am dumb before him. My dear Ada gone—and now God shows me again and makes me feel, how we are all in His hand—O God have mercy upon me, a miserable sinner! When Thou threatenest, then they believe in Thee, says the old poet in the *Veda*—and is it not so even now? How careless my happy life has been—now They terrible thunder, O God, has roused me . . . Oh let me never forget God's mercy—let me enter upon a new life and remain steadfast in it. There cannot be many years to live—let me live them in the sight of God.

Feb. 10. Wilhelm is better, and now that this dark cloud is passing away, the old sorrow returns. I feel as if God had intended to remind me how much is life to me, how much is still entrusted to me, how my life is still blessed above thousands and thousands. I shall not forget this warning—I shall try to do my duty, but I shall keep a sacred place where I can find you, my dear Child, where I can speak to you, and be guided by you . . .

Feb. 17. I often thought, my dear Child, how painful it would be if at any time you *shall* have been brought to think that your father's faith was less orthodox than your own. I know it might have happened, for the distance between my own religious views and yours was great. It could not be otherwise, and it is difficult to bridge over that distance except by love and trust. And yet I always felt that you, as a child, and I, as a man, were only speaking each our language but meaning the same. There is a difference between the childlike faith of a man (all real faith must be childlike) and the childlike faith of a child. The one is Paradise not yet lost, the other Paradise lost but regained. The one is right for the child, and the other is right for the man. It is the will of God that it should be so—but it is also the will of God that we shall all bear with each other, and join, each in his own voice, in the great hymn of praise.

The same day: My dear Child—The more I think of your life upon earth, the more perfect it seems to me. How much have you been spared! Our miseries generally begin at eighteen—our feelings and passions awake, and *oh! how much such hearts as yours were to suffer*, before they find satisfaction and rest. The miseries endured by young girls and young men of deep and intense feelings are beyond all description. How much I suffered myself, and how often do such sufferings blight a whole life. Of all that, you know nothing—you carried away the purest idea of life.

February 22, 1877: My child, how I long for you—every thought of mine seems lame—it always turns to you and then it will not move further.

March 5, 1877: My dear child, I thought I should have taken you to Italy and shown you that beautiful country of sunshine and art—how you would have revelled in both.

September 11, 1877: So many friends come to see me, and they speak to me of what I have lost, and I must listen to what they say—they mean to be kindly, I know—but the heart only knows its own bitterness. Darling child! I was very happy before you were given me—I might have lived a happy life even if I had never known you. That is true, and I try to work myself back into that time when I was alone or when I was alone with your mother, who was not your mother yet. They were happy days, and why shall the days be not be happy again?

October 4, 1877: One often feels tempted to say, Blessed are those who have nothing on earth, for they can lose nothing. There are philosophers who hold that it is the highest wisdom to love nothing. There is some truth in this.

October 21, 1877: We meet friends who have suffered as we have suffered, and who seem so bright and happy. What has time to do with real sorrow? And yet we are like other people, certainly not better or truer. Can the same thing happen to us? Can we too be bright and happy again? One turns away from such a thought, one hopes it is impossible. And yet how happy are our children. Why cannot we be like them? Their time will come later. With me the happy life of my youth, for I was young till I was 53, is gone. Life itself is changed. Nothing seems to be my own.

December 8, 1877: I try to work hard as a help—not that I wish to—it turns my thoughts away from thee, my dear Child, I could not . . . There is much that has to be done, and it will be done. I do not lose my time in idle sorrow—sorrow is good, it strengthens me, only sometimes it overcomes me and revives the sharp pain and brings back the sense of emptiness, of yearning, and hunger.

I was quite drunk with life—then you were taken from me—and now I can see at last, what others have seen long ago, that our home is not here.

December 20, 1877: Today you would have been seventeen.

April 2, 1878: But for you, I should never have felt that this life is an exile—I felt so fully at home in it. Now I know what it is.

June 16, 1878: I am tired now, and long for rest—but there is so much that remains to be done. I want my old life to come back, to be every morning with you again, my dear Child—to live a quiet life with you— but it seems almost impossible. And yet how I have felt your presence and your help.
But for you, I should probably never have undertaken that work. Now I want to finish it for you, and to dedicate it to you, if I can find the right expression.

In April 1878, Max Müller had delivered his Hibbert Lectures on the origin and growth of religion, and he was publishing them in the summer. He told his daughter about this:

> 'To Her
> Whose dear Memory
> Encouraged, directed, and supported me
> In writing these Lectures,
> They are now dedicated
> As a Memorial
> Of a Father's undying Love.'

Thus have I fulfilled something of what I felt I ought to do for you when you were taken from us, my dear Child—What I cannot do for you here on earth I shall try to do for others—that was what I felt then, when I looked everywhere for a meaning and purpose in what seemed, so mysterious, so unnatural.

10

July 18, 1878: One is driven along day after day—but now and then there comes a sudden lull, sometimes for a few minutes only, but in those few minutes Oh what a world of sadness and bitterness. One asks no longer Why—one knows there is no answer to that. It is so, and as it is, it must be borne.

August 3, 1878: 'Our wedding day—nineteen years ago—what happiness then—what happiness ever since—except that one great grief. And yet it is to that grief I cling—it is that grief which has opened a new world before my eyes.

September 12, 1879: I thought I shall find rest—but found none. We travelled about from place to place, saw things and men, but hardly an hour had I to myself. From Sheveningen we went through Holland, saw Leyden, Haarlem, Utrecht, Amsterdam—then to Dessau where the children were very happy. To me, it is a place of the past—I no more belong to it.

September 25, 1879: Grief is a sweet remembrance of happiness that was.

November 16, 1879: Wilhelm is here for his Sunday—and you Darling are not. There is the old riddle always before me—Why was my child taken from me? Human understanding has no answer for it and yet I feel as certain as I can feel of anything, that this is as it is, it is good, it is best, better than anything I can wish for . . . What makes me start sometimes is the returning joyfulness of life. It seems so thoughtless, so forgetful—but I never forget you, my Darling—and the more you are with me, the better I feel.

December 16, 1879: The day is gone—no new light, we cannot know, we cannot even imagine—we can only trust, hope for the best, the wisest.

December 20, 1879: Her nineteenth birthday.

Last night of the year—31 Dec. 1879
My last word, my last thoughts belong to thee—life is heavy, it will never again be what it was. I try hard, but why deceive oneself? I seem to have done . . . Darling child, the bright sun set with you—the evening cannot be like the morning or the noon.

February 22, 1880: Driven on, less and less rest—no time hardly to look back. Yesterday was Mary's 18th birthday—how different all is from what might have been.

October 9, 1880: What gaps—it is work that keeps me away from you to myself! Life is drawing to an end, and I have still more work to finish, if I can. But I long for rest. In a few days my mother will be eighty—is so long a life a blessing? It seems a long and tiring journey to a home which others have reached by a much shorter road.

September 3, 1881: In Dresden again—1876 and now 1881—and all as hard and unintelligible as ever—that one riddle no one can solve—how different life would have been but for that stroke. I have been changed perhaps, I have grown better—more ready to surrender self—but the heart bleeds—bleeds as much as ever, as often as ever. How constantly you are with me . . . Help me, help thy mother who wants help, and I cannot help, do not know how to help her.
How many are gone—and I still full of work. Dean Stanley gone too, he and Rolleston I miss like my left and right arms—they were so trusty.

Sunday, 5 September. Just come back from your grave—full of memories, Darling Child—and are you not to be envied for your short and sunny journey through life?

December 5, 1881: The evening before the 58th birthday—Georgie and Mary gone to a ball—Beatrice in Paris, Wilhelm in Eton—I alone here—and yet no rest—no time to collect my thoughts—my memories —driven, driven on by work that comes to me—I feel I must do it, I feel I ought to do much more, but it is too late.

In April, 1883, whilst at Hastings with his family Max Müller got a telegram that his mother was seriously ill. It was followed by another which announced her death. He at once started for Dessau, and arrived in time to be able to bury her. He described the illness, death and funeral to his wife at length, and wrote about her to all her grand-daughters, dead as well as living. To his dead daughter Max Müller wrote in retrospect in 1885:

My dear Mother—my earliest recollection, my first love—my constant thought these many years taken away—a tie that bound me to the Eternal broken for a time. And yet one fears the law of nature and joins in the old sigh of humanity with a heavy heart but not so crushed and torn as once all seemed so unnatural, so violent, so unintelligible . . . To us the sun seems to set every day—seems to be gone—wasted—yet it is not so. The sun remains—though *our* sun seems to set. We are dazzled when the light is too great, and our eyes too small—we cannot enlarge our mind enough to take in all the light about us—we shut our eyes and trust.

To his living daughters he wrote immediately. To his youngest daughter Beatrice he wrote:

As long as my mother lived, I felt that I belonged to her; now I belong to no one, though others belong to me. You have no idea what a rich life hers has been, rich in joys, rich in sorrows, and rich in love and sympathy for others. In her very last letters to me she was full of interest as to your singing. She always hoped you would have a voice like hers. When she was your age she sang at some great musical festivals, admired by the best judges.

To his second daughter, now the eldest, the intellectual Mary, who was engaged to be married to a young Oxford don whom she passionately loved, he wrote:

I wish you had been able to see your dear grandmother once more if only as I saw her, sleeping on flowers, covered with palm-branches, taking with her some faded tokens of her early happiness, unchanged, calm, beautiful . . . It is curious how forgetful we are of death, how little we think that we are dying daily, and that what we call life is really death, and death the beginning of life, a higher life . . . Even you, in your great happiness just now should feel that what you call your own is only lent to you.

The undergraduates who regarded the freedom of Müller's new house at 7 Norham Gardens as one of the best boons of their Oxford days, probably did so as much for the daughter as for the father. One of them, writing an obituary notice of Max Müller after his death, reserved his most eloquent passages for Mary. He wrote that in her 'the exceptional physical beauty of both parents reappeared in a strangely etherealized form'. He continued:

She was one of those of whom we all seem to perceive, after they are gone, that a hundred mystic signs had always marked them for another world than this. I can see her still, with her classic head and straight, sweet features, with a wreath, in her dark hair, of gold olive leaves beaten flat and thin, which had been copied from an Etruscan model for one of her wedding gifts—a vision of almost incredible human grace, 'a dream of form in days of thought'.

This did honour to the undergraduates of Oxford, who showed that though they could drown themselves for Zuleika Dobson they could also rise to an abandoned admiration of a more spiritual physical attraction.

Mary was endowed with remarkable intellectual gifts. She did not know Greek when she was married, and learnt it from her husband in the course of six weeks while walking with him on long forest and mountain paths in Germany. From his lips she learnt in that short time declension, conjugation, a considerable vocabulary and enough of syntax to be able to construe easy Greek like that of Xenophon at first sight.

She was a good linguist, and translated before her death a very learned philological treatise by Scherer.

From a very young age she was strong-willed, and offered problems to her parents. Mrs Max Müller, a strong character, was sometimes imperious with her, and her husband remonstrated. So one finds him writing to his wife on January 13, 1879, when Mary was just short of being seventeen:

I am so much afraid you will grow out of harmony with Mary, and I sometimes look forward with trembling to the future. She is a very good girl, so honest, so diligent. She is not strong, she has not the feeling of health and strength like Beatrice. But I feel certain she is full of love for us both, only she is shy and frightened.

We must not expect our children [he continued] to be exactly what we should like them to be. They are given us to make the best of we can. We have to conform to them—we are older and wiser, and can bear with them far better than they with us. I do not mean that we should always yield to them. We can be very strict and severe, but always show them our love and our real sorrow when we must spoil their pleasures. If the ways of a mother and daughter once diverge they very seldom meet again. You know I am not preaching to you—I only want to show you a danger. You do not always understand Mary's waywardness.

I could see all the time that she considered the dress you worked for her too showy. There is no harm in that, rather the contrary. But what between seeming to be ungrateful and shrinking from attracting attention the poor child did not know what to do. Many a grown up person would have felt the same difficulty. If you had said one word that you too thought the dress more showy than you had expected, all would have been right. But you only put your authority against her taste, and thus all your kindness in working the dress for her was lost. However, I may have said too much, and particularly in writing one seems to say much more than one wants to say. All I wish is to see you and the children happy together, and that you know.

Three years later it was the turn of the daughter to be remonstrated with. On May 5, 1882, he wrote to Mary:

> Now what I had so often to blame you for was being out of tune, not so much with me as with your mother—particularly not showing her that loving respect that a daughter should show to her mother, thus ennobling a relation which, I believe, forms the highest happiness in life. Though when you were children, I was sometimes given to be very stern with you, your mother has always shown you the greatest kindness, and far too much of indulgences even—yet you were constantly opposing her and even finding fault with her. I never doubted your heart, but I felt very unhappy about your manner. You can say everything to a father and mother, but you should say it as a child, even when you are twice as old as you are now. Now whenever you begin to express an opinion it was never done in a hesitating or inquisitive tone, but always as a determined assertion. That seemed so unnatural. It was almost impossible to argue anything out with you, or exchange opinions—because you simply reiterated your opinion and looked upon those who differed from you, and who at all events were older than you, with a kind of contemptuous smile. Now such things jar on me like wrong notes; but particularly as I felt all the time that it was not real, but only put on. It is quite true that I am often absorbed in my work, and many of the things which interest you have lost interest for me. Yet I have seldom sent you away, and if I have done so I have done it with regret and with kindness, I believe . . . You could make the few remaining years of my life much happier, if you would take your natural place, helping your mother, cheering your father, and practising that self-surrender which is at the root of all true happiness because it makes us feel satisfied with ourselves.

This letter from a father aged fifty-nine to a daughter aged twenty is very creditable to the former. His daughter also caused him some worry when she fell in love with a not very wealthy young don, Fred Conybeare, and wanted to marry him. His own situation in respect of his own marriage was ironically reversed. On June 7, 1883, he wrote to his wife:

> If he [his daughter's lover] really cares for Mary, he should show that he is worthy of her and capable of an effort and a sacrifice. He must work and do something, and show what is in him. A mere 'Coach' would not do for her, nor for me. You will be sorry if you allow yourself to be drawn further and further. I know it is difficult to say No to a lovesick swain and a lovesick maiden—but I feel certain it is for their

good. If F. will only work with a will, I do not see why he should not
marry next year—but if he begins life sighing and dawdling, the chances
of a happy marriage seem to be very distant . . . As to their income, I
know they can live on £800 a year—so could *one*—but whether *you*,
and therefore *I* would be happy is another question. Of course, if we
old people were asked whether we would live on £800 a year, or not
live together at all, we should probably say, Let us live on £800 a year—
but the week after there would be long faces and regrets. And so it will
be with them. I know Mary and her ideas of what is nice, and generous,
and comfortable. I should be sorry for Fred if she had to do without a
maid! [Of course, a lady's maid is meant.]

However, they were married towards the end of the year. Then a
different kind of anxiety arose for Max Müller—whether Mary
would be careful enough when expecting a child. Less than a year
after her marriage she had a child, which did not live, and Müller
wrote to his wife: 'So it was not to be—and the little soul shrank
back from this life . . . Poor Mary seems to have suffered much, and
to have no reward for it is very hard.'

Two years later she was expecting another child, and was ill.
Hearing about it Max Müller wrote to his wife who was with her
daughter at Southwold in Suffolk: 'However one must be prepared
for misfortune.'

On September 2, he wrote again: 'When will people learn that if
women want to be mothers, they must live sensible and natural
lives?' On September 4 the following telegram arrived at his house
for Wilhelm, who was only nineteen, from his mother:
'To Wilhelm Max Muller, Oxford. Mary passed away today in
long faint. Break it to Daddy and Bee. Mummy'
Mrs Max Müller dared not send the news directly to her husband.
On the last page of the diary is pasted this telegram, and underneath
Max Müller wrote: 'Friday, September 3, 1886. Mary left us . . .'

He wrote no more in that diary. His sorrow was too deep for
expression. He gave the news of his fresh bereavement to others but
thought more of the sorrow of others than his own. Thus he wrote
to Sir Robert Collins, Secretary to the Duchess of Albany: 'I have
shared many sorrows, and even now, under this new blow, it is the
misery of that poor husband and the grief of my wife that chokes
the heart far more than my own distress.'

Thirteen years later he wrote to his son: 'I wonder whether you
remember the anniversary of today when dear Mary was taken from

us. Who could understand it and account for it? And yet we must learn to see a meaning in everything, we must believe that as it was it was right.'

That was the last word of philosophy on death. Max Müller's wife was to receive the final blow after his death. When she was writing his biography the third daughter Beatrice died, and the last words of that book were:

'Desolation rests on the earthly home where her father passed so many happy hours.

'And yet "Death is not death, if it gives us to those whom we have loved and lost, for whom we have lived, and for whom we long to live again."'

Chapter 3

INDIA: MEN

WHEN Max Müller told his son to grow fond of someone or something and so be raised to the intensity of a passion, he was thinking
of his own life. Whatever his love for *someone* might have brought
him, his fondness for *something* never disappointed him. That was
India, adopted as a boy's dream and pursued through life as an
object of love. Many people looked upon this as his great illusion.

It could be, for he could create an India of his own, as Pygmalion
did with his Galatea. Though absorbed in India all his life, he never
visited the country. In early life he could not because his mother
thought that England was far enough. His love affair and marriage
also prevented it. In middle age he was too busy at Oxford; and
when old he felt that a visit to India would be too great a physical
strain. Among Indians the legend grew that he believed their
country to have been the land of his previous birth, and that to see
it might prove a fatal shock of joy.

He himself did not think that not to visit a country where lay
one's spiritual or intellectual interest was necessarily a great loss.
Learning that his son had visited Palestine and recalling his longing
to see the East in his young days, he wrote to Wilhelm on April 9,
1898: 'I have had to give up many of these dreams, but somehow
one learns to see with the mind and imagination what we cannot see
with the eyes: nay, in many cases I believe imagination is truer
than what you see. People go to Jerusalem to see the place of some
of the miracles, and they do not see the greatest of miracles, that out
of that small town, in a small country, there should have risen a
light to light the whole world.'

The fact that he had no first-hand experience of India was often
thrown in his teeth by the Englishmen there, who did not like his
advocacy of Indians and his enthusiastic evocations of ancient Hindu
civilization. The charitable among them regarded him as too
idealistic, and the malicious gloated over his disenchantment if he
were ever to visit the country. Referring to this the *Statesman* of
Calcutta, one of the leading English language newspapers in India,
then wholly under English ownership, management and editorial

direction, wrote on May 10, 1903, in reviewing Mrs Max Müller's biography of her husband:

> The conjecture is often hazarded that, had Max Müller seen with his own eyes the India of whose people and thought he wrote with so noble an enthusiasm and so fine a sympathy, the illusion would have fallen from him. We cannot think it. The man whose insight was equal to the task of piercing through all the accretions overlying the Hindu scriptures to the pure gold of the idea and the poetry beneath, would assuredly have been baffled by no obstacle created by the India we know today. Beneath and behind the distorting reality he would have seen the India of his vision; and, although his theories would have been modified, his attitude towards the real contribution which India has made to the intellectual life of the world would have remained unchanged.

This vindication, so far as it went, was correct. But from another point of view it was unnecessary. For one thing, as will be seen presently, Max Müller was not unaware of the actual social, moral and religious condition of the India of his time. Then, the India he idealized, that of the ancient Hindus, could be idealized and made proof against disillusionment, for it was reconstructed from certain ancient religious and philosophical texts which admitted of a wide range of interpretation according to the inclinations of the reconstructor, so that no one who differed from him could charge him either with ignorance or with intellectual dishonesty. Furthermore, it is impossible to check the correctness of any such reconstruction against concrete historical evidence as to cults and beliefs.

For instance, the religious and philosophic ideas to be found in the *Rig-Veda* and the other *Vedas*; to take only three principal interpretations, those of Max Müller, Bergaigne and Keith, there is not a scrap of evidence, except the existence of the texts, that these ideas formed the basis of the religious life of the Hindus in times which properly belong to history. The differences in the interpretations are due to differences in philological exegesis combined with assumptions regarding early religion, and the philological exegesis itself is conjectural. So Max Müller could create his ancient India without being compelled to change his picture. Actually, he did more. He imposed his idea of India and of Hindu religion in its most ancient form on the religious life of the Hindus of his time.

His picture, which he put before Indians and Europeans alike, was built up with the help of a selective principle applied to the

entire body of Sanskrit literature, and the principle led him to for-
mulate his peculiar view of the historical development of this
literature. He expounded it on different occasions, but expressed it
most succinctly and clearly in the lectures delivered by him at
Cambridge in 1882, which afterwards he published under the title:
India: What Can It Teach Us?

According to him, the whole of Sanskrit literature could be
divided into two parts: one preceding the Turanian invasions, and
the other following them. He used the general term 'Turanian' for
the Sakas or Scythians, Kushanas, and all the nomadic or semi-
nomadic peoples who came into India and ruled there from the first
century B.C. to the third century A.D. To the pre-Turanian epoch,
he said, belonged the Vedic literature and the ancient literature of
the Buddhists. To the post-Turanian epoch belonged all the rest of
Sanskrit literature, whether religious or secular. Between the two
periods he assumed a longish period of literary unproductiveness
for the Hindus, and called the later literature that of the Sanskrit
Renaissance.

Moreover, he drew a qualitative distinction between the products
of the two periods, regarding those of the earlier period as 'ancient'
and 'natural', and those of the later as 'modern' and 'artificial'. He
thought that the literature of the second period was never a living
and national literature for the Hindus, though it contained relics of
earlier times. The great mass of it was artificial and scholastic, full
of interesting compositions and by no means devoid of originality
and occasional beauty. Yet all that held appeal for the Oriental
scholar alone, and not for the historian, or philosopher with a broad
human sympathy.

Max Müller set down his deliberate opinion:

> It was a real misfortune that Sanskrit literature became first known
> to the learned public in Europe through specimens belonging to the
> second or what I called the Renaissance period . . . Although the
> specimens of this modern Sanskrit literature, when they first became
> known, served to arouse a general interest, and serve even now to keep
> alive a certain superficial sympathy for Indian literature, more serious
> students had soon disposed of these compositions, and while gladly
> admitting their claim to be called pretty and attractive, could not think
> of allowing Sanskrit literature a place among the world-literatures, a
> place by the side of Greek and Latin, Italian, French, English or
> German.

Conway, who was reporting the war: 'I doubt whether it is wise to weaken France at the very moment that Germany becomes so much more powerful. As to making France harmless, that can never be done, and I doubt whether for the sake of Germany it is desirable.'

Naturally Max Müller's wife was pro-German, and he informed his mother that 'G. [Georgina] is even more German than I am', and also told Abeken that 'she is German through and through, and she and my three girls, the youngest only six years old, work indefatigably for the wounded'. But though Müller's anxiety in regard to the outcome of the war was over, a new cause of anxiety arose for him in the signs that he observed of a misunderstanding between England and Germany.

He was bound to wish for wholehearted friendship between the English and the German people. But he went even further and thought that the peace of the world could only be preserved by creating an alliance of the Teutonic Powers, among whom he included the United States. 'My great anxiety through all this war,' he wrote to Gladstone on October 6, 1870, 'has been the unfriendly feeling that is springing up between England and Germany. The whole future of the world seems to me to depend on the friendship of the three Teutonic nations, Germany, England, and America.' He looked upon France and Russia as the potential disturbers of peace, and set down the idea of an Anglo-German alliance to counteract them.

Already in England a deep suspicion of Germany was taking shape. At first sympathy in England was for Germany as the attacked side, but with the German victories there came about a change. There were some eminent British intellectuals who were wholly pro-German, such as Carlyle, the historian Freeman, and the political writer Goldwin Smith. John Stuart Mill supported Germany from his antipathy to Napoleon III, and at first Gladstone, as Müller reported to Abeken, was on the German side, 'not from natural sympathy, but from a conviction, from a feeling of right and duty.'

The British attitude began to be reversed after Sedan. At the beginning of this change of opinion Max Müller wrote to his mother: 'The best part of the nation was for Germany, but the Aristocracy has strong sympathy with France.' This change was partly the expression of the familiar British inclination to sympathize with the weaker side, but was also due to the tendency to

9

This was virtually falling in with the view of Sanskrit literature taken by Mill and Macaulay, quoted in a previous chapter.

'It is different,' he declared, 'with the ancient literature of India, the literature dominated by the Vedic and the Buddhist religions. That literature opens to us a chapter in what has been called the Education of the Human Race, to which we can find no parallel anywhere else.' He further said that anybody who cared for the origins of language, thought, religion, philosophy, or law and many other human creations 'must in future pay the same attention to the literature of the Vedic period as to the literature of Greece and Rome and Germany'.

Knowledge of this period of Sanskrit literature, he said, began with Eugène Burnouf, who was not likely to spend his life on pretty Sanskrit ditties and wanted to correlate Sanskrit literature to history, human history, world history, and 'laid hold of Vedic literature and Buddhist literature as the two stepping stones in the slough of Indian literature'. As a result of the study of Sanskrit thus inaugurated, something other than a particular literary expression was to be found in Sanskrit literature. So he wrote: 'What then, you may ask, do we find in that ancient Sanskrit literature and cannot find anywhere else? My answer is, We find there the Aryan man, whom we knew in his various characters, as Greek, Roman, German, Celt and Slav, in an entirely new character, a character,' he explained, 'which was the complement of that of the Northern Aryan.'

He elaborated the idea in a very eloquent passage of his lecture:

All then that I wish to put clearly before you is this, that the Aryan man, who had to fulfil his mission in India, might naturally be deficient in many of the practical and fighting virtues, which were developed in the Northern Aryans by the very struggle without which they could not have survived, but that his life on earth had not therefore been entirely wasted. His very view of life, though we cannot adopt it in this Northern climate, may yet act as a lesson and warning to us, not, for the sake of life, to sacrifice the highest objects of life.

There is undoubted truth in the antithesis thus emphasized between the activism of the Northern Aryan and the quietism of the Southern. But Max Müller did not realize that the first was the result of a successful struggle and the second of an unsuccessful and hopeless struggle—both against nature. Yet from the historical point of view he was not right. He was underrating and partly rejecting the whole expression of that ancient Indian civilization of whose existence we have historical evidence from archaeology, inscriptions, art and literary products both religious and secular. And he was treating as the most important and valuable that part which was only prehistoric or protohistoric. And even that was only by inference rather than by direct historic proof.

His view of the two periods of Sanskrit literature is not historical if one excludes the Vedic literature, both in the hymns and the liturgical texts, and the most archaic mystical works. What he regarded as a Renaissance of Sanskrit literature was most probably its first birth. The secular literature was certainly a new appearance, and even in regard to the religious texts, which he assigned to the earlier epoch, we cannot be sure when they received their present form. Many of them must have done only in the so-called age of the Renaissance. Besides, he was wrong in thinking that classical Sanskrit literature was artificial, rhetorical and merely pretty. By the same criterion the whole of Latin literature might be called artificial; and in English literature Shakespeare, Milton and Pope, not to mention others, should be regarded as extravagantly rhetorical or conventional. Max Müller's taste in poetry was neither comprehensive nor eclectic. He regretted that his Oxford friends often forgot that he had been brought up on German poetry and though he knew Heine, Rückert, Eichendorff, Chamisso and Geibel, not to speak of Goethe, Schiller, Bürger and even Klopstock, their allusions to Tennyson, Browning, Shelley or Keats were entirely lost on him. He revealed his preference in poetry by saying that Tennyson's *In Memoriam* remained a treasure for life with him.

But the ancient India which he regarded as the highest and most valuable was his own creation, and thus immune to disillusionment. But since he was presenting that India to the Indians of his time in order to raise them from the cultural condition to which they had reduced themselves, and to revitalize their life, it is quite possible that he would have been saddened by the actual conditions, and had a feeling of despair had he ever visited India.

A man of Max Müller's deep and broad humanity could not fail to be attracted to the men and women of the country he loved so much. In fact, his personal relations with the Indians he met in the course of his long life provide the most touching expression of his devotion to India. I was surprised by the span of time over which he had either Indian acquaintances or Indian correspondents. The first Indian he met was Dwarkanath Tagore, born at the end of the eighteenth century; and one of his last correspondents was an eminent Bengali whom I used to meet in Calcutta in the thirties of this century. In between there were many figures of first rank in modern India like Raja Radhakanta Deb, Debendranath Tagore, Keshub Chunder Sen, Rajendra Lal Mitra, Bhao Daji, Behramji Malabari and K. T. Telang. He particularly sympathized with those who were trying to reform Indian religion and social customs, and were not only working for the cause, but also suffering for it. In doing so and championing them, he did not shrink from courting unpopularity and abuse. A full account will be found in the second volume of his reminiscences, *Auld Lang Syne*. But my accounts are also given from intimate personal correspondence.

The next Indian whom he met was no celebrity, but he had a remarkable history of religious struggle. One day in 1854 Müller was sitting in his room at Oxford copying his MSS, when an Indian dressed in a long black coat was shown in, and he addressed Müller in a language of which he did not understand a single word. Max Müller replied in English, and asked in what language he was speaking. The visitor was surprised: 'Do you not understand Sanskrit?' Max Müller said: 'No, I have never heard it spoken, but here are some MSS of the *Veda* which will interest you.' The Indian read a little, and then remarked that he was not able to translate what he was reading. On Müller's expressing surprise, the man said that he did not believe in the *Veda* any more, he had become a Christian. Then he told a remarkable story. His Hindu name was Nilakantha Goreh, but had been changed to Nehemiah Goreh on his conversion.

On account of his conversion he had lost all, for even his wife and his father had had to repudiate him. Goreh had been placed with a missionary seminary in London, where he found himself among a number of prospective missionaries whom he considered half-educated and narrow-minded. He did not get any sympathy from them, but was blamed for everything he said or did. He was treated as a kind of nigger by those who should have respected him. He saw nothing in London that answered his notion of what a Christian city should be. 'If what I have been seeing in London is Christianity, I want to go back to India; if that is Christianity, I am not a Christian.' Müller thought that all this was very ominous. After a time his friends sent Goreh back to India, feeling that there was a real danger of his falling into utter despair. There, as Müller wrote, what seemed to be almost an innate tendency of the Indian mind developed in Goreh, and he decided to renounce the world altogether and become an ascetic. Still later he joined the Society of the Cowley Brothers which had branches in India. On the day before he was to leave Oxford he came to see Max Müller for a short while and Müller gave the news to his wife on November 3: 'Now and then the old spirit seemed to move in him, but he soon relapsed into formulas . . . it was sad to see the eagle with broken wings.'

In his diary Müller wrote:

> Last Saturday Nilakantha Goreh called on me! It was sad—I had not seen him for I suppose 25 years. He has become a monk, a Cowley Brother! How different from what he was when he stepped into my room in Park Place! He was then a true martyr, a man who had made greater sacrifices for his conviction than any man I knew. And now! The old fire is quenched! 'We must keep to the Creeds', he says—he who had left father, wife, friends, fortune and home to be free of men and creeds.[The year is 1877.]

In the biography of Goreh written by a missionary,[*] he is shown as making harsh remarks about Max Müller, and airing contempt for his knowledge of Hindu philosophy. But Müller in his reminiscences of Goreh, written at the end of his own life, had only praise and affection for him.

Yet a Hindu Bengali, who was a friend of Goreh and knew him intimately, wrote to Müller: 'I really could not understand how a man of Mr Goreh's intelligence and learning, who had discarded Hinduism, could accept, in its stead, popular Christianity which stands on the same level with popular Hinduism. By popular Christianity I mean the Christianity of the Church, as contradistinguished from the Christianity of Christ.'

The next Indian whose connexion with Max Müller I shall describe was also on a religious quest, but he was not an obscure individual like Goreh. He was Keshub Chunder Sen, who, as a religious and social reformer, will always have a place in any history of modern India. He was leading a powerful monotheistic movement, very largely modelled on Christianity, and even before he was thirty was so famous that Lord Lawrence, the Viceroy, invited him to Simla

---

[*] C. E. Gardner, *The Life of Father Goreh*, edited and with a preface by R. M. Benson, London, Longman's, 1900.

as his guest. He was a man of extraordinary and almost wild enthusiasm and eloquence, and spoke English as well as he did Bengali. He was born into a wealthy and very respected family of Calcutta, but had given up, or rather was forced to give up, his family on account of his religious convictions. However, he gave up his secular employment voluntarily, and became a preacher. His very young wife accompanied him both in his religious mission and his break with Hindu society.

Keshub Chunder Sen came to England in 1870, when he was thirty-two. As Max Müller related in his biographical essay on Sen: 'His stay in England was a constant triumph.' He spoke in London and all the principal towns, and produced a deep impression on all his hearers from all classes of society. 'His name', Müller added, 'became almost a household word in England.' It should be mentioned that the reception which Sen got in England was partly the result of the interest in India, both ancient and modern, which Müller himself had created. He was also invited to meet Queen Victoria.

Max Müller met him for the first time at a luncheon given by Dean Stanley, and on April 1, 1870, wrote to his wife: 'We have just come back from London, where we had a very interesting luncheon at the Deanery. No one there but Keshub Chunder Sen, and the Prince [Leopold, son of Queen Victoria] and I. We soon got into a warm discussion, and it was curious to see how we almost made him confess himself a Christian. He will come to Oxford, and then I hope to see more of him.'

Sen went to Oxford and stayed with Müller, who had a good opportunity of watching him, and always found him perfectly tranquil, even when very earnest, with his opinions clear and settled. The highlight of the Oxford visit was Sen's meeting with Dr Pusey. Pusey was not very pleased with his lectures, and still less with his association with the English Unitarians. But there was a long and serious talk between the two in the presence of Müller, who later, when he had to write about Sen, regretted that he had kept no record of that interview. None the less, he remembered the end of the discussion quite distinctly, for it turned on a question of his own. The point at issue was whether those who were born and brought up as members of a non-Christian religion could have salvation in the Christian sense. Pusey did not think so. Müller asked him pointedly whether at the time of Christ a man who believed what Keshub Chunder Sen believed would or would not have been received as a disciple. He and Sen maintained that he would have been. Pusey held his ground. Much depended on what salvation meant, and Sen defined it as an uninterrupted union with God and said: 'My thoughts are never away from God . . . my life is a constant prayer, and there are but few moments in the day when I am not praying to God!' Dr Pusey was softened by this, and remarked with a smile: 'Then you are all right.'

In 1878 there came a crisis in Sen's triumphant religious career. An offer came from an Indian prince, the Maharaja of Cooch Behar, to marry Sen's eldest daughter, who was not yet quite fourteen years old. For the sake of succession the marriage had to be according to Hindu rites. Now, idolatrous rites and child marriage were the very things which Sen as a religious and social reformer had opposed. He had made it a rule for his followers not to observe the former in any circumstances, and not to marry their daughters before they had completed their fourteenth year. In fact, an Act passed in 1872 had legalized marriages performed according to Brahmo rites and fixed the minimum age for it as fourteen.

But Sen fell in with the proposal, and his daughter was married to the prince in February 1878, and some subterfuges were adopted to satisfy the conscience of Sen. At once a storm broke over his head. Many of his followers had already been offended by his dictatorial ways, and now they accused him of apostasy. They seceded from his church and founded a parallel one. The quarrel was continued with extreme bitterness, and Sen's plea that he had given his daughter in marriage to the prince by hearing an *adesh* or command from God, with whom he had communed over the question, was treated as pure opportunism.

Max Müller felt distressed at what Sen had done, or rather by the manner in which Sen did it. But he was not the man to abandon a friend for one act of weakness. So he wrote to another Indian reformer on March 29, 1879:

I have full faith in Keshub Chunder Sen. I cannot bear to see the unforgiving way in which he has lately been treated. He has made a mistake, no doubt. But even if he had committed a crime, would it be impossible to forgive? Are his judges immaculate? Do they know the temptations of a man placed in so exceptional a position? He has been too kind, too yielding as a father—he has himself acknowledged that much. That is enough. You will never find immaculate saints on earth:

we ought to be grateful when we find an honest man, though he may not be free from human weaknesses.

To an English critic of Sen he wrote also: 'I cannot easily give up a man whom I once trusted.' And he wrote to *The Times* in defence of Sen. But the English friends of the new Hindu Theists of the strictest sect were more unrelenting than the early Christians who overlooked St Peter's three denials of Christ.

Sen was deeply touched by Max Müller's defence, and wrote from Calcutta:

> My dear Sir, Allow me to thank you most cordially for having said a good word for us in *The Times*. I have read your letter with very great interest, and thankfully appreciate your heartfelt sympathy with us in our trials and difficulties. You can hardly imagine the troubles I have had during the last two or three years and the grossly false and libellous charges brought against me week after week . . . All this I say to you privately because you have been good enough to give us your sympathy as a friend, and because you have boldly come forward, as few have done, to assert publicly that personal feelings lie at the bottom of the opposition movement. However, God's will be done!

In private Max Müller told Sen what he really thought of his conduct. In principle he did not object to the marriage between the Hindu Maharaja and Sen's daughter. He even quoted St Paul's words about marriages between pagans and Christians: 'The unbelieving husband is sanctified by the wife, and the unbelieving wife is sanctified by the husband; else were your children unclean, but now are they holy.' He was also honest enough to say that had he himself been placed in Sen's position he would probably have acted in the same way. But, he said, Sen should have taken his friends and followers into his confidence, instead of trying to impose his choice on them as God's commandment.

Sen replied that the whole affair was so uncertain, and the marriage appeared so improbable until it was a *fait accompli*, that he really had no time to consult his friends. He also explained that what he called God's commandment was not 'supernatural inspiration', but a 'command of conscience'. In plain words, he thought that the marriage was providential. 'It was very like a political marriage, such as you speak of. A whole kingdom was to be reformed, and all my individual interests were absorbed in the vastness of God's saving economy, or in what people would call public good. The Lord required my daughter for Cooch Behar, and I surrendered her.' In any case, the Maharaja of Cooch Behar, though he remained Hindu in form, became a patron of all the liberal movements in religion, as well as other things including cricket.

Sen wrote to Max Müller that the hostility and the attacks of his detractors had actually helped the progress of his church: 'Our influence spreads on all sides, and there is far greater enthusiasm among us now than in any previous period in the history of our church.' In one sense this was true, for Keshub Chunder Sen was giving a form to his movement, now called the New Dispensation, which in its public expression fell in line with the traditional Vaisnavism of Bengal. This consisted in going through Calcutta and other towns singing and dancing to the accompaniment of drums, exhibiting the maudlin religious enthusiasm of that sect. This is the exhibition, given on a very miniature scale, which now evokes admiration or amusement in Oxford Street, and which I have also seen in the United States. It was a sort of High Church movement among the Hindu Theists, and naturally it drew the condemnation of the seceding Theists who were very much Low Church. It scandalized the supporters of Sen in England, and it was described as 'a combination of dervish dances and Roman Catholicism'.

Max Müller wrote a very sensible letter on this external exhibition to Sen's loyal follower Pratap Chunder Mozoomdar. In it he wrote:

To tell you the truth, I am not fond of such things; but every religion is a compromise between men and children . . . There is no real harm in shaving one's hair. A man must either shave his hair or let it grow, and who shall say which of the two is best? As to leading an ascetic life, what harm is there in that? India is the very country for leading an ascetic life, and a man does not there banish himself from society by it, as he would do in Europe. Pilgrimages too, singing in the open air and carrying flags, seem all so natural to those who know the true Indian life—not the life of Calcutta or Bombay—that I cannot see why people in England should be so shocked by what they call Keshub Chunder Sen's vagaries.

About flag-waving by Sen's followers, Müller, if anything, was even more sensible: 'Because he carries a flag, which was the recognized custom among ancient religious leaders, he is accused of worshipping a flag. I am sure he does not pay half the worship to his flag which every English soldier does to his. It often becomes to him a real fetish; and yet a soldier, when he dies for his flag, is honoured by the very people who now cry out against Keshub Chunder Sen, because he honours his flag, as a symbol of his cause.'

But what Max Müller more seriously objected to was Sen's extreme emotionalism, and he wrote about it to Sen himself. But Sen replied unrepentantly:

The forms of one nation are apt to be repulsive and even shocking to another. Our Oriental nature is our apology for the 'impassioned utterances', the 'language of excessive veneration', 'highflown Language', etc., you speak of. How can I, my friend, destroy my Asiatic nature, how can I discard the language of poetry and emotion and inspiration which is my life and nature? To adopt any other language would cost me much effort, would be artificial, mechanical, unnatural, and, I may add, hypocritical. I must speak as I feel; and you know my devotion is, as a rule, extemporaneous. Our tears during prayer, our fervent and constant apostrophizing, our ascetic habits, our very forms of devotion in which we speak of God as one whom we *see* and *hear*, may be disagreeable to European eyes and ears, but so long as they are natural and national, and not affected or borrowed, we need not be afraid of serious consequences.

In addition to having this sort of enthusiasm ingrained within himself as a Bengali, Sen may also quite sincerely have felt that he should recast the monotheism he was preaching, which was very largely Christian in inspiration as well as spirit, in a national mould. At the height of the agitation against him, his follower Protap Chunder Mozoomdar, who was to take his place after his death as the leader of the New Dispensation, and who had a far more powerful intellect than his leader though he remained perfectly loyal to him, wrote to Max Müller:

'You have watched the agitation on the Cooch Behar marriage. The agitation began from deeper causes, and ended in deeper opposition than a mere protest against the marriage. Keshub Chunder Sen's genius is too Western for his own countrymen, and too Eastern for yours. His mind is so independent and original, so far above conventional proprieties of every sort, that long before the marriage he had begun to make enemies both inside and outside the Brahmo Samaj.' This was very true. The Christian missionaries in India too disliked Sen, though, of course, they never persecuted him. Speaking in England in 1870, Sen had actually said: 'Allow me, friends, to say, England is not yet a Christian nation.' So even in 1873, in the course of his lecture on missions delivered in Westminster Abbey, Müller said: 'They [the missionaries] feel towards Keshub Chunder Sen as Athanasius might have felt towards Ulfilas, the Arian Bishop of the Goths; yet what would have become of Christianity in Europe but for the Gothic races, but for those Arian heretics, who were considered more dangerous than downright pagans?'

In spite of differences of temperament and ways of thinking, neither of them lost respect and admiration for each other. When trying to recuperate in the Himalayas from an illness which led to his death, Sen wrote from Simla on July 20, 1883: 'I am sorry I cannot write to you so often as I wish. But of this I can assure you, that you are often present in my thoughts. The affinity is not only ethnic, but in the highest degree spiritual, which often draws you into my heart and makes me enjoy the pleasure of friendly intercourse. I forget the distance, and feel we are very near each other.'

Sen died less than six months later, and Max Müller wrote an eloquent and touching obituary notice, which he closed with these words: 'As long as there is a religion in India, whatever its name may be, the name of Keshub Chunder Sen will be gratefully remembered, as one who lived and died for the glory of God, for the welfare of mankind, and for the truth, so far as he could see it.'

But Müller's most sincere tribute was paid more than fifteen years later when he himself had come very near death. Sen's aged mother, hearing of Müller's serious illness at the end of 1899, wrote through her grandsons to inquire about his health. He replied on November 27: 'Please to tell your dear grandmother that I feel much touched by her sympathy . . . I miss her son very much . . . He was so kind, so gentle, so good a man too, and his mother ought indeed to be proud to be the mother of such a man.'

Sen was fifteen years younger than Max Müller, and died fifteen years before him.

This very incomplete account of Max Müller's personal relations with Indians should include his tributes to two remarkable Indian women of his time, only one of whom he met. Both were heroic in every sense of the word. The first of them was Rama Bai, called Pandita or Learned, whose Sanskrit leaning had become a legend in India. Her life was even more remarkable and might be called an epic in miniature. Max Müller wrote of her as the 'truly heroic Hindu lady, in appearance small, delicate, and timid, but in reality strong and bold as a lioness'.

She was the daughter of a very learned Brahmin of an ancient and venerated clan, but was born in a forest of the Western Ghats. This Brahmin had as a widower married Ramabai's mother when she was only nine years old. He had tried to teach his first wife, but was not allowed to do so by his family because there was prejudice in traditional Hindu society against educating women. He tried again with his second wife, and when again opposed, he retired to the wilderness to be free. There the wife grew to be learned, and they had three children, one son and two daughters, Ramabai being the younger daughter. His reputation for learning spread, and students began to come to his house. He also attracted visitors.

A traditional Hindu teacher could not take fees, but on the contrary had to house and feed his pupils on what support he got from generous patrons of learning. Ramabai's father lived in his hermitage for some time, teaching his son and elder daughter with the students. Soon the expenses became so heavy that he had to break up his home, and began to wander all over India with his family, earning a livelihood by reciting or expounding the sacred books in palaces or *Maths* (monasteries). His eldest daughter married, and his son and Ramabai helped him in this.

When he died his son supported his widow as well as Rama in the same way, but they earned very little. Then the mother died, and after travelling all over India on foot the brother and sister came at last to Calcutta, where Ramabai's lectures created a sensation. But a new blow fell. The brother died, and left alone she was compelled to marry. However, her marriage was very happy, and she had a daughter whom she named Manorama or Heart's Joy. But after nineteen months she became a widow. In her desperation she decided to fit herself for practical work, and in order to get medical training, helpless as she was, she decided to come to England. She scraped together all she had earned by lecturing and translating Sanskrit for the government, and arrived there, quite destitute at the end of her journey.

With her child and the woman friend who had accompanied her she was taken to the Anglican Sisterhood at Wantage, some members of which she had known at Poona. She told them, however, that she would never become a Christian. She paid a visit to Max

Müller at Oxford at the time, and on October 27, 1883, Müller wrote to his young son: 'We had a nice visit from Ramabai, a Brahmin lady who knows Sanskrit splendidly. She knows books as long as Homer by heart from beginning to end—speaks Sanskrit correctly, and writes Sanskrit poetry. Unfortunately she hears very badly, and as she came to England to study and take a degree, she is very unhappy.'

What actually happened, however, was terrible. Ramabai's companion feared that they might be made Christian by force, and tried to strangle her to death to save her from the calamity. Failing in this she killed herself. It was after this that Ramabai came over to stay with Max Müller at Oxford. Her nervous prostration was such that one of Müller's maidservants had to sleep with her at night. Arrangements were made to enable her to attend medical lectures, but her hearing became suddenly worse, and the idea had to be given up. She then decided to train herself as a nurse, to do some useful work in India.

At this juncture she was invited to America to see the presentation of a doctorate in medicine by the Medical College of Pennsylvania to a young countrywoman of hers, who was the first Indian woman to take such a degree anywhere, and who had known and helped her after her widowhood in India. Ramabai went and found many friends, who helped her to start a home for young Hindu widows in India. But in the meantime she had to become a Christian because she could not stand alone; she had to belong to somebody and somewhere, especially to worship God with those who had been kind to her. Writing about this Max Müller felt sure that she herself would not make any attempts to proselytize among the little widows who were entrusted to her, 'but she lost, of course, the support of her native friends and has to fight her battles alone.'

In 1887 Müller wrote to the reformer Malabari: 'Try to establish schools or refuges for widows. Here you might combine with Ramabai. I suppose she will soon return to India. She has become a Christian, but she is not narrow-minded, and may be made useful.' By the end of the century Ramabai had some two thousand widows in her home. She wrote a very moving book, *Life of a High-Caste Hindu Woman*, describing the treatment of a young Hindu woman in the house of her father-in-law.

The other Hindu woman to whom Max Müller paid a glowing tribute though he never met her, was the friend of Ramabai who had got the medical degree. Her name was Anandibai Joshi. She had been married at the age of nine, and had been very happy in her marriage. So, when asked to speak about child-marriage before an American audience, she stood up and defended it, though of course only as betrothal albeit binding for life. She had seen the suffering of young mothers in India, and resolved to take a medical training in America, saying, however: 'I will go to America as a Hindu, and come back and live among my people as a Hindu.' So at the age of eighteen she went to Philadelphia with her husband, in spite of endless difficulties, and enrolled as a student in the Medical College of Pennsylvania.

Dr Rachel Bodley, who received her, wrote about this coming: 'One day in September 1883, there came to my door a little lady in blue cotton saree, accompanied by her faithful friend, Mrs B. F. Carpenter of New Jersey, and since that hour when, speechless for very wonder, I bestowed a kiss of welcome upon the stranger's cheek instead of words, I have loved the women of India.' Anandibai had very great difficulty in adapting herself to the Western way of life, but she got her degree, and was appointed physician in charge of the female ward at Kolhapur in the province of Bombay. Her health however had been undermined, and she died at the age of twenty-two in 1887. Though she had technically lost caste by crossing the seas, she was received by all, and when she died all Poona mourned with her family. Max Müller wrote about this: 'It shows that even the most inveterate social and religious diseases are not incurable when treated with unselfish love and generosity. If all this could be achieved by a frail young daughter of India, what is there that could be called impossible for the strong men of that country?'

This faith in the men of India was set down by Max Müller only a year before his own death. No one who has the capacity to love deeply and strongly can help extending his love from the general to the particular; or from the particular to the general. The failure to be general denies fullness and breadth, and to a certain extent unselfishness in love, while without particular objects, love is disembodied and remains only a tenuous exhalation. In Max Müller's case love became particular in two ways. His love of the idea of India and for the ancient civilization of India became more specifically love for the people of India as a whole; it then became love for individual Indians.

So what he found most unnatural and vehemently denounced in the relationship between India and Britain was the habitual denigration of the Indian character by those Englishmen who lived in India or had first-hand experience of the country. Müller set himself not only to defend Indians, but also to show in what way the Indian character and outlook could be a complement to those of the European. So, in the very first of the lectures he delivered at Cambridge in 1882, to which he boldly gave the title, *India: What Can It Teach Us?*, he said:

If I were asked under what sky the human mind has most fully developed some of its choicest gifts, has most deeply pondered on the greatest problems of life, and has found solutions of some of them which well deserve the attention even of those who have studied Plato and Kant—I should point to India. And if I were to ask myself from what literature we, here in Europe, we who have been nurtured almost exclusively on the thoughts of Greeks and Romans, and of one Semitic race, the Jewish, may draw that corrective which is most wanted in order to make our inner life more perfect, more comprehensive, more universal, in fact more truly human, a life, not for this life only, but a transfigured and eternal life—again I should point to India.

Those who have not gone into the history of Indo-British personal relations during the most stable days of British rule in that country can have no idea what the British contempt and hatred of Indians was like. By the end of the nineteenth century the Englishman had formulated his Thirty-nine Articles of dogma regarding Indians, and the first and second Articles were of course that they were all liars and all dishonest. These assumptions were communicated in advance to any Englishman who was going to India as an administrator or in any other capacity. Generally speaking they were accepted even before the Englishman saw the country and its people. So the English came with a prefabricated hostility.

Before the Mutiny the attitude was one of more or less passive contempt. But after, an element of fear came into the aversion, and sensing the latent hostility of their subjects the British in India snarled like frightened beasts of prey. When in 1920 a distinguished Bengali, who had been raised to the peerage and was then Under-Secretary of State for India, was justifying in the most moderate language in the House of Lords, the cashiering of General Dyer for shooting hundreds of Indians at Amritsar, a drunken peer was heard to shout: 'If they are all like him, the more they shoot the better.'

It must be added, however, that the Indians fully reciprocated the hatred. No one stated this more clearly than one of the greatest of modern Indians, the famous Bengali writer, Bankim Chandra Chatterji. He wrote in 1873:

> If we take up any English newspaper [i.e., a newspaper edited by Englishmen in India], we are sure to find somewhere in it some abuse of the Natives, some unfair vilification. Again, looking into any Bengali newspaper, we find as a matter of equal certainty anger against the English and denunciation of them. In every Indian newspaper there is unjust criticism of the English, in every English newspaper the same injustice to Indians. This has been going on for a long time, there is nothing novel about it. Conversation in society runs along the same lines.

Chatterji accepted this as inherent in the conqueror-conquered relationship, and he added that so long as this lasted there could not be any lessening of the racial hatred.

Max Müller set himself to fight and if possible to eliminate this misunderstanding. In his second Cambridge lecture therefore he declared that he was going to grapple with a prejudice which was more mischievous than ignorance, because it formed a kind of icy barrier between the Hindus and their rulers, and made anything like a feeling of true fellowship between the two utterly impossible. 'That prejudice,' he continued, 'consists in looking upon our stay in India as a kind of *moral* exile, and in regarding the Hindus as an inferior race, totally different from ourselves in their moral character, and, more particularly in what forms the very foundation of the English character, respect for truth.'

So he devoted the lecture to a demonstration, with facts and testimonies which could not be contested, of the truthful character of the Hindus, and he concluded the lecture with the following words: 'Certainly I can imagine nothing more mischievous, more dangerous, more fatal to the permanence of English rule in India, than for the young Civil Servants to go to that country with the idea that it is a sink of moral depravity, an ant's nest of lies; for no one is so sure to go wrong, whether in public or in private life, as he who says in his haste: 'All men are liars.'''

To the end of his life he continued to defend the Indian character. This championship in the midst of almost universal denigration earned for Max Müller the gratitude of all Indians, and their admiration of him was due no less to it than to his expositions of Hindu life and culture. Thus, speaking after his death at a meeting, R. G. Bhandarkar, a great Sanskrit scholar and a historian, laid greater emphasis on his defence of Indians than on his scholarship. He said: 'The character of all of us Indians had been greatly traduced in Europe. We were described as men given habitually to lying, of no substance or worth in us, possessing no self-respect and incapable of any great effort. Max Müller combated this view.'

The lecture provoked decided antagonism among those Englishmen in England or India who professed to know inhabitants of India. One critic called him a Hindu pervert, but a really scandalous sequel followed. A leading Sanskrit scholar in England sent a communication to Indian newspapers accusing Max Müller of intellectual dishonesty in defending Hindus against the charge of untruthfulness. The first Indian newspaper which published this communication did so in the following news story:

A distinguished Orientalist of England, writing to Babu Protapa Chandra Roy of this city, the enterprising publisher of the *Mahabharata*, says, 'It may perhaps amuse you to learn that in the recently published German translation of *India: what can it teach us?* the passages in praise of Hindu truthfulness have, *with the author's sanction* been suppressed. What will his bosom-friend Dr. Rajendralala Mitra say to this? Why, Dr Mitra, when he sees the work thus mutilated, will simply say that the learned Professor knows the art of being all things to all men at the same time . . . An additional incentive to such suppression might have been found in the little probability of the Professor's Hindu friends reading his work in German, especially after they had once read it in English.

Clearly, this English Orientalist had the animus of Whitney against Max Müller without Whitney's courage. Max Müller could guess the identity of the writer, but did not name him. He called the story a scandalous invention from beginning to end. The facts were at once communicated to the editor of the Indian paper. Max Müller had not seen the German translation before its publication. The German translator had only omitted extracts from English writers whose names were less known to German than to English readers, because the lectures had to be abridged.

Even so the wholesale running down of Indians continued, and those who looked upon Indians as an inferior race protested against Max Müller's description of them as biased. Müller admitted quite frankly that the Indians he had known intimately—Dwarkanath Tagore, Keshub Chunder Sen, Behramji Malabari, Ramabai— were exceptional beings, who would be so in England as anywhere else. He was not an indiscriminate admirer of everything Indian. He had had some unpleasant experiences with the small number of young Indians who came to Oxford. About one very unpleasant experience with them he was driven to write in his reminiscences: 'These men have a very curious way of blushing. If you convict them of a downright falsehood, their bright brown colour turns suddenly greyish, but their eloquence in defending themselves never fades or flags.' If I had not read the vindication of Hindu truthfulness offered by Müller, I should have said that the spirit of this remark was not very far from those made by the hardboiled Anglo-Indians of his times.

What Müller objected to was any sweeping generalization from a small number of personal observations. He said: 'If I hear a man calling all Indians liars, I generally ask how many he has known. I do the same thing when I hear all Frenchmen called monkeys, all Italians assassins, all Germans unwashed, all Russians savages, or even England *Perfide Albion*.' Besides, he knew that the question of Hindu truthfulness, even when considered on the doctrinal or historical plane, was extremely complex. For instance, in establishing the general truthfulness of Hindus he took his stand on the glorification of truth in the sacred books, as well as on the repeated insistence in them on telling the truth and nothing else. Yet he himself in Note C to the printed edition of his lectures gave authoritative citations from the books of Hindu sacred law *(Dharma Sastras)* which treated falsehood uttered in certain circumstances as venial sins. For example, he quoted among many others a passage from the *Vasistha* treatise on law: 'If a man speaks an untruth at the time of marriage, in sexual intercourse, when his life is in danger, or when he is likely to lose all his property, and when a *Brahmana* is in danger, it has been declared that these five untruths are not sins.' There are, of course, many such passages in all Hindu sacred texts. But, on the whole, Max Müller could make out a strong case for the Hindu's love of truth in ancient times from Hindu scriptures and from the testimony of foreign observers such as the Greeks. Moreover, since no direct evidence was then available for what the Hindus actually did, the didactic insistence on truth created a justifiable presumption that they were truthful in their conduct.

In respect of the contemporary situation Max Müller had greater difficulty, not due to lack of evidence but to the contradiction in it. The most vocal opinion of the Anglo-Indians, or the British who were living or had lived in India, was that Indians were habitually and universally given to lying. As against them he was in a decidedly unfavourable position, and he frankly described it. 'Having never been in India myself,' he said in his Cambridge lecture of 1882, 'I can only claim for myself the right and duty of every historian, namely, the right of collecting as much information as possible, and the duty to sift it according to the recognized rules of historical criticism.'

He stated the issue between him and the men on the spot even more clearly in his letter to *The Times* on the Ilbert Bill, which appeared in the paper on August 6, 1883. What he said might be described as a methodological *exposé* in a nutshell. Müller confessed that he could not claim 'the honourable title of Anglo-Indian', but added that he had read the accounts of the most eminent Anglo-Indians of former times, and was acquainted personally with many of his time. According to him, the Anglo-Indians could be divided into two classes: those who never appealed to their residence in India as a title to infallibility, and the others who wrote and spoke on Indian subjects like so many Popes.

If you differ from them [he said], they seem to have but one answer to all facts and all arguments—namely, 'I have been in India; I have spent twenty-five years among the natives—it is all wrong, I know it is wrong, and you would not say so if you had been in India.'

It makes little difference to these invincibles that where they say 'Black' others who have spent quite as many years in India as they have, say 'White'. It only makes them more emphatic, and those who may happen to listen, naturally think it rather impertinent that one who had never been in India should venture to know more of the customs, the prejudices, the laws, and literature of that country than one who has ruined his liver and lost his temper by twenty-five years' residence in Calcutta. I have not as yet been driven by my Anglo-Indian friends to such a pitch of despair as others who have openly declared that no one who has been in India is fit to write a history of India.

'Residence in India,' he pointed out, 'had its dangers as well as its advantages.' Firstly, India is a large country and not even twenty-five years in Calcutta, Bombay or Madras would justify an experienced civil servant in beginning a single sentence with 'the people of India'. Secondly, Anglo-Indians lived in an English environment, and when they saw the Indian environment they saw it in a changing state due to contact with English influences. Thirdly, an observer might be too near as well as too far, and nothing was more difficult than for a soldier to see the battle in which he is fighting as a whole, or for Bismarck to write the history of his time.

It was the privilege and duty of the scholar and the historian, Müller declared, to stand aloof, to choose his own point of view, and to look at both sides of a question. If historians could write about the Peloponnesian or the Crimean War without being in Greece or Russia, surely a man who had studied the evidence carefully could pronounce an opinion on Lord Lawrence's or Lord Lytton's government in India?

Max Müller based his views about the general truthfulness of Hindus on the experience of a large number of eminent Englishmen who had intimate knowledge of Indians, and more especially he depended on the statements of Colonel Sleeman, who as the eradicator of the notorious criminal community of the Thugs, (its members murdered people by strangling them with a handkerchief), was not likely to be ignorant of the darker side of Indian life. And Müller quotes one of Sleeman's sayings: 'I have had before me hundreds of cases in which a man's property, liberty, and life has depended upon his telling a lie, and he has refused to tell it.'

Depending on such testimonies, Max Müller made out a subtle and sophisticated case for the truthfulness of the people of India. He said that in order to judge them fairly the Indian people had to be observed where and when they were *left to themselves*. Historically, he explained, they could be regarded as left to themselves only before the Muslim conquest. This conquest was so cruel and atrocious that the wonder, to his mind, was how a nation could survive such an inferno without being turned into devils themselves. So the truthfulness of the Hindus could be seen best in ancient India, when they were politically independent.

Next, basing himself on the views of Sleeman, he said that Indians could be considered to be left to themselves only when they were in their village communities. He said that Sleeman was one of the first to discover the village communities of India, which later were described more fully by Sir Henry Maine. Sleeman stated that lying between members of the same village was almost unknown.

Lastly, he pointed out that English opinion about Indians was shaped largely by experiences in big cities like Calcutta, Bombay and Madras, and that the native elements in such towns contained the most unfavourable specimens of the Indian population. This might be regarded as the moral counterpart of the military opinion in India that the best Indian soldiers were not to be recruited from the bazaars of the cities. Besides, Müller pointed out, any insight into the domestic life of the more respectable classes, even in towns, was extremely difficult to obtain.

I might add another aspect of the question which Max Müller left open, without stating it explicitly. The concept of 'Hindus left to themselves' should also include their loyalty to their own notion of *Dharma*—righteousness, justice or *dikaiosyne*, or whatever European name might be given to it. This could be found working among rural people. The Hindu peasant, despite his worldly propensities, was also the carrier of a tradition of religious faith and morality which was the ancient Hindu spirituality reduced to its lowest and simplest, but which was also the heritage of the upper classes before British rule. If that rule introduced the European moral consciousness among the Hindus, it also undermined the simple indigenous morality. The Indian Penal Code and the Evidence Act, introduced by the British in India, with all their complexities created more falsehood in India than existed before. And now the professed secularism of the Westernized ruling class in India is dealing the last blows to Hindu morality.

Finally, it has also to be said that among us the notion of verbal truthfulness was never very highly developed and therefore nobody minded a false statement, and often called an incorrect statement a lie. The feeling of moral baseness in lying was roused only in the early days of British rule in India when the English word 'liar' was used, and not when its Bengali equivalent was applied. There is an amusing scene in an early Bengali farce in which a young man rushed to give a beating to his friend who called him a 'liar'. The offender was very much shocked by it, and asked for an explanation. The angry young man replied that had he been called *mithyavadi* (i.e., liar in Bengali) he would not have minded it at all, but to be called a 'liar' was unforgivable. That shows how foreign the idea of verbal falsehood was among us. The European influence also created the white lie in India, prevarication and casuistry, for which before there was hardly any need. Therefore one might say that Max Müller's defence of Hindu truthfulness was as well founded in one way, as was in another the accusation that we Hindus were liars to a man. Modern and Westernized Hindus of the late nineteenth century did not understand this difference, and took Max Müller's defence of Hindu truthfulness with all its Western implications. Therefore when Lord Curzon in one of his convocation speeches admonished the students of Calcutta University to respect truth 'in all circumstances', the whole of educated India was scandalized.

Chapter 4

INDIA: MOVEMENTS

IT has been seen that all the scholarly researches of Max Müller had a practical side, or in any case practical implications. For instance, in editing the *Rig-Veda* he always kept in mind the effect its publication might have on the religious life of contemporary Hindus. He had the same end in view when, after completing his edition of the book, he took up the editorship of a gigantic corpus of the scriptures of the East under the general title of *The Sacred Books of the East*. In addition, he kept himself in touch with all the important religious and social movements in India even when they were not directly connected with his scholarly work, and tried to promote those which he considered progressive. In thus involving himself in the sphere of action from a distance he certainly produced results which were more tangible than those which Plato could bring about either at Athens or Syracuse.

But the deepest and most enduring practical effect of his scholarly effort was produced by that part of it which for him was the most theoretical. His work on Comparative Philology had its political effect, and gave a specific direction and character to modern Indian nationalism.

The contribution made by the European Orientalists to Indian nationalism is now recognized by all. The Hindus had created their own brand of nationalism, a basic chauvinism so to speak, long before the coming of European influences to their country. For example, the great Muslim scholar, Alberuni, who made a special effort to know them and their religion, recorded at the beginning of the eleventh century that: 'The Hindus believe that there is no country but theirs, no nation like theirs, no kings like theirs, no religion like theirs, no science like theirs. They are haughty, foolishly vain, self-conceited.' This megalomania became far more intense and unshakable under Muslim rule, and remained a living passion under British rule. But it had no historical basis, and could not be accepted in its traditional form by the Indians who were receiving a Western education. They wanted a nationalism which would be tenable historically. The Orientalists of Europe supplied the historical basis by revealing to modern Indians their past history and achievements. Max Müller fully supported all legitimate use of history by them. As he put it: 'A people that can feel no pride in the past, in its history and literature, loses the mainstay of its national character.' But the question was whether the pride was being felt rationally. At first, by and large, that was the case.

Comparative Philology entered into the new Hindu nationalism less obviously, but its conclusions were an essential ingredient in its composition. But it has to be pointed out that new science of Comparative Philology created in the nineteenth century had its political effects in Europe as well. Hitlerism was its late and monstrous abortion; and anti-Semitism a deformed and vicious child. Withal, it created other political movements which were not looked upon as illegitimate. These were pan-Germanism, pan-Slavism, pan-Islamism and pan-Turanism. This was pointed out by Sir Henry Maine in his Rede Lecture, delivered before the University of Cambridge in 1875:

> Sanscritic study has been the source of certain indirect effects, not indeed having much pretension to scientific character, but of prodigious practical importance. There is no question of its having produced very serious political consequences, and this is a remarkable illustration of the fact that no great addition can be made to the stock of human thought without profoundly disturbing the whole mass and moving it in the most unexpected directions. For the new Theory of Language has unquestionably produced a new theory of Race.
>
> That people not necessarily understanding one another's tongue should be grouped together politically on the ground of linguistic affinities assumed to prove community of descent, is quite a new idea. Nevertheless, we owe to it, at all events in part, the vast development of German nationality; and we certainly owe to it the pretensions of the Russian Empire to at least a presidency over all Slavonic communities. The theory is perhaps stretched to the point at which it is nearest breaking when men, and particularly Frenchmen, speak of the Latin race.

That Comparative Philology should make an impact on the Indian mind was natural, because that impact was nothing more than a recoil to an impact of India on the European mind. As Sir Henry Maine said: 'India has given the world Comparative Philology and Comparative Mythology.' It is easy to see that in saying so he had the work of Max Müller in mind. In the inaugural lecture which

Max Müller delivered on being appointed to the new chair of Comparative Philology, he brought out the connexion even more forcefully. I have already quoted the passage from that lecture in which he said that 'a Comparative Philologist without a knowledge of Sanskrit was like an astronomer without a knowledge of mathematics'. In the same lecture he elaborated the actual historical connexion between the two by saying: 'We may date the origin of Comparative Philology, as distinct from the Science of Language, from the foundation of the Asiatic Society of Calcutta in 1784. From that time dates the study of Sanskrit, and it was the study of Sanskrit which formed the foundation of Comparative Philology.'

The connexion between modern Hindu nationalism and Comparative Philology was implicit in this purely scholarly affiliation, but it owed its full development very largely to the manner in which Max Müller presented it to his readers. For him this branch of philology was not solely an inquiry into the origin and nature of language, but also a means of exploring the mind of the earliest civilized man, and even more especially the mind of the Aryan man. He employed the phrase 'Aryan Race', frequently, and also idealized the ethnic group to which he gave this name. So, there is a likelihood of his being regarded as what in these days is called a 'Racialist'. The two words 'Aryan' and 'Race' have become some sort of red rag to contemporary Radicals. This makes it necessary to explain what Max Müller meant when he spoke of the Aryan Race. There was no vagueness in his conception at all. In 1872, speaking before the University of Strassburg, he said:

These two sciences, the Science of Language and the Science of Man, cannot, at least for the present, be kept too much asunder; and many misunderstandings, many controversies, would have been avoided, if scholars had not attempted to draw conclusions from language to blood, or from blood to language. When each of these sciences shall have carried out independently its own classification of men and of languages, then, and then only, will it be time to compare their results; but even then, I must repeat, what I have said many times before, it would be as wrong to speak of Aryan blood as of dolichocephalic grammar.

Again, in his book *Biographies of Words*, published in 1888, he wrote:

How then shall we tell from language what races had to learn the language of their Aryan conquerors or their Aryan slaves? There is no Aryan race in blood, but whoever, through the imposition of hands, whether of his parents or his foreign masters, has received the Aryan blessing, belongs to that unbroken spiritual succession which began with the first apostles of that noble speech, and continues to the present day in every part of the globe. Aryan, in scientific language, is utterly inapplicable to race. It means language and nothing but language; and if we speak of Aryan race at all, we should know that it means no more than Aryan speech.

Lastly, addressing the Anthropological Section of the British Association at Cardiff in 1891, he gave a summary of his views on this question from as early as 1847, and declared that 'the unholy alliance between Philology and Physiology' had hitherto done nothing but mischief.

Speaking of his first appearance at a scientific conference at Oxford in 1847, he said that at that time it was taken for granted that in future Comparative Philology would be the only safe foundation for Anthropology. Linguistic Ethnology was a very favourite term used by Bunsen, Pritchard, Latham and others. He protested against this view even then, and published his formal protest in 1853. To Bunsen he said that 'there ought to be no compromise between ethnological and phonological science'.

Curiously enough, he was often supposed to be the strongest advocate of a theory which he was attacking. He made a frank confession, however, in the address of 1891: 'Perhaps I was not entirely without blame, for, having once delivered my soul, I allowed myself occasionally the freedom to speak of the Aryan or Semitic race, meaning thereby no more than the people, whoever and whatever they were, who spoke Aryan or Semitic languages.' He went on to say that as to the colour of the skin, the hair, the eyes of those unknown speakers of Aryan speech, the scholar says nothing. 'If we step once from the narrow domain of science into the vast wilderness of mere assertion, then it does not matter what we say. We may say, with Plenka, that all Aryas are dolichocephalic, blue-eyed, and blond, or we may say, with Pietrement, that all Aryas are brachycephalic, with brown eyes and black hair. There is no difference between the two assertions. They are both perfectly meaningless.'

Holding these views he found it paradoxical that he, a philologist, should be presiding over the Section of Anthropology, and justified that in two ways. First of all, he thought that at some future time some connexion might be discovered between philological and anthropological facts. But he emphasized strongly that anthropologists should know more about language, and ventured to hope that 'the time will come when no anthropologist will venture to write on anything concerning the inner life of man without having himself acquired a knowledge of the languages in which that inner life finds its truest expression'. So it will be seen that in respect of the relationship between language and 'race' zoologically defined, Max Müller held very sound as well as sane views.

Educated Indians of his time who were becoming familiar with these philological discoveries and being influenced by the new ideas, did not accept or apply them with his scientific spirit. On the contrary, they showed every inclination to do so in a manner which could have been called racialist. But even here it is very important to be precise as to the attitude, for the word 'racialist' has become a mere pejorative expression without a correct denotation or comnotation.

What is now called 'racialism' is not a zoological or purely genetic concept at all, but a psychological one. It is nothing but an exaggerated consciousness of group identity based on a common language and a common culture, often accompanied by a sense of superiority to other human groups, and always by a desire to preserve the identity. It should really be regarded as an extreme form of nationalism, and the quarrel between the racialists and anti-racialists is correctly seen as a conflict between nationalism and cosmopolitanism. This form of nationalism is perpetuated by the mental inheritance of a community, but it also has a genetic aspect. All communities with a well-defined sense of identity are overwhelmingly endogamous, and this endogamy furnishes a kind of genetic support to what is really an acquired character. The loyalty to the psychological identity is always heightened and made aggressive towards other groups by any threat to it.

The Hindus certainly had a high degree of group consciousness, a sense of unbridgeable difference from all others, and this was accentuated by their habit of giving to all their social relationships and activities a genetic complexion and cast. In ancient times what might be called Hindu nationalism retrospectively was based on their belief that they were 'Aryas', and as such not only different from other peoples and communities, but also superior. Anyone who is at all familiar with Sanskrit literature cannot be unaware of this, cannot remain ignorant of what the notion of being Arya meant to the Hindu of ancient times.

To begin with, however, the notion of Arya was applied aggressively to the older population of the country, to the non-Aryan internal proletariat. But when other foreigners began from time to time to invade India and rule the original Aryan conquerors, the notion was extended to them. From the Hindu point of view these foreigners in their original homes began to be regarded as an external proletariat, and were all indiscriminately lumped under the name, Mlechchhas or unclean foreigners. Only the Hindu was regarded as Aryan, and as the historical memory was wholly lost, India was regarded as the only Aryan land. This Aryan pride was also seen, though not in so intolerant a form, in Persia as well before the spread of Islam, and it has been resuscitated there in our time.

This Aryan pride ran in the blood of all Hindus and, transformed into a dogmatic megalomania and xenophobia, it enabled them not only to survive under foreign rule, but also to despise their foreign rulers, whether Muslim or British. None the less, it hung in the air, without any historical basis. Comparative Philology supplied that basis, and brought into existence a more rational and also a more self-conscious Aryanism among the modern Hindus.

This was the positive influence of the ideas derived from Comparative Philology on Indians. They had also a defensive application by which the Hindus tried to maintain their national honour against the very vocal British arrogance in India. Whether it was asserted or assumed, they resented the British attitude, and felt deeply insulted by their treatment as inferiors. Comparative Philology came to their rescue by showing that not only in their languages, but even ethnically, they were related to Europeans. This created an immense enthusiasm and confidence among the Hindus, which was noticed by Sir Henry Maine when he was a Member of the Viceroy's Council in India and Vice-Chancellor of Calcutta University. Delivering his Convocation address in 1864 in Calcutta, he said:

Probably, if we could search into the hearts of the more refined portions of the Native Community, we should find their highest aspiration was to be placed on a footing of real and genuine equality with their European fellow-citizens. Some persons have told them that they are equals already, equal in fact as they undoubtedly are before the law. Most of you have heard of one remarkable effort which was made to establish this position. A gentleman, who was then a Member of the Government of India, Mr Laing, went down to the Dalhousie Institute, and, in a lecture delivered there, endeavoured to popularize those wonderful discoveries in philological science which have gone far to lift the hypothesis of the common parentage of the most famous branches of the human family to the level of a scientific demonstration. I do not know that anybody was ever more to be admired than Mr Laing for that act of courage, for I know how obstinate were those prejudices which he sought to overthrow, and to what height they had risen at the moment when he spoke. The effect produced by his lecture on the Aryan race must have been prodigious, for I am sure I scarcely see a single native book or newspaper which does not contain some allusion to Mr Laing's argument.

Maine was, however, conscious that there lay a risk for the future in this enthusiasm. He told the students of Calcutta University whom he was addressing that though Mr Laing taught nothing but the truth, it was a barren truth. Then he explained himself:

Depend upon it, very little is practically gained by the Native when it is proved, beyond contradiction, that he is of the same race with the Englishman. Depend upon it, the true equality of mankind lies, not in the past, but in the future. It may come—probably will come—but it has not come already.

In the meantime [he continued] the equality which results from intellectual cultivation is always and at once possible. Be sure that it is a real equality. No man ever yet genuinely despised, however he might hate, his intellectual equal.

Indians by themselves tried to reach that intellectual equality, and also found that instead of being despised by the Englishman he was being hated. But at the same time they also went on advertising the equality from the presumed common descent. In 1874, a Bengali writer had an article in the *Indian Mirror*, a very influential newspaper edited by an eminent Bengali, in which he brought out the difference that Sanskritic studies in Europe and Comparative Philology had made to the British attitude towards Indians. He said that at the beginning of their rule the British regarded the people of India as little better than niggers, having a civilization

perhaps a shade better than that of the barbarian, but that the discovery of Sanskrit had entirely revolutionized the course of thought
and speculation. 'We were niggers at one time. We now become
brethren.' Then he continued:

> The advent of the English found us a nation low sunk in the mire of
> superstition, ignorance, and political servitude. The advent of scholars
> like Sir William Jones found us fully established in a rank above that of
> every nation as that from which modern civilization could be dis-
> tinctly traced. It would be interesting to contemplate what would have
> been our position if the science of philology had not been discovered ...
>
> We should know that it is to the study of the roots and inflexions of
> Sanskrit that we owe our national salvation . . . Within a few years
> after the discovery of Sanskrit, a revolution took place in the history
> of comparative science. Never were so many discoveries made at once,
> and from the speculations of learned scholars like Max Müller, the
> dawnings of many truths are even now visible to the world . . . Com-
> parative mythology and comparative religion are new terms altogether
> in the world.

There was more than a chance that this reawakening of self-
respect among the modern Hindus could lead them astray. But the
immediate result was something which Max Müller both welcomed and admired, because it showed a line of development which
he himself was urging on Indians. The human urge in all his
scholarly work was that, becoming aware of their great past and
drawing on their legacy, they would revitalize their contemporary
life, and shed the dead wood which had accumulated through the
centuries. He saw that the process was unfolding both in its destruc-
tive and constructive aspects.

So, as President of the Aryan Section of the International Congress of Orientalists held in London from September 14 to 21, 1874
he described the result of the impact made on Indians by the work
of European Orientalists and other scholars. He summed up the
general drift in one significant sentence: 'Thus the religion, the
literature, the whole character of the people of India are becoming
more and more Indo-European.' He amplified the formula by
saying:

> A new race of men is growing up in India, who have stepped, as it were,
> over a thousand years, and have entered at once on the intellectual
> inheritance of Europe. They carry off prizes at English schools, take
> their degree in English Universities, and are in every respect our

equals . . . With regard to what is of the greatest interest to us, their scholarship, it is true that the old school of Sanskrit scholars is dying out, and much will die with it which we shall never recover; but a new and most promising school of Sanskrit students, educated by European professors, is springing up, and they will, nay, to judge from recent controversies, they have already become most formidable rivals to our own scholars . . . They work for us, as we work for them.

But there was also another side to the movement which Max Müller could not see because he did not visit India. Sir Henry Maine did see it, and it seemed so ominous to him that he thought it necessary to warn his young listeners against it in Calcutta in his Convocation address of 1866. In 1870 he said that he had had unusual opportunities of studying the mental condition of the educated class in one Indian province (Bengal), and had found that though this class was so strongly Europeanized as to be no fair sample of native society as a whole, its peculiar stock of ideas was probably the chief source from which certain influences were proceeding. Then he added: 'Here there has been a complete revolution of thought, in literature, in taste, in morals, and in law.'

To the young members of this class he spoke about the strange dichotomy in their ideology. He said that he had no complaint to make of the education which they were receiving, but that he could not help being disappointed at the use to which they were sometimes putting it. 'It seems to me that not seldom they employ it for what I can best describe as irrationally reactionary purposes.' He could see plainly that the educated Indians themselves did not conceal the fact that by their new education they had broken for ever with their past, and abandoned much of the customs and creeds. Yet, he said, he was constantly reading and sometimes hearing elaborate attempts on their part to persuade themselves and others, that there was a sense in which these rejected portions of their history, usage and belief were perfectly in harmony with the modern knowledge which they had acquired, and with the modern civilization to which they aspired.

There were some Indians, he went on to say, who seemed to have persuaded themselves that there was once a time in India when learning was more honoured and respected, and when the career of a learned man was more brilliant, than in British India and under British rule. So that they believed or tried to believe that it was better to be a Brahmin, or a scribe attached to the court of some half-mythical Hindu king, than to follow one of the learned professions which the English had created.

He observed that in point of fact there was no one in the hall in which he was speaking to whom the life of a hundred years ago would not be acute suffering supposing it could be lived over again. Then he declared emphatically:

> It is impossible even to imagine the condition of an educated Native, with some of the knowledge and many of the susceptibilities of the nineteenth century—indeed perhaps with too many of them—if he could recross the immense gulf which separates him from the India of Hindu poetry, if indeed it ever existed. The only India, in fact, to which he could hope to return—and that retrogression is not beyond the range of conceivable possibilities—is the India of Mahratta robbery and Mohammedan rule . . . European influences are, in a great measure, the source of these delusions.

He also said that a similar mistake was being made by them when they called in ingenious analogies and subtle explanations to justify usages which they did not venture to defend directly, or of which in their hearts they disapproved. He saw a tendency on the part of the educated classes to defend practices on the ground that they served some practical end or, more often, because something superficially like them could be found in Europe. Then he said: 'There is no greater delusion than to suppose that you weaken an error by giving it a colour of truth. On the contrary, you give it pertinacity and vitality, and greater power for evil.'

The warning was not heeded, the tendency grew, and by the end of the century a very plausible Hindu apologia was built up, largely on the strength of the very ideas and information supplied by men like Max Müller. This can be seen in the record of a conversation that the French literary critic, André Chevrillon, had with a learned Bengali, the principal of the college at Jaipur. Chevrillon found in him a fund of enthusiasm for the old metaphysics of the country, and he told the Frenchman: 'Within the last five or six years there has been a reaction in its favour. Under English influence writers in Calcutta (the school of Brahmos) have denounced the immoralities and follies of the Hindu religion. We now begin to recognize that under its extravagance is hidden a profound idea, and you will see that it is defended by our scholars and thinkers. We aspire to be *ourselves*.'

Chevrillon commented to himself: 'Does this Hindu speak truly? Is it possible that India, becoming once more conscious of herself, is throwing off the intellectual yoke of England? Is it possible that in the peace enjoyed under English rule, the Hindu brain, so long paralysed by Mohammedan oppression, will once more begin to work? And if so, what will come of it?'

Lord Curzon as Viceroy of India was also observing the movement of the Hindu mind, and on receiving a copy of Max Müller's *Auld Lang Syne*, vol. II, wrote to him on July 26, 1899:

> There is no doubt that a sort of quasi-religious, quasi-metaphysical ferment is going on in India, strongly conservative and even reactionary in its general tendency. The ancient philosophies are being re-exploited, and their modern scribes and professors are increasing in numbers and fame.
>
> What is to come out of this strange amalgam of superstition, transcendentalism, mental exaltation, and intellectual obscurity—with European ideas thrown as an outside ingredient into the crucible—who can say?

Though Curzon was not fully aware of what had actually happened, a strong current of Hindu conservatism with a fairly elaborate ideology of its own, intellectually competent in its higher expression, had already come into existence, and it had put the liberal Hindu movement on the defensive. This revivalist movement became political in the next stage, and pervaded the nationalist movement. Thus it may be said that the transformation Max Müller wanted in Hindu life was turned into a channel of which he could not approve but which he and his fellow-Orientalists had provided.

His role in this movement was passive and involuntary. But he deliberately took up the role of adviser and guide to the movement of religious reform in India. This was natural on account not only of his scholarly interest in Hinduism, but also of his deeply religious nature. He wanted the Hindus to recast their religious life in the light of what he was placing before them as its highest expression. All through his life, in one way or another, he continued his interpretation of Hinduism, so that all his writing may be described as his exposition, direct or incidental, of the religion, and the most formal expositions are to be found in his Hibbert and Gifford Lectures. But from the reformist point of view he stated his position most clearly and briefly in a letter to the Duke of Argyll, written in 1869. It has to be quoted in full for its importance.

It is certainly true that the religion of the Hindus, as far as we can gather from their sacred hymns in the *Veda*, is free from everything that strikes us as degrading in the present state of religion and morality in India. But between the ancient religion of India and the religious worship of the present generation there have been several falls and several rises. Buddhism, in the sixth century before our era, was a reaction against corruptions that had crept into the ancient religion even at that early time. Then, Buddhism, starting with the highest aspirations, degenerated into monasticism and hypocrisy, and a most rigorous form of the old Brahmanic religion took possession of India, and drove Buddhism out of every corner of the country. Since that time there have been several religious reforms, though of a more local character, and this makes it very difficult to generalize and treat the whole religious life of India as one organic body of religious thought. Yet so much may be said with perfect truth, that if the religion of India could be brought back to that simple form which it exhibits in the *Veda*, a great reform would be achieved. Something would be lost, for some of the later metaphysical speculations on religion, and again the high and pure and almost Christian morality of Buddha, are things not to be found in the *Veda*. But, as far as popular conceptions of the deity are concerned, the *Vedic* religion, though childish and crude, is free from all that is so hideous in the later Hindu Pantheon.

As to the potentiality for transformation (in the sense of improvement), Max Müller made a distinction between the natural and historic religion, which he described in this letter as *national* and *personal*. He wrote:

With regard to the inevitable decay of religion, a difference ought to be made between two classes of religion, *national* and *personal*. There are ancient religions, like that of Greece, and that of India, too, which grow up like national languages, where it is impossible to speak of individual influences, because all individual influence is determined by the silent and almost unconscious approval or disapproval of the community. In these religions I think we can watch for a time a decided progress, a general elimination of what is bad, i.e., what is not acceptable to the national conscience.

But religions like Buddhism, Mohammedanism, and Christianity too, belong to a different class. They start with a high ideal conceived by a representative man, representative either of a nation or of the whole of humanity, and that high ideal is hardly ever realized; it has to adapt itself to larger circles and lower levels, and can only be kept from utter degeneration by constant effort at reform.

It will be seen from this letter that Max Müller had no admiration for the post-*Vedic* manifestations of Hinduism, except for the religious aspect of the philosophy of *Vedanta*. He never discussed the orgiastic and erotic aspects of Hinduism which some writers in the West seem now to regard as the brightest light from the East. But we can guess what his opinion must have been, for he could not have remained ignorant of them. As to the beliefs and practices of contemporary Hindus, his unfavourable opinion was openly voiced. In fact, he considered Brahmanism to be dead, and said so in plain language in his Westminster lecture on Missions, delivered on December 3, 1873. Referring to the Brahmanic religion he said:

That religion is still professed by at least 110,000,000 of human souls, and, to judge from the last census, even that enormous number falls much short of the real truth. And yet I do not shrink from saying that their religion is dying or dead. And why? Because it cannot stand the light of day.

The worship of Siva, of Vishnu, and the other popular deities, is of the same, nay, in many cases of a more degraded and savage character than the worship of Jupiter, Apollo, and Minerva; it belongs to a stratum of thought which is long buried under our feet: it may live on, like the lion and the tiger, but the mere air of free thought and civilized like will extinguish it. A religion may linger on for a long time, it may be accepted by the large masses of the people, because it is there, and there is nothing better. But when a religion has ceased to produce defenders of the faith, prophets, champions, martyrs, it has ceased to live, in the true sense of the word; and in that sense the old, orthodox Brahmanism has ceased to live for more than a thousand years.

Here he was speaking of that form of Hindu religion which according to him appeared in India after the degeneration of Buddhism and supplanted Buddhism—the form, that is to say, which is conventionally described as the Puranic. Then he turned to Hinduism as it was practised in his time, and went on to say:

It is true there are millions of children, women, and men in India who fall down before the stone image of Vishnu, with his four arms, riding on a creature half bird, half man, or sleeping on the serpent; who worship Siva, a monster with three eyes, riding naked on a bull, with a necklace of skulls for his ornament. There are human beings who still believe in a god of war, Kartikeya, with six faces, riding on a peacock, and holding bow and arrow in his hands; and who invoke a god of success, Ganesa, with four hands and an elephant's head, sitting on a rat. Nay, it is true that, in the broad daylight of the nineteenth century, the figure of the goddess Kali is carried through the streets of her own city, Calcutta, her wild dishevelled hair reaching to her feet, with a necklace of human heads, her tongue protruded from her mouth, her girdle stained with blood. All this is true; but ask any Hindu who can read and write and think, whether these are the gods he believes in, and he will smile at your credulity. How long this living death of national religion in India may last, no one can tell: for our purposes, however, for gaining an idea of the issue of the great religious struggle of the future, that religion too is dead and gone.

What Max Müller said about the educated Hindu was only partly true. If he had mixed with a large number of them, as Sir Henry Maine did, he would have found that 'the educated youth of India certainly affect a dislike of many things which they do care about, and pretend to many tastes which they do not really share'. If Müller had asked his educated Indian whether, going further than his private scepticism, he was ready to denounce the idol-worship openly, he would certainly have heard the argument that, however unmeaningful to him, it was useful for the common herd. If Müller further asked whether image-worship took place in his house, he would have heard the plea that he could not hurt the feelings of his mother or wife by putting an end to that. Müller would perhaps have been too polite to ask if the scoffing Hindu himself did not at times descend to this worship and to practices much worse, but if he had he would have got only discreet evasion.

However that may be, Max Müller's view that Brahmanism was dead led him into a controversy with Sir Alfred Lyall, whose knowledge of India was both wide and deep. He replied to Müller in an article in the *Fortnightly Review* (July 1, 1874), and contended that so far from being dead Hinduism was very much alive.

Müller replied in the next issue of the *Fortnightly Review*, and tried to explain himself rather than to contradict Lyall. He admitted that objections raised against his describing Brahmanism as already dead had force, and wrote: 'The word was too strong; at all events, it was liable to be misunderstood. What I meant to say was that the popular worship of Siva and Vishnu belongs to the same intellectual stratum as the worship of Jupiter and Apollo, that it is an anachronism in the nineteenth century.' In support of his position Müller quoted Lyall's opinion: 'That Brahmanism may possibly melt away of a heap and break up, I would not absolutely deny.' This has not happened, nor is likely to happen. In expecting its eventual disappearance both Max Müller and Sir Alfred Lyall were wrong. If one is not thinking of *becoming*, but only of *being*, Hinduism is what the Hindus describe it to be: the *Eternal Way*.

Nevertheless, holding his own view of the religious life of contemporary Hindus, Müller naturally would consider how it could be reformed and revitalized. In his early days he thought that Hinduism could not be reformed, and must be replaced by Christianity. Thus on August 25, 1856, he wrote to Bunsen from Oxford: 'India is much riper for Christianity than Rome or Greece were at the time of St Paul.' But he added that he would not like to go to India as a missionary because that would make him dependent on the parsons, and he did not care to go as a civil servant as that would make him dependent on the government. What he preferred was this: 'I should like to live for ten years quite quietly and learn the language, try to make friends, and then see whether I was fit to take part in a work, by means of which the old mischief of Indian priestcraft could be overthrown and the way opened for the entrance of simple Christian teaching.' He thought he could manage to go to India with Maharajah Dalip Singh, son of Ranjit Singh. Dalip Singh, he knew, was much at Court, and it seemed to him that this prince, who had become a Christian, was destined to play a political part in India.

But of course, nothing came of this, and Müller did not pursue the scheme seriously. If he had he would have found that it was not practical. Not that he was wrong in thinking that Christianity would appeal to the Hindus, for at that time most educated Hindus with a religious bent were feeling the need for a living monotheistic faith. But the obstacle to Christianity was not religious, it was political and social. The British authorities in India were right in dismissing the idea of creating a religious mission for their rule. The mere suspicion of an interference with religious taboos gave rise to serious disaffection among their Hindu soldiers, and was one of the causes of the rebellion next year.

Max Müller subsequently rested his hopes for a religious reform in India on the *Vedic* studies in the West. He had already learnt about the monotheistic movement of Rammohun Roy, who was preaching a new form of Hinduism based on the latest products of the *Vedic* canon, the *Upanishads*, and had established a monotheistic society in Calcutta. Rammohun Roy came to England in late life, and died at Bristol in 1833. He had seen Rosen, the compiler of the first printed edition of the *Rig-Veda*, though a partial one, at work on the manuscripts, and told him that instead of wasting his time on it, he should study the *Upanishads*.

In Calcutta, however, some of his followers thought that in order to strengthen the movement among the less educated people they could not depend solely on the *Upanishads*, whose doctrines were too pure and sublime to suit the gross ideas of common people. They began to uphold the *Vedas* as revelation. But they soon found that the *Vedic* corpus was so heterogeneous that as revelation they had either to be adopted as a whole or rejected as a whole. They rejected it formally in 1850.

The lead in this action was taken by Debendranath Tagore, who himself had found release from his religious doubts in the *Upanishads*. When he became the leader of the monotheistic society which was called the Brahmo Samaj, he thought it necessary to find out the real character of the *Vedas* by sending four young Brahmins to Benares to study them at this centre of Hindu learning and religion. It was upon hearing their account that Debendranath decided to make no use of the *Vedic Samhitas* for the new monotheism.

Max Müller thought that the sending of the Brahmins might have had a connexion with his own work on the *Rig-Veda*, and so wrote to Debendranath. Upon reading the letter, Debendranath wrote to Max Müller that he had received no intimation regarding Müller's work on the *Rig-Veda*, and that the idea of sending the Brahmins to Benares had originated with him independently.

Thus the *Vedic Samhitas*, or the *Vedas* strictly so-called, did not form the basis of the Brahmo monotheistic movement, which took its stand on the *Upanishads*. Even of them the son of Debendranath Tagore, Satyendranath Tagore, who was the first Indian to enter the I.C.S., wrote that his father's spiritual aspirations were awakened and fed by the 'sublimer portions of those *wild treatises*'. This was as far as the Brahmos in the first stage of their movement would go to draw support from the *Vedic* texts. The *Upanishads* continued to be the theoretical basis of the Brahmo doctrine. But spirit and liturgy as well as devotions were soon taken over from Christianity, and Brahmoism in its spirit though not in its form became an adaptation to Hinduism of Christianity. This was due primarily to Keshub Chunder Sen, the next leader of the Brahmo movement and a friend of Müller.

In India the acceptance of the *Vedas* as a basis for any form of modern Hinduism was due to another Hindu reformer, who, however, had nothing to borrow from the West. This was Swami Dayananda Saraswati, the founder of the Arya Samaj, a very nationalistic and somewhat fanatical sect of Hindu monotheists, virtually confined to the Punjab and Punjabis. He did not know English, but he knew the *Vedas* by heart, and interpreted them in his own way. He regarded the *Vedas* as revelation, divinely inspired, and supra-human. He died in 1883, after the publication of Max Müller's edition of the *Rig-Veda*, and it was reported that he carried the edition with him. But in his commentary on the *Rig- -Veda* in Sanskrit he was very hard on Müller. He could not understand why Müller cared for the *Vedas* at all if he did not accept their divine origin.

Though Max Müller's hope that his work on *Vedic* literature and religion would help towards the creation of a new and purer form of Hinduism for modern Hindus was not realized, it should not be assumed that it made no impact on their religious thought. How contemporary Hindus regarded his *Vedic* enterprise has already been described. Over and above, there is no doubt that his researches and ideas acted as a catalyst on the mind of the Hindus. More especially, his conception of the history of Hinduism, which presented an antithesis between its *Vedic* form and the later so-called Puranic form as the most important fact of the evolution, was accepted both by liberal and conservative Hindus. Though it is no longer historically tenable, it still survives in a modified version.

It is possible that if Max Müller had descended to the claptrap about Hinduism ladled out by Western bigots or charlatans of Eastern and Hindu spirituality he might have become the founder of a school of Hinduism in India. But he wholly disapproved of and almost despised this Western infatuation with Hinduism, which was displayed in his time by Madame Blavatsky in a very assertive form. Max Müller first heard about her from his Parsee friend, Malabari, to whom he wrote in 1879: 'I was much amused at your "theosophic Russian countess". If she would learn Panini while she is in India she might do more useful work.' Soon he knew much more about her, and grew suspicious. Madame Blavatsky had not gone to India to learn, but to teach her version of Buddhism and Hinduism.

She was ignorant of Sanskrit and Sanskrit literature, but was proclaiming to the world that Hindu philosophy, particularly that of the Vedanta and of Buddhism (she could not always distinguish one from the other) were infinitely superior to all the philosophies of Europe, and even at that time the Brahmans were the depositories of the primeval wisdom of the world. At one stage she was with Dayananda Saraswati, the founder of the Arya Samaj, and she declared that between them they would soon promulgate a new theosophy which would eclipse all former systems of thought. But Dayananda was soon disillusioned and would have nothing to do with the Polish countess. But she founded a Theosophical Society in India, with its headquarters at Adyar in Madras.

After her death one of her associates, Colonel Olcott, protested to Max Müller, and wanted to know whether he held that there was no esoteric interpretation of the Sanskrit *Sastras*.

Max Müller's reply was straightforward. He flatly contradicted that there was anything esoteric in Buddhism, for it was a religion for the people at large, for the poor and the suffering and the downtrodden. He pointed out that Buddha himself protested against the idea of keeping anything secret. He admitted that there was more esotericism in Brahmanism; but even in that there was no such thing as an esoteric interpretation of the *Sastras*. These, he said, had but one meaning, and all who had been properly prepared by education had access to them.

As to the countess herself, Müller regretted that he had hurt the feelings of Colonel Olcott, but he was unmoved as to his general judgement. He said in a letter to Colonel Olcott written on June 10, 1893:

I felt it my duty to protest against what seemed to me a lowering of a beautiful religion. Her name and prestige were doing real mischief among people who were honestly striving for higher religious views, and who were quite willing to recognize all that was true and beautiful and good in other religions. Madame Blavatsky seems to me to have had the same temperament, but she was either deceived by others or carried away by her own imaginations.

In India the so-called Theosophy she preached was taken up by a number of educated Hindus with somewhat immature ideas about religion, especially as proclaimed through the writings and speeches of Mrs Annie Besant. Max Müller knew that the educated Hindus were showing a great readiness to succumb to the Western charlatanry regarding their religion, and he described it in a parable or *drishtanta* (example) taken from an Indian story.

Once there was a man with a peculiar power to grunt exactly like a pig, and he made a good deal of money by showing off his power of mimicry to the common people. In one village where he was giving an exhibition, a holy man passed by, who decided to teach a lesson to these credulous people. He advertised that he would show them a better performance, with much better grunting, free of cost. People flocked to him, and, producing a real pig, he squeezed it to make it grunt. But the people said: 'Is that all? We hear that every day, what's there to it?' And they all went away. The sage said: 'Here is a splendid lesson. We seldom care for reality, and always go in for imitation.'

At that time the counter-charlatanry of the Hindus had not yet reached the West and found victims. Hinduism in a new form was being preached by men like Swami Vivekananda, and it was largely Vedantic. Max Müller welcomed this preaching. As he himself has said: 'From what I have seen and read of Vivekananda and his colleagues, they seem to me honestly bent on doing good work.' But even in Vivekananda's teaching Müller perceived now and then something of the old Blavatsky leaven that had not been entirely discarded. And on more general grounds he gave an opinion which was very sound. He looked upon Vedanta as an expression of the *Way of Knowledge* of the Hindus, and did not like the dependence of the new preachers on Ramakrishna, who belonged to the *Way of Love*. He admired Ramakrishna, and wrote a book on him at the end of his life, but he could not approve of the mixing up of Ramakrishna's teaching with the Vedanta. As he put the matter:

> Vivekananda and the other followers of Ramakrishna ought, however, to teach their followers how to distinguish between the perfervid utterances of their teacher, Ramakrishna, an enthusiastic *Bhakta* (devotee) . . . and the clear and dry style of the Sutras of Badarayana. However, as long as these devoted preachers keep true to the *Upanishads, the Sutras,* and the recognized commentaries, whether of Samkara or Ramanuja, I wish them all the success they deserve by their unselfish devotion and their high ideals.

But this has not happened so far as the popular reception of Vivekananda's teaching is concerned. It has resulted for their followers in a personality cult of both Ramakrishna and Vivekananda.

With the realization that he could not influence the Hindu revival in the way he desired, Müller's practical interest in the religious life of India took another direction. Towards the very end of his life he tried to persuade that section of the Hindu monotheists who owed their inspiration and zeal largely to Christianity, or at all events to Christ, to declare themselves formally as Christian. That was, of course, that branch of the Brahmos which was led by his friend Keshub Chunder Sen, and after Keshub's death by his friend and disciple, Protap Chunder Mozoomdar.

The Hindu theists had a great diversity of opinion regarding Jesus and Christianity, ranging from intense hatred on the one hand to profound respect and personal attachment on the other. Sen belonged to the latter group. Throughout his life he remained devoted to Christ, though in his own way. He gave an idea of what that was in many of the speeches he made in England during his visit in 1870. 'Why,' he asked, 'have I cherished respect and reverence for Christ? Why is it that, though I do not take the name of Christian I still persevere in offering my hearty thanksgivings to Jesus Christ?' He gave his answers:

> There must be something in the life and death of Christ—there must be something in his great gospel which tends to bring comfort and light and strength to a heart heavy-laden with iniquity and wickedness.
>
> My first inquiry was, What is the creed taught in the Bible? Must I go through all the dogmas and doctrines which constitute Christianity in the eye of the various sects, or is there something simple which I can at once grasp and turn to account?
>
> I found Christ spoke one language and Christianity another. I went to him prepared to hear what he had to say, and was immensely gratified when he told me: 'Love the Lord thy God with all thy heart, with all thy mind, with all thy soul, and with all thy strength, and love thy neighbour as thyself.'
>
> Christ never demanded from me worship or adoration that is due to God, the Creator of the Universe.
>
> He places Himself before me as the spirit I must imbibe in order to approach the Divine Father, as the great Teacher and guide who will lead me to God.
>
> Christ demands of us absolute sanctification and purification of the heart. In this matter, also, I see Christ on one side, and Christian sects on the other.
>
> To be a Christian then is to be Christ-like. Christianity means becoming like Christ, not acceptance of Christ as a proposition or as an

outward representation, but spiritual conformity with the life and character of Christ. By Christ I understand one who said, 'Thy will be done.'

I feel I must love Christ, let Christians say what they like against me; that Christ I must love, for he preached love for an enemy.

It was in the light of all this that he said that the so-called followers of Christ were not yet Christian.

After the controversy over the schism in the Brahmo Samaj and Max Müller's defence of Keshub Shunder Sen in his letter to *The Times*, the nature of Keshub's adherence to Christianity was discussed between them. It arose from a complaint by Keshub Chunder Sen about an attack on him by Professor Monier Williams, who had replied to Müller's defence. About this Sen wrote:

> The manner in which he has treated us is so utterly unworthy of him, and is marked with such vacillations, wavering, and duplicity, that I can have no misgivings in accepting your verdict . . . It seems rather strange that Professor Monier Williams, who professes to be a devout Christian, should withhold his regard and sympathy from that section of the Brahmo community which is most allied to Jesus and makes the nearest approach to the religion founded by Him. As for his arguments, they have been smashed times beyond number. In private letters to me he professes friendship, and I have simply warned him in the most kindly spirit to ascertain facts before rushing into print.

Though Max Müller had his own opinion of Professor Monier Williams, he did not wholly condemn him. On the other hand he tried to make Sen understand why, despite his attitude to Christianity, many sincere Christians felt unsympathetic to him. In fact, it was Sen's Christianity itself which was the cause. So Müller himself wrote to Sen that in order to discuss this question he thought that a perfect understanding was necessary between the two as to the true character of Christ. He wrote:

> It may seem strange that a son of India, one who calls himself a believer in *Brahman* (the Absolute Spirit), and who therefore, in strict theological phraseology, would be called a non-Christian, should have given offence to men who call themselves Christians by what seems to them language of excessive veneration for Christ. Yet it is so, and that is why, in the case of some of your critics at least, the objections to your deeply impassioned utterances about Christ arise from good and honest motives.

The difficulty was Sen's rejection of the very Kerygma of Christianity. Müller gave him a rather long explanation according to his own understanding of it, which he said would be regarded by many theologians of his day as very strange. Even so he set it forth, and the crucial passage was:

> Christianity is Christianity by this one fundamental truth, that as God is the father of man, so truly, and not poetically or metaphorically only, man is the son of God, participating in God's very essence and nature, though separated from God by self and sin. This oneness of nature (homoousia) between the Divine and the Human does not lower the concept of God by bringing it nearer to the level of humanity; on the contrary, it raises the old concept of man and brings it nearer to its true ideal.

This was Müller's interpretation of the notion of *homoousia* put into the Christian creed at the Nicene Council at the suggestion of Constantine. Then he observed: 'After these remarks you will better be able to understand the danger of speaking of Christ in language which carries us back to the panegyrics addressed by pagan poets to their gods and idols. If you speak of Christ as not perfectly human, in His own sense of the word, you make a new idol of Him, and you utterly destroy the very soul of His religion.'

Sen replied:

> 'There is hardly a syllable in your last epistle which I should hesitate to endorse. You have said exactly what I should have said, only in a more learned and philosophical style. So far as your intellectual estimate of Christ is concerned I do not think there is much difference between us . . . I am so glad and thankful that the Spirit of God has helped me to work my way through Hinduism to the point where an enlightened Christianity has brought you . . . I have always disclaimed the Christian name, and will not identify myself with the Christian church, for I set my face completely against the popular doctrine of Christ's divinity.

There the matter rested so far as Keshub Chunder Sen was concerned. More than this he would not concede. But eighteen years later Max Müller raised the question of the affiliation of the Brahmo movement, led by Keshub Chunder Sen, with Christianity. In 1899, when he was in Germany, he wrote from Ems a long letter to Protap Chunder Mozoomdar, making an appeal to him formally to declare his community as Christian.

My dear friend, You know for many years I have watched your efforts to purify the popular religion of India, and thereby to bring it nearer to the purity and perfection of other religions, particularly of Christianity. You know also that I have paid close attention to the endeavours of those who came before you, of men like Rammohun Roy, Debendranath Tagore, Keshub Chunder Sen, and others, in whose footsteps you have boldly followed . . . I know that you have met with many disappointments and many delays, but you have never lost heart and never lost patience. I confess that I have several times felt very unhappy about the mischances that have befallen your good cause; but even when Keshub Chunder Sen was forsaken by a number of his friends and followers, on utterly insufficient grounds, as far as I could judge, and again, when he was taken from us in the very midst of his glorious work, I never lost faith in the final success of his work, though I began to doubt whether I should live to see the full realization of his hopes.

He then spoke about what the Brahmo movement had accomplished and what, as he saw the matter, they had still to do:

You have given up a great deal, polytheism, idolatry, and your elaborate sacrificial worship. You have surrendered also, as far as I can judge, the claim of divine revelation which had been so carefully formulated by your ancient theologians in support of the truth of the *Vedas*. These were great sacrifices, for whatever may be thought of your ancient traditions, to give up what we have been taught by our fathers and mothers, requires a very strong conviction, and a very strong will. But though this surrender has brought you much nearer to us, there still remain many minor points on which you differ among yourselves in your various *samajes* or congregations. Allow me to say that these differences seem to me to have little to do with real religion; still they must be removed, because they prevent united action on your part . . . If you are once united among yourselves, you need no longer trouble about this or that missionary, whether he come from London, Rome, Geneva, or Moscow. They all profess to bring you the Gospel of Christ. Take the New Testament and read it for yourselves, and judge for yourselves whether the words of Christ as contained in it satisfy you

He reassured Mozoomdar about Christian doctrine and organization.

Christ comes to you [he wrote] as He comes to us in the only trustworthy records preserved of him in the Gospels. We have not even the right to dictate our interpretation of these Gospels to you, particularly if we consider how differently we interpret them ourselves. If you accept His teachings as recorded, you are a Christian. There is no necessity whatever for your being formally received into the member-ship of one or other sect of the Christian Church, whether reformed or unreformed. That will only delay the growth of Christianity in India.

He recalled Sen's words to him that after all Christ was in many respects an Oriental who might be better understood by Orientals. He also said that he saw nothing in the proclaimed Brahmo creed or the view of God held by the Brahmos which was not Christian. After developing all his points at length, he closed with this earnest and eloquent exhortation:

> From my point of view, India, at least the best part of it, is already con-verted to Christianity. You want no persuasion to become a follower of Christ. Then make up your mind to act for yourselves. Unite your flock, and put up a few folds to hold them together, and to prevent them from straying. The bridge has been built for you by those who came before you. Step boldly forward, it will not break under you, and you will find many friends to welcome you on the other shore, and among them none more delighted than your old friend and fellow labourer.

Mozoomdar did not answer this letter for a long time, but he pub-lished it with a public rejoinder from himself, in which among other things he wrote about the attitude of the official representatives of Christianity in India:

> What disconcerts me is the half-expressed contempt which the Christian leaders, even of the liberal school, seem to have of the Hindu ideal, and spirituality. When I express my ardent love for Christ and Christianity, they are kindly in sympathy: but the moment I say that Christ and His religion will have to be interpreted in India through Indian antecedents and the Indian medium of thought, I am suspected of trying to bend Christianity down to heathenism.

Later he wrote to Max Müller:

> A wholesale acceptance of the Christian name by the Brahmo Samaj is neither possible nor desirable, within measurable time; it would lead to misconception, which would do only harm. But the acceptance

of the Christ spirit, or, as you term it, 'the essential religion of Christ', is not only possible, but an actual fact at the present moment. Liberal souls in Christendom will have to rest content with this at least *now*, and let the *name* take care of itself.

In the meanwhile, Max Müller had fallen very seriously ill, and his life was despaired of. But as soon as he was recovered a little, he wrote a second letter to Mozoomdar, even before receiving his personal answer. He had seen the Indian papers and had gathered from them that his letter had produced a certain impression. He had been abused for it both in India and in England. He wrote: 'But surely you owe much to Christ and Christianity, your very movement would not exist without Christianity. One must be above public opinion in these matters, and trust to truth which is stronger than public opinion. However, the name is a small matter. Only I thought that truth and gratitude would declare in favour of Christian Brahmos, or Christian Aryas.'

However, on March 11, 1900, less than eight months before his death, he again wrote to Mozoomdar: 'You ought to know me enough to know that I am not trying to *convert* you to Christianity. If you are not a Christian you must not call yourself a Christian.' He repeated that he did not want the Brahmos to join any existing Christian church or sect:

You say there that your country cannot do without Christ—that India is Christ's, and Christ is India's. You speak actually of an Indian Church of Christ. Now these words can have one meaning only. You are Christ's, and in that sense you are Christians, without being Roman Catholics, or Anglicans, or Lutherans. I do not want you to join any existing church or sect, I only wish you to give honour to the name of Christ to whom you owe the best part of your present religion.

This was Max Müller's last testament to India about religion. There can be no doubt that in this he spoke from the heart. But it embroiled him with the orthodox and dogmatic section of the Anglican Church. In the Diocesan Conference held at Oxford in the autumn of 1899, the Principal of Pusey House denounced Max Müller for his letter to Mozoomdar, and declared that Müller had asked the Brahmos to call themselves Christian without believing in the central doctrine on which the faith and life of the Church was founded.

The Rev. H. J. Bidder, Vicar of St Giles and a close friend of Max Müller, at once replied to the accusation on behalf of his sick parishioner, saying that 'as one privileged to minister to his closing days, and well acquainted with his religious convictions, I cannot allow the reckless assertion made against Professor Max Müller to go uncontradicted in his own city'. Some more correspondence followed, and Mr Bidder wound up in the *Oxford Times* with this remark: 'Perhaps I ought to have remembered that he enjoys a position in the greater world of religious thought—to say nothing of inward strength and serenity—which places him beyond the reach of attack either from private bigotry or from the Oxford Diocesan Conference.'

But the more dogmatic elements in the Anglican Church were from the first prejudiced against Max Müller. This prejudice burst out in public condemnation of him after his lecture on the Missions in the nave of Westminster Abbey on December 3, 1873, at the invitation of Dean Stanley.

From the next day Müller began to receive both congratulations and vituperation. Liddon, one of the most eminent Anglican divines of that time, seized his hand and told him: 'I rejoice from my heart that you have been helping us.' Ruskin approved. But there were others who wholly disapproved of what he said. Some papers wrote that he should be sent to prison for having brawled in church, and after reading some of these an Oxford tradesman rushed out when he saw Müller passing and said to him: 'Well, sir, when they send you to prison, count on a hot dinner from my table every week.' Henry Reeve, the editor of the *Edinburgh Review*, though a friend, wrote to Müller: 'By the law of England, as I read it, an unordained person who preaches or lectures in a church is guilty of a misdemeanour, punishable with three months' prison.' However, Dean Stanley had taken the opinion of Lord Coleridge, the Lord Chief Justice, and so Müller could write to his friend George Bunsen: 'There is no going to prison yet.'

The main offence was that he deprecated the excessive emphasis on the creeds, and also the attempts of some missionaries to uproot the converts from their own society. In regard to doctrine he had said: 'The fundamentals of our religion are not in these poor creeds; true Christianity lives, not in our belief, but in our love—*in our love of God, and in our love of man, founded on our love of God.*' On this Sir Alfred Lyall commented somewhat ironically: 'Missionaries will even yet hardly agree that the essentials of their religion are not in the creeds, but in love; because they are sent forth to propound scriptures which say clearly that what we believe or disbelieve is literally a *burning question.*'

Max Müller's relations with other Indian movements have now to be considered, though briefly. A man of his humanitarian outlook could not be indifferent to the social abuses in India, some of which were very cruel. Earlier in life he had carried on a controversy with Raja Radhakanta Deb, whose opinion of the *Vedic* work of Max Müller has been quoted earlier, about the burning of Hindu widows, of which the Raja approved theoretically. Max Müller was puzzled by this, though he had an explanation for it. He wrote:

> That an educated Hindu should defend the burning of widows seems strange; still, if Popes and Cardinals could defend *autos-da-fé* or the burning of heretics, nay even of witches, because the fire would purify and save their souls which could not be saved otherwise, why should not an Indian Raja have been convinced that the burning of widows could not be wrong, believing, as he did, that it was enjoined by a lost *Sakha* of the *Veda*, and that the poor women could not be saved unless they followed their husbands on their heels into another world?

He also referred to ancient Teutonic mythology, according to which Nanna and Brunhilda were burnt with their husbands.

But in his later life the movement of social reform in which he was most interested was the prevention of child marriage in Hindu society. He had heard of its inhumanity from Rama Bai, as well as from his friend the Parsee reformer Malabari. Malabari was trying to induce the Government of India to stop this by legislation, which it was most unwilling to do. Its policy was not to interfere with Hindu customs and beliefs, and this policy had been formally announced in the Proclamation of Queen Victoria to the peoples of India. So when Malabari wrote to him about his disappointment Müller asked him not to consider the battle lost, but also said that for the moment nothing more could be expected from the government.

About this custom two questions arose. Firstly, whether it was sanctioned and made obligatory by the Hindu sacred law; on this Müller was positive that no Hindu scripture sanctioned it, and he added that no Hindu Pandit now gainsaid his opinion. Secondly, whether such a widespread Hindu custom should be interfered with by the government. On this too Müller had a definite view. He was no advocate of social and cultural neutrality on the part of the British Government in India. He held that *Pax Britannica* should be supplemented by *Lux Britannica*, and made out his case against Hindu infant marriage on the ground of humanity. He wrote to Malabari on October 26, 1886:

> Government does not deserve the name of Government, if it declares itself unable to protect each individual subject against personal torts, whether sanctioned by customs or not. Now, infant betrothal is a tort— it is a contract made without consent of one of the parties. If therefore the party suffers and wishes to be released from an unjust contract, the government ought so far to protect him or her. Whether the Government is foreign or native, does not matter. It is *your* Government, so long as you accept it and enjoy all the advantages of it; and to turn round and say that your Government should not prevent and punish iniquity is self-contradictory.

He declared emphatically that the 'custom of infant betrothal is unjust, the custom of infant marriage criminal'. But he also knew that he would be abused by the Hindus for his opinion, yet he could not remain silent, and he said: 'The more my friends in India abuse me, the more proud I shall feel. If they call you ignorant, because you are a Parsee, what will they call me—a mere Mlechchha?'

The question came up again in 1890, when Malabari proposed to come to England to interest the British Government in his efforts to put an end to infant marriage. Early in that year Max Müller wrote to him, giving his views on child marriage from another angle:

> I have never doubted that early marriage is the greatest impediment in the natural development of a woman's character, and I am equally certain that your stunted wives and mothers are the chief cause of the slow, the very slow social progress in India. You have made rapid progress in everything else, but you do not know yet what light an educated, healthy and thoughtful wife can spread over every home, whether rich or poor . . . I have nothing to say about the physiological side of the question; but from a psychological point of view, marriage at ten, at twelve, even at fifteen, seems to me the surest means to stunt the natural growth of the mind in its various phases. The law should prevent all that is really noxious to physical health; no individual effort on the part of men of light and leading in India can effect a change in the long-established custom.

Later in the year Malabari came to England and established contacts with leading persons in the country to find out what could be done from England to discourage child marriage. One of them, Lord Northbrook, who was a former Viceroy of India, wrote to Müller:

> I believe Mr. Malabari to be worthy of encouragement, and I am disposed to think the time has arrived when the question of how far the Government of India might so alter the law as to discourage infant marriages should be seriously considered by practical men.
> Would you support Mr. Malabari's assertion that infant marriage is not a Hindu religious institution, but a custom to which no religious authority is attached?

Muller's opinion on this subject was, of course, definite. He tried to establish contacts for Malabari with, for instance, Princess Christian, the daughter of Queen Victoria. But he also told him that, though she had agreed to see him, Malabari should not expect her to express any opinion in public, whatever her feelings might be about the question. Regarding explorations in governmental quarters, Müller wrote to Malabari:

> Lord Lansdowne has been written to about the enabling clause. You understand what I mean—a clause enabling a father to keep his daughter till the time has come for her to leave her father's house. That clause will probably be carried by Lord Lansdowne in Council. There ought to be no pressure brought to bear on him. He ought to be allowed to do it himself, spontaneously. Any public demonstration to bring this about would, under present circumstances, do harm. The other question, as to raising the age of consent, is much more serious— is in fact, a political question, that will have to be fought out openly in India.

By that time however social reform had become of secondary interest in Indian politics, and the nationalist movement had emerged. Max Müller watched it from a distance, but did not think of intervening in current Indian politics, except on one occasion when he thought a deeper issue of Indo-British human relations was involved. The occasion was indeed significant, for it not only created the Indian National Congress as the organized mouthpiece of Indian nationalism, but also brought into being a strong sense of alienation of the new Indian intelligentsia from British rule.

The occasion was the introduction of the so-called Ilbert Bill, technically a bill to modify the Criminal Procedure Code, by Sir Courtenay Ilbert, Legal Member of the Viceroy's Executive Council, at the instance of the Viceroy, Lord Ripon. It sought to remove an anomaly in the judicial system of India which seemed to perpetuate a racial discrimination between the British and Indian members of the judiciary. At that time Indian magistrates and judges could not try European (mostly British, of course) accused persons in the district courts, though they did so in the capital cities of the provinces.

At once there was a furore among the British in India. They not only started a violent agitation against the bill, but even threatened to kidnap the Viceroy and hold him to ransom. This resistance was encouraged from inside the government even by the members of the Indian Civil Service. It had a strong backwash in England as well. What induced Max Müller to join this controversy was a report by the judges of Calcutta High Court, which was an implicit condemnation of the bill. The report was accepted, not as polemics, but as a clear, impartial and judicial pronouncement which had to be accepted.

This Max Müller disputed in a letter to *The Times*, published on August 6, 1883, refuting the conclusions of the judges paragraph by paragraph. What surprised him was not so much the loud clamour which was taken as a unanimous condemnation of the bill by British public opinion both in India and in England, but the number of eminent members of the Indian Civil Service and the Indian Army who supported Lord Ripon. Lord Ripon himself wrote a letter to Max Müller, thanking him for his letter. On September 3, 1883, he wrote from Simla:

Dear Professor Max Müller, I hope that you will excuse me for troubling you with a few lines to thank you very much for the able letter which you have addressed to *The Times* in reply to the Report of the Judges of the Calcutta High Court upon the so-called 'Ilbert Bill', and also for the very valuable support which you have given to my policy in this country.

I can assure you that I appreciate very highly the assistance with you have rendered to me. It is a great satisfaction to me to find that the course of policy which I am pursuing meets with your approval. I have need of all the aid which I can receive from England, for I am assailed here with a storm of bitter and unscrupulous hostility, which you, who dwell in a calmer atmosphere, can scarcely realize.

Believe me,

Yours faithfully

Ripon.

Müller thanked the Viceroy, and said that his letter was evoked by the fear that *The Times* 'would go on quoting that Opinion of the Judges as unanswerable, till people who did not take the trouble to read it would believe that it was so'. The bill was passed finally with a compromise clause under which a British accused could demand half the jury to be European. The agitation left a permanent legacy of misunderstanding with Indians.

However, Max Müller was a realist, and he disapproved of the eagerness of educated Indians to get into the Indian Civil Service, that is, to be employed in the administration at the highest level on a footing of equality with the British members of the Service. So he wrote to his friend Malabari on September 5, 1884, when the question of the equality of Indians with the British in all matters of government was provoking a particularly bitter agitation. He wrote:

With regard to your countrymen, I wonder that they care so much for the Indian Civil Service. If I were a Hindu, I should look out for very different work to benefit my countrymen. To tell you the truth, I do not believe in the efficiency of a *mixed* Civil Service. Oil and water will not mix—let the oil be at the top, there is plenty of room for the water beneath.

On the whole, Max Müller immensely admired British rule in India, and looked upon it as a political *tour de force*. His description of it in his reminiscences was very graphic.

The government of India by a mere handful of Englishmen [he wrote] is, indeed, an achievement unparalleled in the whole history of the world. The suppression of the Indian Mutiny shows what stuff English soldiers and statesmen are made of. If people say that ours is not an age for Epic poetry, let them read Lord Roberts's *Forty-one Years in India*. When I see in a circus a man standing with outstretched legs on two or three horses, and two men standing on his shoulders, and other men standing on theirs, and a little child at the top of all, while the horses are running full gallop round the arena, I feel what I feel when watching the government of India. One hardly dares to breathe, and one wishes one could persuade one's neighbours also to sit still and hold their breath. If ever there were an accident, the crash would be fearful, and who would suffer most? Fortunately, by this time the people of India know all this.

He felt too that under the British Parliament's rule, the Government of India was not what it was under the East India Company. The motive power, he said, had passed from the highest authority in India to people 'at home'; by which he meant that India had become enmeshed in British party politics. He even felt that 'Mill, who was so much abused for his defence of the old East India Company, was right after all, and that it was a misfortune for India when it was drawn into the vortex of party government'.

After the Ilbert Bill Müller laid the blame for the disturbed political atmosphere in India partly on the Opposition, and said: 'There are some politicians who would not shrink from saying, "Perish India, if only we can oust Gladstone!" What India wants, and will want for many years to come, is rest and quiet work.' He considered the British residents in India even more responsible. As he wrote to Malabari in 1884: 'The fault, however, lies not with you, but with the new race of English settlers in India. Unless they are taught how to behave, and kept under control by a strong hand, government in India will become impossible . . . the whole blame for the present disturbed state falls on the English settlers in India, and on the scheming politicians in England.' In this he was right.

But Max Müller was not yet prepared to envisage an India independent of British rule. Considering the renewed political dissatisfaction among Indians in 1896, this time over the cost of the Indian troops sent to Egypt, he wrote to Malabari:

I wish there was more English feeling in India, and that it would show itself in words and deeds. What is the use of haggling over the pay of an Indian regiment in Egypt? It is a mere nothing compared with the true interests, the peace, and prosperity of India. I can understand Indian patriots who wish to get rid of England altogether, but those who see what that would mean should take to their oars manfully, and pull a good English stroke. You are in the same boat—you can float together, and you would go down together. So it strikes me, though you know that I am generally on the Indian side.

It has to be added that in expressing this kind of opinion at the end of the century, Müller was not saying something with which the greatest Indians of the age did not agree. Bankim Chandra Chatterji, who is regarded as an apostle of Bengali nationalism and revolutionary activity, tried to drive the moral home in his famous novel *Ananda Math*; namely that British rule in India was providential. Before him the great Indian reformer Rammohun Roy, who is looked upon as the precursor of Indian nationalism, had said to Victor Jacquemont that 'India requires many more years of English domination so that she may not have many things to lose while she is reclaiming her political independence'.

Max Müller also pleaded for leniency to those who were considered to be dangerous extremists among the nationalist leaders in India. So, when the famous nationalist Tilak was imprisoned for sedition in 1898, he put his signature to a petition which urged consideration to be shown to him. Müller wrote to Sir John Lubbock explaining why he spoke for Tilak:

> My interest in Tilak is certainly that of a Sanskrit scholar, for though I do not agree with the arguments put forward in his *Oñon, or Researches into the Antiquity of the Vedas* (Bombay, 1893), I cannot help feeling sorry that we should lose the benefit of his labours. I sent him my edition of the *Rig-Veda*, but I am told now that he is not allowed to read even his Bible and Prayer-book in prison. You see, from the wording of the petition, that we do not question the justice of the sentence . . . But the warning has now been given, and none too soon, though I do not believe that there is any sedition lurking in India at present, not even in the hearts of such men at Tilak.

Max Müller was in his fundamental inclinations an enthusiast, and remained one till his last day. But what was equally pronounced in him as an intellectual was his balance of mind and capacity to see both sides of any question. He could thus support British rule in India and also champion India and Indians.

Chapter 5

VANAPRASTHA

THE heading of this chapter is a Sanskrit word, which means to a Hindu the stage of life to be spent in a forest as enjoined by his sacred law. This is the third state; the two preceding it are *Brahmacharya* (education and observance of chastity) and *Garhasthya* (family life), and that following *Vanaprastha* is *Sannyasa* (wanderings as a vagrant ascetic). Max Müller described the state in the following words in one of his books:

> Then followed the third stage after a man had fulfilled all his duties, had performed all necessary sacrifices, and had seen the children of his children. Then and then only came the time when he might retire from his house, give up all that belonged to him, and settle somewhere in the forest near, with or without his wife, but still accessible to his relations, and chiefly occupied in overcoming all passions by means of ascetic exercises, and withdrawing his affections more and more from all the things of this life.
>
> During that third station, that of the *Vanaprastha* or *Hylobios*, the mind of the hermit became more and more concentrated on that higher philosophy which we call religion, and more particularly on the *Vedanta*, as contained in the *Upanishads,* and similar but later works. Instead of merely dipping into the waters, the philosophical baptism became then a complete submergence, an entrance into life with Brahman, where alone perfect peace and a perfect satisfaction of man's spiritual desires could be found.

When I speak of the *Vanaprastha* of Max Müller I have this spiritual quest in mind, and the description is wholly applicable to the last twenty-five years of his life. He himself seems to have had the notion that the highest utterances of Hindu philosophy were sent out by the sages in their station of *Vanaprastha*. As he wrote to Renan in 1877: 'The *Upanishads* and the *Vedanta*, if looked into seriously, contain, I believe, the solution of many difficulties which perplex our philosophy. Only it is not enough to translate them, they require the shoulder of a Christophorus to carry them over the channel of two thousand years that runs between the old *Vanaprasthas* and us.'

For the rest, Max Müller did not intend to abandon the world or its duties and obligations. He did not even give any public exhibition of grief. So those who came to see him could not have any inkling of the crushing sorrow which had undermined his will to live, though not his tenacity in work. To the world at large he showed a cheerful and at times even a gay manner, and never failed in courtesy, sympathy and hospitality. He even extended his social life. When his daughter Mary left school in 1880, for her sake he received much more company at home, and this enabled him to see more of the younger members of the university. One of them, Henry Newbolt, wrote long afterwards:

I have seldom met anyone so entirely different from my imagination of him as Mr Max Müller. I had pictured a burly, bearded German Professor, carelessly dressed, possibly brusque in manner, certainly of unavoidable learning, the author of all those books.

This figure still lies—without its label—in some back cupboard of my mind; the gracious and genial presence of the real man could never be pieced on to it. As to the books, I hardly feel sure who wrote them after all; I never heard anything of them from the true Max Müller. I remember talks on music, dogs, poetry, Hindu ceremonies, pictures, sweetmeats, and fairy tales: never a professorial or pedantic word.

Newbolt also wrote that only once did he hear Müller speaking of religion with a guest, and that was when he was staying at Norham Gardens in August 1885. He talked in the garden with great vivacity of Darwin and Haeckel, and when the guest went into the house Müller turned upon Newbolt, looking up with a flash through his gold-rimmed glasses and burst out: 'If you say that all is not made by design, by Love, then you may be in the same house, but you are not in the same world with me.' That was, of course, the gauntlet thrown down by the teleologist to those who say that emergences are brought about by wholly accidental permutations and combinations. Newbolt's more vivid memory was of the lover of dogs:

I can see him now, standing at the window, when a picnic day had turned out wet, grumbling, not to us but to the dogs, Waldmann and Nännerl, and in a manner most sympathetically dog-like. I see him, too, genuinely disturbed over the absence of Nännerl, sallying out late at night to find the prodigal, with a lantern: like a figure in one of Richter's charming prints, or Hans Andersen's tales.

The historical pedigree of these two dachshunds was a favourite topic with him. When an American scholar, Ethelbert D. Warfield, Principal of Lafayette College, came to see him, Müller related that three types of dogs were plainly distinguished on the pyramids, and among them was the type to which these highly specialized dogs belonged.

Another acquaintance, describing his life at Oxford, wrote that Max Müller was usually at his best as a host; especially at All Souls, where this writer said: 'I recall him upon a warm April day, "in such a time as comes before the leaf", but when the tall windows of the college hall were thrown wide open to an expanse of emerald English turf, bordered by a blaze of jonquils, and *Pyrus japonica*, enthusiastically doing the honours of that stately place.'

In 1894 when he was over seventy an interviewer wrote of him: 'The Professor, for all his long laborious years, retains the vigour and vivacity of youth. His manner of speech is rather that of a frolicsome undergraduate than of the typical University Don.' That was the picture painted of him when he attended the Students' Club meeting in Glasgow while delivering his third Gifford Lecture. The journal of the students reported him as saying:

> I have tasted a little of the professorial life of Glasgow, but this is the first time I have shared its student life, and I feel a student at Leipzig once again . . . Later in the evening [the report continues] Mr MacLaren sang *Die Wacht am Rhein*, and Mr Buchanan *Rhine Wine* at the request of Professor Müller. On their conclusion, he asked the company to join him in singing a song, known in every college in the world— a song that had come down for hundreds of years, the *Gaudeamus igitur*. The Professor then took his seat at the piano, and in grand style led the splendid old song, the company joining with the greatest heartiness.

I have read a number of Gifford Lectures, and could never imagine that anyone could have the energy to do such a thing after delivering not one but a series of three lectures.

Max Müller's courtesy and hospitality were particularly marked towards foreigners. As Henry Newbolt wrote to Mrs Max Müller: 'This quaint simplicity, the charm of the perfectly child-like character, always seemed to me the one un-English part of him. It carried with it the power, which we as a nation lack, of entering with ease and sincerity into relations, however sudden and unexpected, with strangers or foreigners.'

He was always ready to wecome Indians, whether known or unknown. Young students and visitors were received into his house
with the same courtesy as he showed to the most distinguished
figures from India. One of them wrote to Mrs Max Müller after
his death: 'I do not know whether you still remember it, but I had
the pleasure and privilege of passing a few hours in the company of
your late illustrious husband in the middle of May 1882, at your
hospitable residence in Oxford. To you and to your husband it was
only one of the numerous visits Indians of all castes and creeds, of
all shades and colours, paid to the great Rishi of Oxford, but to me
it has been one of the most memorable incidents of my whole life.'

Even immediate sorrow would not prevent him from receiving
an unknown Indian. In 1886, soon after the death of Max Müller's
daughter Mary, a Bengali came to see him at Oxford, and he left
the following description of the visit in his travel diary, published
in 1889. His name was Trailokya Nath Mukharji. This is what he
wrote:

> So one day in November 1886 . . . I rang the visitor's bell at the door
> of his cottage in the suburbs of Oxford.* Mrs Max Müller herself
> opened the door. An elderly gentleman of venerable appearance soon
> appeared in the passage, who received me with the utmost kindness.
> It needed not an introduction to tell me that I stood in the presence of
> the man who would vie with Sayanacharya and Yaska in his profound
> love of *Vedic* learning, and with Panini in his power of critical investi-
> gation and intelligent collation of facts. Still I asked: 'Have I the
> honour to speak to Professor Müller?' He quietly said: 'I am that indi-
> vidual.' Then we sat for a long time in his cosy drawing room where a
> cheerful fire was burning, but, alas! deep sadness reigned over the
> whole house. The Professor constantly talked of India and the Hindus
> for whom . . . he has the deepest sympathy and love. He told me that
> although his body lived in England his mind and soul were in India.

Distinguished foreign visitors were always coming to his house
to see him or to stay with him. Among those who came during the
last twenty-five years of Müller's life were Renan, Darmesteter and
even Turgenev from Paris, the Grand Duke of Baden, the Crown
Prince of Sweden, a Red Indian chief named Strong Buffalo and
Prince and Princess Christian. The well-known American author
Oliver Wendell Holmes came in 1886, and Lowell, the American

---

* 7 Norham Gardens was big enough to house Max Müller's 13,000 books, and
is now a school. At that date 'north of the Parks' was a suburb of Oxford.

critic who represented his country in England as Minister, came often.

Max Müller felt that he had a moral obligation to his foreign visitors. As the American scholar Dr Warfield put it: 'It seemed as though the foreigner enjoyed an especial welcome in that home. Perhaps it was because he remembered the time when he, too, was a stranger in a strange land; remembered the loneliness of his own lot; remembered, too, and sought to return, the kindness which had been shown to him.'

It was during this station of *Vanaprastha*, as I have called it, that he turned out all his major works of scholarship and thought, with the exception of the first edition of the *Rig-Veda* and his volumes on the *Science of Language*. Work was a matter of habit and principle with him, and after the death of two of his daughters it had become a refuge from sorrow, though often he longed for rest.

The major work of editing which he undertook was the series *The Sacred Books of the East*, and the original contributions to science and scholarship were his books on religion, mythology and thought. Besides, he had the habit of continuously revising and rearranging his older works, and these often called for very strenuous work.

Quite early in life he had laid down for himself a systematic programme of philosophical inquiry, and he described it in the preface to the two volumes on the science of mythology, published at the very end of his life in 1897. In it he said that he had planned as the work of his life an exposition, however imperfect, of the four sciences of Language, Mythology, Religion and Thought, 'following each other in natural succession, and comprehending the whole sphere of activity of the human mind from the earliest period within the reach of our knowledge to the present day.' He elaborated the assumptions underlying this programme in these words:

> There is nothing more ancient in the world than language. The history of man begins, not with rude flints, rock temples or pyramids, but with language.
> The second stage is represented by myths as the first attempts at translating the phenomena of nature into thought.
> The third stage is that of religion or the recognition of moral powers, and in the end of One Moral Power behind and above all nature.
> The fourth and last is philosophy, or a critique of the powers of reason in their legitimate working on the data of experience.

He had already put in a comprehensive form what he had to say about three of these, namely language, religion and thought, in the following books:

  I. The Science of Language, two volumes, last edition, 1891
 II. The Science of Religion,
    1. Introduction to the Science of Religion, 1870
    Hibbert Lectures:
    2. The Origin and Growth of Religion, 1878
    Gifford Lectures: Four Series
    3. Natural Religion, 1888
    4. Physical Religion, 1890
    5. Anthropological Religion, 1891
    6. Theosophy or Psychological Religion, 1892
III. The Science of Thought, 1887
    To this is to be added his translation of Kant's *Critique of Pure Reason*, with an introduction by Müller himself.

He wanted to supplement these by presenting his systematic view of mythology, but at first felt that he did not have the time and strength needed for it in the midst of other work. But at last he was almost provoked to write the book by the continuous attacks on his views on this subject by critics who said that they were completely out of date. He took all this almost as a personal challenge, and in 1897 brought out his *Contributions to the Science of Mythology* in two massive volumes, running to a total of 864 pages.

Some account must be given in this chapter of his dealing with religion, thought and mythology. But before that it is necessary to describe another editorial undertaking of his, the publication of *The Sacred Books of the East*, which finally ran to forty-nine volumes.* It occupied him over the last twenty-five years of his life in collaboration with specialists and fellow-workers in many countries.

Soon after he had published the sixth and last volume of his *Rig-Veda* (1874), the idea of supplementing this work with translations from the sacred writings of other religions, as a comprehensive source for the study of religion, entered his mind. The first reference by him to such a project is to be found in a letter to the Sinologist Legge, which he wrote on February 13, 1875. In it he informed Legge that he was trying very hard to get a number of

---

* One index volume was added later, and it was compiled by Dr Winternitz.

scholars together for making translations of the other sacred writings, but at the same time expressed the fear that it might not be an easy task. The same year the project became more concrete. He received an invitation from the Austrian Government to transfer his services to Vienna and to publish a series of translations as envisaged by him under the auspices of the Imperial Academy. It was this proposal which, apart from personal reasons, lay behind his decision to resign from his chair at Oxford. But, as has been related, his friends saw to it that he should get the time and facilities to carry out the project at Oxford.

He at once prepared a prospectus of the series, and sent it to all those who might be interested in the project. He had already ensured the support of a number of scholars, but many more had to be found. Looking at the matter from the point of view of the translators, he said that the work could be undertaken by them at a certain sacrifice, for they must leave for a time their own special researches. He also observed that 'there was the most serious difficulty of all, a difficulty which no scholar could remove, viz., the difficulty of finding the funds necessary for carrying out so large an undertaking.' However, through the interest taken in it by Lord Salisbury, who was for some time Secretary of State for India, Sir Henry Maine, a former member of the Viceroy's Executive Council, and Dean Liddell, Vice-Chancellor of Oxford, it was decided to publish the series at the expense jointly of the University Press and the Government of India.

Twenty-four volumes were contemplated, and they were to be apportioned between six religions: two from India, Hinduism and Buddhism; two from China, Taoism and Confucianism; Zoastrianism from Persia; and Islam. The Christian and Judaic scriptures, though eastern in their origin, were excluded for fear of offending orthodoxy, and even the publication of the others gave offence to many English Christians. Progress at first was slow, but three volumes of *The Sacred Books of the East* were published in May 1879, and were dedicated to Lord Salisbury, Sir Henry Maine, and Dean Liddell, 'to whose kind interest and exertions this attempt to make known to the English people the sacred books of the East is so largely indebted'.

When the first three volumes were being bound Max Müller was provided with a very striking and significant 'motto, figurehead, flag', as he described it (I will call it a manifesto), for the

whole series by a lady who at the time was only a casual acquaintance of his but was to become a close friend. She was Lady Welby,
who was very much interested in religious and philosophical questions. She had heard of the project and had been roused to great
indignation by the accusations that in publishing the series, which
she called a 'signal service' to religion, Max Müller had only wished
to discredit Christianity. One day, looking through her book-
shelves, the first book she drew out was the work of a seventeenth-
century divine, Bishop Beveridge (1636–1707), entitled *Private
Thoughts on Religion.* Almost the first passage that caught her eyes
was one which she thought was strikingly applicable to the work
Müller had undertaken:

> The general inclinations which are naturally implanted in my soul to
> some religion, it is impossible for me to shift off [wrote Bishop
> Beveridge], but there being such a multiplicity of religions in the
> world, I desire now seriously to consider with myself which of them all
> to restrain these my general inclinations to . . .
>
> Indeed there was never any religion so barbarous and diabolical, but
> it was preferred before all other religions whatsoever, by them that did
> profess it; otherwise they would not have professed it . . .
>
> And why, say they, may you not be mistaken as well as we? Especi-
> ally when there is, at least, six to one against your Christian religion;
> all of which think they serve God aright; and expect happiness as well
> as you . . .
>
> I am resolved to be more jealous and suspicious of this religion, than
> of the rest, and be sure not to entertain it any longer without being
> convinced by solid and substantial arguments, of the truth and cer-
> tainty of it. That, therefore, I may make diligent and impartial inquiry
> into all religions and so be sure to find out the best, I shall for a time,
> look upon myself as one not at all interested in any particular religion
> whatsoever, much less in the Christian religion; but only as one who
> desires, in general, to serve and obey Him that made me, in a right
> manner, and thereby to be made partaker of that happiness my nature
> is capable of.

She at once sent the passage to him, and called afterwards. She
herself described that meeting:

> I can never forget that picture.
> He was sitting at his writing-table. After a kindly greeting he said,
> 'I was sitting just there when your letter came. It had all the effect
> upon me of what is called a miracle . . . It was a bolt out of the blue; it

was exactly what was wanted, and if it had reached me but a few hours later it would have been too late. As it was, I had to wire to the binder to stop work.

Completing *The Sacred Books of the East* was like extending the principle of criticism of life formulated by Plato to religion and belief. Max Müller certainly thought that the corpus of the religious texts he was preparing would not only bring criticism into the study of religion, but also revalidate religion by means of the same criticism. Müller wrote a detailed exposition of the aims in the first volume of *The Sacred Books*, which contained his translations of some of the *Upanishads*. Only a summary can be offered here.

The basic aim was quite clearly historical. Müller thought that the texts might be of use to theologians, and might also help missionaries by giving them an accurate knowledge of other religions, as indispensable to them as is the knowledge of an enemy country to a general. Nevertheless, he explained, the texts had assumed quite a new importance in his time as historical documents. He declared that it could not be emphasized strongly enough that the chief interest of these books was historical, and only the historian would be able to understand the important lessons which they taught.

But, in order to be of value to the historian, a very strict principle of selection of the texts had to be followed, and the limitations of the translations frankly recognized. The principle was that the texts or passages translated should not be one-sided, presenting only the brighter aspects of the religions dealt with; and that they should never omit what could appear as primitive, crude, childish and even repulsive to modern readers. There was nothing Max Müller disapproved of more strongly than uncritical admiration, and especially of the Eastern religions.

In his introduction he referred to the books which had already been published in which these texts were described as full of primeval wisdom, religious enthusiasm and also sound and simple moral teaching. He observed that this illusion had to be dispelled and the study of the ancient religions of the world had to be placed on a more sound and truly historical basis. 'The time has come,' he said, 'when the study of the ancient religions of mankind must be approached in a different, less enthusiastic, more discriminating, in fact in a more scholar-like spirit.'

In the report on the progress of the series which he submitted to
Dean Liddell in 1882, he emphasized the principle even more
strongly in the light of the criticism of his editing:

> I have been blamed for not making this Series of Sacred Books more
> attractive and more popular, but to do so would have been incompatible
> with the very object I had in view in publishing these translations. I
> thought the time had come when the ancient religions of the East
> should be studied in their own canonical texts, and that an end should
> thus be put to the vague assertions as to their nature and character,
> whether coming from the admirers or the detractors of those ancient
> creeds. To have left out what seems tedious and repulsive in them
> would have been to my mind simply dishonest, and I could have been
> no party to such an undertaking. The translations as here published,
> are historical documents that cannot be tampered with without destroy-
> ing their value altogether.

Even so he was attacked for suppressing some of the objectionable
sides of these religions. In 1886 the Bishop of Colombo wrote to
Max Müller about the method of presenting the Buddhist Vinaya
texts by omitting to reproduce the parts which could be regarded as
objectionable. A journal in India violently attacked him for giving a
false idea of the real character of some of the Buddhist teaching.
These charges were repeated by Professor T. M. Lindsay of
Edinburgh.

Whatever might have been his editorial decision in regard to
particular passages, Max Müller had laid down the general principle
governing the inclusion or exclusion of what might have been regarded as obscene details in the introduction to the first volume. In
it he said:

> There are in ancient books, and particularly in religious books, frequent
> allusions to the sexual aspects of nature, which, though perfectly harm-
> less and innocent in themselves, cannot be rendered in modern lan-
> guage without the appearance of coarseness. We may regret that it
> should be so, but tradition is too strong on this point, and I have there-
> fore felt obliged to leave certain passages untranslated, and to give the
> original, when necessary, in a note.

But he felt that on the whole he had tried not to suppress the outspoken simplicity of the ancient man, because he felt that this man
as he really was, that is, as an animal with all the strength and weaknesses of an animal, must be studied in all his aspects.

As to his general attitude, he rather feared that his fellow-workers would think that he had used very strong and irreverent language with regard to the ancient sacred books of the East. But he justified his approach by saying that in the days of anthropological research when no custom was too disgusting to be recorded, it would be strange if the few genuine relics of ancient religion which had been miraculously preserved should be judged from an aesthetic, and not from an historical point of view.

After setting down this caution for those who might expect to find nothing but gems in the sacred books of the East, he went on to describe the difficulty which in the best circumstances might prevent a full and accurate understanding of these books. Translations, he said, could never take the place of the originals, because they could never be more than an approximation of one language to the other. Then he observed: 'The translator, however, if he has once gained the conviction that it is impossible to translate old thought into modern speech, without doing some violence either to the one or to the other, will hardly hesitate in his choice between two evils. He will prefer to do some violence to language rather than to misrepresent old thoughts by clothing them in words which do not fit them.'

He illustrated his principle later in his report to Dean Liddell by describing his method of translating the *Upanishads*, which were not only obscure but also repellent in many places. He wrote:

> If, as has been pointed out, my translation often differs so widely from previous translations as to seem hardly based on the same original text, this is due chiefly to my venturing to steer a course independent of native commentators. I have little doubt that future translators of the *Upanishads* will assert their independence of Sankara's commentary still more decidedly. Native commentators though indispensable and extremely useful, are so much under the spell of the later systematic Vedanta philosophy that they often do violence to the simplest thoughts of ancient poets and philosophers.

By the beginning of 1882 fourteen volumes of *The Sacred Books* had been published, eight more were in the press, and the translation of the remaining two of the first series of twenty-four was sufficiently advanced to be ready by 1884. So Max Müller thought it necessary to put before the Delegates of the Clarendon Press and the Secretary of State for India the question of continuing the work in a second series, as was the wish of a large number of scholars

whom he had sounded. He could also say that, though the first
series was not launched as a commercial proposition, the sales had
been such that not only the recoupment of the expenditure by the
Clarendon Press, but also a profit could be expected.

But objections to the undertaking, as has already been mentioned,
had been raised from the start. The translations had been welcomed
by Dr Pusey himself, and Lord Lytton, as Viceroy of India, had
formed an opinion on them which he expressed to Müller in a letter
written in 1885, after his retirement. 'Your own enterprise,' he
wrote, 'with *The Sacred Books of the East* is colossal. It takes one's
breath away. Never was an *Introducteur des Ambassadeurs* on so vast
a scale, nor with such great personages dependent on his good offices.'
But the orthodox of the narrow type persisted in their opposition.

Nevertheless, the second series was sanctioned. Max Müller's
faith in the undertaking was founded not only on its historical importance but also on an assessment of its general significance for
religion, and was as unwavering as it was firmly asserted. Even in
1879, when only the first volumes had been published, he had
written to Lady Welby: 'Of one thing I feel very certain, that this
translation of *The Sacred Books of the East*, which some of the good
people here consider most objectionable, will do a great deal towards lifting Christianity into its highest historical position. I look
forward to the time when those who objected to my including the
Old and New Testaments among *The Sacred Books of the East* will
implore me to do so.'

After the second series was sanctioned he wrote even more confidently. In a letter to Renan on April 21, 1883, he described the
opposition, explained his own stand, and incidentally sought the
support of the great French scholar.

> The first series of twenty-four volumes is nearly finished, and when I
> proposed the second series, *mes amis les ennemis* did all that they could
> to prevent it. They have not succeeded, and the second series will
> appear, but I shall be glad of an authoritative voice like yours to tell
> the English public the real purpose of the undertaking. Most of my
> English critics say '*Les Bibles de l'humanité ne sont pas amusantes*'.
> Certainly not! they are not amusing; on the contrary, they are the very
> saddest books to read. But they must be read, they must be meditated
> on, if we want to know what kind of creature homo sapiens is.

Then followed a passage which might be described as Müller's
credo for the series:

The Bibles were considered by him [homo sapiens] as the best he could produce as superhuman and Divine; let that be one lesson. But there is another, and a more cheerful lesson; amid all this scoria there are the small grains of gold—be good, be true, be patient, trust—the same everywhere, in the highest and the lowest religions, and these grains are the *quod semper, quod ubique, quod ab omnibus,* which will form the eternal religion of the world. These *Sacred Books of the East* will become in future the foundation of a short but universal religion, they will remain the most instructive archives of the past, studied or consulted when thousands of books of the day are forgotten, and yet my wise friends say *'ce n'est pas amusant'*!

Finally he observed that it reflected great credit on the Oxford University Press and the Secretary of State for India that they had not been frightened by the vulgar clamour. 'A few words,' he added to Renan, 'from you to the *Academie des Inscriptions* would be a great help to them and to me. So if you could find time for saying a few weighty words, I should feel grateful.'

When the two series were nearing completion, his Indian friends sent him an address of appreciation signed by Hindu Pandits, to which distinguished Indians of all religions added their signature. In it they spoke of *The Sacred Books* in these words:

Your series of *The Sacred Books of the East* is calculated to generate and strengthen in the minds of those who read it a conviction that God's ennobling and elevating truth is not the monopoly of any particular race. It unfolds the gradual evolution of religious thought, the different stages of which were developed by different races or by the same race at different times. It has already communicated a strong impetus to the unifying movement alluded to above, and we are glad to observe that the philosophic writers of England have begun to avail themselves of the information therein laid before them.

The next year there was one Anglican divine of great spiritual sensitiveness who conveyed his impression of the value of *The Sacred Books.* He was Archdeacon Wilson, who wrote in January 16, 1894: 'Science has discovered much in the Victorian era, but I think that no discovery will bear such lasting fruits as yours, and your great edition of *The Sacred Books of the East.* So in case the new year finds you lonely and discouraged, I send you a word of thanks and love from this smoky, foggy town of Rochdale.'

While Max Müller was carrying on this vast task of compiling a source-book of religion, he was also giving out his own ideas on the nature and history of religion, thought and mythology in a series of impressive books. Some of them were lectures printed in book form. Max Müller was never slipshod or obscure in the presentation of his ideas. On the contrary, his expositions were always striking by means of their style. It is, however, not always easy to present all ideas so as to be intelligible to everybody, because some ideas are intrinsically difficult to grasp, and not even always accessible to reason without the help of intuitive sympathy. This difficulty would face the reader when reading Max Müller's more abstruse books.

His first important series of lectures were the Hibbert Lectures on religion, delivered from April 1878, and published in book form immediately afterwards. These Hibbert Lectures *On the Origin and Growth of Religion as Illustrated by the Religions of India* were delivered in the Chapter House of Westminster Abbey. The whole series was finished in three months.

Shortly before the day of the first lecture Max Müller got a telegram from the Chapter that 1,400 applications had been received for tickets (which were gratis), while the hall could hold only 600. So, not to disappoint those who wanted to hear him, he lectured twice, morning and afternoon. Of the first lecture a leading paper wrote: 'The place, the lecturer, and the occasion were all alike remarkable. Under the shadow of one of the noblest buildings ever raised by medieval Christianity, an Oxford Professor came forward to deal with the deepest problems of historical religion in the "dry light" of modern science, and in the name of a trust which was intended by its founder to promote "the unfettered exercise of private judgement in matters of religion".' Another paper said: 'The Chapter House was thickly crowded with perhaps the most remarkably eclectic audience ever assembled within that majestic old building. To very many the thought must have occurred, with what astonishment the old monks of Westminster would have looked upon such an audience gathered in their Chapter House for such a purpose.'

The tone of these notices, shows that in religion, as with language, Max Müller could suddenly open up for his hearers wide and unsuspected mental horizons. Naturally, there were adverse as well as appreciative comments, and some in strong and unsparingly severe language. Max Müller was prepared for the attacks. Thus on

December 7, 1878, he wrote to Stanley: 'Of course I know that many people will be angry with my *Lectures*. If it were not so, I should not have written them. The more I see of the so-called heathen religions, the more I feel convinced that they contain germs of the highest truth. There is no distinction in kind between them and our own religion. The artificial distinction which *we* have made has not only degraded the old revelation, but has given to our own almost a spectral character.'

A few months later he repeated this at greater length to Malabari: 'As I told you on a former occasion,' he wrote on January 29, 1882, 'my thoughts were with the people of India. I wanted to tell those few at least whom I might hope to reach in English, what the true *historical* value of their ancient religion is, as looked upon, not from an exclusively European or Christian, but from an *historical* point of view.'

At the same time he was aware of a certain risk of being the bearer of a misunderstood message to the Hindus of his age. As he wrote:

> I wished to warn against two dangers, that of undervaluing or despising the ancient national religion, as is done so often by your half-Europeanized youths, and that of overvaluing it, and interpreting it as it was never meant to be interpreted, of which you may see a painful instance in Dayananda Saraswati's labours on the *Veda*. Accept the *Vedas* as an ancient *historical* document, containing thoughts in accordance with the character of an ancient and simple-minded race of men, and you will be able to admire it, and to retain some of it, particularly the teaching of the *Upanishads*, even in these modern days. Accept the past as a reality, study it and try to understand it, and you will then have less difficulty in finding the right way towards the future.

To put it crudely, but not untruly in its essential purport, the path taken by the Hindus, with the help of the work on their religion by Western scholars and more especially by Max Müller, gradually revealed itself to be the very opposite of the right way as understood by him.

Already before his death modern Hindus were falling into four different groups in their application of the results of Western investigations into their past religion. The first group was made up of the traditional Hindus who were acquiring dogmatism with a strong infusion of intolerant fanaticisms in their beliefs and attitudes. The second group had in it men of genuine religious sensibility who had been awakened to a new conception of God and spirituality by Christianity, but who tried to clothe their basically Christian spiritual life under the cover of *Upanishadic* teaching. There was a third group formed by men who were religious in their way, but unable to stand on their own feet. So they were carried away both by their own inclinations and by the prestige of Europe in that age to accept their religion from the hands of European charlatans, and to drift towards extremely spurious groups like the Theosophists. Lastly, the half-Europeanized part of the Hindu intelligentsia made use of the West's discovery of their religion to bolster up a peculiarly xenophobic nationalism, without any realization of its spiritual value.

However, for the present his Hibbert Lectures were translated and published in some Indian languages at the initiative of Malabari, and as he could not bear the expenses of getting this done himself he had to appeal for subscriptions.

Max Müller's next full-length presentation of his own thoughts was an attempt to understand the process of thought itself, which resulted in a large book entitled *The Science of Thought* published in March 1887. He was fully conscious of what he was doing, and did not expect the same kind of reaction to it as he had seen to his books on religion or language. Even before the publication of the book he wrote to his friend Dr Prowe: 'It contains much that is old, and much that is new; but whether the present-day people will read it or not, I do not know.' So far as the book was a reassertion of his thesis of the inseparability of thought and language which he had put forward in all his treatment of language, it did draw on itself adverse comments. For the rest, it caused less trouble for him than his previous books, and the subsequent ones.

'I feel convinced,' he said, 'that the views put forward in this book, which are the result of a long life devoted to solitary reflection and to the study of the foremost thinkers of all nations, contain certain truths which deserve to be recorded . . . I have written some of my books as a pleader, and, if I may judge by results, I have not pleaded quite in vain. But the present book is not meant to be persuasive. All I can say of it is, *Dixi et salvavi animam meam.*'

Since the reading public always give every system of thought a hallmark and label, he thought it necessary to explain that his system might be called Nominalism, which it would not be in any strict sense. It might also be regarded as being materialistic. And he might be asked whether he was a Darwinian. One special concept of thought, as arrived at by him, he thought it necessary to make explicit. He said that 'thought in the sense in which I have defined it and used it in my book, represents one side of human nature only, the intellectual, and there are two other sides, the ethical and aesthetical, on which I have not touched'.

After finishing his book on thought he wrote to Noiré: 'There is a book on mythology to follow, and perhaps the preparation of a new edition of *Lectures on the Science of Language*, and then I may be allowed to say, "Now lettest Thou Thy servant depart in peace".' But his *nunc dimittis* had to be postponed by a chance circumstance which led him for four years to devote himself to a consideration of the history of religion in the most lengthy and elaborate set of books he ever wrote.

In January 1888, his friends had urged on the University of Edinburgh the election of Max Müller as the first Gifford Lecturer. But an old Edinburgh man, Hutchinson Stirling, was elected. The University of Glasgow, which had also been endowed by Lord Gifford, immediately offered its Lectureship to Müller at the instance of Principal Caird. He accepted the invitation.

Lord Gifford had been a distinguished Scottish lawyer, whom the outside world took to be no more than a keen, hard-working, and judicious professional man, who after gaining wealth, and a good deal of it at the Bar, had taken a place on the bench. His intimate friends knew him as a man of philosophical temperament, who was devoted to Plato, Spinoza and other philosophers. But his will when opened, surprised even them. After providing for his relatives, he gave the residue, a very large sum, to the four Scottish universities of Edinburgh, Glasgow, Aberdeen and St Andrews, to establish Lectureships on religion. He wanted through these lectures to promote what he called Natural Theology among the people of Scotland, and he defined Natural Theology in the widest sense of that term as 'the knowledge of God, the Infinite, the All, the First and only Cause, the One and the Sole Substance, the Sole Being, the Sole Reality, and the Sole Existence, the Knowledge of His Nature and Attributes, the Knowledge of the Relations which men and the whole universe bear to Him, the Knowledge of the Nature and Foundation of Ethics and Morals, and of all Obligations and Duties hence arising'.

To give away one's money for such a purpose was indeed remarkable, but even more remarkable were the terms which were to be complied with in electing the lecturers. The will declared:

The lecturers shall be subject to no test of any kind, and shall not be required to take any oath, or to emit or subscribe any declaration of belief, or to make any promise of any kind; they may be of any denomination whatever, or of no denomination at all (and many earnest and high-minded men prefer to belong to no ecclesiastical denomination); they may be of any religion or way of thinking, or, as is sometimes said, they may be of no religion, or they may be so-called sceptics or agnostics or free-thinkers, provided that the 'Patrons' will use diligence to secure that they be able, reverent men, true thinkers, sincere lovers and earnest inquirers after truth.

With equal boldness Lord Gifford laid down the principle of treating the subjects. He wrote: 'I wish the lecturers to treat their subject as a strictly natural science, the greatest of all possible sciences, indeed, in one sense, the only science, that of Infinite Being, without reference to or reliance upon any supposed and so-called miraculous revelation. I wish it to be considered just as astronomy or chemistry is.'

In view of these directions in the will of Lord Gifford, Max Müller called the Lectureships a sign, and a very important sign, of the times.

The first series of Gifford Lectures at Glasgow was delivered by Müller in 1888, and he was elected three times after that and delivered the Lectures in 1890, 1891 and 1892. In these four sequences he presented a stupendous synthesis of the evolution of religion in an ascending process in four stages, which he called Natural Religion, Physical Religion, Anthropological Religion and Theosophy or Psychological Religion.

He tried to observe Lord Gifford's directions, but was attacked for that very reason. No public protest was raised against the first lectures, though when they were published one critic said that 'the learned professor found something good in every religion, *except in Christianity*'.

A more comminatory attack was made on Max Müller from the Roman Catholic side. Monsignor Munro in the Catholic St Andrew's Cathedral took his text from Matthew's account of the betrayal of Christ by Judas, and announced that he was going to apply that terrible narrative to the subject he was going to deal with that evening. Then he said:

> The Gifford Lectures delivered by Professor Max Müller were nothing less than a crusade against Divine revelation, against Jesus Christ, and against Christianity. The guilt of those who permitted that anti-Christian doctrine in a university founded to defend Christianity, was simply horrible. It was a strange thing that in a Christian university, public feeling should have tolerated the ostentatious publication of infidelity.
>
> As to Max Müller: 'Professor Max Müller was incapable of a philosophical idea, and ignorant of Christianity he sought to overthrow. His theory uprooted our idea of God, for it repudiated the idea of a personal God.'

He added that the lectures were blasphemous, and even Müller's pantheism was atheism in disguise.

However, that made no difference either to Max Müller or to the university, and he was able to give his fourth series of lectures in 1892. The last words of the last series were:

> I do not believe in human infallibility, least of all, in Papal infallibility. I do not believe in professorial infallibility, least of all in that of your Gifford Lecturer. We are all fallible, and we are fallible either in our facts, or in the deductions which we draw from them. If therefore any of my learned critics will tell me which of my facts are wrong, or which of my conclusions are faulty, let me assure them, that though I am now a very old Professor, I shall always count those among my best friends who will not mind the trouble of supplying me with new facts, or of pointing out where they have been wrongly stated by me, or who will correct any arguments that may seem to them to offend against the sacred laws of logic.

It remains to consider only his last major work, his lengthy treatise on mythology published in 1897, when he was seventy-four. For Max Müller mythology, language and religion were cognate subjects. In fact, his excursion into mythology was an extension of his work on language, and that fact conditioned his whole approach to mythology and his method of dealing with it. Actually, his essay on comparative mythology preceded his formal lectures on language. It was published in 1856, five years before them. But not less important were his conclusions about mythology, incidentally but quite formally set down in all his books on language and religion. It was these which really drew the fire of a different school of mythologists on him. So one might say that his formal book on mythology, published when he was almost approaching death, was like the legitimization of a dearly loved natural son.

In this chapter I shall give only the external framework of his work on mythology. Max Müller was extremely tenacious about his conclusions on any subject after he had arrived at them as a result of prolonged study and thinking. That might be looked upon as dogmatism, but as has been shown by his final remarks in his last Gifford Lecture, he did not admit he was dogmatic. He sincerely believed that he kept an open mind. He always believed and said that the claim to have uttered the *dernier mot* was wholly baseless.

In any case, his treatise on mythology began with a fanfare, and it is heartening to feel the gusto of the counter-attack delivered by him. He did not fight back with spleen and rancour but with cool-ness. To begin with, he was very forthright about the nature of the attacks on his views:

It is easy to say such things [he wrote in his preface to the book] in a number of daily papers, but they do not become true for all that. If, as happens sometimes, the same critic is on the staff of many papers, and has to supply copy every day, every week, or every month, the broken rays of one brilliant star may produce the dazzling impression of many independent lights, and there has been of late such a galaxy of sparkling articles on Comparative Mythology and Folklore, that even those who are themselves opposed to this new science, have at last expressed their disapproval of the 'journalistic mist' that has been raised, and that threatens to obscure the real problems of the Science of Mythology.

He conceded readily that the writers of such articles were fully persuaded of the truth of their opinions, but at the same suggested gently that they might also consider the judgement of real scholars not wholly undeserving of their attention.

Then he set forth his position in the controversy:

In what I am going to say I am not defending myself, though I am always represented, if not as the true founder, at all events as the only champion left to defend the Science of Mythology. I can therefore speak with all the more freedom and without fear of being considered egotistical. I am pleading pro domo, but not for myself. Scholars come and go and are forgotten, but the road which they have opened remains, other scholars follow in their footsteps, and though some of them retrace their steps, on the whole there is progress.

After that he went on to mention the names of many eminent scholars in Italy, Holland, Germany, America and France to show how the science was being carried on.

The whole dispute was over method. Max Müller followed the philological method, whereas his critics followed the anthropological. Max Müller's contention throughout was that whatever detritus mythology may carry along with it, its original constituent elements were words and phrases about the most striking phenomena of nature, such as day and night, dawn and evening, sun and moon, sky, earth and sea, in their various relations to each other and to man. As his wife defined it in her biography: 'Max Müller's highest object was to discover reason in all the unreason of mythology, and thus to vindicate the character of our ancestors, however distant.'

As far back as 1869 in a letter to Sir George Cox, another mythologist, he had emphasized the connexion between Sanskrit, Comparative Philology and Comparative Mythology. He wrote: 'The most minute criticism of etymological coincidences seems to me the only safe foundation of Comparative Mythology . . . If, therefore, you ask me, I tell you openly, do not make Comparative Mythology the principal work of your life, unless you make up your mind first to study Sanskrit and Comparative Philology.'

He said the same thing to Andrew Lang, the most sparkling among his critics, in a letter written in 1897: 'Still less could I understand why you should have attacked me, or rather my masters, without learning Sanskrit, which is by no means so difficult as people imagine. You must have a rapier to fight a man who has a rapier, otherwise it becomes a row.'

He asserted at the same time that he did not dispute the value of the anthropological approach, and observed: 'I don't say that I should go to the stake for it, but I am perfectly certain that some good may be got from the study of savages for the elucidation of Aryan myths. *L'un n'empêche pas l'autre.*'

Continuing, he paid a warm tribute to Frazer of *The Golden Bough*: 'Frazer has never attacked me, and I have always touched my hat to him. He works his mine, I work mine: why should we quarrel?'

Andrew Lang had the good sense and the good manners to recognize the urbanity of Max Müller in controversy, and also to perceive the basic cause of their differences. After the death of Müller he wrote to Mrs Max Müller: 'My own relations with Mr Max Müller were those of an amateur, or casual inquirer, who ventured, on a single point, to oppose the conclusions of a man eminently learned. We approached the subject, that of the origin of myths, from different quarters, and saw different sides of the shield as in the old apologue. Neither of us was fortunate enough to convert the other.' Then followed his tribute:

But what I am anxious to say is, that Mr Max Müller always met my criticisms, often petulant in manner, and perhaps often unjust, with a good humour and kindness perhaps unexampled in the controversies of the learned and the half-learned. I shall always remember with pleasure certain occasions when Mr Max Müller turned my own laugh against myself, with victorious humour and good humour . . . History would offer reading much more agreeable, if discussions were always conducted (they almost never are) in the genial and humane temper which Mr Max Müller displayed in dealing with an 'opposite' so unworthy as myself.

Such letters keep up one's faith in and respect for writers and scholars.

Though Max Müller was always ready to go on with his work without the world's praise, it could never be said that those who conferred position in the world were indifferent to his merits. From a fairly early age he had been receiving academic and other honours which would have satisfied the yearning for recognition of any scholar. Though he had never sought or canvassed for them, he was not above feeling a certain pride in them. Actually he delighted in them from a childlike desire for praise, regarded them as a precious reward, and above all as a strong incentive to further work.

However, one grievance lingered vaguely in his heart and rankled more actively in the mind of his wife, who could not understand why when foreign countries were vying with one another to grant him distinctions, nothing had been given him in his adopted country. She smarted under this sense of injustice. The death of his first daughter made him somewhat indifferent to such things, and he wrote to his wife in 1883: 'There was a time when I should have liked to have been made Sir Frederick and you Lady Max

Müller. Dear Stanley wrote to me years ago that a baronetcy or a life peerage would be the right thing—however, we do very well without, and want nothing more from the world.'

In one very high place in the world there was great regard both for him and his work. The Queen herself and the entire royal household were always very kind to him. So in 1886 the Queen suggested to Gladstone that he might receive some public mark of her favour. The Prime Minister suggested a knighthood. Upon this the Queen wanted to know privately what Max Müller's feeling might be. Neither Max Müller nor his wife could look upon this as an adequate recognition when foreign countries had given him their highest honours reserved for literary work. So the objection was explained to the Queen, and she fully appreciated Müller's motives in not accepting a knighthood.

Ten years later it was obviously the Queen again who took the initiative. On May 17, 1896, Lord Salisbury as Prime Minister wrote in his own hand to Max Müller:

Dear Professor Max Müller,
I have great pleasure in informing you that Her Majesty has been pleased to mark her sense of the great services you have rendered to philological science in this country and of your singular eminence in the world of letters, by directing that you should be summoned to the Privy Council. I am very glad to be the channel of this communication. Believe me,
Yours very truly,
Salisbury

The announcement was made among the Birthday Honours on May 20. The Times commented that it was 'a fitting recognition of distinguished services to literature and philology extending over the half-century he has lived amongst us.' It is not clear whether on May 20 Max Müller had as yet received Salisbury's letter and was keeping the matter confidential even from his wife. In any case, he came down to the drawing-room that morning with The Times in hand, and said to his wife: 'Don't faint', and handed her the paper. The announcement was in three places on the editorial page. There was great joy for both, because it was felt that the recognition was exceptional. Max Müller knew that he was going to be the only non-political Privy Councillor, and that might cause jealousy among scientific workers. But congratulations poured in all day long.

Max Müller was duly grateful. He wrote to Sir Robert Collins, Secretary to the Duchess of Albany: 'I am really quite upset. I had so little expected anything of the kind, and it is, of course, far too much. However, it shows the Queen's very kind heart. I confess there always was something bitter when I received so many favours from other countries, and nothing from the country of my choice and love. *One* enemy can do more harm than many friends can mend.' What he felt no less strongly was the death of those friends who would have rejoiced most at the event.

His only surviving daughter Beatrice was greatly pleased, but she was not forgetful of her mother and brother. So she wrote: 'Dear Daddy P.C., I suppose now they will soon make you a baronet which would be nice for Billy and Mama, I am so sorry this gives her nothing.

Though Max Müller's life was despaired of during his serious illness in the autumn of 1899, he was sufficiently recovered in the next spring to give his friends and family an impression of renewed vitality. It was during this intermezzo of energy that he carried on his vigorous polemics with Mommsen over the Boer War. He was also receiving many visitors. A professor from Vienna, after visiting him at his home, wrote about him in a German paper: 'He keeps his Oxford home hospitably open for foreign birds of passage, who find their way to Oxford from all corners of the universe.' Among the visitors at this time were a number of Indian princes, including the Gaekwar of Baroda.

At this time he was also interviewed by the representative of a magazine (Hugh W. Strong, for the *Temple Magazine*), and the account was published in June 1900. Speaking to this interviewer in answer to his questions, Max Müller gave what might be called a valedictory message. I shall quote a few of the questions and answers.

Q. 'Your seventy-seventh year, Professor?'
A. 'Yes, and I never felt old until this illness.'
Q. 'From which you are making an excellent recovery. May I be permitted to ask, what are your literary plans for the future?'
A. 'My work is done. All I can do in the future is to look on. There is the *Rig-Veda* in six large volumes, and *The Sacred Books of the East* in fifty volumes of translations, my commission from the Oxford University. These really form my life's work. Beyond them are numerous other books and translations, my *History of Sanskrit*

Literature, my *Science of Language, Science of Religion, Science of Mythology, History of Indian Philosophy*, etc., while most of my shorter writings are collected in *Chips from a German Workshop*. Now I feel it is high time I drew in my sails—which hitherto have been for ever spread to the favouring gale.'

Q. 'May we next discuss your methods of work?'

A. 'They are very simple. When I have nothing to do I work.'

Q. 'But your recreations, Professor?'

A. 'Oh! I didn't want them. As soon as I felt exhausted I gave up and rested. Absence of occupation is not rest.'

Q. 'And now may I ask what progress your special studies are making?,

A. 'Most satisfactory on the whole. The three main branches especially well: the Science of Language here in Oxford; the Science of Comparative Mythology in Germany; and the Science of Comparative Religions in England. The latter is, of course, a subject which naturally appeals to English thought and interest.'

Q. 'A last word as to Oxford, Professor?'

A. 'Oxford the unchangeable! Why, it has simply been revolutionized in appearance and character since I first saw it. Fancy, there were no married dons in those days! And now! [He did not tell the interviewer that he was the first married Fellow.] The Vice-Chancellor and heads of houses were little kings. If you happened to catch them in good humour at dinner, they would mention your wish at the Hebdomadal Council. We have changed all that.'

In the next summer his health declined, and it was soon apparent that he was going. At this time a visitor came to his house by a very curious chance, but the visit was symbolic of his life and of its main interest, for the visitor was an Indian Holy Man.

On August 7, 1900, quite early in the morning Mrs Max Müller was told that two Hindus were at the door, and going down she found two strange figures, one dressed in a flowing robe, with his bare feet in slippers, and a turban on his head. The other was a much younger man, and could speak a little English. He explained that his companion was a most holy Yogin, by name Agamya Yogindra, who had arrived in England from India a few days ago, and had now hastened to Oxford to meet the only man in England whose name they knew. They were told that Max Müller could not come down before 11 o'clock, and so they went away to come back at the time given.

From information received later from India, Max Müller came to know that he was a genuine Mahatma, who, as a holy man, had a

very high position in India, and had mastered all that was to be
gained by the ascetic discipline of Hinduism. He had braved the
voyage to England impelled by the pure desire to impart what he
believed to be the highest knowledge, and in his innocence had
thought that his name and fame would be so known in England
that admiring crowds would meet him in London. But at the station
he found nobody and was sitting bewildered, when a porter saw the
Yogin and his chela (disciple) amid the bundles which contained
their food and cooking pots, formed an idea according to his knowledge what sort of persons they might be, and sent them to the
Psychic Society, whose members passed them on to Oxford.

When he met Müller, Dr Carpenter and Mr Bidder, the Vicar of
St Giles, were present. Protap Chunder Mozoomdar, the Brahmo
leader who was also in England then, arrived soon after as he was
invited to spend the day with the Müllers. Mozoomdar was in total
disgrace with the Yogin, for he had been summoned to the presence
in London, but had been unable to go on account of a previous
speaking engagement. Yogin could not understand how a mere engagement could interfere with his command, and treated Mozoomdar with great severity. It amused Mrs Max Müller to observe that
Mozoomdar seemed to accept his position without reserve and
acknowledge the crime which he had unwittingly committed. She
did not, of course, know that these Hindu holy men were the equiva-
lents of kings in another dimension of the world, and were absolute
monarchs by Divine right in that dimension. That was why they
were always addressed as Maharaj, great king, by all.

Anyhow the interview proceeded. Max Müller spoke in Sanskrit
unfamiliarly pronounced for the Yogin, and the Yogin spoke English in an imperfect manner and Sanskrit with a pronunciation
Müller could not understand. The others observed the powerful
personality of the teacher. He was a tall, strongly built man, with a
face of unusual breadth with sunken eyes, a wide, but firmly closed
mouth, a resolute chin, all of which spoke of long practices of medi-
tation and self-control.

After talking for some time with Müller, he turned to Mr Bidder
to denounce the country to which he had come: 'I had come to teach
men the subtle enigmas of existence, but England was like a poison-
ous fruit, fair and attractive to view, but full of deadly juice; there
were no good men, no one who wanted to understand knowledge;
only in this house have I found a good man and *one who knows*.'

It was found that Max Müller was tired out by this difficult conversation, and wanted a little rest before lunch. But when he sat at lunch he talked with animation. The Yogin would not sit down to eat with them, but remained in the library. But they all met again at the coffee-table on the garden terrace. Dr Carpenter did not want to overstrain Max Müller, and went away with the Yogin, who in October was sent back to India.

While sitting with Max Müller, Dr Carpenter observed that the Yogin was looking fixedly at his host, 'almost as one who could read the lines of destiny'. Max Müller observed: 'My life is nearly over, I shall never be able to do any more work.' The Yogin went up to him, placed a hand on either shoulder, looked long and fixedly into Müller's face, and replied: 'Yes, I see death has come near you, friend. He has looked you in the face.'

Mr Bidder recalled this parting in these words: 'I shall never forget the scene on the garden terrace, when this representative of ancient India took a last farewell of India's friend and champion.'

On October 28, 1900, Max Müller died, and in his condolence letter Anagarika Dharmapala, the Ceylonese Buddhist monk who lived in Calcutta, wrote to Mrs Max Müller: 'I now offer the deepest sympathy of all Buddhists in your bereavement; and I repeat the noble words of our Lord Buddha, which he uttered 2,489 years ago, "Do not grieve at my passing away, since it is natural to die".'

Conclusion

THE MAN AND THE THINKER

How much of a man's inner life can remain wholly unperceived even when sufficient information about it has been provided from letters and other intimate papers can be judged from a remark made in a review of Mrs Max Müller's biography of her husband, published in 1902. The reviewer said:

> There are no subtle recesses of psychology to be explored in this eminently sane, open, unembarrassed Teutonic nature, certain of himself, his work and the world. Such a nature makes for the happiness of its owner, but there is nothing salient or picturesque which the reader's interest can lay hold of.

Though the remark was not made in malice, anything more wide of the mark about Max Müller could not be imagined, because there was enough material in the two volumes of the biography to show, despite a wife's natural reticence in the presentation of her husband, how complex his personality was.

There was greater scope for imperfect understanding during his lifetime, for as seen from the outside his was a career of uninterrupted successes and growing fame. If he had died before Dr Samuel Smiles published his *Self-help* his example would certainly have been included in the book. Success through self-help and perseverance was the most obvious feature of Müller's life. So, reviewing the biography, the *Daily Telegraph*'s critic wrote with greater appreciation than the other reviewer just quoted: 'His career possesses the dramatic interest of a hard-fought battle, its vicissitudes, its momentary despondency, its rekindled enthusiasm, its final and decisive victory.'

But the account I have given would also show that besides this—an unquestionable achievement because Müller obtained his worldly success by obstinately pursuing the most unworldly and even unpractical ideal—there were other remarkable things in him. A man's life is led at different levels. In a notice of the life of Baron Bunsen, his friend and patron, Max Müller himself wrote: 'All really great and honest men may be said to live three lives: there is one life which is seen and accepted by the world at large, a man's outward life; there is the second life which is seen by a man's most intimate friends, his household life; and there is a third life, seen only by the man himself and by Him who searcheth the heart, which may be called the inner or heavenly life.'

Quoting this passage the distinguished Dutch Arabic scholar, de Goeje, who succeeded to his place in the Institut as Associate Member, said in his *éloge* that he could speak only about the first aspect of Müller's life, and he paid him a most handsome tribute. It would, however, be wrong to think that the most conspicuous merit would be recognized as such by everybody. During his life Max Müller had his share of belittling. After his death stories were printed about him which for fear of a contradiction or an action of libel would never have been published before. Even very respectable papers carried these tales. He has also been disparaged in autobiographical books published in our times when nobody remembers him. It was not on the supposed inadequacies of Max Müller's scholarship that the more piquant dismissal of him was based. It was on the attribution to him of ridiculous weaknesses like personal vanity. For example, de Goeje in his *éloge* said:

> One of my colleagues at Leyden one day saw me surrounded by Max Müller's books and expressed his surprise. When I informed him that I was preparing myself to write a notice of his life and work he exclaimed: 'Ah! I do not like your Max Müller. He was a vain man who was only after his own glory.' I protested against this judgement, which I have heard pronounced by others.

De Goeje added:

> It needs the sacred fire to sustain a man in such stupendous activity; only a sincere scientific conviction can create such eloquence. *Pectus est quod disertum facit*. [It is the heart which makes eloquence.]

All this attribution of vanity, especially in respect to clothes, was known to Mrs Max Müller, and about it she wrote in her biography: 'Some of his critics, who never knew him personally, speak of his vanity, because he dwelt with pleasure and gratitude on the honours and successes that came to him in later life. Any really vain man would have shrunk from showing his enjoyment of the good things that fell to him, for fear of being thought vain.' She explained that to the end of his life Müller showed 'the child's pure delight in little things, that gave a constant zest to his life, and he had the power of rejoicing in every little luxury and pleasure which he could afford himself.' The poverty in which his boyhood and youth was passed made him all the more disposed to do so. In his school days when he came home in the vacations he did not wear his expensive school boots, but to save them put on the home-made shoes provided for him by his mother.

The real test of a man's character is his uncensored private correspondence and diaries, and I have read a good deal of both from Müller. I have not found one passage which shows him different from what he appeared to be in the public eye. His was too transparent a nature for any kind of disguise. But I have also found that he was not ignorant of the ways of the world, nor disposed to be its victim. He had acquired much worldly experience in the course of his early struggles, and in later life he was as much a man of the world as he was a studious recluse. Besides, a man of his keen mental powers was not likely to prevent these powers from playing on the life that he saw around himself. He gave the benefit of that experience to his son, though he did not always employ it for his own advancement.

Many examples of worldly wisdom are found scattered liberally in Max Müller's correspondence with his son, and they would qualify him as another Polonius or a Victorian Chesterfield. If he wanted to satisfy his penchant for generalization from his experience of the world he could easily have become a writer of maxims like La Rochefoucauld, Vauvenargues, or Chamfort, because there was a vein of sententiousness in him. But his interest was elsewhere, and his sententiousness was exhibited differently.

Max Müller took life and the world too seriously to be capable of becoming worldly. He was very much like the other Anglo-German he so much admired, that is, Prince Albert. And he would always repeat to himself, as to his son,—*Das Leben ist ernst*. That made him disinclined even to make life an art. As he wrote to his son: '*Das Leben ist eine Kunst*, is Goethe's doctrine, and there is some truth in it also, as long as *Kunst* implies nothing artful or artificial.' His moral preoccupation was always dominant in his response to the visual arts, though not to music, which being abstract and absolute was tied up with his religious sentiment. So, in painting he felt drawn towards works in which he could see a clear moral content, and this drew him strongly towards the picture of La Carità by

Andrea del Sarto, whose face he assumed to be that of Andrea's wife Lucrezia. In Florence, as he was passing along a narrow street after seeing the frescoes of Andrea in the Collegio dello Scalzo, he suddenly saw against a wall in one of the shops the face of la Carità with the rain streaming on it—'silver grey, placid and perfect. And there was the boy holding her hand, and the other boy on her arm, and the third boy hiding behind her dress.' He bought it for a nothing. He thought it might be a contemporary replica, though it was later ascertained to be a nineteenth-century copy.

He wrote an essay on the picture, sent copies to his friends Browning and Ruskin, and asked their opinion. The writer of 'Andrea del Sarto, the Perfect Painter' wrote to him appreciatively, but Ruskin almost snarled out: 'Andrea and his story are alike out of my range of work or care. You never find him named by me, during the whole course of my Oxford lectures—nor do I recognize any worth in him but that of a dexterous schoolman. I liked your paper extremely—but it seemed to me late in the life of a man of your power to be either first discovering or first asking in what Beauty consists.' Perhaps in this particular area of Müller's sensitiveness Ruskin was not far wrong.

Religion, morality, and thought where his three preoccupations. A disciple of Kant was not likely to be anything but firm in his morality, and so firm that he saw no necessity for revalidating his trust in it by means of criticism, whose application he considered indispensable in the case of religion. His respect for morality also made him almost a worshipper of Buddha, more a moral than a religious prophet. But, as between religion and intellection, he was throughout given to that 'dialogue' or dialectic he so much valued as a method. The man of faith in him was unceasingly holding an argument with the man of reason. He was as cerebral as he was religious, and though he never perceived it, this perpetuated an unresolved dichotomy in him.

As has been noted before, at the end of his life Max Müller set down that he was never troubled by the religious doubts which assailed his distinguished contemporaries, and that he was carried along by the simple Protestant faith which was instilled into him at Dessau by his mother. But there was enough evidence in all his writings to show that this was not the whole story for him. His works on religion, which constitute the most voluminous part of his immense literary output, was as much communing with himself as communication to others. He often dwelt on the nature of a child's faith.

'There is certainly no happier life,' he once wrote, 'than a life of simple faith; of literal acceptance, of rosy dreams . . . But can we prevent the light of the sun and noises of the street from waking the happy child from his heavenly dreams? Nay, is it not our duty to wake the child?'

Again, 'There is a difference between the childlike faith of a man (all real faith must be childlike) and the childlike faith of a child. The one is Paradise not yet lost, the other Paradise lost but regained. The one is right for the child, the other is right for the man.' (See also pp. 277–78.)

Yet again, 'Who, if he is honest towards himself, could say that the religion of his manhood was the same as that of his childhood, or the religion of his old age the same as the religion of his manhood? It is easy to deceive ourselves, and to say that the most perfect faith is a childlike faith. Nothing can be truer, and the older we grow the more we learn to understand the wisdom of the childlike faith. But before we can learn that, we have first to learn another lesson, namely, to put away childish things.'

There it was—the entire motivation of his stupendous inquiry into religion, with its philosophical, scientific, and historical facets. But the question arises: Where did all this land him? Did it lead him back to the Paradise of the child Max Müller's faith, to an acceptance of Christianity? Some of the basic conclusions about religion to which he arrived would have startled him if he had in him any attachment to the kind of Christian orthodoxy asserted by every Church or denomination of Christianity. Here, in his own words, are a few of them:

1. The more we study the history of the religions of the world, the clearer it becomes that there is really no religion which could be called an individual religion, in the sense of a religion created, as it were *de novo*, or rather *ab ovo*, by one single person. This may seem strange, and yet it is really most natural. Religion, like language, is everywhere an historical growth, and to invent a completely new religion would be as hopeless a task as to invent a completely new language.

2. From a comparative study of religion we shall learn that there hardly is one religion which does not contain some truth, some important truth; truth sufficient to enable those who seek the Lord, and feel after Him, to find Him in their hour of need.

3. A belief in God, in the immortality of the soul, and in a future retribution, can be gained, and not only can be, but has been gained, by the right exercise of human reason alone, without the assistance of what has been called a special revelation.

4. If there is one thing which a comparative study of religions places in the clearest light, it is the inevitable decay to which every religion is exposed.

5. Of Max Müller's many pronouncements on Christ I shall cite only two. He said that those who deprived Jesus of His real humanity in order to exalt Him above all humanity were really undoing His work. Christ came to teach us, not what He was, but what we are. He had seen that man, unless he learned himself to be the child of God, was lost. Max Müller could see that this would raise a question for the Christian: Is not Christ God? He answered: Yes, He is, but in His own sense, not in the Jewish nor in the Greek sense, nor in the sense which so many Christians attach to that article of their faith. Christ's teaching is that we are of God, that there is in us something divine, that we are nothing if we are not that.

6. Last of all Max Müller believed that the study of all the religions of the world, however high or low, however primitive or developed, would enable Christians to appreciate better than ever what they had in their own religion and declared that no one who had not examined patiently and honestly the other religions of the world could know what Christianity really was, or could join with such truth and sincerity in the words of St Paul, 'I am not ashamed of the gospel of Christ.'

It is hardly to be wondered that in the light of such opinions incessantly repeated by Max Müller, orthodox Christians would consider him both un-Christian and anti-Christian, for certainly these views disregarded, if they did not reject, the whole central kerygma of Christianity as a special dispensation of God for man. His wide and catholic inquiry into all religions gave Max Müller a profound veneration for all religious inclinations and aspirations, and also sympathy and tolerance for them. But it also made him blind to the particularity of Christianity as a religion, and this is surprising in a man of his historical consciousness. Not only to Christians but even to non-Christians, if the latter have studied the religion at all, Christianity should appear as a unique religious phenomenon, different even from the two religions to which it was the nearest, namely, Judaism and Islam. Christianity does not take its stand on a general concept of God's relations with man, but on a

particular act of His for the redemption of man. Müller's concept
of Christianity as embodied in his writings almost ignored the ideas
of Incarnation, Mediation, Expiation, and Resurrection. It made
him forget that intolerance of other religions was of the very essence
of Christianity. The Christian was bound to be even more uncompromising in his attitude to unbelievers than the Muslim or the
Communist. To make Christianity tolerant of all religious beliefs is
to destroy it in its most characteristic aspect.

Why was Max Müller led to this position intellectually and
ethically, whatever he might have been as a believer? To begin at
the very beginning, that was in obedience to the trend which made
its appearance as soon as Christian preachers thought of taking it
to the Gentiles. They were forced to philosophize in order to
justify to the Greeks what was foolishness to them. That brought
Christianity to an unquiet marriage with reason, to which no other
religion had come. They kept faith and reason quite apart. After that
came the entire intellectual tradition created by the Graeco-Roman
elements in European culture, with its philosophical as well as
scientific sides, which taught that question and analysis are the
beginning of knowledge.

Belief in examination and revalidation made Max Müller think
that even atheism made a contribution of great value to religion and
faith. 'There is an atheism', he wrote, 'which is unto death, there is
another atheism which is the life-blood of all true faith. It is the
power of giving up what, in our best, in our most honest, moments,
we know to be no longer true; it is the readiness to replace the less
perfect, however dear, however sacred it may have been to us, by the
more perfect, however much it may be detested, as yet, by the world.
It is the true self-surrender, the true self-sacrifice, the truest trust
in truth, the truest faith. Without that atheism religion would long
ago have become a petrified hypocrisy; without that atheism no new
religion, no reform, no reformation, no resuscitation would ever
have been possible; without that atheism no new life is possible for
any one of us.'

This is putting faith in reason above faith in dogma or even
belief. From the religious point of view this application of the intellect is like Abraham's sacrifice of his son to his Lord. But Max
Müller does not seem to have realized that the sacrifice would have
run its course except for the intervention of the Lord. Any thoroughgoing application of reason to faith can only destroy the latter. So

Christian faith, incapable of existing without reason, had to propound a new view of reason: *Le cœur a ses raisons que la raison ne connait pas.* To say *Credo ut intelligam* is typically Christian, to reverse the formula and say *Intellego ut credam* is also partly Christian, but only on the assumption that understanding is only an instrument of believing. Taken without this limitation and reservation, the intellect could only destroy religious life. Max Müller was certainly conscious of that too, for he wrote: 'True religion, that is practical, active, living religion, has little or nothing to do with logical or metaphysical quibbles. Practical religious life, is a new life, a life in the sight of God, and it springs from what may be called a new birth.'

Despite this, the duality which divided him between faith and reason persisted, and this was due not only to the hold on him of the intellectual tradition of the Greeks taken over by the Christian apologists, but also to something innate in him, to his temperament, which was Apollinian and not Dionysiac. This distinction is seen not only in the antithesis between the man of action and the man of contemplation, but also among the intellectuals themselves. Some of them can immerse themselves in their experience and project their response to it in a manner which in spite of its logical trappings is intuitive, and is therefore akin to prophetic utterances. These are the Dionysiacs of thought, and Hegel, Nietzsche, Marx, or even Freud might be classed as such. Against them stand the intellectuals who want to reduce experience to order, and present even the suprarational as rational, or at any rate in a form which would be accessible to human intelligence. Kant was of that type, the Apollinian among thinkers. Müller, the disciple of Kant was also bound to be such.

So, he was as religious as he was philosophical, and as philosophical as he was religious. He wanted to bring the two as near as possible. As he wrote:

Religion is not philosophy; but there never has been a religion, and there never can be, which is not based on philosophy, and does not presuppose the philosophical notions of the people. The highest aim towards which all philosophy strives, is and will always remain the idea of God, and it was this idea which Christianity grasped in the Platonic sense, and presented to us most clearly in its highest form, in the Fourth Gospel.

This made him put forward his dialectic concept of the evolution of religion. In the very first series of lectures on the 'science of religion' which he delivered in 1870 he said:

From first to last religion is oscillating between two opposite poles, and it is only if the attraction of one of the two poles becomes too strong, that healthy movement ceases, and stagnation and decay set in. If religion cannot accommodate itself on the one side to the capacity of children, or if on the other side it fails to satisfy the requirements of men, it has lost its vitality, and it becomes either mere superstition or mere philosophy.

It was natural therefore that he should accept and exalt the idea of Logos, both in its Greek and Christian form. As embodied in the Fourth Gospel, it revealed to him not only the unbreakable bond between word and thought, but also their continuation as the Son of God and, finally, Jesus.

In this aspect of Müller's speculations about religion he was a participant in religious experience, and, in an age which is irreligious (not anti-religious) and faithless, not much interest is likely to be felt in his views on religion as a phenomenon of human experience with an intrinsic value for all men. Nobody can say now whether that kind of interest will come back. In the meanwhile, there is interest in religion as a phenomenon to be observed scientifically from the outside. Max Müller in another aspect of his inquiry into religion was, or at least claimed to be, a scientist. In fact, comparative study of ancient religions scientifically was very largely his creation, and in spite of the presence in them of philosophical or devotional utterances, he called all his books 'Science of Religion' in its varied aspects.

First of all, according to him, religion, like all other objects of scientific inquiry, was based on sense perception. As he put it, 'religion, if it is to hold its place as a legitimate element of our consciousness, must like all other knowledge, begin with experience'. Secondly, he thought, religion was based on an innate urge in man for the Infinite. So the most general definition he could give of religion was this: 'Religion consists in the perception of the infinite under such manifestations as are able to influence the moral character of man.' He admitted that this definition of religion covered only its origin, but explained that 'if we once admit a continuity in the historical growth of religion, the same definition ought to remain applicable to all later developments'. In any case, he was not ready to surrender the claim science had on religion, and so he wrote: 'To those who maintain that religion is chiefly *modus cognoscendi Deum,* a way of knowing God, we should reply that there is no conceptual knowledge which is not based first of all on perceptual knowledge.'

I shall not discuss here the merits of Max Müller's scientific conclusions about religion, but only describe one of its controversial aspects. The workers who followed him in the study of comparative religion began to poke fun at him, and especially at his solar myth. The more serious charge was that he was idealizing early religions too much for a scientist.

Now, this challenge came mostly from the Christian school at first and then from the anthropological school. To take the Christian view first: he said that the ancient non-Christian religions of the world, though professed by highly civilized peoples, had been most unfairly treated by most historians and theologians. Every act of the life of their founders which showed that they were but men had been eagerly seized and judged without mercy; every doctrine that was not carefully guarded had been misinterpreted and distorted; every act of worship that differed from the Christian had been held up to ridicule. Hence, he declared, there had arisen a complete misapprehension of the real character of ancient religions, and Christianity itself had been torn away from its 'sacred context of the history of the world'.

With the emergence of the anthropological inquiry into religion this attack was resumed from another direction: the anthropological Blücher joined the theological Wellington to bring about a twilight of the ancient gods. Max Müller had no quarrel with anthropology where it was applicable. But he would not admit that it was applicable to the ancient civilized religions. As he had said, Frazer worked his mine, and he worked his. His method of dealing with the ancient religions was philological and historical; he would not admit that the notions derived from the observation of the religion of contemporary primitive peoples could be read back into the old religions.

As it happens, this quarrel has recently been witnessed apropos of a reinterpretation of ancient Roman religion offered by the English Latinist, Rose. In the light of the description of the religion of the Melanesians by Codrington he has equated their *mana* with the *numen* of the Romans, and represented Roman **religion** as manaistic in origin, and even character. Georges Dumézil, who in our time is continuing the historical and philological method of Müller in his monumental studies of the religion of the Indo-Europeans, has vigorously contested this 'primitivizing' of ancient civilized religions, raising the question: Numen or god? He observes very cogently that 'in all religions, even the highest, one finds that in the same epoch and in the same society the faithful who practise, so far from placing their practices on the same level, have a wide gamut of interpretations ranging from pure automatism to the most unfettered mysticism?' He cites the opinion of a fellow-worker who has written on Yoga that the manipulations of the holy are necessarily ambivalent, at times taking place on the religious plane and at others on the magical without any awareness on the part of the manipulator as to whether he is performing an act of worship or a magical operation. Dumézil also points out that the linguistic and material resources for embodying the invisible are limited, and therefore from the words and the apparatus of a cult no one can be sure whether he is seeing devotion or magic. This is amplifying the argument of Müller against the application of anthropological methods to civilized religions. William James also warned students of religion against taking the origins of a religion too literally in assessing it in its full development.

Max Müller would have nothing to do with this 'dis-idealization' of religion. He was also led to idealize the ancient religions on account of his respect and love for mankind. Some of his sayings illustrate this strikingly. 'Human nature is divine nature modified.' 'God comes to us in the likeness of man—there is no other God.' 'Next to our faith in God there is nothing so essential to the healthy growth of our whole being as an unshaken faith in man.' So, all his interpretations of religion and mythology, based on his love for man, can be called his Canticles, for in spite of their scientific and philosophical form there is a fervour and vocal exultation in them which come only from religion.

Meanwhile, what had happened to his childlike faith? There is no doubt that he cherished it. But there are no records of it in his feelings and thoughts set down in late life. Even in his most intimate confessions there is no trace of his radiant faith. They only show a stoical resignation to God's will. *Wie Gott will* was inscribed on his tombstone.

Was it his stupendous intellectual effort to understand man and his religion which had brought him to this state? His personal mood was very much like that of the Preacher: 'In much knowledge *is* much grief: and he that increaseth knowledge increaseth sorrow.' Perhaps, imitating Plato, one might apply a Greek fable to the quest for knowledge, especially for scientific knowledge of religion and love. Blameless Actaeon was torn by dogs for having inadvertently caught a glimpse of the bathing Artemis. The Artemis of life perhaps visits those who pry into her mysteries with the same punishment. Freud and Havelock Ellis, coming after Max Müller, seem to indicate that.

In any case, his colossal labour thoroughly tired out Max Müller. His last words were, 'I am tired.' As in a dying man the bodily sensation is paramount, these words perhaps should not be taken too seriously. But they echoed the refrain of his last years—that he was very tired. In the letter to his son written just over a year before his death (quoted on page 252) he said that he wanted rest but added that so far as his life was concerned it might be a hopeless fight, it could hardly be otherwise.

The same letter contains what might be called his last testament. 'I am prepared to go,' he wrote, 'it would be strange if I were not, with such a long life behind me, and most of it devoted to religious and philosophical questions. And having lived this long life, so full of light, having been led so kindly by a fatherly hand through all storms and struggles, why should I be afraid when I have to make the last step? I have finished all my work, and what is more I see that it will be carried on by others, by stronger and younger men. I have never piled mud in the market, I gladly left that to others, but I have laid a foundation that will last, and though people don't see the blocks buried in a river, it is on these unseen blocks that the bridge rests. I cannot do any more work.'

That was as much as any scholar or scientist could say of his work. Max Müller was a pioneer and explorer, and he will be remembered as such. But he was also a man, and in our idea of him as such we need not assess the value of his life as only relative.

SOURCES OF THE BIOGRAPHY

(Citations from Max Müller's writings and correspondence are in his *own* English, except when a book or a letter is in German. The lists in this and Appendix II specify which are in that language. The languages of his non-British correspondents [except Indians, who wrote in English] were their own. All citations from any source in German are given in Mrs Max Müller's translation.)

Printed Sources:

1. Max Müller's recollections of European and Indian personalities published under the title *Auld Lang Syne* I and II, in 1898 and 1899.
2. His autobiography written in fragments in his last years, and revised with the help of his son during the last months of his life, down to October 19, i.e., nine days before his death. Published posthumously in 1901.
3. *The Life and Letters of the Rt. Hon. Friedrich Max Müller,* by his wife, and published in two volumes in 1902.

These are the basic printed sources. Very little has been written on him since then. There seems to be a revived interest in him at present, and I have read two recent works: an essay by J. H. Voigt and an article by Joan Leopold.

Manuscript Sources

A large volume of Max Müller's papers and other material is in the Bodleian, and is fully catalogued. They are classified under the following heads:

A. Letters; B. Journals; C. Writings of Max Müller; D. Honours conferred on Max Müller; E. Miscellanea; F. Printed Material; G. Papers of Other Members of the Family; H. Coins and Medals.

The most important papers are the following:

Letters to his mother *in German*	5 volumes
Letters to his wife	5 volumes
Letters to Bunsen *in German*	1 volume
Letters to various British Personages	4 volumes
Letters connected with his resignation of the Oxford Professorship	1 volume

Letters from Royal Personages   1 volume
Letters from Indians   1 volume
'Funny Letters' from various correspondents   1 volume
Letters to and from Relatives   1 volume
Letters to Children   1 volume
Letters of Condolence after Death   1 volume
Max Müller's early Journal   1 volume
Journals of Mrs Max Müller   3 volumes
Max Müller's Thoughts on the Death of his Daughter   1 volume

Among the printed material there are contemporary notices and articles as well as extensive reviews of Mrs Max Müller's biography. There are also albums of pictorial and photographic material.

CHRONOLOGICAL LIST OF MAX MÜLLER'S WORKS

1844.	Hitopadesa, translation. (German)
1847.	Meghadûta, translation in verse. (German)
	Relation of Bengali to the Aboriginal Languages of India.
1849–73.	Rig-Veda and Sâyana's Commentary.
1853.	Essay on the Turanian Languages.
	Essay on Indian Logic.
1854.	Proposals for a Uniform Missionary Alphabet.
	Languages of the Seat of War.
1856.	Essay on Comparative Mythology.
1857.	Deutsche Liebe (14th edition, 1901). (German)
	(English translation by his wife, 1877)
	Buddhist Pilgrims.
1858.	German Classics
1859.	Ancient Sanskrit Literature.
1861.	Lectures on the Science of Language, Vol. I (14th edition 1886).
1862.	Ancient Hindu Astronomy.
1864.	Lectures on the Science of Language, Vol. II
1866.	Hitopadesa, Text, Notes, etc.
	Sanskrit Grammar.
1867–75.	Chips from a German Workshop, four vols.
1868.	Stratification of Language.
1869.	Rig-Veda, translation, Vol. I.
	Rig-Veda Prâtisâkhya.
1870.	Dhammapada, translation.
1871.	Letters on the War.
1873.	Rig-Veda in Samhitâ and Pada Texts.
	Darwin's Philosophy of Language.
	Introduction to Science of Religion.
1875.	J. B. Basedow. (German)
	Schiller's Briefwechsel. (German)
1876.	On Spelling.
1878.	Hibbert Lectures.
1879.	Upanishads, translation.
1881.	Selected Essays.
	Kant's Critique, translation.
1882.	India—What can it teach us?

1884. Biographical Essays.
1887. Science of Thought.
       La Carità of Andrea del Sarto.
1888. Biographies of Words.
       Science of Thought, three Lectures.
1888–92. Gifford Lectures, four vols,
1889. Science of Language, three Lectures.
1890–2. Rig-Veda, new edition.
1893. Âpastamba Sûtras, translated.
1894. New Edition of Chips, four vols. much altered.
       Lectures on the Vedânta Philosophy.
1897. Science of Mythology, two vols.
1898. Auld Lang Syne, Vol. I.
       Râmakrishna.
1899. Auld Lang Syne, Vol. II.
       Six Systems of Indian Philosophy.
       Das Pferdebürla. (German)
1900. Transvaal War.
1901. Posthumous. Autobiography and Last Essays, two vols.

Appendix III

IMPORTANT EVENTS IN
MAX MÜLLER'S LIFE

Born   6 December 1823
At school in Leipzig   1836–41
University career in Leipzig   1841–1843
Doctorate of Leipzig University   September 1843
In Berlin   1844
In Paris   1845–46
In London   1846–47
Settles at Oxford   May 1848
Taylorian Professor of Modern European Languages   1854
Fellow of All Souls   1858
Marriage   3 August 1859
Fails to get Boden Professorship   December 1860
Professor of Comparative Philology   1868
Death of first daughter   1876
Death of second daughter   1886
Privy Councillor   1896
Serious illness   1899
Death   28 October 1900
Death of (Mrs) Georgina Adelaide Müller née Grenfell   17 July 1916

INDEX

(M.M. in the index stands for Max Müller.)

14